Pomeroy & Burstein, Ancient History

Selected Reading Lists and Course Outlines from American Colleges and Universities

Ancient History

edited by Sarah B. Pomeroy
Hunter College, C.U.N.Y.
&
Stanley M. Burstein
California State University,
Los Angeles

Second updated and expanded edition, 1986

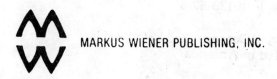
MARKUS WIENER PUBLISHING, INC.

Second updated and expanded edition, 1986

© 1984 by Markus Wiener Publishing, Inc.

ISBN 0-910129-57-6

Library of Congress Card No. 83-61356
Printed in America

Table of Contents

Introduction...3

I.   Chronological Courses

      Ancient Civilization
            JoAnn McNamara, Hunter College, CUNY.............................7

      Ancient History Expanded, 1200 B.C.E.-600 C.E.:
      A Macro-Historical Survey.
            Lee Daniel Snyder, New College of the Univ. of San Francisco.....13

      Bronze Age in Greece and the Emergence of Civilization.
            Virginia Hunter, York University.................................14

      Greek History from the Late Bronze Age to the
      Peloponnesian War.
            Ralph J. Sealey, University of California, Berkeley..............21

      History of Greece.
            James M. Heath, Bucknell University..............................26

      Greek History 550-400 BCE.
            Donald Lateiner, University of Syracuse..........................37

      The Roman Republic.
            Erich S. Gruen, University of California, Berkeley...............40

      The Roman Empire.
            Erich S. Gruen, University of California, Berkeley...............45

      The Near East from Alexander to Cleopatra.
            Stanley M. Burstein, California State University, L.A............51

      The Aftermath of Alexander the Great.
            Erich S. Gruen, University of California, Berkeley...............56

      Hellenistic Greece.
            Erich S. Gruen, University of California, Berkeley...............61

      Ancient Greece and Rome.
            Pericles B. Georges, Harvard University..........................68

      The Ancient World.
            Arthur M. Eckstein, University of Maryland.......................75

      Greek and Roman History from Alexander to Caesar.
            Susan M. Treggiari, Stanford University..........................78

      History of Rome.
            James M. Heath, Bucknell University..............................79

History of the Roman Republic.
    Kurt A. Raaflaub, Brown University................................92

A Survey History of Ancient Italy (esp. 500 BCE to 150 BCE).
    Donald Lateiner, University of Syracuse.........................114

History of the Roman Empire.
    Susan M. Treggiari, Stanford University.........................115

The Eastern Roman Empire.
    John Meyendorff, Fordham University.............................123

The Byzantine Empire.
    John Meyendorff, Fordham University.............................125

II.   Social History

Roman Society in the Age of Cicero and Augustus.
    Susan M. Treggiari, Stanford University.........................127

The City in the Greek, Roman and Byzantine World.
    Bruce R. Hitchner, University of Virginia.......................128

Classical Civilization.
    Kenneth Pratt, California State University, Los Angeles.........130

Ancient Dreams and Dream Interpretation.
    Donald J. Hughes, University of Denver..........................135

Greek and Roman Medicine.
    John Scarborough, University of Kentucky........................139

Greek and Roman Athletics.
    Thomas F. Scanlon, University of California, Riverside..........145

III. Women's History

Greek Women.
    Sarah B. Pomeroy, Hunter College, CUNY..........................161

Roman Women.
    Susan M. Treggiari, Stanford University.........................164

IV. Special Topics

The Environmental History of the Ancient Mediterranean World.
    Donald J. Hughes, University of Denver..........................167

Sparta from the Beginnings until 371.
    Raphael J. Sealey, University of California, Berkeley...........171

The Discovery of Freedom in Ancient Greece.
    Kurt A. Raaflaub, Brown University..............................174

Foundations of Athenian Democracy.
Virginia Hunter, York University..............................198

Greek History 478-338 B.C..
Raphael J. Sealey, University of California, Berkeley...........208

The Constitution and Society of Athens.
Raphael J. Sealey, University of California, Berkeley..........217

The History of Ancient Athenian Law.
Raphael J. Sealey, University of California, Berkeley..........223

Alexander the Great.
Valerie French, American University............................228

Causes of War in Antiquity.
Valerie French, American University............................248

Greek and Roman Warfare.
Janice Gabbert, Wright State University........................272

Politics and Culture in the Age of the Hannibalic War.
Erich S. Gruen, University of California, Berkeley..............276

Political and Social Upheaval in the Age of the Gracchi, Marius,
and Sulla.
Erich S. Gruen, University of California, Berkeley..............281

The Age of Cicero.
Erich S. Gruen, University of California, Berkeley..............290

The First Imperial Dynasty of Rome.
Erich S. Gruen, University of California, Berkeley..............295

Roman Law.
Ronald Mellor, University of California at Los Angeles..........303

Religion and Society from Alexander to Julian.
Pericles B. Georges, Harvard University........................310

The Dialogue of Paganism and Judaism in the Greek
and Roman World.
Louis M. Feldman, Yeshiva University...........................313

The Classical and Christian Worlds.
Carole Straw, Mount Holyoke College............................327

About the Editors...329

Documents have been reproduced from the originals as submitted.

INTRODUCTION TO THE FIRST EDITION

A colleague recently remarked that one of the attractions of a career in college teaching was that you did not have to take any education courses during your university career. When you got a job, they just threw you into a classroom the first day and you began teaching. The statement is true and the sentiment common, but, as is often the case, there is another and less attractive side to this situation. The would-be college teacher's freedom from the need to take "stultifying" education courses also means that he or she also usually has no training in the planning of a course. The first year of teaching, not surprisingly, becomes a hectic struggle to put together syllabi for courses. Old notes and syllabi, if one were lucky enough to have had a professor who prepared good ones--those of friends and colleagues if not--are eagerly sought out in the urgent need to have something for the students on the first day of class and, worst of all, the crisis recurs every time a new class has to be taught. The purpose of this collection is to assist new teachers in surmounting this formidable hurdle as well as to suggest opportunities to experienced teachers for innovative course offerings by making available syllabi whose value has been tested in the classroom.

Before being included in this volume, syllabi had to meet certain specific criteria. First and foremost, they had to be intelligible by themselves. Numerous courses of demonstrable excellence had to be rejected because either they required

3

special teaching materials not generally available such as readers prepared by their instructors specifically for the course or their syllabi contained only information concerning the course's goals and requirements without any indication of its instructional content. Considerable attention in choosing syllabi was also given to the special position an ancient historian tends to occupy in departments of history or classics. Typically, such departments have only one or, at most, two ancient historians whose responsibilities, therefore, tend to be much broader than those of other colleagues. Where an American or European historian may only be required to teach advanced courses within his or her own rather narrow specialty, perhaps the American Civil War or post-World War II Europe, the ancient historian is expected to be a generalist, offering courses at both the introductory and advanced levels on the whole of Greek or Roman history or even both, as well as courses dealing with special topics of current scholarly or student interest. Accordingly, a special effort was made to include syllabi dealing with the various chronological survey courses that are the ancient historian's bread and butter as well as a generous selection of special topics courses.

The successful completion of a project always brings a feeling of accomplishment and satisfaction. That is true for this volume, but paging through these syllabi also brings a sense of encouragement. Once ancient history was in the forefront of historical studies, but for much of the twentieth century that

4

had not been true. While scholars in other fields of historical inquiry boldly ventured into new areas of study such as social history, and enthusiastically experimented with new methodologies, ancient history remained focused on narrative political history and wedded to the empiricism characteristic of nineteenth-century scientific history. What was not clearly and explicitly documented in the ancient sources could not be studied; and the few scholars who turned to the social sciences in an attempt to escape from this tyranny of the "sources" were dismissed as "unsound." Although some may still hold such views, these syllabi suggest that they are in the minority, and that ancient historians today are vigorously expanding the boundaries of their field, that they are, in fact, studying and teaching the "unstudiable." To be sure, courses in political history are well-represented, and properly so, since they remain the staple of the ancient historian, but so also are courses in such diverse and exciting areas as the history of women in antiquity, ancient sports, environmental history, and urban history. Ancient history clearly has once again rejoined the mainstream of twentieth-century historical studies.

For the editors, the preparation of this volume has been a rewarding and gratifying experience. In particular, we would like to thank our many colleagues who so generously responded to our requests to share their syllabi with us and a new generation of teachers. We only regret that limitations of space have prevented us from including more of them. In the end, however,

books have their own fate. It is the hope of the editors that
this volume of syllabi will assist teachers of ancient history to
communicate to their students something of the exciting
developments in ancient studies that are documented in it.

Sarah B. Pomeroy   March 1984

Hunter College, CUNY

Stanley M. Burstein

California State University, Los Angeles

History 201: Ancient Civilization   Professor   McNamara
M 5:40-7:00; W 5:40-7:05   Room 631N

Text: Sinnigen and Robinson, Ancient History

Midterm Examination: March 31

Final Examination: May 21

Two Book Reports: March 3
                   April 21

The book reports are to be about five pages each. One is to deal
with a primary source (something written in ancient times) and
the other with a secondary source (written in modern times).
Each is to follow the appropriate instructions accompanying the
syllabus.

Use a style manual for guidance in treatment of footnotes,
bibliography and other questions of presentation. Attribution of
material is to be footnoted.   Failure to use appropriate footnotes will be regarded as plagiarism.   Please supply notes for
all statements, even material taken from class lectures and
discussion, in order to familiarize yourselves with the procedures. Proper forms for footnotes and bibliography must be
observed.   You are advised to consult The MLA Handbook for
Writers of Research Papers, Theses and Dissertations for these
forms and for all stylistic problems.   Copies are available in
the bookstore.

Grades for the essays will be scaled to content and to style
(grammar and spelling included).   Errors in the latter will
reduce your grade half a point (i.e., from A to A-).

7

Primary Sources are the raw materials of history. They represent the direct, "eye witness" testimony of the past conveyed to us in the present through literary and material remains. Letters, diaries, chronicles, contracts, laundry lists and tax rolls are among the varieties of written primary sources available to the historian. Works of art, monuments, broken pots, traces of plowing patterns in the soil are also among the primary sources which give historians clues to what has happened in the past.

Primary sources often survive by accident and only in part. Often their meaning is unclear because of linguistic difficulties or cultural differences. Often no primary source, or no adequate primary source, survives for a given time or place. Even more often, only one source survives and we have no means of checking its reliability. Thus many historical problems remain unsolved and impenetrable. Where evidence is insufficient or the testimony of the witnesses is unreliable, a historian can only guess at what may have happened.

Your report is to be concerned with problems of evidence. For practical purposes, I have restricted your choice of primary sources to written works available in English in New York. But be aware of the problems of translation and edition inherent in most of them. You are to consider the work you choose from the point of view of its value to a historian not as a work of art or philosophy. To do so, consider the following questions, with properly footnoted illustrations from the source itself to substantiate all your arguments.
1. What is the nature of the source? Is it a novel,. a political tract, a letter, a work of history or something else? What makes it suitable as a primary source and what special difficulties does it present?

2. Who was the author? When and where was the work produced?Did the author have any special bias which would affect the value of the work (for example, can you see a religious, political, social or racial prejudice in the work? Is the author a partisan of any special idea?)

3. Are their any unconscious assumptions which affect the value of the work (for example, a belief that the sun revolves around the earth, or that human nature naturally tends toward the good)?

4. What sort of historical information does the source provide. How does it illuminate social habits or ideological principles as well as specific events?

5. How reliable is the author? How close was the author to the events observed? How involved in them? How good are the author's sources?

6. What is the relationship of this work to other sources from the same period? Are there other sources to check against this one? Do they tend to corroborate your source or contradict it?

Secondary sources are books written by historians based on the
study and interpretation of surviving primary sources. They
represent the guesses, estimates and opinions of individual
scholars based upon their view of the evidence available and
shaped by the questions they have addressed to the evidence. In
a modern court of law, they would be classified as "hearsay" or
"circumstantial" evidence. Historians constantly re-write or
re-design the past in the light of new evidence, new approaches
to old evidence or new questions arising out of their own
contemporary concerns.

You are to analyze the historian's use of evidence. Pay careful
attention to the way in which the data was selected, organized
and interpreted. Your report is to examine the author's method
of presenting and arguing a case from the available evidence.
This should include a consideration of the following questions.
with footnoted illustrations to substantiate your argument.

1.   What is the subject of the book? Why has the author chosen
it and how has it been formulated?

2.   Who is the author? What personal circumstances of time,
place, class, gender, or belief are likely to have influenced the
choice of subject and the conclusions presented?

3.   How is the material organized (chronologically, geographi-
cally, topically?) A thoughtful consideration of the Table of
Contents may be helpful at this point.

4.   What primary sources does the author employ. Do they appear
to be adequate and appropriate to the problem?

5.   What secondary sources does the author cite? How do the
arguments in this book differ from those expressed in other
secondary sources?

Part I.   The Stone Age and the Bronze Age.
1.   Human Prehistory.
2.   The Agrarian Revolution
3.   Mesopotamian Civilization.
4.   Egyptian Civilization.
5.   The Spread of Bronze Age Civilization
6.   The Indo-Europeans: Hittites and Hurrians
7.   Crete and Mycenae to the Homeric Age.
8.   The Amarna Age.

Primary Sources:
Driver, G.R., and Mills, John C., _The Assyrian Laws_.
Finkelstein, J.J., _Late Old Babylonian Documents and Letters_.
Epic of Gilgamesh
The Code of Hammurabi
Homer, _The Iliad._ _The Odyssey_.
The Hittite Laws, ed. Neufield.
Lichtheim, Miriam, _Ancient Egyptian Literature_.
Old Testament. The book of Judges; Kings.

Secondary Sources:
Albright, W.F., _From the Stone Age to Christianity_.
Batto, Bernard F., _Studies on Women at Mari_.
Chadwick, Hector M., _The Heroic Age_.
Chadwick, John, _The Decipherment of Linear B_.
Chadwick, John, _The Mycenean World_.
Childe, Gordon, _What Happened in History_.
Cohen, M., _The Food Crisis in Prehistory_.
Daniel, Glyn, _The Megalith Builders of Western Europe_.
Diop, C.A., _The African Origin of Civilization_.
Eliade, Mircea, _From the Stone Age to the Eleusinian Mysteries_.
Emery, W.B., _Archaic Egypt_.
Finley, M.I., _Early Greece: The Bronze and Archaic Ages_
Frankfort, H., et al., _The Intellectual Adventure of Ancient Man_.
Ghirschman, I., _Iran_
Gray, J., _Archaeology and the Old Testament World_.
Jacobsen, Thorkild, _The Treasures of Darkness._
Jaynes, Julian, _The Origins of Consciousness in the Breakdown of the Bicameral Mind_.
Jeffery, L.H., _Archaic Greece: The City-states ca. 700-500 B.C._
Kramer, S.N., _The Sumerians_
Leakey, Richard, _The People of the Lake_.
Meek, T.M., _Hebrew Origins_
Mellaart, J., _The Earliest Civilizations of the Near East_.
Page, Dennis, _History and the Homeric Iliad_.
Pfeffer, John E., _The Creative Explosion_.
Renfrew, Colin, _The Radiocarbon Revolution and Prehistoric Europe_.
Saggs, _The Greatness that was Babylon_
Seibert, Ilse, _Women in the Ancient East_

Part II.   The Mediterranean Melting Pot.
     9.   The Iron Age.
    10.   The Hebrews.
    11.   The Assyrian and Persian Empires.
    12.   Sixth Century Spiritual Revolution.
    13.   The Emergence of Greece.
    14.   The World of the Polis: Athens and Sparta.
    15.   The Golden Age of Classical Greece.
    16.   Alexander the Great and the Hellenistic World.

Primary Sources:
Aeschylus, The Persians
Aristophanes, The Acharnian Farmers
Aristotle, Politics
Arrian, Life of Alexander
Demosthenes, The Philippics
Euripides, The Trojan Women
Herodotus, The Persian Wars
Hesiod, Works and Days. Theogony.
Pausanius, A Guide to Greece (Penguin Books: 2 vols).
Plato, The Symposium
Thucydides, The Peloponnesian Wars
Xenophon, Oeconomicus. Anabasis.

Secondary Sources:
Andrewes, A., The Greek Tyrants
Chadwick, Hector M., _he Heroic Age.
Chadwick, John, The Decipherment of Linear B.
Chadwick, John, The Mycenean World.
Dodd, E.R., The Greeks and the Irrational.
Dover, K.J., Greek Homosexuality.
Eliade, Mircea, From Buddha to the Triumph of Christianity.
Finley, M.I., The Ancient Economy.
Finley, M.I., Early Greece: The Bronze and Archaic Ages
Fustel de Coulanges, N.D., The Ancient City.
Ghirschman, I., Iran
Huxley, G.L., The Early Ionians.
Kirk, J.S., and Raven, J.E., The Presocratic Philosophers.
MacDowell, Douglas M., The Law in Classical Athens.
Michel, R., Sparta
Pomeroy, Sarah, Goddesses, Whores, Wives and Slaves.
Pomeroy, Sarah, Women in Hellenistic Egypt.
Sainte-Croix, G.E.M. de, The Class Struggle in the Ancient Greek
          World.
Simon, Bennett, Mind and Madness in Ancient Greece.

Part III. The Roman Mediterranean.
           17.   The establishment of the Republic.
           18.   The Conquest of the Mediterranean.
           19.   The Roman Revolution.
           20.   The Augustan World.
           21.   Pax Romana.
           22.   Cultural Conflict and Reintegration.
           23.   The Christian Empire.
           24.   Romanizing the Germans.
           25.   Justinian and the Legacy of the Ancient World.

Primary Sources:
Augustine, _Confessions_
Caesar, _The Civil War_
Cicero, _Letters to His Friends_
Gaius, _Institutes_.
Johnson, Coleman-Norton, and Bourne, _Ancient Roman Statutes_
Josephus, _The Jewish War_.   _Jewish Antiquities_.
Juvenal, _Satires_
Livy, _History_ (any available volume)
Petronius, _The Satyricon_
Pliny the Younger, _Letters_
Suetonius, _Annals_
Tacitus, _The Histories_
Vergil, _The Aenead_.

Secondary Sources:
Barrow, R.H., _Slavery in the Roman Empire_ .
Brown, Peter, _The World of Late Antiquity_ .
Brunt, P.A., _Social Conflicts in the Roman Republic_.
Crook, J.A., _Law and Life in Rome_.
Dudley, Donald R., and Webster, Graham, _The Rebellion of Boudicca._
Gaudemet, Jean, _Les institutions de l'antiquité_.
Guignebert, Charles, _The Jewish World at the Time of Jesus_.
Holum, Kenneth, _Theodosian Empresses_.
Jolowicz, H.F., _Roman Foundations of Modern Law_.
Jones, A.H.M., _Studies in Roman Government and Law_
MacMullen, Ramsay, _Paganism in the Roman Empire_.
Maine, Henry Sumner, _Ancient Law_.
Momigliano, A., _The Conflict Between Paganism and Christianity_
Schulz, Fritz, _Classical Roman Law_.
Syme, Ronald, _The Roman Revolution_

Ancient History Expanded, 1200 B.C.E.-600 C.E.
A Macro-Historical Survey

Lee Daniel Snyder
Fall Semester, 1982-83
New College of USF

Course Outline:

A. Theoretical Approach to Ancient History

1) Aug. 30 - Introduction: various approaches to Ancient History
2) Sept. 2 - Macro-History theory
3) Sept. 6 - An overview of the Second Era

B. Formative Cycles:

4) Sept. 9 - The Mesopotamian Heritage: Divine Kingship and Law
5) Sept. 13 - Age of Hittites and Patriarchs
6) Sept. 16 - India, A Slow Beginning: Tribe and Ritual
7) Sept. 20 - The Greek Heroic Age
8) Sept. 23 - A wandering King: Man against Nature, Disc. of Odyssey

C. Classical Cycles:

9) Sept. 27 - Rise of Classical Greece: Age of the Polis
10) Sept. 30 - Athenian Empire, Democracy and Nationalism
11) Oct.   4 - Assyria and Israel, An Age of Small States
12) Oct.   7 - A Religious King: The Epic of David, Disc. of I and II Samuel
13) Oct. 11 - India Reorganized in States and Empire: The Age of Buddha
               and the Maurays
14) Oct. 14 - A Questing King: The Epic of Rama, Disc. of Ramayana

D. Renewal Cycles:

15) Oct. 25 - Reshaping of India: Foreign Invasions and the Resurgence
               of Religion
16) Oct. 28 - Turning Inward, Disc. of Bhagava Gita
17) Nov.   1 - Assyrian Imperialism and the Prophetic Protest against
               Injustice
18) Nov.   4 - Turning Upward, Disc. Amos
19) Nov.   8 - Crisis and Reorganization in the Greek World
20) Nov. 11 - Turning Rational, Disc. of Plato's Symposium
21) Nov. 15 - Rise of Rome and Hellenistic Monarchies

E. Secularization Cycles:

22) Nov. 18 - Roman Civil War, Struggle for a New Constitution
23) Nov. 22 - Roman Empire: Climax and Exhaustion
24) Nov. 24 - The Persian Empire, Unification of the Near East
25) Nov. 29 - Age of the Guptas in India

F. Post Secularization Developments:

26) Dec.   2 - India and the Mediterranean Contrasted
27) Dec.   6 - Persia, The Parthian Frontier Empire and the Sassanian
               Renewal
28) Dec.   8 - Conclusions: The Broad Comparison of Cultural Traditions

V. Hunter
Dpt. of History
York University   1980 - 1981

The Bronze Age in Greece and the Emergence of Civilization - History 410

Sept. 24 - Problems of Chronology, Method and Interpretation

      Sir Arthur Evans, The Palace of Minos.* Peruse
      S. Hood, The Minoans, Introduction and chapters 1, 2, and 4
      Pictures, beautiful pictures (Marinatos, von Matt, or Warren)

      Recommended:
      L.R. Binford, "Archaeological Perspectives."*
      M.I. Finley, "Archaeology and History."*
      E.G. Trigger, Beyond History: The Methods of Prehistory. New York, 1968,
         GN33T73.

      Individual reports on:
      A.D. Lacy, Greek Pottery in the Bronze Age, London, 1967, NK 3843L3.
      J.W. Michels, Dating Methods in Archaeology, chapters 2, 7, 9.* See, too,
         Colin Renfrew, Problems in European Prehistory, Cambridge, 1979, ch. 17.

Oct. 1 -   Problems of Chronology, Method, and Interpretation

      Hood, ch. 5
      E.R. Service, Origins of the State and Civilization. Introduction and chs. 3,

      One of:
      L.R. Binford, ed. For Theory Building in Archaeology. Essays on Faunal
         Remains, Aquatic Resources, Spatial Analysis, and Systemic Modeling.
         New York, 1977, Ch. 10. "Theory Building and the Study of Evolutionary
         Process in Complex Societies." CC75F59.
      C. Renfrew, "Beyond a Subsistence Economy: The Evolution of Social
         Organization in Prehistoric Europe." in Reconstructing Complex Societies.
         edited by C.B. Moore, Supplement to the Bulletin of the American Schools
         of Oriental Research 20, 1974, 69 - 85, CC75R416.
      M. Sahlins, "On the Sociology of Primitive Exchange." in The Relevance of
         Models for Social Anthropology, edited by M. Banton, London 1965,
         139 - 238, GN27C65.

      Individual reports on:
      V.G. Childe, "Retrospect." Antiquity 32, 1958, 69 - 74
      B.G. Trigger, Gordon Childe. Revolutions in Archaeology, New York, 1980.
      B.G. Trigger, "Determinants of Urban Growth in Pre-industrial Societies."
         and K. Branigan, "Minoan Settlements in East Crete" in Man, Settlement and
         Urbanism, edited by P. Ucko, R.Tringham, and G.W. Dimbleby, London, 1972,
         575 - 599 and 751 - 759, HT113B47.

* Full reference found in syllabus handed out for reference only.

                                      Sept. 17, 1980

Oct. 9 -   Crete in the Early Bronze Age.

            K. Branigan, The Foundations of Palatial Crete. A Survey of
                Crete in the Early Bronze Age. London, 1970, Chapter 4,
                "The Economy," 67 - 91 (handout).
            Hood, Chapter 3.
            C. Renfrew, The Emergence of Civilisation. The Cyclades and the
                Aegean in the Third Millenium B.C. London, 1972, DF77R35,
                part II, Culture Process.

            one of:

            Chapter 14, "Patterns of Settlement," 225 - 264.
            Chapter 15, "Natural Environment," 265 - 307.
            Chapter 16, "The Development of Aegean Metallurgy," 308 - 338.

            Recommended:
            P. Warren, Myrtos. An Early Bronze Age Settlement in Crete,
                Chapter 6, "Economy and Society," 255 - 268, London, 1972
                (handout). *
            Renfrew, The Emergence of Civilisation, Chapter 4, "The Minoan-
                Mycenaean Civilisation and its Origins," 45 - 60.

            Individual reports on:
            K. Branigan, The Tombs of Mesara. A Study of Funerary Architecture
                and Ritual in Southern Crete, 2800 - 1700 B.C., London, 1970 *
            and
                The Foundations of Palatial Crete.
            P. Warren, Myrtos.

Oct. 16 -   The Great Palaces of Crete: Materials, Technology and Crafts and
            their Purpose in the late Bronze Age.

            J. Betts, "New Light on Minoan Bureaucracy," Kadmos 6, 1967, 15 - 40
                (handout) *
            J. Boardman, Greek Gems and Finger Rings, Chapter 2, "Minoans and
                Mycenaeans," 19 - 46 and 62 - 65. *
            J.W. Graham, The Palaces of Crete, Princeton, 1962 (handout) *
            Hood, Chapters 6, 7, and 8.

            Recommended:
            Evans, The Palace of Minos, vol. 1, Chapters 10, 15, and 17.
            Renfrew, The Emergence of Civilisation, Chapter 17, "Craft Specialisation,
                339 - 361.

            Individual reports on:
            J.W. Graham, The Palace of Crete.
            V.E.G. Kenna, Cretan Seals, Oxford, 1960, Chapter 4, "The Late Minoan
                Age," 49 - 67. *

Oct. 23 - The Great Palaces of Crete: Social System and Institutions

Hood, Chapters 9 and 10.
Renfrew, The Emergence of Civilisation, Chapter 18, "Social
    Systems," 362 - 403 (handout).

Pictures from one of:
S. Marinatos and M. Hirmer, Crete and Mycenae, London, 1960, N5660M35.
L. von Matt, Ancient Crete, London, 1968, DF221C8M253.
P. Warren, The Aegean Civilisations, Oxford, 1975, DF220W3.

Individual readings

Individual reports on:
D.W. Packard, Minoan Linear A, Berkeley and Los Angeles, 1974,
    P1035P28, and K. Branigan, "The Earliest Minoan Scripts -
    The Pre-Palatial Background," Kadmos 8, 1969, 1 - 22.
N. Platon, Zakros. The Discovery of a Lost Palace of Ancient Crete,
    New York, 1971, DF221C8P586.

Nov. 5 - The Great Palaces of Crete: Social System and Institutions

Individual assignments
Service, Origins of the State, part 2, "The Modern Primitive States,"
    104 - 164.

Recommended:
Evans, PM, vol. 1, Chapter 21, 436 - 447 and Chapter 25, 495 - 522;
    vol. 3, Chapter 70, 71, 74, 75, and/or 77.
M.P. Nilsson, The Minoan-Mycenaean Religion and its Survival in Greek
    Religion, second edition, Lund, 1950, BL793M8N51971.
Renfrew, EC, Chapter 19, "Symbolic and Projective Systems," 404 - 439.

* Full reference found in syllabus handed out for reference.

16

HISTORY 410

Wed., Nov. 12 - Greece in the Early Bronze Age

J.L. Caskey, "The Early Helladic Period in the Argolid,"
Hesperia 29, 1960, 285 - 303 (handout)
J. Chadwick, The Mycenaean World, Chapter 1, "The Hellenization
of Greece."
C. Renfrew, EC, Chapter 7, "Mainland Greece in the Third
Millenium B.C." (handout)
E. Vermeule, Greece in the Bronze Age, Chicago 1964, Chapter 2,
"Early Bronze Age Greece and the Islands," 24 - 44 and 58 - 65.

Recommended:
R. J. Howell, "The Origins of the Middle Helladic Culture"
in Bronze Age Migrations in the Aegean, edited by R.A. Crossland
and A. Birchall, London, 1973, 73 - 101, DF220C5851970.

Individual report on Lerna.

Bibliography on the Mycenaean World:

J.T. Hooker, Mycenaean Greece, London, 1976, DF220H65.
G.E. Mylonas, Mycenae and the Mycenaean Age, Princeton, 1966,
DF221M9M93.
H. Schliemann, Mycenae, New York, 1967 and Tiryns, New York 1885,
DF221M9S351967 and DF221T5S3.

Wed., Nov. 19 - The Citadels of Greece and the Mycenaean World

R.J.C. Atkinson, "Neolithic Engineering," Antiquity 35, 1961,
292 - 299 (handout).
Chadwick, The Mycenaean World, Chapters 2 and 7.
W.A. McDonald, "The Problems and the Program," Chapter 1 in The
Minnesota Messenia Expedition, Reconstructing a Bronze Age
Regional Environment, edited by W.A. McDonald and G.R. Rapp,
Minneapolis, 1972, DF261M45M56 (handout).
H.J. van Wersch, "The Agricultural Economy," Chapter 11 in MME
(handout).

Recommended:
D. Kaplan, "Man, Monuments, and Political Systems" (xerox no. 27368).

Individual report on:
Mylonas, Mycenae and the Mycenaean Age and N. Scoufopolis,
Mycenaean Citadels, Goteborg, 1971, DF89S391971.

Bibliography on the Mycenaean World:
R. Hope Simpson, A Gazeteer and Atlas of Mycenaean Sites, London,
1965
A.J.B. Wace, Mycenae, Princeton, 1949, DF221M9W331964.

Ventris and Chadwick, <u>Documents</u>. Individual readings.

Individual reports on:
G.F. Bass, "Cape Gelydonya" in <u>Marine Archaeology</u>, edited by
   J. de P. Taylor, New York, 1965, 119 - 140, DE61N3T31965a.
L.R. Palmer, "The Mycenaean Tablets and Economic History,"
   The Economic History Review 11, 1958, 87 - 97, HC10E4.
N.K. Sandars, The Sea Peoples, Warriors of the Ancient Mediterranean,
   1250 - 1150 B.C., London, 1978, Chapters 3 and 8, DE73.2S4S46.

Recommended:
R.M. Adams, "Anthropological Perspectives on Ancient Trade,"
   Current Anthropology 15, 1974, 239 - 258, No. 27753.
C. Renfrew, "Trade and Culture Process in European Prehistory,"
   Current Anthropology 10, 1969, 151 - 169, No. 22721.

Wed., Jan. 7 - Hostility, the State, and the End of the Mycenaean World

Chadwick, The Mycenaean World, Chapters 10 and 11.
J.V. Luce, "Thera and the Devastation of Minoan Crete: A New
   Interpretation of the Evidence," AJA 80, 1976, 9 - 18 (handout).
Service, Origins of the State, part 3 (one or two civilizations)
   and part 4, "Conclusions."

Individual reports on:
J.V. Luce, The End of Atlantis, London, 1969, DF220L76.
L. Palmer, Mycenaeans and Minoans, second edition, New York, 1965,
   Chapter 8, "The Conflict of Scholars," 287 - 320, DF220P31965.
P.M. Warren, "The Miniature Fresco from the West House at Akrotiri,
   Thera, and its Aegean Setting," JHS 99, 1979, 115 - 129.

Recommended:
Renfrew, EC, Chapter 21, "The Multiplier Effect in Action."

Other works on the state:
M. Fried, The Evolution of Political Society, New York, 1967,
   Chapter 6, "The State", GN490F71967.
L. Krader, Formation of the State, Englewood Cliffs, N.J., 1968,
   JC11K73.
E.R. Service and R. Cohen, eds., Origins of the State. The Anthro-
   pology of Political Evolution, Philadelphia, 1978, GN492.607.

Jan. 14 - 28 - For three weeks no seminar will be held. Instead, we shall visit
U of T library. In order to ensure some discussion of individual
projects and progress on them, the class will be divided into four
groups, with visits taking place on Tuesday and Friday afternoons.
This will also allow us to consider the resources of the library
in relation to individual projects.

During these visits there will be a general discussion about planning
a design for research. In addition, every student will be assigned
a journal and be expected to peruse current numbers for new bibliography of potential use to him/herself or to other members of the
seminar.

Wed., Nov. 26 - <u>The Linear B. Tablets: the economy and society of Mycenaean Greece</u>

> S. Aschenbrenner, "A Contemporary Community," Chapter 4 in <u>MME</u>
>   (handout).
> Chadwick, <u>The Mycenaean World</u>, Chapters 3 and 8.
> M.I. Finley, "The Mycenaean Tablets and Economic History," <u>The</u>
>   <u>Economic History Review 10</u>, 1957, 128 - 141 (22722).
> M. Ventris and J. Chadwick, <u>Documents in Mycenaean Greek</u>, second
>   edition, Cambridge, 1973, CN 362V4 1973. Individual readings.
>
> Recommended:
> C.H. Gordon, <u>Forgotten Scripts</u>, New York, 1968, P211G6.
> E.A. Havelock, <u>Origins of Western Literacy</u>, Toronto, 1976, Chapter 2,
>   "The Pre-Greek Syllabaries," 22 - 38, P211H38.
>
> Individual report on:
> C.W. Blegen and M. Rawson, <u>The Palace of Nestor at Pylos in Western</u>
>   <u>Messenia</u>, vol. 1, <u>The Buildings and Their Contents</u> (in two parts,
>   text and illustrations), Princeton, 1966 and M. Lang, vol. 2,
>   <u>The Frescoes</u>, Princeton, 1969, NA277B55.

Wed., Dec. 3 - <u>The Linear B Tablets: lists and the "redistributive" economy</u>

> Chadwick, <u>The Mycenaean World</u>, Chapters 4 - 6.
> Finley, "The Mycenaean Tablets and Economic History."
> Ventris and Chadwick, <u>Documents in Mycenaean Greek</u>. Individual readings.
>
> <u>One</u> of the following works of K. Polanyi on redistribution:
>
> "The Economy as Instituted Process" in <u>Trade and Market in the Early</u>
>   <u>Empires</u>, edited by K. Polanyi, C.M. Arensberg, and H.W. Pearson,
>   Glencoe, Ill, 1957, 243 - 270, HC31P6.
> "On the Comparative Treatment of Economic Institutions in Antiquity,
>   with Illustrations from Athens, Mycenae, and Alalakh" in <u>City</u>
>   <u>Invincible, a Symposium on Urbanization and Cultural Development</u>
>   <u>in the Ancient Near East</u>, edited by C.H. Kraeling and R.M. Adams,
>   Chicago, 1960, CB311S91958.
> <u>Dahomey and the Slave Trade. An Analysis of an Archaic Economy</u>. Seattle
>   and London, 1966, a chapter or chapters in part 2, "Patterns of the
>   Economy."
>
> Recommended:
> J. Goody, <u>The Domestication of the Savage Mind</u>, Cambridge, 1977,
>   Chapter 5, "What's in a list?", esp. 80 - 103, GV451G66.

Wed., Dec. 10 - <u>The Linear B Tablets: trade and war in the Mycenaean world</u>

> Chadwick, <u>The Mycenaean World</u>, Chapter 9.
> Renfrew, <u>EC</u>, Chapter 20, "Trade, Communication and Innovation," 455 -
>   475 (handout).

The general areas of research are as follows:

Culture Process, Trade, and the Development of Writing in Crete (EM-MM) - Ron Judd
Lerna: a Helladic proto-urban complex of the Korakou culture - Malcolm MacLachlan
Linear B: sheep, wool, textiles, and trade at Knossos - John Scutt
Linear B: flax at Pylos - Dennis Caron
Linear B: women at Pylos -
      (i) crafts, craftswomen, and craftsmen - Doris Hertzke
      (ii) women and slavery - Mira Bondar
      (iii) Women and religion - Poppy Cobanoglu
Pylos as a redistributive center - Dan Thorpe
Late Bronze age tombs at Knossos and Pylos - Louis Koutsaris
Directional trade in the late Bronze age - Lesley Hunt

February 4 - 11 - The seminar will resume for two weeks and concern itself
        with three matters:

        a) the sharing of bibliography amassed from current periodicals
        b) the presentation of two individual designs for research
        c) discussion of the nature of the research reports to be presented
          after Reading Week.

        Note:

        Each student will hand in a design for research before Reading Week.
        It constitutes the second small assignment.

        I will be in my office for consultation during the regular seminar
        hours from Jan. 14 - 28.

RESEARCH REPORTS

March 11 - Culture Process, Trade, and the Development of Writing in Crete - Ron Judd
        Lerna: a Helladic proto-urban complex of the Korakou culture - Malcom
                                            MacLachlan
March 18 - Women at Pylos: crafts, craftswomen, and craftsmen - Doris Hertzke
        Women and Religion at Pylos - Poppy Cobanoglu

March 25 - Directional Trade in the Late Bronze Age - Lesley Hunt
        Late Bronze Age Tombs at Knossos and Pylos - Louis Koutsaris

April 1 - Linear B: sheep, wool, textiles, and trade at Knossos - John Scutt
        Linear B: flax at Pylos - Dennis Caron

April 9 - Women and Slavery at Pylos - Mira Bondar
        Pylos as a Redistributive Centre - Dan Thorpe

        The papers will be due Tuesday, April 14.

20

Greek History from the Late Bronze Age
till the Peloponnesian War

– – – – – – – – – – – – – – – – – – –

This course is intended as an introduction to the subject. Participants are advised
to familiarize themselves with the texts of Herodotus and Thucydides. Attention is
also drawn to the following two collections:

   G.F. Hill: Sources for Greek History 478-431 (revised by R. Meiggs and
      A. Andrewes)
   R. Meiggs and D. Lewis: A Selection of Greek Historical Inscriptions·

The class will meet once a week, probably on Tuesdays, in the instructor's office,·
2317 Dwinelle. At the first meeting tasks will be distributed and a little will·
be said about sources. The other meetings will treat in turn the subjects listed
below. Each participant will be required to write papers on two of the subjects.
The written version of each paper should be handed in about a week after it was
presented for discussion in class, but the paper presented at the last meeting
should be handed in no later than the last Friday of instruction.

1.   The Greek migrations into Greece

   Hdt. 1. 56; 1. 145-147
   Thuc. 1-12
   Sterling Dow, "The Greeks in the Bronze Age," Rapports (II) du XIe Congrès
      International des Sciences Historiques (1960) 1-34 (also available in·
      the series of reprints in European History published by Bobbs-Merrill)·
   Ernst Risch, "Die Gliederung der griechischen Dialekte in neuer Sicht,"
      Museum Helveticum 12, 1955, 61-76
   William F. Wyatt, Jr., "The Prehistory of the Greek Dialects," Transactions of
      the American Philological Association 101, 1970, 557-632

   Further readings, if desired:

   Ernst Risch, "Frühgeschichte der griechischen Sprache," Mus. Hel. 16, 1959,
      215-227
   Franz Hampl, "Die Chronologie der Einwanderung der griechischen Stämme und das
      Problem der Nationalität der Träger der mykenischen Kultur, "Mus. Hel.
      17, 1960, 57-86

   (Dow and Risch represent the two competing views)

2. Colonization

   Homer: Odyssey 6. 7-10
   Hdt. 2. 178; 4. 145-161
   Thuc. 6. 1-5
   Meiggs/Lewis No. 5
   R. M. Cook, "Ionia and Greece in the Eighth and Seventh Centuries
       B.C.," Journal of Hellenic Studies 66, 1946, 67-98
   A. J. Graham, "The Date of the Greek Penetration of the Black Sea,"
       Bulletin of the Institute of Classical Studies (University of
       London) 5, 1958, 25-42
   L. H. Jeffery, "The Pact of the First Settlers at Cyrene," Historia
       10, 1961, 139-147
   Oswyn Murray: Early Greece (Atlantic Highlands, N.J. 1980)
       69-79, 100-119
   Michael Zahrnt: Olynth und die Chalkidier = Vestigia 14 (München
       1971) 12-27

   further reading, if desired:
   A. J. Graham: Colony and Mother City in Ancient Greece (Manchester
       1964)

   (What method is to be followed in determining dates of foundation?
   What conclusion is to be drawn about the direction and causes of
   Greek expansion?)

3. The hoplite phalanx

   Hdt. 1. 16-24; 3. 39-53; 5. 67-68; 5. 92; 6. 126-130
   Thuc. 1. 126
   Plutarch: Lykourgos 6-7
   A. Andrewes: The Greek Tyrants 31-42, 66-77
   A. M. Snodgrass, "The hoplite reform and history," JHS. 85, 1965,
       110-122
   J. Salmon, "Political Hoplites?" JHS. 97, 1977, 84-101

   (When was the hoplite phalanx adopted? What, if any, were the
   social and political consequences?)

4. The rise of Peisistratos

   Hdt. 1. 59-64; 5. 55-65; 6. 34-41; 6. 103-104
   Thuc. 6. 54-59
   Aristotle: Athenaion Politeia 13-19
   Meiggs/Lewis Nos. 6 and 11
   A. Andrewes: The Greek Tyrants 100-115
   R. J. Hopper, "'Plain', 'Shore' and Hill' in Early Athens," Annual
       of the British School at Athens 56, 1961, 189-219
   H. T. Wade-Gery, "Miltiades," JHS. 71, 1951, 212-221 = Essays in
       Greek History 155-170

   further reading, if desired:
   P. J. Rhodes, "Pisistratid Chronology Again," Phoenix 30, 1976, 213-233

   (What sources of power did Peisistratos draw on?)

22

5. The reforms of Kleisthenes at Athens

Hdt. 5. 55-97
Ar. AP. 20-22
D. W. Bradeen, "The Trittyes in Cleisthenes' Reforms," TAPA. 86, 1955, 22-30
D. M. Lewis, "Cleisthenes and Attica," Historia 12, 1963, 22-40
P. J. Bicknell: Studies in Athenian Politics and Genealogy = Historia Einzelschriften Heft 19, 1972, 1-53 and 60-61
B. L. Bailey, "The Export of Attic Black-Figure Ware," JHS. 60, 1940, 60-70

(What features of the reforms demand explanation?)

6. The work of Solon
Hdt. 1. 29; 5. 113
Ar. AP. 1-13
Plutarch: Solon
C. Hignett: A History of the Athenian Constitution 1-27, 316-321
A. French: The Growth of the Athenian Economy (London 1964) 10-29, 181 note 14
A. Andrewes: The Greeks (London 1967) 104-110
H. T. Wade-Gery, "Eupatridae, Archons and Areopagus," Classical Quarterly 25, 1931, 1-11 and 77-89 = Essay in Greek History 86-115
J. Day and M. Chambers: Aristotle's History of Athenian Democracy = University of California Publications in History, vol. 73, 1962, 200-201
J. R. Ellis and G. R. Stanton, "Factional Conflict and Solon's Reforms," Phoenix 22, 1968, 95-110
M. Chambers, "Aristotle on Solon's Reform of Coinage and Weights," California Studies in Classical Antiquity 6, 1973, 1-16
R. Stroud: The Axones and Kyrbeis of Drakon and Solon = University of California Publications in Classical Studies, vol. 19, 1979, 41-44

attention is drawn to the following collections:
E. Ruschenbusch: Solonos Nomoi. Die Fragmente des solonischen Gesetzeswerkes mit einer Text- und Ueberlieferungageschichte = Historia Einzelschriften Heft 9, 1966
M. L. West: Iambi et Elegi Graeci, I - II (Oxford 1971-72); the fragments of Solon's poems are in II, 119-145

(What was the date of Solon's work? What two views can be held about the economic problem confronting him? What changes, if any, did he make in the constitution? How well was information about his work preserved into the classical period?)

7. The strategy of the resistance to Persia in 480

Hdt. 7. 131-152; 7. 172-177; 7. 179-183; 7. 188-195; 8. 1-2; 8. 21; 8. 40-82
Meiggs/Lewis Nos. 23 and 27

C. Hignett: Xerxes' Invasion of Greece (Oxford 1963) 201-215, 345-355
J. A. S. Evans, "Notes on Thermophlae and Artémisium," Historia 18, 1969, 389-406
C. Habicht, "Falsche Urkunden zur Geschichte Athens im Zeitalter der Perserkriege," Hermes 89, 1961, 1-35
K. S. Sacks, "Herodotus and the dating of the battle of Thermophlae," CQ. NS 26, 1976, 232-248

further reading, if desired:
P. A. Brunt, "The Hellenic League against Persia," Historia 2, 1953,
    135-163
W. K. Pritchett, "Herodotus and the Themistokles Decree," American
    Journal of Archaeology 66, 1962, 43-47
C. W. Fornara, "The Value of the Themistocles Decree, American
    Historical Review 73, 1967-68, 425-433

(How did the resistance plan to check the Persian advance? What
difference does the decree attributed to Themistokles make to
reconstruction of strategy? With what confidence can the
chronology of operations be determined?)

8. The origins of the Delian League

    Hdt. 8. 2-3; 9. 106
    Thuc. 1. 89-102; 1. 128-138; 4. 102
    Ar. AP. 23
    Plutarch: Kimon 9
    scholion to Aischines 2. 31, accessible in Hill's Sources, page 3
    J. A. O. Larsen, "The Constitution and Original Purpose of the Delian
        League," Harvard Studies in Classical Philology 51, 1940, 175-213
    A. W. Gomme: A Historical Commentary on Thucydides I (Oxford 1945)
        289-295
    B. D. Merritt, H. T. Wade-Gery, M. F. McGregor: The Athenian Tribute
        Lists III, 94-224
    R. Sealey, "The Origin of the Delian League," in E. Badian, editor:
        Ancient Society and Institutions -- Studies presented to Victor
        Ehrenberg (Oxford 1966) 233-255
    A. H. Jackson, "The Original Purpose of the Delian League," Historia
        18, 1969, 12-16
    Kurt Raaflaub, "Beute, Vergeltung, Freiheit? Zur Zielsetzung des
        Delisch-Attischen Seebundes," Chiron 9, 1979, 1-22

    (What was the purpose of the Delian League? How extensive
    was its original membership? What circumstances led to its formation?)

9. Disaffection in the Athenian Empire ca. 454 - ca. 443
    Thuc. 1. 98-117
    Meiggs/Lewis Nos. 40, 43, 52
    Hill/Meiggs/Andrewes B30
    R. Meiggs: The Athenian Empire (Oxford 1972) 109-128, 234-254
    J. C. Barron, "Milesian Politics and Athenian Propaganda, c. 460-440 B.C.",
        JHS. 82, 1962, 1-6
    B.D. Meritt, "The Tribute Quota List of 454/3 B.C.," Hesperia 41,
        1972, 403-417
    C. W. Fornara, "The Date of the Regulations for Miletus," American
        Journal of Philology 92, 1971, 473-475
    M. Pierart, "Milet dans la premiere lists de tributs," Zeitschrift
        für Papyrologie und Epigraphik 15, 1974, 163-167

    further reading, if desired:
    Hans-Joachim Gehrke, "Zur Geschichte Milets in der Mitte des
        5. Jahrhunderts v. Chr.," Historia 29, 1980, 17-31
    R. Meiggs, "The Crisis of Athenian Imperialism," HSCP, 67, 1963, 1-36

attention is drawn to the lists of tribute-payments in
Hill-Meiggs/Andrewes 403-426 and in Meiggs, Athenian Empire 538-561

(What happened at Miletos? How widespread was disaffection? What
opportunities did the disaffected take advantage of ?)

10. The hypothesis of class-struggle in the Athenian Empire

Thuc. 3. 1-51; 3. 82; 4. 78-88; 4. 102-116; 4. 120-135; 8. 21;
     8. 73
G. E. M. de Ste. Croix, "The Character of the Athenian Empire,"
     Historia 3, 1954-55, 1-41
D. W. Bradeen, "The Popularity of the Athenian Empire," Historia
     9, 1960, 257-269
C. W. Fornara, "I. G. I^2, 39. 52-57 and the Popularity of the
     Athenian Empire," CSCA 10, 1977, 39-55

further reading, if desired:
H. W. Pleket, "Thasos and the Popularity of the Athenian Empire,"
     Historia 12, 1963, 70-77
T. J. Quinn, "Thucydides and the Unpopularity of the Athenian Empire,"
     Historia 13, 1964, 257-266
J. de Romilly, "Thucydides and the Cities of the Athenian Empire,"
     BICS. 13, 1966, 1-12
T. J. Quinn, "Political Groups at Chios: 412 B.C.," Historia 18,
     1969, 22-30
R. P. Legon, "Samos in the Delian League," Historia 21, 1972,
     145-158

(Were political struggles in the Athenian Empire due to a constant
conflict between rich and poor or to other causes?)

CLASSICS 229: History of Greece   Fall 1982

                        Course Description

James M. Heath   Bucknell University
Aims of course

   This course will present you with an overview of Greek history and try
to elicit from you reactions from that presentation. The textbook, Sealey,
A History of the Greek States, 700-338 B.C., has a rather traditional
approach that concentrates on political institutions and their development.
Such other factors as the economic, religious, literary, artistic, social,
and so on are mentioned but not given the emphasis they would be given in
the history of a modern state. There are perhaps two reasons for this
emphasis: the author's interests and, more important, the nature of the
sources on which we depend for our knowledge of Greek history. These
sources reflect the concerns of the ancients. It is our task to try to
extrapolate from those sources to answer a different set of questions.

   The course, then, presents you with this textbook and with other sources
of information on the ancient Greek world, ancient works in translation and
modern works. Your task will be to go beyond the textbook: to pose questions
that the textbook and other works do not seem to be aware of and to reinter-
pret the information you are given in ways other than the authors interpret
it. In a sense the task is to develop an approach to and concern for Greek
history that is unique and individual, but which still places due reliance
upon the information you have access to. You will be expected not so much
to absorb facts (though some such absorption is necessary) as to use
information in critical and imaginative ways.

Grading Scheme

   Your final grade in the course will be based on the following factors;
they are described in greater detail later:

   1) a short analytical essay, due Oct. 15, 15%

   2) the midterm exam, tentatively scheduled for Wed., Oct. 13, 20%

   3) a map project, due by Oct. 22, 10%

   4) a second essay on one of several structured types, 25%, due Nov. 12

   5) another piece of work, for 30% of your final grade, one of
        the following:

      a) the final exam, whenever scheduled by Registrar's Office;
      b) a paper (described later) on Mary Renault's Nature of
         Alexander, due by end of final exam;
      c) another essay, on either another of the suggested topics or a
         topic selected by you and approved by me, due Dec. 3;
      d) a creative project, involving a combination of art work, music,
         etc. with a written description or analysis of what you are
         about, due Dec. 3
   Note: If you choose option c or d for the final 30%, you should have the
         topic or project discussed with and approved by me by Nov. 17.

General notes on work for grades

1) The due dates are spread throughout the semester to enable you to concentrate on one matter at a time. The last piece is due either before dead week or by the end of the final exam, depending on which option you pick. The dates are firm: but I shall permit each of you to exceed the deadline for _one_ work project (not an exam) by one week. But let me know that you are availing yourself of this option before the deadline.
   I urge you to try to get work to me before the various deadlines. I should have more time to read it and return it to you quickly, with comments.

2) I am anxious to help you develop your ideas and to critique your work in its early stages, on the essays. Make an appointment to see me in my office for this. But be aware that if you wait until close to a deadline to see me you will have to wait in line and won't get the kind of help that you need. If you want to develop a topic for a paper I shall ask you for a starting point on which to build. If you leave written work, in rough form, with me I shall get it back to you as soon as I can.

3) In your written work organization and argument are essential. Find a theme, a point to make, and select pieces of information that can be used to develop that theme. Build structure into your work, don't just list and juxtapose facts. Let one idea lead into another, an answer to one question to a new question.

4) The writing style is important. Try above all to be clear and direct. After that you should aim for liveliness. Avoid passive verb forms; specify who does, says, thinks things.
   Watch your proofreading. Accurate spelling contributes to a good visual impression an essay conveys. If you are weak in this area, have a more literate or observant colleague read through a draft. Then make the necessary corrections, retyping whole pages if too many corrections are needed.

5) Essays should be typed. Typing creates a more effective visual impression than even good handwriting. This need makes it all the more important to plan ahead. I will accept the Alexander paper due at the final exam time in written form if typists are unavailable, with these provisos: alternate lines vacant, margins on all four sides, length corresponding to the typed requirement.

Paper topics

1) Short essay, due Oct. 1. Length: about 3 pages (i.e., 2-4). This work is to be an _essay_ in the etymological sense, an _attempt_ to explore the meaning of and the problems in understanding, some fact or remark in something you have read so far in the course. You have to pose a question, think about relating the general and the specific, the theoretical and the factual.
   For example, on p. 10 of Sealey, four lines from the bottom, you read the sentence: "Communications by land were difficult." What does this mean in practice? You might have to consider first what "communications" can refer to: trade, travel, messenger services, diplomacy. Which of these (if any)

comes to mind first, and why? Why would people in those places and times want to communicate? On what occasions? At what times of the year? Who (in the society) would want to communicate?

When you have posed and investigated some questions regarding communications you are in a better position to approach the second part of the sentence, with the emphasis on land communications and their difficulty. You can now suggest some kinds of land communication that are possible and the reasons for their difficulty--and necessity.

For this essay you should not look outside yourself and what you have read in the course for data. The exercise requires you to isolate a problem and to bring to it your powers of analysis. First, find the point that conceals a problem; second, see how your own resources can help you throw light on that problem. Try to introduce examples of phenomena in Greek history that illuminate your problem. In the "communications by land" question, for example, you might bring in the changes of techniques of warfare that Sealey talks about on p. 29.

I'll be happy to try to help you develop a question. But you must take the first step: come to see me and point to a passage that interests you.

Second or alternative paper topics

a) Summary and comment essay

This essay should be about 5 typed pages (i.e., 4-6) and should both summarize and, more important, comment upon a short passage in a scholarly work or ancient source that you locate for yourself outside the materials assigned in the course. The passage may come from a book (not a "textbook" but a work on a specific topic relating to Greek civilization); it may be a part of or a whole article in a periodical, or a book review, or a passage from an ancient source you haven't seen officially. The passage you choose should be short, about 2 or 3 pages minimum and 5 or 6 maximum, and it should be complete in itself somehow. Attach a xerox copy of the passage you choose to your essay.

Your task in the essay is, first, to summarize the point the author is making. Explain what question(s) s/he is addressing, what kinds of information are used, what attitudes and assumptions the author shows, what conclusions are reached in the passage. This part should take up less than half the paper. The second part of your paper should comment on what you have summarized, and raise questions about it. Are there aspects of the author's question you don't understand or the author doesn't make clear? Are the author's attitudes and assumptions unusual--different from your own? Does anything in the argument differ from what Sealey or some other author you are reading the course, ancient or modern, indicates? In other words, you are to write a short essay that comments on the passage you choose on the basis of your own reasoning fortified with what you are encountering in this course. Your essay should open up areas for discussion.

For suitable materials you may refer to the footnotes following the chapters in Sealey or Finley, or look for books in the library (Greek History is DF, in the basement, Classics is PA on the first mezzanine). You may want to consult one of the following periodicals in the Periodical Room:

American Historical Review

American Journal of Archaeology

American Journal of Philology

Antiquity

Archaeology

Classical Journal

Classical Philology

Classical Quarterly

Classical Review

Classical World

Comparative Studies in Society and History

Greece and Rome

Hesperia

Historia

History and Theory

Phoenix

Past and Present

See also: Journal of Hellenic Studies, DF 10..J8

b) Tragedy/History essay.

This essay too should be about 5 pages in length. The task for you is to explore the historical nature of a tragedy, or at least a section of one. First, you must choose a particular play, or a particular passage within that play that appears significant as offering some kind of contemporary reference: a passage discussing justice, individuals who seek power, war, the vengeance of the gods, etc. Next, you have to attempt to make sense of this reference in the play. To do so you have to place the play in time: this is not always possible with pin-point accuracy, but a time range can be proposed. When you know when, or about when, the play was composed you can start finding out what was going on in the world then, especially in or affecting Athens, that the play reference could apply to. This ends the information-gathering phase; a summary of this should introduce your essay.

The second part of the essay then will try to make sense of this information, to see what kind of statement the author of the play is making to the Athenian audience. Discuss how the author structures a situation, what attitudes and assumptions he holds, whether he expects the views expressed in the play to differ from and criticize those of the wo/man in the theater of Dionysus, in what way the audience is being educated.

Identify the play you choose and the translation you use, and the particular passage you concentrate on. For general assistance on chronology and plot, refer to John Ferguson, A Companion to Greek Tragedy (PA 3131 .F4, on reserve) or Crowell's Handbook of Classical Drama (PA 3024 .H35, in the Reference Room), or a work you locate on the library shelves. Be sure to footnote information you receive from such works.

NOTE: This is not an exercise in literary criticism (aesthetic)!

c) An essay relating an aspect of the Greek and contemporary worlds

This five-page essay involves you in attempting to compare an aspect common to Greek and contemporary civilization. Let us say, for example, that you choose law. The first thing to do is to isolate a particular feature of law that lends itself to comparison: let's say the treatment of murder cases. Now first you need to specify how Greeks treated murder. But law differed from polis to polis, so you should choose one: Athens, say. Now you need to pick a time, since the treatment of murder changed over time in Athens. The fifth century offers a critical time: as you gather from the Aeschylean trilogy, murder is changing from a crime against a family to one against the state. It was to be handled as a public matter rather than as a private one—and obviously many people were upset by this change and thought that traditional religion and values were destroyed.

Now you need to pick a contemporary feature that offers a comparison. It is not now the challenge to religious forces that arouse popular concern but the means to deter murderers. Will capital punishment do the job, or life imprisonment? Would greater attention to ignorance, poverty, and discrimination have some effect? What role should the courts of law play, as an arm of the police forces of the state or the guardians of the legal process, even when that appears to hinder attempts to reduce crime?

Your job, then, is to present a facet of Greek society, one that illustrates a dilemma preferably, and an analogous contemporary situation. Then as a conclusion you can comment on how the Greek resolution of the classical dilemma may (or may not) assist in resolving the contemporary one.

Midterm exam (tentatively set for Wednesday, Oct. 13)

This exam will ask for short responses (a sentence or so) to questions that elicit your understanding of important fundamental points made in the textbook and the sources you have been assigned. I might, for example, ask what is unusual about the Spartan kings (See Sealey, pp. 70ff.) or the meaning of tyranny in the Greek sense (p. 38). Examples should be cited. There will be a good bit of choice on the exam.

Map project

Attached to this course description you will find two copies of an outline map of the Aegean world. You are to enter on these maps 100 geographical features of the Greek world (50 on each) according to the scheme below and also to write a page or two (see later).

On one, enter the following (see ways of identifying below):

a) 15 geographical <u>areas</u> of the Greek world (e.g., Attica)--sketch in rough boundaries;
b) 15 mountains or mountain ranges in the Greek world of historical or cultural significance;
c) 10 rivers or water channels important in Greek history;
d) 10 battle sites in Greek history.

On the other map enter:

e) 15 islands that play important roles in Greek history;
f) 15 communities (cities, etc.) that are not the most well known but play roles in Greek history;
g) 8 sites whose importance in the Greek world is as international centers;
h) 12 waterfront features of the land (capes, gulfs, etc.) that have played roles in Greek history.

Develop a scheme for identifying each feature on the map, by type. For example, you might use different colors, or different symbols. Number each feature within its type (e.g., River 1, 2, etc.)

Written work

a) Draw up a list of the 100 features you place on the maps, keyed to them and indicating the symbols, colors, etc. you use. Number each entry.

30

b) Choose one feature from each of the 8 types and write a 3 or 4-sentence statement about a role that feature played in some specific incident in Greek history. Try to be as specific and descriptive as you can.

For assistance in locating features, refer to maps in your textbook or other works on the library shelves. In particular I recommend you ask at the Reference Desk for atlases of the classical world kept there.

Alexander the Great paper (final exam alternative)

This paper should be a bit more substantial than the second paper. It should reflect both a reading of Mary Renault's The Nature of Alexander and the whole course. Your task is to pick out an episode or theme in the Renault work that demonstrates some kind of continuity or lack of continuity throughout Greek history. You will then describe some feature of civilization a) as it appears in the book, b) as it appears at one or more points in Greek history. You will then discuss how the feature has changed over the time period--even if it appears the same, this may be an illusion. As you do this you will have to consider the artistic aims of Mary Renault and the extent to which her attitudes are shaped by the needs of the modern reader.

Other final exam alternatives

These too should be more substantial than the second paper. You should check with me in plenty of time for help and for an OK.

Final exam

The exam schedule appears in November usually. The exam will be of the essay type. The questions will be of a comprehensive nature, asking you to develop themes characteristic of the whole sweep of Greek history. I attach a copy of an exam of a couple of years ago with this course description to give an idea of the kind of thing I ask. I shall attempt to give a sheet with sample questions by the last class. It may also be an open book exam. The best preparation for this kind of exam is to follow the course along rather than to cram at the end. It will ask you not to regurgitate facts but to present information in interesting conformations. You will use information to illustrate points not to fulfill my need to know.

Transliterating Greek

You probably will not need it, but in case you do or are just interested, I attach a sheet explaining a bit about the writing and transliterating of Greek.

CL 229 History of Greece   Fall 1982   Detailed assignment list

Week no.	Dates	Readings	Topics
1	9/3		Introduction
2	9/6-8-10	Finley, World of Odysseus, pp. 15-141 Portable Gk. Historians, pp. 63-81 (Herodotus)	The prelude to Greek history: themes and assumptions
3	9/13-15-17	Finley, World of O, pp. 142-77 Sealey, pp. 10-35; 38-59; 66-86	Archaic Greece
4	9/20-22-24	Sealey, pp. 89-105; 107-28; 134-59; 164-66(top) Port. Gk. Hist., pp. 26-62	The development of Athens; Herodotus as historian
5	9/27-29-10/1	Sealey, pp. 169-92; 195-228 PortGrHist., pp. 81-100	Persian and Greece: historicity?
6	10/4-6-8	PGrHist, pp. 100-215 Sealey, pp. 232-64 (Fri.)	Between the major wars

7	10/11-13-15	Mon.: Sealey, pp. 268-94
		     PortGrHist, pp. 218-32
		Wed.: Midterm exam
		Fri.: Greek Drama, pp. 14-54
		     (ed. Moses Hades)
			Mid-fifth century
			
			Aeschylus

8	10/18-20-22	Sealey, pp. 297-321; 324-33 PortGrHist., pp. 232-65, 290-98 Greek Drama, pp. 111-149 or 188-221	Start of Peloponnesian War; Sophocles and Euripides
9	10/27-29	(Monday is part of fall break) Lang, The Athenian Citizen PortGrHist, pp. 265-90 Greek Drama, pp. 55-79 or 222-55	Life and concerns of Athenians
10	11/1-3-5	Sealey, pp. 333-46; 348-58 PortGrHist., pp. 298-379	Course of Peloponnesian War
11	11/8-10-12	Sealey, pp. 358-67; 369-84 Greek Drama, pp. 151-87 or 256-87 Gk Drama, pp. 288-337	The end of the war.
12	11/15-17-19	Sealey, pp. 386-98; 404-21; 423-36 PGrHist, pp. 381-439; 489-95	The fourth century Xenophon Constitutions

32

List of readings (continued)

Week	Dates	Readings	Topics
13	11/22	Menander, Dyscolus (The Grouch): on reserve.	Late fourth century Athenian society
14	11/29-12/1-3	Sealey, pp. 438-61; 469-92 Renault, Nature of Alexander, pp. 3-124	The rise of Macedon and end of the classical period in the Greek world.
15	12/6-8-10	Finish Renault, Nature of Alex.	Alexander and his legacy, the Hellenistic world.

CL 229   History of Greece   Final Exam, Fall 1980

   This final exam is to consist of four essays, one from each of the four
sections below. Ideally, they should be what you might write in a half
hour, though you may have the full three hours for the exam. They should
be essays in the sense that you develop a question or topic or approach
and explore its ramifications. Develop paragraphs and connect points within
paragraphs by some kind of logic. In all the essays you should attempt to
consider changes over time in both external conditions and events and in
internalized attitudes. Try, too, to make specific reference to some actual
events and reflections of events in written works; show that you are aware
of the time relationships within and among these events or accounts of events.
   In each section, develop a topic for an essay that is either one of the
questions asked or something more comfortable for you that you can derive
from what is asked.

                                  A

   How do Greeks distinguish themselves from non-Greeks and members of
particular city-states from those of other city-states? How do the Greeks'
definitions of themselves and "others" differ at one time and over time?
In what ways do Greeks discover identity?

                                  B

1. In what ways are both independence and dependence and interdependence
characteristic of Greek citizens and states in different periods?

2   In what ways does Greek civilization offer opportunities for individuals
to distinguish themselves? In what ways is the group more dominant than
the individual?

                                  C

1. In what ways might a Greek (male or female) conceptualize his or her past?
How might this conception of the past differ at 500 B.C., 400 B.C., 300 B.C.?
In what particular ways might the past contrast or conflict with the present
at those times?

2. How might one reconcile the beauty of the Parthenon with the brutality
of Athenian rule? What problems does this paradox introduce? Is this paradox unusual in Greek history or at other times and in other places?

3. In what ways is tragedy or Aristophanic comedy a phenomenon unique to
fifth century Athens? In what ways is it universal? In what ways is it im-
possible for that particular form to exist in other Greek times?

                                  D

   It might be said that Alexander's assuming the throne of Macedon marked
the death of the city-state in the Greek world. (This may be an overstatement.)
What does this statement involve? What are the steps that lead to the downfall of the Greek city-state? Did the city-state have a built-in flaw from
the beginning? Do you think a Greek of Alexander's time or after would have
agreed with the statement?

                                  34

Some guidelines for transliterating Greek words into English.
Below is the alphabet: capital form, lowercase, name, usual English
transliteration (sometimes with alternatives).

A α   alpha   a (fa̱ther)

B β   beta   b

Γ γ   gamma   g (always hard)

Δ δ   delta   d

E ε   epsilon e (ge̱t)

Z ζ   zeta   zd or dz or z

H η   eta: as in sheep's ba̱a̱

Θ θ   theta: th (thin)

I ι   iota   i (bi̱t)

K κ   kappa   c (hard) or k

Λ λ   lambda l

M μ   mu m

N ν   nu n

Ξ ξ   xi x (ks, both letters)

O o   omicron o (not in U.S. dialects)

Π π   pi p

P ρ   rho r

Σ σ,ς sigma s (ς at end of words)

T τ   tau t

Υ υ   upsilon y or u (French u,
                        German ü)

Φ φ   phi ph (Philip)

X χ   chi ch, kh (Scottish loch)

Ψ ψ   psi ps (both letters)

Ω ω   omega long o (ocean)

There is also a way to represent initial h: ' over the opening vowel or
diphthong (a double vowel combination). This is called "rough breathing."

Diphthongs: αι: ai, ae, ει: ei, i οι: oi, oe, υι: ui
                     e   e
            αυ: au   ευ: eu   ου: ou, u

Initial υ always has the rough breathing (hence the large number of English
words that begin hy-). Initial r also has the rough breathing, hence is
written in English rh- (pronounced like hr-).

The accent marks indicate change in musical pitch not stress.

Some examples (Hatzfeld, p. 29):

   ἔξοχοι ἄνδρες; exochoi andres   ἄριστοι : aristoi

   Εὐπατρίδαι: Eupatridae

   ἀγορά, ἀπελλά, ἐκκλησία: agora, apella, ecclesia

   συνοικισμοί : synoikismoi (there is an English word synoecism)

NAME: _____

36

University of Syracuse

HISTORY 50   Don Lateiner
Fall 1985   Syllabus

        GREEK HISTORY 550-400 BCE

WEEK   TOPIC   READINGS

1. Introduction to the study of ancient history   Ehrenberg. SS I.1-3
   a. Sources: archaeology, inscriptions, texts
   b. Geography of Greek lands
   c. Background: Prehistory, Minoan-Mycenean.   Fornara. AP 1,3,4
      Dark Ages

2. Archaic Greece: Community and Communities
   a. Economic and Social Organization & Conflicts
      Rich and poor, aristocrat and peasant   AP 11
   b. Expansion: trade and colonization   SS I. 4-5,Thuc.I.1-23
            (& piracy)   AP 4-6, 8,14,17 18, 29,33. 17
   c. Hoplite warfare and the rise of tyranny   AP 7-8,10, 16,24,25. 36

3. Chief centers of mainland power
   a. Sparta: Lycourgos, rhetra, and the military SS II; [Plut.Lyc.]
                                                    AP 2,9,12,13, 27,38
   b. Corinth: Cypselid tyranny   AP 21. Hdt.V.91 92
   c. Athens: Drakon, Solon, Peisistratus: Social
      Justice   SS III-IV.1;[Plut Sol.]
                                                    AP 15,22-23,26,30-31,37,39

4. Asia Minor: Greek development and foreign powers
   a. Athens still: Cleisthenes' reforms   IV.2; AP 40-44
   b. Ionia: tyranny and greatness   Hdt. I; AP 19,20, 32, 63
   c. Lydia: Croesus; Medeo-Persian Empire: Cyrus, AP 28,34. 35, 45-46, 72; Hdt.
      Cambyses, Darius   III

5. Revolutionary (=Archaic) Greece
   a. Archaic art: Geometric, Orientalizing. Attic
   b. Lyric Poetry and Ionian rationalism   SS IV.3
   c. Exam I

6. Conflict between Greek mini-powers and Persian Super-power
   a. The Ionian rebellion   SS. V.1; Hdt. V-VI.1-35
   b. Marathon Campaign   SS. V.2, AP 48-51
   c. Battle of Marathon: Case Study in anc. warfare SS. V.3; Hdt. VI.94-140

7. Xerxes' Invasion and Herodotus' Histories
   a. Preparations and the march. Greek Defense.   SS. V.4; AP 41,52-53. 56
      Athenian ostracism.   Hdt.VII.1-172
   b. Thermopylae & Artemision   Hdt. VII.173-VIII.1-40

   c. Salamis & Plataea; Mycale   Hdt.VIII.41 IX.104
                                                    SS V.5; AP 55,57-60

37

8. Hellenic Defense League > Athenian alliance
    a. Formation   SS VI.1; AP 61, 63,65
                                            Hdt.IX.105-122; Thuc. I. 89-97
    b. Expansion & revenues. Instruments of imperialism AP 62,66,68,69, 71, 85,97-103,1
    c. Internal and external campaigns   Thuc.I. 97-117; AP 77,
                                            78, 95, 108, 110, 112-15

9. The Athenian democracy   SS. VI.2
    a. Evolution and organization   AP 105-106
    b. Participation in civil & military affairs   AP 86
    c. Criticism: Aristophanes, "Old Oligarch"   AP 107 (OO), 111,
                                            Aristoph. Wasps

10. Perikles: "Golden Age"?   SS. VI.3
    a. The man and his influence   Thuc. II. 34-46, AP 74, 75
                                          76,79, 96, 104,109,
                                          116; [Plut. Per.]
    b. Classical art, Sophists. Hippocratic Medicine   SS. VIII.1-2; AP 117-118
                                           120-21
    c. Exam II

11. The causes of the Peloponnesian war   SS. VII.1
    a. Sparta's Allies   AP 73, 80, 89
    b. Sparta and its territory   AP 67, 104
    c. Athens & its allies & subjects   Thuc. I. 118-46
                                           AP 81-85, 86, 90, 92-94, 95
                                           119, 122-125

12. Phase I: The Ten Years War   SS. VII.2
    a.Corcyra, Potidaea, Platea   Thuc. I, II
                                           AP 126-30, 133-38
    b. Greek Revolutions: Athenian Plague, Kleon
        Corcyra, Chalcidice   AP 131, 139-41;Thuc.III. IV.75-V.24
    c. Phase II: The Temporary Peace; Melos   Thuc. V. 84-116;AP 132, 142-44

13. Phase III: Sicily and South Italy   Thuc. VI-VII
    a. Development of Greek Cities in the West   SS. VI.4; AP 5,29, 52,54,64,91
    b. Athenian Invasion   SS. VII.3,VIII.5
                                           Aristoph. Birds; AP 146-47
    c. Revolution in Athens   SS.VII.4; Thuc. VIII.1-57;
                                           AP 145, 148-51, 155

14. Phase IV: Sparta's Triumph   Thuc. VIII.58-109
    a. The Aegean War, The Decelean War   AP 152-54, 156-65, 166
    b. Peace and its consequences   SS VIII.3, AP 167-70;
                                           [Xen. Hell. I-II]
    c. A New Athens: Aristophanes. Socrates. Plato   SS. VIII.6; Arist. Clouds

15. Fifth-century Greece: An Assessment
    a. Politics. Law and Economy   AP 70,87,88, 97, 137,147
    b. Cultural life: Religion, Sport, drama, literature AP 75, 90
    c. ?

DONALD LATEINER
HUMANITIES & CLASSICS
OHIO WESLEYAN UNIVERSITY
DELAWARE, OHIO 43015

INFORMATIONAL

PURPOSE: To acquaint students with the critical period of Ancient Greek history
from 550-399 BCE, the Archaic and early Classical phases. We investigate social
and economic structures (slavery, law, etc.) as well as political history
(tyranny, democracy, civil wars, the invasion of Greece) from Croesus to
Socrates. Archaeology will be featured; classes include lectures, slides, and
discussion.

BOOKS: V. Ehrenberg, From Solon to Socrates (New York 1973) 2nd ed. SS
Ch. Fornara, Archaic Times to the End of the Peloponnesian War (NY 1983) 2nd
ed. AP
Herodotus, The Persian Wars (Penguin, tr. A. de Selincourt)
Thucydides, The Peloponnesian War (Penguin, tr. R. Warner)
Aristophanes, Three Comedies (U Mich., tr. W. Arrowsmith)

Ehrenberg has written our basic text, a modern synthesis of
ancient information (literary and inscriptional texts), papyri,
coins, art, etc.) and modern reconstruction (archaeology,
historical analysis, etc.). Fornara generally presents the
ancient governmental documents unaffected by tranmission
(medieval copying, destruction, etc.). Hdt. and Thuc. offer the
first historical accounts in Western history--they invented the
subject. Aristophanes writes political, often scabrous comedies
about democracy,imperialism, and intellectual fads. We shall
read much but not all in each volume. All knowledge must be based
on the ancient--PRIMARY--sources.

TESTS: The syllabus includes three exams, one at the end of each
third of the course (five weeks). Each will provide a choice of
"identifications" (5 of 8?) and essays (1 of 3). We shall try to
review before exams. A weekly brief and easy quiz is likely. One
"make up" exam will be given in the last week; it will be
"comprehensive". No "make up" quizzes.

PAPERS: Two short papers (4 pages typed and double-spaced)--or
one long paper in two final drafts--will give you a chance to
write history. I will suggest problems, topics as well as ancient
and modern sources. You may choose a different topic but be sure
to get my approval for it.

CLASSES: Please participate in class discussion. Attend every
class without fail. Three absences will not be penalized; the
fourth will cost a full letter grade.

GRADE FORMULA: Class contribution 20%; Exams 30%; Quizzes 30%;
Papers 20%.

This information and the syllabus are subject to change. Any
suggestions?

History 106A
Mr. Gruen

Spring, 1985
MWF 10-11

The Roman Republic

Book List

Caesar, The Conquest of Gaul (Penguin pb)
Cary, M. and Scullard, H.H., A History of Rome (3rd ed.) (St. Martin's)
Catullus, The Complete Poetry (U. of Michigan pb)
Cicero, Letters to Atticus (Penguin pb)
Cicero, Selected Political Speeches (Penguin pb)
Cicero, On the Good Life (Penguin pb)
Lewis, N. and Reinhold, M., Roman Civilization: Source Book I: The
    Republic (Harper Torchbooks pb)
Livy, The Early History of Rome (Penguin pb)
Livy, Rome and the Mediterranean (Penguin pb)
Lucretius, On the Nature of the Universe (Penguin pb)
Plautus, Pot of Gold and Other Plays (Penguin pb)
Plutarch, The Makers of Rome (Penguin pb)
Plutarch, The Fall of the Roman Republic (Penguin pb)
Polybius, The Rise of the Roman Empire (Penguin pb)
Sallust, The Jugurthine War, the Conspiracy of Catiline (Penguin pb)

Lecture and Reading List

First Week (Jan. 21-27)

Jan. 21: Holiday

Jan. 23: Introduction

    Cary, pp. 3-6

Jan. 25: Prehistoric Italy

    Cary, pp. 7-15

Second Week (Jan. 28 - Feb. 3)

Jan. 28: Greeks and Etruscans

    Cary, pp. 16-28

Jan. 30: Legends and Facts of Early Rome

    Cary, pp. 31-56
    Livy, Early History of Rome, I (entire), II, 1-21
    Lewis and Reinhold, pp. 46-62

Feb. 1: The Struggle of the Orders

    Cary, pp. 57-69, 75-79
    Lewis and Reinhold, pp. 89-129

Third Week (Feb. 4-10)

Feb. 4: Roman Expansion in Italy

        Cary, pp. 70-74, 84-94
        Livy, Early History of Rome, V (entire)
        Lewis and Reinhold, pp. 70-88

Feb. 6: The Roman Confederation and the War with Pyrrhus

        Cary, pp. 94-95, 99-107

Feb. 8: The First Punic War and its Aftermath

        Cary, pp. 113-122
        Polybius, I, 1-15, III, 22-26

Fourth Week (Feb. 11-17)

Feb. 11: The War with Hannibal

        Cary, pp. 124-137
        Polybius, III, 1-17, 20-21, 27-35, 77-89, 106-118

Feb. 13: The Constitutional and Political Structure

        Cary, pp. 79-83, 97-99
        Polybius, VI, 2-18, 43-58

Feb. 15: Discussion

Fifth Week (Feb. 18-24)

Feb. 18: Holiday

Feb. 20: Roman Comedy: The Advent of Latin Literature

        Cary, pp. 194-198
        Plautus, The Brothers Menaechmus, The Swaggering Soldier,
            Pseudolus

Feb. 22: Roman Religion

        Cary, pp. 109, 198-199
        Lewis and Reinhold, pp. 129-150, 466-482

Sixth Week (Feb. 25 - March 3)

Feb. 25: The Origins of Roman Involvement in the East

        Cary, pp. 123, 150-154
        Polybius, II, 2-12, III, 16-19
        Livy, Rome and the Mediterranean, XXXI, 1-9, 14-18

Feb. 27: Rome and the Hellenistic Monarchies, 200-188 BC

       Cary, pp. 154-157, 161-165
       Polybius, XVIII, 1-12, 44-46
       Livy, <u>Rome and the Mediterranean</u>, XXXII, 8-12, XXXIII, 1-10,
           30-35, 39-42, XXXIV, 48-52, 57-59, XXXV, 12-19,
           XXXVI, 15-21, XXXVII, 34-45, 52-56, XXXVIII, 8-11, 37-39
       Lewis and Reinhold, pp. 309-313

March 1: Tradition and Change in the East, 188-168 BC

       Cary, pp. 157-159, 165-166
       Polybius, XXIV, 11-13
       Livy, <u>Rome and the Mediterranean</u>, XXXIX, 23-29, 33-37, 46-48, 53
           XL, 2-24, 54-58, XLII, 5-6, 11-18, 29-30, XLIV, 30-46
       Lewis and Reinhold, pp. 314-316

Seventh Week (March 4-10)

March 4: Rome, Greece, and Asia Minor, 167-129 BC

       Cary, pp. 159-160
       Polybius, XXIV, 11-13
       Livy, <u>Rome and the Mediterranean</u>, XLV, 17-33, 44
       Lewis and Reinhold, pp. 316-323

March 6: Rome and the West, 200-133 BC

       Cary, pp. 138-149
       Polybius, XXXVI, 9
       Livy, <u>Rome and the Mediterranean</u>, XXXIV, 8-21, 60-62,
           XLII, 23-24

March 8: Discussion

Eighth Week (March 11-17)

March 11: Domestic Politics, 200-133 BC

       Cary, pp. 177-185
       Plutarch, <u>Cato the Elder</u>
       Livy, <u>Rome and the Mediterranean</u>, XXXVIII, 43-60, XXXIX, 40-46

March 13: Midterm Examination

March 15: The Economic Background to the Gracchan Era

       Cary, pp. 186-193
       Lewis and Reinhold, pp. 227-234

Ninth Week (March 18-24)

March 18: Tiberius Gracchus

> Cary, pp. 203-206
> Plutarch, Tiberius Gracchus
> Lewis and Reinhold, pp. 237-240

March 20: Gaius Gracchus

> Cary, pp. 206-211
> Plutarch, Gaius Gracchus
> Lewis and Reinhold, pp. 243-251

March 22: The Age of Marius

> Cary, pp. 212-226
> Plutarch, Marius
> Sallust, Jugurthine War, 1-46, 63-65, 82-86
> Lewis and Reinhold, pp. 256-267

Tenth Week (March 25-31)

March 25: Sulla

> Cary, pp. 226-238
> Plutarch, Sulla,
> Lewis and Reinhold, pp. 269-271

March 27: The Breakdown of the Sullan Constitution

> Cary, pp. 239-244
> Plutarch, Sertorius

March 29: The Conspiracy of Catiline

> Cary, pp. 244-248
> Cicero, Orations against Catiline, I, II, IV
> Sallust, The Conspiracy of Catiline

Eleventh Week (April 1-7)

April 1: The First Triumvirate

> Cary, pp. 248-249, 255-256, 265-266
> Cicero, Letters to Atticus, #12-14, 16-19, 21, 23, 27, 29, 30, 36, 38-42

April 3: Caesar and the Gallic War

> Cary, pp. 258-264
> Caesar, The Conquest of Gaul, I-II (entire)

April 5: Discussion

43

Twelfth Week (April 8-14)

April 8: The Coming of Civil War

    Cary, pp. 266-269
    Cicero, _Letters to Atticus_, #88-95, 104, 122, 124, 126-132

April 10: Civil War and Dictatorship

    Cary, pp. 270-282
    Cicero, _Letters to Atticus_, #134, 135, 139, 144-146, 151,
        153, 158, 161, 163, 165A, 171, 174, 178A, 185, 187
        199, 199B, 217
    Cicero, _In Support of Marcellus_

April 12: Rhetoric and Political Theory

    Cicero, _On the Orator_, I
    Cicero, _The Dream of Scipio_
    Plutarch, _Cicero_

Thirteenth Week (April 15-21)

April 15: Lucretius and Ciceronian Philosophy

    Cary, pp. 311-312
    Cicero, _On Duties_, II
    Lucretius, _On the Nature of the Universe_, II

April 17: Catullus and the New Poetry

    Cary, pp. 308-309
    Catullus, #2, 7, 8, 11, 29, 49, 53, 57, 58, 68, 76, 79,
        83, 85, 86, 93

April 19: Holiday

Fourteenth Week (April 22-28)

April 22: Sallust and Historical Writing

    Cary, pp. 309-310
    Sallust, _Jugurthine War_, 1-4, 41-42, 84-85

April 24: Economic Developments and Upper Class Society

    Cary, pp. 299-303
    Lewis and Reinhold, pp. 439-466, 482-513

April 26: The Roman Plebs

Fifteenth Week (April 29-May 3)

April 29: Why did the Republic Fall?

May 1: Discussion

44

The Roman Empire

Book List

Required

Acts of the Apostles

Aurelius, Marcus, _Meditations_

Birley, _Lives of the Later Caesars_

Cary, M. and H.H. Scullard, _A History of Rome_, 3rd ed.

Eusebius, _The History of the Church_

Horace, _The Complete Odes and Epodes_

Josephus, _The Jewish War_

Juvenal, _Sixteen Satires_

Lewis, N. and M. Reinhold, _Roman Civilization: The Empire_, II

Petronius/Seneca, _The Satyricon/The Apocolocyntosis_

Suetonius, _The Twelve Caesars_

Tacitus, _Annals of Imperial Rome_

Tacitus, _The Agricola and the Germania_

Vergil, _The Aeneid_

Recommended

Apuleius, _Golden Ass_

Lucian, _Selected Satires_

Oliver, _The Ruling Power_

Ovid, _The Erotic Poems_

Pliny the Younger, _Letters_

Lecture and Reading List

1st Week (Aug. 26 - Sept. 1)

August 26: Introduction

August 28: The Triumph of Octavian

Cary, pp. 283-298

August 30: The Augustan Principate

Cary, pp. 315-321, 343-347
Lewis and Reinhold, pp. 3-19, 72-79

2nd Week (Sept. 2-8)

Sept. 2: Holiday

Sept. 4: Society and Morals under Augustus

Cary, pp. 321-330, 347-350
Lewis and Reinhold, pp. 24-31, 47-49

Sept. 6: Literature and the Augustan Regime: Vergil and Livy

Vergil, Aeneid, I, VI, XII

3rd Week (Sept. 9-15)

Sept. 9: Literature and the Augustan Regime: Horace and Ovid

Horace, Odes, I, 2, 12, 21, 35, 37; II, 1, 7, 9, 15;
        III, 3, 5, 6, 14, 16, 24; IV, 5, 14, 15
Horace, Epodes, 1, 7, 9, 16
Ovid, Art of Love, I, III

Sept. 11: Discussion

Sept. 13: Tacitus and the Emperor Tiberius

Cary, pp. 351-354
Tacitus, Annals, I, 1-15, 72-81; II, 27-32, 43-88;
         II, 1-19; IV, 1-12

4th Week (Sept. 16-22)

Sept. 16: Caligula and Claudius

Cary, pp. 354-357, 360-365
Tacitus, Annals, XI, 23-28; XII, 1-9, 59-69
Suetonius, Caligula   **46**

Sept. 18: Nero

> Cary, pp. 359-360
> Tacitus, Annals, XIII, 1-5; XIV, 1-13; XV, 38-74

Sept. 20: Literature in the Age of Nero

> Cary, pp. 385-397
> Petronius, Satyricon, 26-78 ("Dinner with Trimalchio")
> Seneca, Apocolocyntosis

5th Week (Sept. 23-29)

Sept. 23: The Army and the Empire

> Cary, pp. 331-343, 366-376
> Lewis and Reinhold, pp. 31-47, 104-114

Sept. 25: The Year of the Four Emperors

> Cary, pp. 402-408
> Suetonius, Galba; Otho; Vitellius

Sept. 27: Discussion

6th Week (Sept. 30 - Oct. 6)

Sept. 30: Vespasian and the Making of a New Dynasty

> Cary, pp. 409-415, 418-420
> Lewis and Reinhold, pp. 88-90
> Suetonius, Vespasian

Oct. 2: The Flavians and the Frontiers

> Cary, pp. 420-424
> Tacitus, Agricola
> Suetonius, Domitian

Oct. 4: Economics and Society

> Cary, pp. 377-385
> Lewis and Reinhold, pp. 156-175, 222-238, 242-270

7th Week (Oct. 7-13)

Oct. 7: Women in the Roman Empire

> Lewis and Reinhold, pp. 252-254, 282-290, 379-383, 407-409
> Juvenal, Satires, VI

47

Oct. 9: Literature and Society: The Age of Juvenal

Juvenal, Satires, III, IV, V, VIII, IX, XI, XIV

Oct. 11: The Varieties of Roman Religions

Cary, pp. 397-400, 482-484
Lewis and Reinhold, pp. 552-581

8th Week (Oct. 14-20)

Oct. 14: Discussion

Oct. 16: Midterm Examination

Oct. 18: Judaism in the Early Roman Empire

Cary, pp. 367-368, 400, 415-417
Josephus, The Jewish Wars, I, 1-6, 120-158, 364-430;
II, 178-220, 271-344, 402-410; III, 1-8, 340-408;
IV, 1-83; VII, 252-406

9th Week (Oct. 21-27)

Oct. 21: The Birth of Christianity

Cary, pp. 400-401
Acts of the Apostles, 1-15

Oct. 23: The Social World of Early Christianity

Cary, pp. 484-485
Acts of the Apostles, 16-28

Oct. 25: Pliny and Trajan

Cary, pp. 425-426
Lewis and Reinhold, pp. 98-100, 336-347
Pliny, Letters, X

10th Week (Oct. 28 - Nov. 3)

Oct. 28: Crime and Christianity in the Roman Empire

Cary, pp. 486-488

Oct. 30: Hadrian

Cary, pp. 426, 432-438
Lives of the Later Caesars: "Hadrian"

Nov. 1: Discussion

11th Week (Nov. 4-10)

Nov. 4:   The Antonine Age: Expansion and Imperial Policy

> Cary, pp. 427-429
> Aristides, <u>Roman Oration</u> (<u>The Ruling Power</u>)
> M. Aurelius, <u>Meditations</u>, I-VIII

Nov. 6:   The Antonine Age: Social and Intellectual Aspects

> Cary, pp. 451-484
> Apuleius, <u>Golden Ass</u>, III, V, XI
> Lucian, <u>Satires</u>: "Alexander the Quack Prophet"; "The Death
>   of Peregrinus"

Nov. 8:   The End of the Antonines and Civil War

> Cary, pp. 489-492
> <u>Lives of the Later Caesars</u>: "Commodus", "Pertinax"; "Didius"

12th Week (Nov. 11-17)

Nov. 11:   The Severan Dynasty

> Cary, pp. 492-503
> <u>Lives of the Later Caesars</u>: "Septimius Severus"

Nov. 13:   Emperors and the Constitution

> Cary, pp. 427-429
> Lewis and Reinhold, pp. 82-98, 118-124

Nov. 15:   The Army and the Civil Administration

> Cary, pp. 429-433, 448-450
> Lewis and Reinhold, pp. 124-155, 490-531

13th Week (Nov. 18-24)

Nov. 18:   Discussion

Nov. 20:   The Crisis of the 3rd Century: Military and Political

> Cary, pp. 507-516
> Lewis and Reinhold, pp. 419-440

Nov. 22:   The Crisis of the 3rd Century: Social and Economic

> Cary, pp. 536-543
> Lewis and Reinhold, pp. 440-455

14th Week (Nov. 25 - Dec. 1)

    Nov. 25: Christianity under Fire

                Cary, pp. 485-486, 544-546
                Lewis and Reinhold, pp. 584-598
                Eusebius, <u>History of the Church</u>, V, 1-5; VI

    Nov. 27: Diocletian and the New Regime

                Cary, pp. 517-520, 524-535, 546-547
                Lewis and Reinhold, pp. 455-474, 598-602
                Eusebius, <u>History of the Church</u>, VIII-IX

    Nov. 29: Holiday

15th Week (Dec. 2-8)

    Dec. 2: Constantine and the Triumph of Christianity

                Cary, pp. 520-524, 547-549
                Lewis and Reinhold, pp. 475-489, 602-610
                Eusebius, <u>History of the Church</u>, X

    Dec. 4: Discussion

    Dec. 6: Did the Roman Empire Decline and Fall?

                Cary, pp. 550-558

SYLLABUS: HISTORY   413:   THE   NEAR   EAST   FROM   ALEXANDER   TO
             CLEOPATRA

PROFESSOR: Stanley M. Burstein, California State University, Los
            Angeles

     However different they may be in other ways, modern western
and Islamic civilizations share a common core,   the Greek
intellectual tradition in its Hellenistic form.   The purpose of
this course is to analyze the historical environment in which
that cultural legacy developed.

Texts:

     Michael Grant, From Alexander to Cleopatra: The Hellenistic
       World (Scribner).
     Plutarch, The Age of Alexander (Penguin).
     Polybius, The Rise of the Roman Empire (Penguin).
     The Apocrypha (Vintage Paperback).
     Menander, Plays and Fragments (Penguin).
     Theokritos, The Idylls of Theokritos (Purdue Univ. Press).

Course Outline:

1. Significance of the Hellenistic Period of Greek History:
    Hellenism and the decline of Ancient Near Eastern
    Civilization.

2. The   Reign of Alexander the Great   (336-323   B.C.):
    Destruction of the Ancient Near Eastern state system.

3. From Babylon to Lysimachia: The wars of Alexander's
    successors and the emergence of the Hellenistic kingdoms
    (323-277 B.C.).
    a. Phase I: The failure of Perdiccas (323-321 B.C.).
    b. Phase II: The rise and fall of Antigonus the One-Eyed
        (321-301 B.C.).
    c. Establishment of the three great kingdoms--Macedon,
        Egypt and Syria (301-277 B.C.).

4. Asia under Macedonian Rule to 223 B.C.
    a. Egypt under Ptolemy II and Ptolemy III.
        (1) Foreign policy: Security through empire.
        (2) Internal policy
             (a) Organization--a managed economy?
             (b) Society--co-operation or co-existence in a multi-
                  ethnic state?
    b. Seleucid Asia.
        (1) Holding the line: the reign of Antiochus I (281-
             261 B.C.).
        (2) Disintegration: from Antiochus II to Seleucus III
             (261-223 B.C.).
             (a) Secession in the west: the founding of the
                  kingdom of Pergamum.
             (b) Secession in the east: the founding of the

kingdoms of Parthia and Bactria.

5. Hellenistic Greek Culture: Cosmopolitan and Professional.
   a. Art, literature and scholarship--the importance of patronage.
   b. Science
      (1) Geography--an expanding world.
      (2) Astronomy and astrology--west meets east: the assimilation of Babylonian astronomy.
      (3) Medicine--the study of human physiology and the Alexandrian doctors.
      (4) Technology--theoretical progress, practical stagnation.
   c. Hellenistic philosophies: strategies for personal survival.
   d. Hellenistic religion.
      (1) The cult of deified kings.
      (2) Mystery cults: Near Eastern wine in Greek bottles.

6. Restoration and Collapse in Asia: From Antiochus III to Antiochus IV (223-164 B.C.).
   a. A new Alexander: Antiochus III and the restoration of the patrimony of Seleucus I (223-196 B.C.).
   b. A new factor: Rome (200-189 B.C.).
   c. The reign of Antiochus IV (175-164 B.C.).
      (1) Antiochus IV and Egypt: the limits of independence.
      (2) Antiochus IV and the Jews: the limits of Hellenization.

7. Rome and the Destruction of the Hellenistic State System.
   a. Europe: the failure of Greek freedom (196-146 B.C.).
   b. Asia: From Pelusium to Actium (168-31 B.C.).

8. Epilogue: The Triumph of Hellenism in the Roman East.

Recommended Paper-back Books on Hellenistic History

Source Books

M.M. Austin, The Hellenistic World from Alexander to the Roman Conquest (Cambridge).
C.K. Barrett, The New Testament Background (Harper).
Roger S. Bagnall & Peter Derow, Greek Historical Documents: The Hellenistic Period (Scholars Press).

Translations

Apollonius of Rhodes, The Voyage of the Argo (Penguin).
Arrian, The Campaigns of Alexander (Penguin).
S. Burstein, The Babyloniaca of Berossus (Undena Press, Malibu, California).
Gordon H. Clark, Selections from Hellenistic Philosophy

(Appleton-Century-Crofts).
Theodore H. Gaster, *The Dead Sea Scriptures in English Translation* (Doubleday).
The Greek Anthology (Penguin).
Josephus, *The Jewish War* (Penguin).
M. Lichtheim, *Ancient Egyptian Literature*, vol. 3, *The Late Period* (University of California Press).
Teles: The Cynic Teacher (Scholars Press).

Modern Studies

F.E. Adcock, *The Greek and Macedonian Art of War* (Univ. of California Press).
E. Badian, *Roman Imperialism in the Late Republic* (Cornell University Press).
H.I. Bell, *Cults and Creeds in Graeco-Roman Egypt* (Ares Press).
Elias Bickerman, *From Ezra to the Last of the Maccabees* (Schocken).
E. Borza, *The Impact of Alexander the Great* (Dryden Press).
G.T. Griffith, *Mercenaries of the Hellenistic World* (Ares Press).
J.B. Bury, *The Hellenistic Age* (Norton).
R.M. Errington, *The Dawn of Empire: Rome's Rise to World Power* (Cornell University Press).
J. Ferguson, *The Heritage of Hellenism* (Harcourt).
Moses Hadas, *Hellenistic Culture* (Norton).
J.R. Hamilton, *Alexander the Great* (Univ. of Pittsburgh Press).
C.M. Havelock, *Hellenistic Art* (Norton).
J.A.O. Larsen, *Representative Government in Greek and Roman History* (Univ. of California Press).
G.E.R. Lloyd, *Greek Science after Aristotle* (Norton).
A.D. Nock, *Conversion* (Oxford).
J. Onions, *Art and Thought in the Hellenistic Age* (Thames & Hudson).
F.E. Peters, *The Harvest of Hellenism: A History of the Near East from Alexander the Great to the Triumph of Christianity* (Scribner).
W.W. Tarn, *Alexander the Great* (Beacon).
W.W. Tarn & G.T. Griffith, *Hellenistic Civilization* (New American Library).
W.W. Tarn, *Hellenistic Naval and Military Developments* (Ares Press).
F. W. Walbank, *The Hellenistic World* (Harvard Univ. Press).
C.B. Welles, *Alexander and the Hellenistic World* (Hakkert).
Ulrich Wilcken, *Alexander the Great* (Norton).

Recommended Paper-back Books on Hellenistic History

Source Books

M.M. Austin, *The Hellenistic World from Alexander to the Roman Conquest* (Cambridge).
Roger S. Bagnall & Peter Derow, *Greek Historical Documents: The Hellenistic Period* (Scholars Press).
C.K. Barrett, *The New Testament Background* (Harper).
S. Burstein, *The Hellenistic Age from the Battle of Ipsos to the Death of Kleopatra VII* (Cambridge Univ. Press).

Translations

Apollonius of Rhodes, *The Voyage of the Argo* (Penguin).
Arrian, *The Campaigns of Alexander* (Penguin).
John R. Bartlett, *Jews in the Hellenistic World: Josephus, Aristeas, The Sybylline Oracles, Eupolemus* (Cambridge Univ. Press).
S. Burstein, *The Babyloniaca of Berossus* (Undena Press, Malibu, California).
Gordon H. Clark, *Selections from Hellenistic Philosophy* (Appleton-Century-Crofts).
Quintus Curtius Rufus, *The History of Alexander* (Penguin).
Theodore H. Gaster, *The Dead Sea Scriptures in English Translation* (Doubleday).
The Greek Anthology (Penguin).
Josephus, *The Jewish War* (Penguin).
M. Lichtheim, *Ancient Egyptian Literature*, vol. 3, *The Late Period* (University of California Press).
Polybius, *The Rise of the Roman Empire* (Penguin).
Teles: The Cynic Teacher (Scholars Press).

Modern Studies

F.E. Adcock, *The Greek and Macedonian Art of War* (Univ. of California Press).
E. Badian, *Roman Imperialism in the Late Republic* (Cornell University Press).
H.I. Bell, *Cults and Creeds in Graeco-Roman Egypt* (Ares Press).
E. Bevan, *The House of Ptolemy* (Ares Press).
E. Bevan, *The House of Seleucus* (Ares Press).
Elias Bickerman, *From Ezra to the Last of the Maccabees* (Schocken).
E. Borza, *The Impact of Alexander the Great* (Dryden Press).
J.B. Bury, *The Hellenistic Age* (Norton).
R.M. Errington, *The Dawn of Empire: Rome's Rise to World Power* (Cornell University Press).
J. Ferguson, *The Heritage of Hellenism* (Harcourt).
E. Gruen, *The Hellenistic World and the Coming of Rome* (Univ. of California Press).
G.T. Griffith, *Mercenaries of the Hellenistic World* (Ares Press).

Moses Hadas, _Hellenistic Culture_ (Norton).
J.R. Hamilton, _Alexander the Great_ (Univ. of Pittsburgh
    Press).
C.M. Havelock, _Hellenistic Art_ (Norton).
J.A.O. Larsen, _Representative Government in Greek and Roman
    History_ (Univ. of California Press).
G.E.R. Lloyd, _Greek Science after Aristotle_ (Norton).
Grace Harriet Macurdy, _Hellenistic Queens_ (Ares).
A.D. Nock, _Conversion_ (Oxford).
J. Onions, _Art and Thought in the Hellenistic Age_ (Thames &
    Hudson).
F.E. Peters, _The Harvest of Hellenism: A History of the Near
    East from Alexander the Great to the Triumph of
    Christianity_ (Scribner).
S.B. Pomeroy, _Women in Hellenistic Egypt from Alexander to
    Cleopatra_ (Schocken).
S. Sandmel, _Philo of Alexandria: An Introduction_ (Oxford).
W.W. Tarn, _Alexander the Great_ (Beacon).
W.W. Tarn, _The Greeks in Bactria and India_ (Ares Press).
W.W. Tarn & G.T. Griffith, _Hellenistic Civilization_ (New
    American Library).
W.W. Tarn, _Hellenistic Naval and Military Developments_ (Ares
    Press).
F. W. Walbank, _The Hellenistic World_ (Harvard Univ. Press).
C.B. Welles, _Alexander and the Hellenistic World_ (Hakkert).
Ulrich Wilcken, _Alexander the Great_ (Norton).

The Aftermath of Alexander the Great

1st Session: Alexander as Ruler of Asia

Arrian, Anab. IV. 7-14, 19-20, VII. 4-12
Diodorus, XVII. 77, 107-110
Plutarch, Alex. 27, 34, 45, 47, 50-55, 70-71, 74
Curtius, VI. 6.-11, VIII. 1.1-2.12, 4.21-8.23, X. 2.1-4.3
Justin, XII. 3.8-4.6, 6.1-7.3, 10.9-12.10

Fox, Alexander the Great, 308-330, 416-432
Goukowsky, Essai sur les origines du mythe d'Alexandre, 43-60, 182-184
Hamilton, Alexander the Great, 103-108, 133-135, 142-144
Hamilton, Plutarch: Alexander, 139-157, 194-199
Hammond, Alexander the Great, 193-199, 242-245, 257-264
Milns, Alexander the Great, 189-200, 239-240, 245-248
Ritter, Diadem und Königsherrschaft, 41-55
Schachermeyr, Alexander der Grosse,
Tarn, Alexander the Great, II, 359-362, 399-449
Wilcken, Alexander the Great, 166-172, 206-209, 218-222

Tarn, PBA (1933) [Griffith, Alexander the Great, 243-286]
Berve, Klio (1938) [Griffith, Alexander the Great, 103-136]
Brown, AJP [Griffith, Alexander the Great, 29-52]
Balsdon, Historia (1950) [Griffith, Alexander the Great, 179-204]
Robinson, D.M. Robinson Studies (1951)
Wüst, Historia (1953-54)
Andreotti, Historia (1956)
Robinson, AHR (1956-7) [Griffith, Alexander the Great, 53-72]
Badian, Historia (1958) [Griffith, Alexander the Great, 287-306]
Bickermann, PP (1963)
Thomas, CJ (1968)
Heckel, AJP (1978)
Bosworth, JHS (1980)
Carney, GRBS (1981)
Carney, CJ (1981)
Badian, Studies for Edson (1981)

2nd Session: Alexander as God

Arrian, Anab. III. 3-5, IV. 7, 15, V. 26, VI. 19, VII. 1, 14-17,
    19-23, 29; Ind. 35.8
Diodorus, XVI. 92, 95, XVII. 37, 49-52, 115, XVII. 4
Curtius, IV. 7.5-32, X. 1.1-19, 5.1-37
Justin, XI. 11.1-13, XII. 12
Plutarch, Lys. 18; Alex. 7, 27-28, 33, 68, 72, 75; Mor. 210C-D, 219E,
    804B
Val. Max. 7.2.ext.13
Hypereides, Contra Dem. 30-31; Epitaphios, 20-22
Strabo, XVII.1.43
Athenaeus, 6.251b
Polybius, XII.12b.3
Aelian, VII. 2.19, 5.12

56

Fox, _Alexander the Great_, 194-218, 436-448, 454-460, 473-478
Goukowsky, _Essai sur les origines du mythe d'Alexandre_, 60-68
Habicht, _Gottmenschentum und griechische Städte_, 3-16, 21-36, 243-250
Hamilton, _Alexander the Great_, 75-77, 138-141, 148-158
Hamilton, _Plutarch: Alexander_, 71-75, 187-189
Hammond, _Alexander the Great_, 122-128, 246-249, 253-254
Milns, _Alexander the Great_, 98-109, 242-244, 251-254
Schachermeyr, _Alexander der Grosse_,
Taeger, _Charisma_, I, 171-224
Tarn, _Alexander the Great_, II, 347-398
Wilcken, _Alexander the Great_, 113-129, 222-238

Robinson, _AJP_ (1940)
Robinson, _AJP_ (1943)
Balsdon, _Historia_ (1950) [Griffith, _Alexander the Great_, 179-204]
Taeger, _HZ_ (1951)
Hampl, _D.M. Robinson Studies_ (1953) [Griffith, _Alexander the Great_, 308-21
Schachermeyr, _JOAI_ (1954) [Griffith, _Alexander the Great_, 322-344]
Hamilton, _CQ_ (1953) [Griffith, _Alexander the Great_, 235-241]
Classen, _Historia_ (1959)
Bickermann, _Athenaeum_ (1963)
Daskalakis, _StudClass_ (1967)
Badian, _HSCP_ (1967)
Edmunds, _GRBS_ (1971)
Atkinson, _Athenaeum_ (1973)
Bosworth, _Studies for Schachermeyr_ (1977)
Rosen, _Historia_ (1978)
Fredericksmeyer, _AJAH_ (1979)
Pugliese Caratelli, _PP_ (1979)
Badian, _Studies for Edson_ (1981)
Fredericksmeyer, _Studies for Edson_ (1981)
Langer, _Ancient World_ (1981)

3rd Session: _The Breakdown of Concord (323-320 BC)_

Arrian, _Succ._ fr. 1.1-45 (Roos, pp. 253-269)
Heidelberg Epitome (_FGH_, 155)
Diodorus, XVII. 117, XVIII. 1-39
Appian, _Syr._ 52-53
Curtius, X. 6-10
Justin, XIII. 2-8
Plutarch, _Eum._ 1, 3-8
Pausanias, I. 6

Bengtson, _Die Strategie_, I, 15-26, 49-59, 63-81, 94-96
Briant, _Antigone le Borgne_, 125-211, 229-279
Cloché, _La dislocation d'un empire_, 10-77
Engel, _Untersuchungen zum Machtaufstieg des Antigonos_, 4-28
Fontana, _Le lotte per la successione di Alessandro_, 103-183
Fortina, _Cassandro_, 7-17
Goukowsky, _Essai sur les origines du mythe d'Alexandre_, 75-92, 193-198
Granier, _Die makedonische Heeresversammlung_, 58-75
Manni, _Demetrio_, 70-81
Müller, _Antigonos Monophthalmos_, 17-22
Schachermeyr, _Alexander in Babylon_, 134-186
Seibert, _Untersuchungen zur Geschichte Ptolemaios_ I, 27-38, 96-128
Wehrli, _Antigone et Demetrios_, 30-36

Will, _Histoire politique du monde hellénistique_, I, 19-38

Schachermeyr, _Klio_ (1925)
Ensslin, _RhM_ (1925)
Schwan, _Klio_ (1929)
Schwan, _Klio_ (1930)
De Sanctis, _StudClass_ (1931)
Miltner, _Klio_ (1932)
Neppi-Modona, _Athenaeum_ (1932)
Schur, _RhM_ (1934)
Manni, _RendAccadLinc_ (1949)
Smith, _AJP_ (1961)
Wirth, _Helikon_ (1967)
Rosen, _Acta Classica_ (1967)
Rosen, _Acta Classica_ (1967)
Kanatsoulis, _Makedonika_ (1968)
Errington, _JHS_ (1970)
Habicht, _Akten des VI Int. Kongr. f. Epigraphik_ (1972)
Pareo, _MemIstLomb_ (1975)
Hauben, _Ancient Society_ (1977)

4th Session: Alliances and Hostilities (320-315 BC)

Diodorus, XVIII. 40-75, XIX. 11-44, 49-52
Plutarch, _Eum._ 9-19; _Phoc._ 30-37
Justin, XIV. 1-3, 5-6
Appian, _Syr._ 52
Pausanias, I. 25
Nepos, _Eum._ 5-12; _Phoc._ 3-4

Bengtson, _Die Strategie_, I, 60-63, 81-88, 96-111, 119-125
Cloché, _La dislocation d'un empire_, 80-137
Engel, _Untersuchungen zum Machtaufstieg des Antigonos_, 29-48
Fontana, _Le lotte per la successione di Alessandro_, 184-245
Fortina, _Cassandro_, 21-42
Goukowsky, _Essai sur les origines du mythe d'Alexandre_, 93-102
Granier, _Die makedonische Herresversammlung_, 75-91
Macurdy, _Hellenistic Queens_, 39-45, 48-52
Müller, _Antigonos Monophthalmos_, 22-30
Seibert, _Untersuchungen zur Geschichte Ptolemaios I_, 129-137
Wehrli, _Antigone et Demetrios_, 36-40
Will, _Histoire politique du monde hellénistique_, I, 39-47

Smith, _RevAssyr_ (1925)
Macurdy, _JHS_ (1932)
Cloché, _AntCl_ (1948)
Manni, _RendAccadLinc_ (1949)
Westlake, _BaliRylandsLibr_ (1954)
Smith, _AJP_ (1961)
Rosen, _Acta Classica_ (1967)
Kanatsoulis, _Makedonika_ (1968)
Habicht, _Akten des VI Int. Kongr. für Epigraphik_ (1972)
Briant, _REA_ (1973)
Pareo, _MemIstLomb_ (1975)
Errington, _Hermes_ (1977)

5th Session: Antigonus the One- Eyed and the Coalition (315-311 BC)

Diodorus, XIX. 45-48, 53-64, 66-69, 73-75, 77-100, 105
Justin, XV. 1-2
Appian, Syr. 53-55
Plutarch, Demetrius, 5-7
OGIS, 5 (Welles, RC, #1), 6

Bengtson, Die Strategie, I, 88-93, 111-119
Cloché, La dislocation d'un empire, 140-178
Engel, Untersuchungen zum Machtaufstieg des Antigonos, 48-58
Fortina, Cassandro, 45-80
Granier, Die makedonische Heeresversammlung, 91-97
Manni, Demetrio Poliorcete, 5-15, 98-105
Müller, Antigonos Monophthalmos, 30-77
Seibert, Untersuchungen zur Geschichte des Ptolemaios I, 138-151, 157-163
Wehrli, Antigone et Demetrios, 40-55, 103-129
Will, Histoire politique du monde hellénistique, I, 48-57

Smith, RevAssyr (1925)
Momigliano, StudItalFilClass (1930)
Nepi-Modona, Athenaeum (1933)
Heuss, Hermes (1938)
Cloché, AntCl (1948)
Manni, RendAccadLinc (1949)
Simpson, JHS (1954)
Simpson, Historia (1957)
Cloché, CRAI (1957)
Aucello, RivFilol (1957)
Simpson, Historia (1959)
Smith, AJP (1961)
Rosen, Acta Classica (1967)
Rosen, Acta Classica (1968)
Hauben, AJP (1973)
Errington, Hermes (1977)
Hauben, Historia (1977)

6th Session: The Aspirations of Antigonus and the Resistance (311-301 BC)

Diodorus, XIX. 105, XX. 19-21, 27-29, 37, 45-53, 73-76, 81-88, 91-100, 102-103, 106-113; XXI. 1
Plutarch, Demetrius, 7-19, 21-23, 25, 28-30
Appian, Syr. 54-55
Justin, XV. 2, 4
Pausanias, I.6.6
Suidas, s.v. "Demetrius"
IG, IV, 1, 68 (Schmitt, Staatsverträge, III, #446)

Cloché, La dislocation d'un empire, 179-220
Fortina, Cassandro, 83-107
Granier, Die makedonische Heeresversammlung, 98-114
Habicht, Gottmenschentum und griechische Städte, 42-50, 58-75
Manni, Demetrio Poliorcete, 17-39, 82-83, 105-106, 111-114
Müller, Antigonos Monophthalmos, 78-121
Ritter, Diadem und Königsherrschaft, 79-108

Robert, <u>Hellenica</u>, II, 15-33
Seibert, <u>Untersuchungen zur Geschichte des Ptolemaios I</u>, 176-189, 225-234
Wehrli, <u>Antigone et Demetrios</u>, 56-73
Will, <u>Histoire politique du monde hellénistique</u>, I, 57-70

Roussel, <u>RevArch</u> (1923)
Smith, <u>RevAssyr</u> (1925)
Scott, <u>AJP</u> (1928)
Cloché, <u>AntCl</u> (1948)
Simpson, <u>Historia</u> (1959)
Rosen, <u>Acta Classica</u> (1967)
Cohen, <u>Athenaeum</u> (1974)
Hauben, <u>Ancient Society</u> (1974)
Hadley, <u>JHS</u> (1974)

University of California, Berkeley   Spring, 1986

Hellenistic Greece

Works from which reading is assigned

*Apollonius of Rhodes, The Voyage of Argo, Penguin paperback
 Appian, Roman History (Loeb Classical Library), vol. II
*Arrian, The Campaigns of Alexander, Penguin paperback
*Austin, M.M., The Hellenistic World, Cambridge paperback
 Callimachus, Hymns and Epigrams (Loeb Classical Library)
 Callimachus, Aetia and Other Fragments (Loeb Classical Library)
*Cary, M., A History of the Greek World, 323-146 BC, 2nd ed., Univ. paperback
 Diodorus Siculus (Loeb Classical Library), vols. IX-X
 Diogenes Laertius, Lives of the Eminent Philosophers (Loeb Cl. Lib.), vol. II
*Hamilton, J.R., Alexander the Great, U. of Pittsburgh paperback
*McEleney, N., First Book of Maccabees, Paulist-Newman, paperback
*McEleney, N., Second Book of Maccabees, Paulist-Newman, paperback
 Menander, The Plays (translated by L. Casson)
*Plutarch, Age of Alexander, Penguin paperback
*Polybius, On Roman Imperialism (ed. by A. Bernstein), Regnery/Gateway
                                                          paperback
*Theocritus, Idylls, Purdue U. paperback

* signifies that book should be purchased, if possible; others may be read in
  Moffitt

Lecture and Reading List

First Week (Jan. 20-26)

Jan. 20: Holiday

Jan. 22: No class

Jan. 24: Introduction

Second Week (Jan. 27 - Feb. 2)

Jan. 27: Alexander the Great: The Rise to Power and Glory

Hamilton, pp. 29-79
Arrian, I, 1-16; II, 2-15; III, 1-5
Plutarch, Alexander, 1-28

Jan. 29: Alexander the Great: Conquest and Retreat

Hamilton, pp. 80-133
Arrian, III, 5-27; IV, 7-14; VI (entire)
Plutarch, Alexander, 29-67

Jan. 31: Alexander the Great: Aims and Aspirations

Hamilton, pp. 133-166
Arrian, VII (entire)
Plutarch, Alexander, 68-77
Austin, pp. 34-38

Third Week (Feb. 3-9)

Feb. 3: Discussion

Feb. 5: The Age of the Successors: A Question of Legitimacy

Cary, pp. 1-20
Diodorus, XVIII, 2-4, 14, 16, 22-25, 28-37, 48-49, 54-57; XIX, 11,
35-36, 49-52
Austin, pp. 41-46

Feb. 7: The Age of the Successors: The Achievement of Antigonus the One-Eyed

> Cary, pp. 21-32, 34-41
> Diodorus, XIX, 55-62. 80-86, 90-92, 105; XX, 45-53, 106-113
> Austin, pp. 57-60, 76-78

Fourth Week (Feb. 10-16)

Feb. 10: The Passing of the Old Order

> Cary, pp. 42-64
> Plutarch, Demetrius, 1-7, 15-22, 28-32, 35-53
> Austin, pp. 83-92

Feb. 12: Athens in the Age of Alexander and the Successors

> Cary, pp. 4-10, 18-19, 32-34
> Plutarch, Demetrius, 7-14, 23-27, 33-34, 46
> Austin, pp. 44-45, 48-49, 78-83

Feb. 14: Macedonia and Greece in the 3rd Century

> Cary, pp. 125-146, 253-255, 282-286
> Plutarch, Pyrrhus, 1-12, 26-34
> Austin, pp. 93-97

Fifth Week (Feb. 17-23)

Feb. 17: Holiday

Feb. 19: Federalism and the Polis

> Cary, pp. 147-164
> Austin, pp. 100-113

Feb. 21: Discussion

Sixth Week (Feb. 24 - March 2)

Feb. 24: The Seleucid Kingdom in the 3rd Century

> Cary, pp. 65-69, 79-90, 95-112, 255-259
> Austin, pp. 239-241, 245, 303-304, 307-308, 363-365

Feb. 26: Ptolemaic Egypt in its Golden Age

>Cary, pp. 259-267
>Austin, pp. 359-362, 368-369, 400-407, 412-413

Feb. 28: The Greeks of Sicily

>Cary, pp. 167-176
>Diodorus, XIX, 1-9, 65, 70-71, 102-104, 107-110; XX, 3-18, 29-34,
>   38-44, 54-72, 101
>Plutarch, _Timoleon_

Seventh Week (March 3-9)

March 3: Hellenistic Society and the Native Reaction

>Cary, pp. 268-282
>Austin, pp. 418, 422-423

March 5: The Nature of the Economy

>Cary, pp. 287-306
>Austin, pp. 151-156, 180-185, 198-201

March 7: Hellenistic Philosophy

>Cary, pp. 354-362
>Diogenes Laertius, _Lives of the Philosophers_: "Diogenes", "Epicurus",
>   "Zeno"

Eighth Week (March 10-16)

March 10: Religion and Ruler Worship

>Cary, pp. 363-374
>Austin, pp. 64-65, 67-68, 438-440

March 12: Discussion

March 14: Midterm Examination

Ninth Week (March 17-23)

March 17: Artistic Patronage, Pomp, and Propaganda

    Cary, pp. 307-317
    Diodorus, XVIII, 26-27
    Athenaeus, Deipnosophists, V, 196a-208d (25-41)

March 19: Science and Technology

    Cary, pp. 343-353

March 21: Hellenistic Women

Tenth Week (March 24-30)

March 24: The Literature and Learning of Alexandria

    Cary, pp. 318-327, 338-342
    Theocritus, Idylls, I, II, V, VII, VIII, X, XII, XIV, XV, XVI, XVII, XXI, XXIII,
        XXVII, XXIX, XXX

March 26: Callimachus and Apollonius: The Battle of the Books

    Cary, pp. 327-330
    Apollonius, The Voyage of the Argo, III-IV
    Callimachus, Hymns, I, IV, V, VI
    Callimachus, Epigrams, 2, 5, 6, 11, 15, 22, 30, 52, 53, 59, 64
    Callimachus, Fragments, 1, 110, 203, 228, 230-263, 384, 392

March 28: The New Comedy and the Mime

    Cary, pp. 331-332
    Menander, The Grouch, The Arbitration, She Who was Shorn

Eleventh Week (March 31 - April 6)

March 31: Hellenistic Historiography

    Cary, pp. 332-338
    Polybius, I, 1-15

April 2:   Discussion

April 4:   The Crossroads of Hellenistic History: 220-200 BC

        Cary, pp. 69-73, 90-94, 112-114, 164--166
        Polybius, IV, 1-8, 22-27; V, 9-12, 31-40, 60-67, 79-87, 101-107;
                VII, 9-14; X, 26; XIV, 11-12; XV, 20, 24-33
        Austin, pp. 117-119, 251-252

Twelfth Week (April 7-13)

April 7:   The Origins of Roman Involvement in the East

        Cary, pp. 182-189
        Polybius, II, 2-12; III, 16, 18-19; VII, 9; XVI, 24-35
        Austin, pp. 121-124, 254-255

April 9:   Rome and the Hellenistic Monarchies, 200-188 BC

        Cary, pp. 189-196, 206-213
        Polybius, XVIII, 1-12, 33-39, 44-52; XXI, 10-17, 29-32, 43-48
        Austin, pp. 255-256, 258-260

April 11: Tradition and Change: The Interplay of Rome and Greece, 188-168 BC

        Cary, pp. 196-203
        Polybius, XXII, 8-9, 13-18; XXIII, 1-4, 7-9; XXV, 3; XXVII, 1-10, 14-15;
                XXVIII, 1-7
        Austin, pp. 133-134, 136-141, 268-269

Thirteenth Week (April 14-20)

April 14: Holiday

April 16: Holiday

April 18: Holiday

Fourteenth Week (April 21-27)

April 21: Hellenism and the Jews

        Cary, pp. 227-230
        Maccabees, I, 1-9, 12-16; II, 3-6, 8-11
        Austin, pp. 274-277

April 23: Discussion

April 25: The Twilight of the Ptolemies and Seleucids

> Cary, pp. 216-222
> Polybius, XXIX, 23-27; XXXI, 5, 9, 12, 18-23; XXXII, 1, 6-7
> Austin, pp. 280-283, 378-381

Fifteenth Week (April 28 - May 4)

April 28: Rome, Greece, and Asia Minor, 167-129 BC

> Cary, pp. 203-205, 213-216
> Polybius, XXIX, 5-11, 19; XXX, 1-5, 19-20; XXXI, 7-10, 13-14; XXXII, 5,
> 19-22, 27-28; XXXIII, 1-3, 7, 12-13; XXXV, 6; XXXVII, 2-3,
> 5-6; XXXVIII, 7-11; XXXIX, 8-17
> Austin, pp. 144-150, 331-332, 338-339, 343-347

April 30: Roman Imperialism: the Greek View

> Polybius, I, 1-6, 12, 37, 63-64; VI, 50, 57; IX, 10; X, 36; XV, 9-10;
> XVIII, 34-35; XXI, 16; XXXI, 11; XXXVII, 1; XXXIX, 5, 13, 17, 19

May 2: The End of Greek Freedom

> Cary, pp. 225-227
> Appian, Mithridatic Wars, 10-23, 28-38, 46-48, 56-63, 67-71, 79-86,
> 90-91, 97-113

Sixteenth Week (May 5-11)

May 5: Cleopatra: Last of the Hellenistic Rulers

> Cary, pp. 222-225

May 7: Discussion

May 9: Retrospect

This course addresses the thought and action contained in more than one
thousand years of history, including periods when some of the works fundamental
to our ways of thinking and feeling were written. This means, in terms of the
cash nexus, a burdensome book order.

However, it is possible to mitigate the shock. (i) All of the required and
recommended readings are on reserve, some of them in multiple copies, at the
Hilles and Lamont libraries. (ii) Used copies of some of the readings are
available in book stores near the Yard: Harvard Bookstore (1248 Mass. Ave.)
and the Book Case (42 Church near Brattle) are two. (iii) In practice you may
find that you need to buy only those readings which are most relevant to your
paper topic, if you are diligent about using the reserve collections. (iv) Whatever translations and editions you eventually lay hands on - used, borrowed, or
new - will do as long as they are complete (not abridged or expurgated) and
sufficiently recent to use modern English (e.g. Crawley's Thucydides but not
Hobbes's, Rawlinson's Herodotus, Church and Broadribb's Tacitus). If in doubt,
keep your receipt and see me.

A word about the items on the Recommended list:

Starr, A History of the Ancient World is perhaps the least unsatisfactory of the
    available surveys of the ancient world. Use it for a continuous general
    narrative and description at a basic level. It does contain excellent and
    up-to-date bibliographies at the ends of the chapters and on pp. 717 - 729.
    Via the index, Starr is also a useful general reference. (For more information
    go first to the Oxford Classical Dictionary, 2nd ed., in the reference rooms
    of Lamont and Hilles)

Andrewes, The Greeks, is an exemplary essay on classical Greek civilization; if
    you can afford it after you've supplied yourself with the early readings, buy
    it and orient yourself if you're unfamiliar with the Greeks by reading it
    through at the outset of the course. Ditto with Brunt at midpoint (below).

Brunt, Social Conflicts etc., is a masterpiece of compression which discusses,
    with lucidity and grace, the history and fate of the Republic from a social
    and economic standpoint. It is the best short introduction to the range of
    problems and considerations which exercise historians of the Republic today
    (late-ordered, not in COOP at this writing).

Millar, The Roman Empire and its Neighbours, is only second to Starr in being far
    too expensive for what it offers. It is nevertheless a very clear and
    knowledgeable survey of the fabric and structure of the Roman Empire, and
    (unlike Starr) is worth reading for itself alone. It contains valuable chapters
    on Roman imperial administration and on the individual provinces; you may
    want to read it at one go at about the ninth week of the course. (I shall
    try to persuade the library to buy more reserve copies.)

(Nilsson, Greek Piety, is now out of print as a Norton paperback, but is on
    reserve. This book is a meditation full of insight, by a master of the field,
    on the religious history of antiquity from the period ca. 800 BC - AD 300,
    i.e. from Homer to Christianity. A.D. Nock, Conversion, and E.R. Dodds, The
    Greeks and the Irrational (a landmark in scholarship) are also worthy starting
    points for those of you with a particular interest in the history of religions
    in antiquity.)

There will be three one-half hour quizzes, on the Thursdays of the third, sixth, and ninth weeks, which will consist of short identifications (chosen from a longer list to be announced on the Tuesdays of the preceding week) and a short essay question. The final examination will consist similarly of identifications, from a previously announced list, plus essay questions both announced and unannounced. Some of the identifications may well be places on the map.

The quizzes will be worth 25% of the grade, with the final and the paper counting equally to make up the rest of the grade.

Saturday classes: None are scheduled. However, the lecture schedule is very tight for a course of this scope, so I reserve the right to call a few Saturday classes late in the course (after the football season is over); but I hope this will not be necessary.

The readings: The weekly readings are set out below. I have tried to keep them within reasonable compass, at the cost of dissecting assignments out of organically whole works. If you are not already familiar with some of these works, especially Herodotus, Thucydides, and the Annals of Tacitus, then you should read them through, if not during the term then at least during reading period. If you are forced to choose only one book for a complete reading, I would make it Herodotus.

Note: Optional readings are in parentheses.

Required:

Homer, 'Iliad' and 'Odyssey' (preferably tr. Lattimore)
Herodotus
Thucydides
Sallust, 'Conspiracy of Catiline' (to be found most conveniently in Penguin ed., with his 'Jugurthine War')
Plutarch, Lives of Solon, Lycurgus, Pericles, Alexander, Pyrrhus, Flamininus, Ti. Gracchus, Sulla, and Caesar. (The last two are contained in the Penguin vol. titled Fall of the Roman Republic, which also contains the Lives of Marius, C. Gracchus, Pompey, and Cicero. If your paper topic takes you into the later Roman Republic, then you will want to read them all and will probably do best to buy this book, which has been ordered; the other Lives are on reserve.
Tacitus, Annals and Life of Agricola (the Modern Library College Edition of his Complete Works contains both)
Plato, The Republic (Cornford's translation, Oxford paperback, is much the best).
Many hands: The New Testament (esp. Acts and the apostolic Epistles; widely available, though not ordered).

Recommended:

A. Andrewes, The Greeks (Norton), ppb.
P.A. Brunt, Social Conflicts in the Roman Republic (Norton), ppb.
F. Millar, The Roman Empire and its Neighbours (Norton), ppb.
(M.P. Nilsson, Greek Piety (Norton), ppb: o.p.)
C.G. Starr, History of the Ancient World (3rd ed., Oxford 1983)

Week 1: Sources, methods, and meanings of ancient history.
Mediterranean landscapes and the Mediterranean year: the immemorial
conditions of life.
The downfall of the Mycenean palace states and the emergence of a new
pattern of society. 'Homeric' society and its values. Homer as history.

Readings: 'Iliad' (Lattimore's introduction if you are reading from his edition),
books i.1 - iii.164 (viii.335 - ix.713, xxi.514 - xxxiii.249), xxiv entire.
Thucydides i.2 - 12.
'Odyssey' (Lattimore's introduction ditto), books xv - xxii.
Hesiod, Works and Days (Lattimore's introduction ditto), lines (1 - 285,
370 - 616), 695 - end.
Recommended: Andrewes, xi-51, 231 - 246; (Nilsson, 1 - 64); Starr, 99 -
111 (top), 185 - 204.

Week 2: The archaic renascence of the Greek world: revolutionary assumptions
about order, system, and necessity in the cosmos.
Politics and society in the archaic Greek polis. "Tyrannies," their
psychology, substance, and significance. A case study: Peisistratid
Athens

Readings: (Hesiod, Works and Days, lines 201 - 285); Presocratic texts: handout.
Herodotus, iv.145 - 167, 200 -205; Thucydides, i.12 - 18.1, ii.15 - 16,
vi.54 - 59.
Plutarch, Life of Solon; Herodotus, i.39 - 64, vi.103 and 34 - 41,
v.55 - 78, iii.80 - 82.
(Aristotle, Constitution of Athens, 2 - 19)
Recommended: Andrewes, 52 -60, 76 - 82, 89 - 118, 247 - 252, 196 - 207
(note also the table of dates at the rear of the book); Starr, 204 - 272.

Week 3: Antidotes to tyranny. Two models: Cleisthenic Athens and "Lycurgan"
Sparta. The Persian world empire and its failure in Europe.
The great age of Athens: a revolutionary society and its critics.

Readings: Aristotle, Constitution of Athens, 19 - 28.2; Plutarch, Life of Lycurgus.
Aeschylus, Persai ('The Persians'); Herodotus, iii.28 - 38, v.96 - vi.33,
QUIZ ON   vi.42 - 45, 48 - 50; vi.95 - vii.57 and 91 - 104; vii.127 - viii.99.
THURSDAY   Thucydides, i.89 - 108; Plutarch, Life of Pericles; pseudo-Xenophon,
Constitution of Athens (handout)
Recommended: Andrewes, 60 - 62, 82 - 89, 147 - 155, 207 - 216, 161 - 195;
Starr, 275 - 338.

Week 4: Herodotus and Thucydides: the invention of history and the two poles
of the historical temper.
A generation of war and its aftermath.
Private lives: love and the family in classical Greece.

Readings:	Herodotus i.1-56 and 71-91; Thucydides 1.18.2.-88; i.109-ii.17; ii.59-65; iii.1-84; v.84-116 (vi.1, 6-29, 53, 60-61, 88.9-92; vii.72-viii.8) viii.63.3-77, 81-82, 86, 89-98; Xenophon, Hellenics (Penguin title: 'History of my Times') i.6 to end of book II. Aristophanes, Clouds; Plato, Defense ("Apology') of Socrates. Lysias, Orations 12, 1, and 3. (Aristophanes, Ecclesiazousai)

Recommended: Andrewes 119-146, 156-161, 217-229; (Nilsson 66-84); Starr 339-356.

Week 5: Irresolute conflicts of the fourth century: Persia's diplomatic hegemony, Athenian ambitions, and the eclipse of Sparta. The shadow of Philip of Macedon. Plato and his critics.

Readings: Plato, Republic 237a-398b and 412b-521b (Cornford's tr. if possible: his pages are 1-85 and 102-235); Aristotle, Politics: excerpts (handout). (Demosthenes, First Philippic; Isocrates, To Philip)

Recommended: Andrewes 68-73, 252-266, 152-154; Starr 359-393.

Week 6: World conquest (I): Philip and Alexander of Macedon. Alexander's successors: the new kingdoms and the new culture of Hellas abroad.

Readings: Plutarch, Life of Alexander; Arrian, Anabasis of Alexander i.1-ii.17;
QUIZ ON iii.1-4 and 16-30; iv.7-14; v.25-end.
THURSDAY Recommended: Andrewes 72-75, 165-166; (Nilsson 84-121); Starr 394-434.

Week 7: Early Rome: historical myths and social realities. The conquest of Italy.
The defeat of Hannibal; the eclipse of peasant Italy and the rise of a slaveholding society.
World conquest (II): Polybius, Livy, and the moderns on Rome's domination of the Hellenistic world. The motives and character of Roman imperialism.

Readings: Livy xxi.1-21, 35-49, 52-58; xxii.34-57. Polybius i.1-35; ii.1-36; iii. 1-15 and 30-76; vi.11-42; vi.51-end of book vi; ix.22-26; x.2-20; xviii.28-32.
Livy xxxi.1-9; xxxiii.30-35 and 38-40; xxxiv.1-8.

Recommended: Brunt, preface-73; Starr 437-499.

Week 8: Italy after Hannibal: deepening social crisis and the Gracchan putsch; the aristocratic reaction.
Civil wars and revolution: from Marius to Caesar.
Caius Octavius of Velitrae (="Caesar Augustus").

Readings: Plutarch, Life of Ti. Gracchus (Life of C. Gracchus); Appian, Civil Wars 1.1-26.
Plutarch, Life of Sulla; Sallust, Conspiracy of Catiline.
Plutarch, Life of Caesar; Cicero, Letters (a selection ed. by Wilkinson: on reserve) pp. 101-122, 135-140, 152-159, 173 (bottom)-192 (note the glossary of technical terms on pp. 193-195).
Augustus: 'Res gestae divi Augusti': handout.

Recommended: Brunt 74-156; Starr 503-552.

71

Week 9: The imperial system and the imperial ideology.
Palace history: "good" emperors and "bad" emperors: their servants, their victims, their enemies real and imagined.
Tacitus: the historian as prosecuting attorney.

Readings: Tacitus Annals i.1-14, 33-53, 72-74; ii.26-43, 53-59, 69-81; iii.1-18, 44-57, 64-49; iv.1-12, 27-41, 52-54, 57-60, 67-71; v.1-9; vi.1-30, 45-51.

QUIZ ON Suetonius, Lives of Nero, Vespasian, Titus, Domitian.
THURSDAY Pliny, Letters, book 10. Aelius Aristides, To Rome, excerpts (handout).

Recommended: Millar 1-80, 294-317; Starr 553-591.

Week 10: Imperial Rome: the streets, the baths, the games. Art and life. The social pyramid.
The fabric of the Empire and the Mediterranean economy: cities, ships, roads.
The army of the Empire and the creation of Roman Europe.

Readings: Petronius, "Trimalchio's Feast" from the Satyricon; (Pliny, Letters, books 8 and 9).
Jevenal Satires 1, 2, 4, 5, 6, 7, 14; Seneca Moral Epistle 47 (handout).
Tacitus Life of Agricola.

Recommended: Millar 81-220; Starr 591-602.

Week 11: Spiritual crisis? Philosophical paganism and the mystery cults.
The Jews of the empire and the first gentile Christians; the social and literary background of the New Testament.
Platonism and Platonic Christianity.

Readings: Acts of the Apostles; Hebrews; I & II Corinthians; I Timothy; Titus.
Plotinus On Beauty (En. 1.6), On Contemplation (iii.8), On the Hypostases (v.1).
Porphyry Life of Plotinus: handouts.

Week 12: Imperial crisis: barbarian invasions and civil wars; the new generals and the new army.
The price of salvation: Diocletian and the tyranny of the new order.
Retrospect and prospect: freedom in history and the Christian Empire.

Readings: None. TERM PAPERS ARE DUE at my office (Robinson L-15) by 5 PM Monday 19 December.

Recommended: Millar 211-220, 317-320, 220-267.

TENTATIVE date of final examination: Thursday 19 January; consult printed Examination Schedule, available about 3 January.

The term paper has a single main object: to introduce you to several
worthwhile works in a broad category of study that interests you. Accordingly,
your paper will be judged to a considerable extent from the point of view of
erudition, i.e., the depth of reading which it reflects. A critical attitude
is, of course, essential, and you are free to agree with, or to criticize, any
particular author's approach or conclusions, giving your own arguments. In length,
the paper should fall between 12 and 20 pages, exclusive of notes which may
include commentary of subsidiary points. It is due <u>at the beginning of reading
period</u>, Tuesday, January 3, at my office: Robinson L-15. You are welcome to talk
with me about your paper whenever you may feel the need; in particular, I will
look over with you any drafts, rough or otherwise, which you bring to me <u>before</u>
Christmas Recess, i.e., effectively before Friday, December 19.

(i) <u>The Ruler.</u> Consider and compare four types of monarchy in the ancient world:
                (a) tyranny in the person of Peisistratus; (b) a Hellenistic king;
                (c) Augustus; (d) Constantine. How did each type of autocrat
                present and justify his rule, on the one hand; and on the other,
                what were the actual social, ideological, and power basis of his
                rule? Do you find any organic relationships between the propaganda
                and the reality in each case? Do you detect any lines of historical
                relationship or progression from (a) to (d)?

Bibliography: A. Andrewes, chapters 43 and 44 in <u>Cambridge Ancient History</u>[2], vol.
                    iii, part 3.
               V. Ehrenberg, <u>The Greek State</u>[2].
               H.L. Bell, <u>Egypt from Alexander the Great to the Arab Conquest.</u>
          <u>or</u> E.R. Bevan, <u>The House of Seleucus.</u>
          <u>or</u> E.V. Hansen, <u>The Attalids of Pergamum.</u>
               M. Rostovtseff, <u>Social and Economic History of the Hellenistic World.</u>
               A.H.M. Jones, <u>Augustus.</u>
               R. Syme, <u>The Roman Revolution.</u>
               A.H.M. Jones, <u>Constantine and the Conversion of Europe.</u>

(ii) <u>Imperialism.</u> Compare the techniques of imperial control (or their absence if
                that is the case in your view) developed by Athens in the 5th
                century with those of Rome in Italy and abroad down to the
                settlement which followed the so-called Social War of 90-89 BC.
                What were the strengths and weaknesses of each power's system?
                What rewards and penalties existed for the allies/subjects under
                each, and how did these operate to promote or hinder the aims
                of the hegemonial power?

 Bibliography: R. Meiggs, <u>The Athenian Empire.</u>
                A.N. Sherwin-White, <u>The Roman Citizenship.</u>[2]
                W.V. Harris, <u>War and Imperialism in Republican Rome.</u>
                E. Badian, <u>Foreign Clientelae.</u>
                R.M. Errington, <u>Dawn of Empire.</u>
                E. Badian, <u>Roman Imperialism in the Late Republic.</u>
                P.D.A. Garnsey and C.R. Whittaker, eds., <u>Imperialism in the Ancient
                World</u>, introduction, chs. 5 and 8 (by M.E. Finley on Athens and
                P.A. Brunt on Rome, resp.)

(iii) Slavery and the Ancient Economy. Describe and estimate the effects of the
                                         wide existence of slavery and other forms
of dependent labor on the culture, political developments, economy, and
technology of (a) classical Athens, and (b) the Graeco-Roman world from the
end of the Hannibalic War onward. Is there a relationship between the
slave economy and Athenian democracy? Between the low level of technology
and slavery? Between the social psychology of the aristocracy, the
opportunities for economic investment which they identified, and slavery?
What conditions in later antiquity appear to have promoted the decline of
slavery?

Bibliography: M. Rostovtseff, Social and Economic History of the Hellenistic World.
               M. Rostovtseff, Social and Economic History of the Roman Empire.[2]
               W.L. Westermann, The Slave Systems of Greek and Roman Antiquity.
               M.I. Finley, The Ancient Economy.
               M.I. Finley, Ancient Slavery and Modern Ideology.
               P. Anderson, Passages from Antiquity to Feudalism.

(iv) Religion. Consider the nature of pagan belief (notably the so-called mystery
                 cults) in terms (a) of its satisfactions for the individual soul,
                 (b) social satisfactions (the character of common worship, aspects
                 of mutual support of votaries, simple friendly relations, e.g.),
                 and (c) its place in public life (the ruler cult, public festivals,
                 etc.). Contrast paganism with Christianity as a real danger to
                 the security of the Empire. What aspects of Christianity made it
                 increasingly attractive to pagans as time went on? Did Christianity
                 satisfy felt needs that pagan Roman society failed to meet? Why
                 did pagan emperors from time to time evidently regard Christianity
                 as a real danger to the security of the Empire? Is there a case to
                 be made for the "inevitable" triumph of Christianity? Or failing
                 its promotion by imperial favor would it simply have remained part
                 of the spectrum of ancient religions, or even faded away?

Bibliography: C.H. Dodd, The Founder of Christianity.
               A.J. Festugiere, Personal Religion among the Greeks.
               A.D. Nock, Conversion.
               A.D. Nock, Early Centila Christianity.
               E.R. Dodds, The Greeks and the Irrational.
               E.R. Dodds, Pagan and Christian in an Age of Anxiety.
               W.H.C. Frend, Martyrdom and Persecution in the Early Church.
               R. MacMullen, Paganism in the Roman Empire.

Some of these works may appear to overlap in their treatment of your subject.
This is all to the good: apart from the fact that each version represents a different
scholarly viewpoint, it is only the short nail that goes in with one blow.

Two suggestions: (i) read through the (admittedly heavy) bibliography on your topic
swiftly once over to identify chapters and sections most relevant to your proposed
treatment; this will save time in the long run. (ii) Don't agonize over what
you really can't follow (this should be a relatively small proportion of the whole);
make the most of what you do understand. If you are baffled, just bash on and come
back to the problem passage after you've done the rest of the reading. If you still
can't get the point, ask me.

The new Cambridge Ancient History will be found in the reference rooms of Lamont
and Hilles. The other volumes are being put on reserve at both libraries.

University of Maryland

History 130   The Ancient World   Dr. Eckstein

This course serves as an introduction to the cultures of Ancient Greece and Rome, upon which much of our own Western Civilization is itself based. The major emphasis in the course is on
attempting to see the people of the ancient world as real people,
dealing with horribly real problems--and in their struggle, creating
much of the particular political, cultural and philosophical orientation which still characterizes the West.

After a brief discussion of agriculture--the basis of all
settled, urban life--we will then begin our extensive examination
of Classical Greece and Rome. We will first analyze the Iliad
of Homer, as an introduction to what it meant to be a Greek. We
will then examine the most important and typical Greek political
institution, the city-state (or polis). It was in the polis that
the concept of the citizen--free and independent, but politically
responsible--first developed. As an examination of polis-culture
at its height, we will then discuss the play Oedipus the Tyrant,
by Sophocles. In the end, polis-culture pretty much destroyed
itself in a great war between Athens and Sparta; we will read
selections from the historian of that war, Thucydides. The Republic of Rome eventually conquered all the Greeks, and our examination of Greek civilization will in turn be followed by an
examination of Rome. The Romans were by far the most materially
successful people of the ancient world. We will look first at
the political institutions of the Roman Republic (especially
as seen through the eyes of a Greek observer, Polybius), then
at the Romans' rise to domination of the entire Mediterranean
world, and then at the replacement of the Free State by one-man
rule (i.e., the Emperors). For the Roman reaction to Roman history, we will read selections from the Aeneid, by Virgil.

Students taking History 130 will naturally be expected to
absorb a substantial amount of purely factual knowledge. However, more important than "names and dates history" will be your
development of a real understanding of ideas, concepts, people,
and (often tragic) historical processes. While there is a textbook, the emphasis in the reading for the course is on works by
ancient Greeks and Romans--the ancient people themselves.

There will be two Hour Examinations, and a Final Examination.
Each of the Hour Examinations will count for 25% of your final
grade; the Final Examination will count for 40% of your final
grade. Now, in addition to the lectures, there will also be discussion sections, meeting once a week. These discussion sections
will help you gain a better understanding of the material, and
of what is going on in the course. Attendance in these discussion
sections is absolutely required. And your contribution to your
discussion section (or your lack of contribution to your discussion section) will count for the final 10% of your final grade.
It's only 10%, but that 10% can mean the difference between (say)
an "A" and a "B", or a "B" and a "C".

History 130

Schedule of Lectures and Readings

Week I (Jan. 23-25)

    Jan. 23--Introduction to the Course
    Jan. 25--The Invention of Agriculture

    Reading: Hollister (textbook), Introduction and Ch. 1

Week II (Jan. 28-30)

    Jan. 28--The Invention of Civilization
    Jan. 30--Homer and History

    Reading: Hollister, Chs. 2-3; Homer, Iliad, Book I

Week III (Feb. 4-6)

    Feb. 4--Homer and History, II
    Feb. 6--Achilles and the Problem of Being Greek

    Reading: Homer, Iliad, Books VI, IX, and XVI (lines 1-100)

Week IV (Feb. 11-13)

    Feb. 11--Achilles and the Problem of Being Greek, II
    Feb. 13--The Origins of the Greek City-State (Polis)

    Reading: Homer, Iliad, Book XXIV; Hollister, Ch. 5

Week V (Feb. 18-20)

    Feb. 18--The Polis, II; The Origins of Athenian Democracy
    Feb. 20--Athenian Democracy, II

    Reading: Hollister, Chs. 6 and 7

Week VI (Feb. 25-27)

    Feb. 25--HOUR EXAMINATION #1
    Feb. 27--Drama at Athens; Sophocles

    Reading: begin Sophocles, Oedipus the Tyrant

Week VII (March 4-6)

    March 4--Oedipus the Tyrant, I: Guilt and Innocence
    March 6--Oedipus, II: The Spirit of Fifth-Century Greece

    Reading: finish Sophocles, Oedipus; Hollister, Ch. 8

Week VIII (March 11-13)

    March 11--Athens and Sparta
    March 18--The Coming of the Great Peloponnesian War

Reading: Thucydides, The Peloponnesian War, pp. 35-87

Spring Break

Week IX (March 25-27)

   March 25--The Coming of the Great War, II
   March 27--Thucydides

   Reading: Thucydides, The Peloponnesian War, pp. 107-164

Week X (April 1-3)

   April 1--Thucydides and Political Science
   April 3--HOUR EXAMINATION #2

   Reading: Thucydides, The Peloponnesian War, pp. 194-223;
             236-245; 400-408 (before the examination)

Week XI (April 8-10)

   April 8--Alexander the Great and the Hellenistic Age
   April 10--The Political Institutions of the Roman Republic

   Reading: Hollister, Ch. 10; Polybius, The Histories, Book VI (begin)

Week XII (April 15-17)

   April 15--Roman Political Institutions, II; The Culture of
             the Roman Aristocracy
   April 17--The Roman Aristocracy, II

   Reading: finish Polybius, Book VI; Hollister, Ch. 11

Week XIII (April 22-24)

   April 22--The Rise of Rome to World Power
   April 24--The Rise of Rome, II

   Reading: Plutarch, The Life of Cato the Elder

Week XIV (April 29-May 1)

   April 29--The Decline of the Republican Consensus
   May 1--The Final Crisis: Caesar

   Reading: Hollister, Ch. 12

Week XV (May 6-13)

   May 6--Augustus and the "Restored Republic": Pax Romana
   May 8--Roman Responses to Roman History: Optimism in Virgil
   May 13--Roman Responses to Roman History: Pessimism in Virgil

   Reading: Virgil, Aeneid, Books 1, II, IV and VI

   FINAL EXAMINATION: May 18, 1:00 p.m.

GREEK AND ROMAN HISTORY

STANFORD UNIVERSITY   WINTER 1983
CLASSICS 102   FROM ALEXANDER TO CAESAR

Syllabus

Jan. 4-6	Rome in geographical setting.
10-13 ROME	The period of the kings 753-510 (trad.) Legend and archaeology. Historical institutions which survive. Etruscan culture and influence
17-20 ROME	The early Republic 509-275. Constitution. Citizenship. Expansion: control of peninsular Italy. The Greeks of southern Italy.

24-27
ROME
AND THE
GREEK
EAST
	Alexander's successors.
	The Greek powers.
	Third-century Greek culture.
	The Punic Wars 264-201: Roman expansion in the
	  Western Mediterranean.
	Rome and the Greek East: conflict and cultural
	  influence.

Jan. 25-
  Feb. 3
ROME
	Second-century crisis: war, slavery, agriculture,
	  manpower.
	The legislation of the Gracchi (133, 123-122).

Feb. 7-10 ROME AND THE EAST	First-century: decay of Greek monarchies. The Roman constitution and its workings. Power structure, reform, reaction, civil war (121-80).
14-17	The late Republic from Sulla to Pompey (80-60). Literary sources. Culture. The rise of a New Man (Cicero).
23-25	Internal politics at Rome in the 50's.
Feb. 28- Mar. 8	Provincial administration: Cicero. Civil War: Pompey v. Caesar (49-45). Caesar's reforms and plans.
Mar. 9-10	Summing-up.

Classics 230   History of Rome   Spring 1983
James M.Heath   Bucknell University

   Instructor: James M. Heath, 206 Marts Hall, phone 1335. Home phone 524-9479.

               Office hours: daily 8:45-9:30. Afternoon hours to be arranged
                           when I have my schedule set. Any other suitable
                           time by arrangement.

Course texts (all will be used):

               Finley Hooper, Roman Realities (Detroit: Wayne State Univer-
                           sity Press, 1979), "Hooper"
               Livy, The Early History of Rome (Baltimore: Penguin Books, 1971
                           and reprints), "Livy"
               Suetonius, The Twelve Caesars (Baltimore: Penguin Books, 1957
                           and reprints), "Suetonius"
               Naphtali Lewis, Greek Historical Documents: The Roman Prin-
                           cipate, 27 B.C.-285 A.D. (Toronto: Hakkert, 1974),
                           "Lewis"
               Chester G. Starr, The Roman Empire 27 B.C.-A.D. 476: A
                           Study in Survival (New York: Oxford University
                           Press, 1982), "Starr"

NOTE: I am offering this course as a W2 writing course. When the writing
       program becomes an official University requirement, this course (if
       approved) will fulfil the second level of the requirement. I intend
       to adapt my teaching methods to permit you to learn while you write
       a lot and have your writing commented on by me and by other students.
       Although you will be expected to write a lot, only carefully specified
       pieces of writing will be the basis of your final grade. I expect
       you to find that the actual work load in the course is the same or
       less than that in a similar non-writing-intensive course; more of
       the work will be shifted into the classroom.

Basis of Final Grade:

               Three papers, 3 to 5 pages each, 20% each.........60%
               In-class writing projects, one during semester
               . (10%) and final exam (at scheduled time) (20%)..30%
               Other (class participation, fulfillment of deadlines)10%
                                                                   100%

I shall grade the final version of each paper; you will be producing several
drafts of each before the final version. I shall look at these drafts as
they progress, and they will accompany your final version, but they will
not be graded. They are for your assistance, to be commented on and reacted
to in various ways that should assist not only the development of each paper
but also your understanding of the material of the course.

CL 230, History of Rome, spring 1983: Course Objectives

The principal objective of the course is the development of your understanding of the ways to learn about a particular civilization of the past. Roman history provides a specific example within which to pursue that general objective.

Here are some particular aspects of the general objective that can make it more workable:

--To experience, analyze, and sense the different kinds of reading materials, literary and nonliterary, Romans and later writers produced on Roman history.

--To gain insight into the different viewpoints, attitudes, and purposes of authors of these various kinds of historical documents, ancient and modern.

--To become aware of historical progression: the sense that documents belong to a particular context and may refer to that or to an earlier context, or even to an imagined context.

--To become aware of one's own presence as a reader, with attitudes and pre-conceptions that may be reinforced or challenged by the attitudes and pre-conceptions of the historical materials.

--To develop ways of raising questions about aspects of Roman history, society, and historical documents.

--To find connections: between literary works and historical contexts; between narrative and interpretation; between phenomena of another civilization and those of your own experience; between "fact" and imaginative reconstruction.

--To develop the facility of your writing as a means to your becoming familiar with the processes that earlier objectives require.

--To develop your facility as an organizer of ideas by leading you through the tasks of reading, reporting, commenting, questioning, and, ultimately, answering in sequence.

--To develop a sense of how development of your writing and your organization of ideas can be assisted by cooperative efforts.

CL 230-spring 1983: schedule of course expectations

The activities planned for each day are given. Readings should be read prior to class. During the class we shall be doing things to make sense of these readings, so bring the books containing the readings to class. Don't hesitate to come to class if some calamity prevents you from completing the readings: you should still get something out of the class. But don't make a habit of skipping the readings. Abbreviations as on cover sheet.

The notation "writing" for an assignment means that some work on writing will be expected in class; usually you will bring a paper in some stage of development and will engage in discussion and rewriting of your own and others' papers. Other pages detail the specific activities for each day.

Week	Day/date	Activity	Topic
1	W 2/2	Introduction: you will get to see what we shall do.	
	F 2/4	Read Livy, pages 33-51; Hooper, pages 15-28	Roman history and myth
2	M 2/7	Read Livy, pp. 51-74; Hooper, pp. 28-61	Romulus and authority
	W 2/9	Read Livy, pp. 378-402; Hooper, pp. 62-76	Romans and Gauls: order and disorder
	F 2/11	Writing: preliminaries for first paper	
3	M 2/14	Read Livy, pp. 128-51 (middle); Hooper, pp. 76-89	War, politics, economics
	W 2/16	Read Livy, pp. 74-121; Hooper, pp. 90-101	Rome's romantic enemies
	F 2/ 8	Writing: first draft of first paper	
4	M 2/21	Read Livy, pp. 341-68; Hooper, pp. 101-27	Rome's greatest enemies
	W 2/23	Read Livy, pp. 196-216; Hooper, pp. 128-53	Patrician images
	F 2/25	Writing: second draft of first paper	
5	M 2/28	Read: Livy, pp. 231-48; Hooper, pp. 154-76	Images of revolution
	W 3/2	In-class writing exercise: counts 10% of final grade	
	F 3/4	Writing: third draft of first paper	

This ends the first segment of the course, on the Roman Republic. We begin now to study the transitional period that leads into the principate of Augustus and the Roman Empire.

Week	Day/date	Activity	Topic
6	M 3/7	Read Suetonius, _Julius Caesar_	Biography and history
	W 3/9	Read Hooper, pp. 177-230	The prelude to Caesar
	F 3/11	Writing: preliminaries to second paper	
7	M 3/14	Read Hooper, pp. 230-74	Relating Suetonius to Hooper's Caesar
	W 3/16	Read Hooper, pp. 275-328	Portrait of an age
	F 3/18	Writing: first draft of second paper	
8	M 3/21	Read Suetonius, _Augustus_	Compare with his _Julius_
	W 3/23	Read Hooper, pp. 329-51	The historical Augustus
	F 3/25	Writing: second draft of second paper	

This ends the course's second segment and brings us to the spring break.
After the spring break we take up the third segment, the Roman Empire.

9	M 4/4	Suetonius, _Tiberius_ Lewis: Look at documents number (_not_ page): 1, 2, 5A-D, 21, 22, 31A, 36, 40C.	The nature of the Roman Empire and of documentary sources on it.
	W 4/6	Read: Hooper, pp. 352-91; look at Lewis, numbers 3A, 5A-E, 7A-8B, 14, 18, 26A, 28B,E, 31, 34, 37A-B, 39A,C, 40	Relating text and documents
	F 4/8	Writing: preliminaries to third paper	
10	M 4/11	Read: Suetonius, _Claudius_ and _Nero_	Differing images of emperor
	W 4/13	Read: Hooper, pp. 392-413; Suetonius, _Vespasian_, _Titus_, _Domitian_ Look at Lewis numbers 5F, 8C, 12, 20, 25A, 26B,C, 27A, 30B, 37C,D, 38A,B, 42	A new dynasty: change
	F 4/15	Writing: first draft of third paper	
11	M 4/18	Read: Hooper, pp. 414-58	The imperial peace
	W 4/20	Look at Lewis nos. 2B, 4, 5G, 6 8D-9B, 10B,C, 11, 15, 19, 23, 24, 25B,D, 26D-N, 27B-E, 28A,C,D, 30A, 31B,C, 32, 33, 35, 37E,F, 38C, 39B, 43, 44	Documentary evidence of the peace
	F 4/22	Writing: second draft of third paper	

Schedule, page 3

12 M 4/25   Read; Hooper, pp. 459-88   The age of military
              Look at Lewis, nos. 3B-D, 5H, 10A,   control
                 13, 16, 17, 25C, 26 O-P, 27F, 29,
                 31D, 41, 45

    W 4/27   Read: Hooper, pp. 489-549   The end of the story

    F 4/29   Writing: third draft of third essay

This ends the formal presentation of the chronological sequence of
Roman history. The course concludes with a two-week coda that summarizes
and synthesizes the concerns of the last two segments of the course. As
we read and discuss Starr's book, I want you to try to make connections,
between historical periods in Rome, between the approaches of different
disciplines, and between the world of Rome and our contemporary world.

13 M 5/2   Read: Starr, pp. 3-52

    W 5/4   Read: Starr, pp. 54-107

    F 5/6   Probably no class. I hope to go to the Ancient Historians's
                 meeting in Madison, WI.

14 M 5/9   Read: Starr, pp. 109-60

    W 5/11   Read: Starr, pp. 162-81. Be prepared to discuss the whole
                 of Starr.

    F 5/13   Discussion leading up to final writing exercise in final
                 exam, whenever that is scheduled.

CL 230   Spring 1983

<h2 style="text-align:center">Instructions for first paper, Myth and History</h2>

Schedule (details and explanations below):

     A. Preliminary work: Friday, 11 Feb.

     B. First draft: Friday, 18 Feb.

     C. Second draft: Friday, 25 Feb.

     D. Third draft: Friday, March 4

     E. Final draft to be handed in: Monday, 7 March

Details and Explanations

A. **Preliminary work.** Come to class Feb. 11 with at least tentative responses to these instructions:

1. This is a must. Choose a short (one or two paragraphs long) self-contained segment in Livy's Book I: a segment of a speech, myth, battle narrative, historical comment, etc. Identify this segment, e.g., "Page 46, "The last to attack . . . coin that paid her.""

2. Find out how much surrounding context you need to read and understand to increase your sense of what your segment is about. Identify this context and describe it in a sentence or two, e.g., "Pages 40-51, the reign of Romulus, especially Roman relations with their neighbors."

3. Pick an audience for your essay: another student, a parent or other relative, a faculty member in a discipline unlike Classics, etc. <u>Don't pick me!</u> You will be addressing this person in your work on this essay from this moment on.

4. Assume the person you chose ("your audience") has read your segment, but not too carefully, and wants to understand it better.

5. Tell your audience these things:

    a. What sort of person is the author of your segment, from what Livy says?

    b. What sort of an audience is Livy writing for? What does he expect them to know and believe?

    c. Is there a character in your segment whose personality is important and different from Livy's or the audience he is addressing? If so, describe that character.

    d. Is Livy making a concealed or implied point in your segment? Express it if you can.

    e. Describe any function your segment appears to have in the context you described in A2 above.

A. 5.f. List any things you don't understand about your segment or its context. Can you tell whether your misunderstanding is due to your lack of information or to the way Livy is writing?

   g. What kinds of information or understanding might help help you give your audience better answers to questions 5 d,e,f?

   h. Give any information that the textbook or your own experience of life provide that bears on the problems in 5fg.

   i. The class session will be devoted to responses to other people's work and hearing their comments on yours. Be sure to bring Livy and the textbook to class.

B. **First draft**

1. From your responses to the instructions in A, and from the comments you heard on those responses, develop a thesis statement--an argument, theory, adage, belief--that your segment illustrates somehow. Make this a general one. In my Tarpeia example I might have picked "women are untrustworthy," "treachery brings its own reward," "there's no honor among thieves," or "wise plans include treachery," and several others. You are working toward an essay topic by this choice.

2. List some statements that illustrate peculiarly Roman aspects of your thesis, as your segment suggests. For my example I might say:

    "The daughter of a Roman could endanger her father by treachery. Enemies of Rome try to subvert Rome through its women. Roman women are easily deceived."

3. Try to find other examples, in Livy or in Hooper as you are reading along, of the operation of your thesis or illustrative statements. Try especially to locate examples that contradict the statements.

4. When you have done the preceding, lay out your essay in some rough form. You might give a fairly detailed outline, or a tree diagram, or a rough written form of the essay. Suit the method you use to your usual work methods.

5. Give a tentative essay title that takes the form:

    ". . . . . . .: Myth and History in (your segment) of Livy Book I"

    (I might title my essay "Women and Treachery: Myth . . .")

C. **Second draft**

Come to class with a rough draft of your essay, typed or legibly handwritten, with margin space for notations. The class activity will focus on the clarity of your ideas, the tightness of your organization, and the sequence of your thought.

D. <u>Third draft</u>

Come to class with a typed or <u>very</u> neatly handwritten form of your essay.
The class will look briefly at the same elements C deals with, but will
go on to give attention to linguistic matters: spelling, syntax, use of
the right words, punctuation, and other mechanical and stylistic features.

E. The final draft is due March 7. The text should be about 4 pages long.
It must be typed, double spaced, preferably not on corrasable bond paper.
You may use your third draft if you are happy with it after the class
session, but the copy you turn in should be neat. One or two minor
handwritten corrections are acceptable, but major revisions require
retyping your manuscript.

    Provide a title sheet that includes this information, neatly arranged:

                course number and title
                instructor's name
                your name
                your campus address
                date paper is submitted
                full title

    After the title page and text, append all other materials that you
have brought to class that relate to it; especially:

                earlier drafts
                evaluation sheets
                editorial sheets

CL 230, instructions for second paper

Schedule:
- A. Preliminary work, by Friday, 11 March
- B. First draft, Friday, 18 March
- C. Second draft, Friday, 25 March
- D. Final draft due Tuesday, 5 April, 4 p.m. (my office)

(I don't give these instructions as exhaustively as I did those for the first paper. For general guidance, and for the form of the final draft, refer to those earlier instructions.)

A. **Preliminary work**

1. Choose an audience different from the one you chose for the first paper and make it a small, identifiable group: Biology majors, a football team, a church group, residents of a retirement home. Define and describe your audience, and keep them in mind through the final draft of this paper.

2. Choose a single numbered section ("chapter") of the 89 chapters in Suetonius's _Julius Caesar_. This will be your chapter.

3. What is the subject of the chapter?

4. Describe the voice the author of the chapter adopts and the audience he seems to be addressing. What attitudes to Caesar do you see? Describe any sources that Suetonius seems to be adapting or transmitting directly.

5. If the chapter is not isolated and unique in subject, list the other chapters that deal with the same subject.

6. Describe the point that this chapter (along with others on the same subject) makes.

7. Consider the subject of your chapter and pick one specific feature of the earlier Roman republic that shares the subject of your chapter in some way. You might pick an actual event, or specific political or religious practices. List your sources for this feature, in Livy and Hooper.

8. Describe the feature you have chosen: give all essential defining factors, including, as appropriate, date, people involved, unresolved questions, traditional attitudes of the Romans to your feature.

9. Start noting down similarities and differences between your chapter in Suetonius and the historical feature you have chosen.

87

B. First draft

1. From your work in A and from responses to it, choose a general thesis statement on the common subject of your chapter and your historical feature.

2. List statements arising out of your two sources that explore dimensions of your thesis.

3. Begin to rough out an essay, in any of the alternatives suggested in the instructions for the first paper.

4. Devise a tentative title for your paper. The title of the final draft will take the form:

    ". . . . . . . : Continuity and Change in Roman Republican history

        as reflected in chapter ____ of Suetonius's Julius Caesar"

    (Example: chapter 20 suggests the title "The Autocratic Roman Noble: . . .")

C. Second draft

As you did with your first paper, write out or, preferably, type out a version of your essay for comment on organization and coherence. The class will help you clarify what you are going to do, and how.

Since the spring break follows, we shall not have a third draft to go over in class. Instead, you have the opportunity to get reactions from friends and relatives elsewhere. Please ask them to put any comments they have in writing and to sign them, and then include them in the file you turn in with your final draft. This exercise tries to get you to seek aid from quarters you may not have looked to before.

D. Final draft

This is due to me at my office by 4 p.m. on Tuesday, 5 April, to give you a bit of leeway after the vacation.
Follow instructions for final draft for the first paper; adapt your title to the form I give in B4 above.

88

CL 230, instructions for third paper, Romanization in the East as shown
by nonliterary documents.

<u>Schedule</u>: A. Preliminary work, by Friday, 8 April

B. First draft, Friday, 15 April

C. Second draft, Friday, 22 April

D. Third draft, Friday, 29 April

E. Final draft due Monday, 2 May

A. <u>Preliminary work</u>

1. Choose your audience. This time it is to be a less defined group:
college students, parents of teenagers, suburbanites, Southerners, . . .

2. Choose one nonliterary document in Lewis, preferably a short, dated
one. Note that some selections are from "literary" authors, such as
Dio Cassius and Aelius Aristides. Choose something clearly "official."

a. Tell what you know or can figure out about the nature of the
document. Is it a government form, a public notice; on paper or
marble; for private individuals or for public display, etc.?

b. What can you discover about the author(s) of the document and the
audience(s) to which it is addressed? Are any attitudes expressed
in it?

c. Summarize the content of the document: who has done or is to do what,
and to whom? What is it about?

d. What is the purpose, obvious and concealed, of the document? Consider
especially the combination of message and its medium.

3. Try to locate, in Hooper or elsewhere, a historical feature (as you
did in your second paper) that deals with a topic similar or related
to that of your document. It may come from any period of Roman
history.

a. Describe the essentials of this feature.

4. Jot down a series of statements that refer to the presence or absence
of features of "Romanness" (as you understand that rather vague term)
in your document and the historical feature you chose for comparison.
Note especially ways in which Romanism differs or is similar in the two.

B. <u>First draft</u>: as before. Title will take the form: ". . . . .: Romanization
in (your document's identification in Lewis) and (your example)."

C-E: as before. We shall attempt closer work on linguistic features in the
session on the third draft.

Chester Starr's investigation of the reasons for the survival of the Roman Empire as long as it did leads him into many interwoven aspects of the political, military and economic history of the Empire, not all of which are easily penetrated" (p. 5). Investigating these aspects involves asking how imperial policy was set and carried out, but he is concerned particularly with the "justice" of the imperial system, the ways in which it is or is not fair to the inhabitants of the Empire. He keeps coming back to the question posed by Saint Augustine, "Justice being taken away, then, what are kingdoms but great robberies?" (p. 68).

For your final project, I want you to write an essay that has two dimensions, i) how one particular group of people in the Roman world does and does not receive justice from the imperial system, ii) how the treatment of this group (also its constitution) changes over time, from Republic to late Empire. You might pick the common people of the city of Rome, the senatorial nobility, equestrians, women of some defined group, slaves (describe the type), and so on. First, make sure you limit your group in some way, then examine how the group is treated or affected by the systems of the Roman world. Start from some clear point in time and consider a few points in time at which change in this treatment or being affected by the Roman system may take place. In particular, discuss how Rome's administrative structure affects your group, but don't forget less formal structures: family, economy, and so on. As these structures change, how does your group fare?

Try to develop a general argument in your essay (e.g., "Developments in the Roman world from c. 200 B.C. to A.D. 300 proved to be increasingly favorable to . . .") and then develop particular aspects of this thesis. Be as concrete as you can about the ways the system affects your group. Try to start each of your paragraphs (about 4 to 8 in the middle, I'd guess) with a thematic sentence, too (e.g., "The emperors of the second century A.D. made decisions that led to less favorable treatment for the . . ."), and then explain and expand upon the sentence in your paragraph. The first paragraph should be introductory, the last should draw points together for a conclusion. I don't want a listing of pieces of information, but a set of connected paragraphs, each investigating one step of your argument, for example, the complex situation at one point in time. I don't expect you to use library resources, though I'm not forbidding that. I prefer you to extrapolate from the materials you have read in the course and the class discussions. Do give citations for direct quotations and cite materials not assigned.

The essay should be about 4 to 6 pages in length. This means you have to select the points you will discuss. The essay is not an exhaustive treatment of your topic but a suggestive argument about it. I should prefer it typed—that makes a better impression—but if you cannot get it typed, you may write it by hand. If so, write in ink on lined paper, leave alternate lines blank, and leave left and right margins. Deliver them to my office (Marts 206) at your earliest convenience. I shall have finished papers on the table by door or in my office as soon as they are done.

Classics 230   History of Rome   Spring 1983

Final exam: in-class version

The exam will end at 5 p.m. sharp. Feel free to leave the classroom for a while now and then if you want to go out and walk around to think about your essay, or just for exercise.

For the final exam you are to write an _essay_ on _one_ of the following topics. Your essay should display these characteristics:

1. Length: 5 paragraphs, including an introduction and a conclusion. This works out to about 5-8 blue book pages or 500-750 words.
2. Comprehensiveness: it should involve different periods of Roman history; some reference should be made to both Republic and Empire.
3. Focus: you should pick a focus within the assigned topics for concreteness. Your title should suggest this focus (see some examples below).
4. Interdisciplinary approach: try to introduce different aspects of Roman history (e.g., economics and religion).
5. Selectivity: choose a few important facts or ideas to illustrate the focus you have chosen.
6. Demonstration of your writing process: separate your preparatory work from your final result. Turn in two blue books, one with your outlines, practice sentences, and so on, a second one with your finished essay.
7. Polish: read your final version over for its readability and accuracy (spelling, punctuation, etc.). Imagine a potential employer will read it.

Topics (Taken generally from Starr's Roman Empire 27 B.C.-A.D. 476)

A. In what ways are the common people of the city of Rome and of the provinces different and/or similar?
B. In what ways does the central government of Rome respond to issues brought up from lower levels?
C. In what ways do leading Romans make themselves symbolic?
D. How are peace and order related in the Roman world?
E. If you wish, ask your own question. It should be of this same "general" type. Write it out, make it short. Don't ask a question on a topic on which you have already worked in a paper for the course.

Examples of possible titles:

A. "The common people of Rome and the Greek East: relations with aristocrats"
B. "Debtors and creditors: responses to their conflicts in Republic and Empire"
C. "Roman noble, municipal magnate, and emperor: picture and reality"
D. "Military peace and economic order: tensions throughout Roman history"

Kurt A. Raaflaub
Department of Classics, Box 1935
Brown University
Providence, RI 02912

Semester I, 1984/85

CLASSICS 131 (= HISTORY 105)

HISTORY OF THE ROMAN REPUBLIC

A. COURSE ANNOUNCEMENT

The political and social history of Rome from its origin to the death of Augustus. Focus on the social conflicts of the early Republic, the conquest of Italy and the Mediterranean, the economic and social repercussions of expansion, the crisis and breakdown of the Republic, and the emergence of monarchy. Special attention to constitutional and ideological developments, to the beginnings of Roman law and historiography, and to other cultural achievements of the period. Aim is to understand the historical causes and specific conditions that led to the unification of the whole Mediterranean world under the rule of one city: Rome. The course work will to a great extent be based on ancient sources, which will be read in translation.

B. REQUIRED READING

1. F.M. Heichelheim - C.A. Yeo - A.M. Ward, *A History of the Roman People*, 2nd ed., Englewood Cliffs, NJ, 1984 (= HYW)
   Alternatively, for graduate or advanced undergraduate students: M. Cary - H.H. Scullard, *A History of Rome Down to the Reign of Constantine*, third ed., New York, 1975 (= CS)

2. *Roman Civilization, Sourcebook*, ed. by N. Lewis - M. Reinhold, Vol. I: *The Republic*, New York, 1966 (= LR)

3. Ancient historians in translation (Penguin)
   - (a) Livy, *The Early History of Rome*
   - (b) Polybius, *The Rise of the Roman Empire*
   - (c) Sallust, *Jugurthine War, Conspiracy of Catiline*
   - (d) Plutarch, *Fall of the Roman Empire*

4. Handout with additional texts and maps (see below part E)

C. EXAMINATIONS

1. Tues., Oct. 9: first classroom exam (30 minutes covering classes 1-10)

2. Tues., Oct. 9: topics of first take-home essay announced

   Tues., Oct. 16: first take-home essay due

3. Tues., Oct. 30: topics of second take-home essay announced

   Tues., Nov. 6: second take-home essay due

4. Tues., Nov. 13: second classroom exam (30 minutes, covering classes 9-20)

5. Choice between term paper or long take-home essay
   (a) Tues., Nov. 13: topics of term papers due (preferably earlier)
       Fri., Dec. 14: term papers due
   (b) Thur., Nov. 29: topics of take-home essay announced
       Fri., Dec. 14: take-home essays due

6. Thur., Dec. 6: third classroom exam (30 minutes, covering classes 21-26 and readings for class 27)

7. Occasional short quizzes are to be expected.

D. SYLLABUS

PART I: FOUNDATIONS

1. Tues., Sept. 4: Introduction - Geography of Italy and the Mediterranean - Roman history: a survey and some questions

2. Thur., Sept. 6: Methodological introduction: nature and interpretation of ancient sources

Sources:
   HYW ch. III, 1-2; V, 1; or CS ch. 6.
   LR pp. 3-16, 40-45; no.9 (pp.62-65)
   Livy, Preface (pp.33-34 or LR pp.8-10)
   Livy I.16-18 (pp.51 bottom - 53 end)
   R.M. Ogilvie, Introduction to *Livy*, in: Penguin, pp.7-17
   Handout no. 5-8

Recommended Reading:
   W. Laistner, *The Greater Roman Historians* (Berkeley and Los Angeles, 1947, pb)
   M. Grant, *Roman History from Coins* (Cambr., 1968)
   M.I. Finley, "The Ancient Historian and His Sources," in: E. Gabba (ed.), *Tria Corda, Scritti in onore di A. Momigliano* (Como, 1983) 201ff.
   T.J. Cornell, "The Foundation of Rome in the Ancient Literary Tradition," in: *Papers in Italian Archaeology* I (*British Archaeol. Reports*, Suppl. Ser.41, 1978) 131ff.
   E.J. Phillips, "Current Research in Livy's First Decade," in: *Aufstieg und Niedergang der römischen Welt*, vol. II.30.2 (1982) 998ff.
   T. Pinsent, "Antiquarianism, Fiction and History in the First Decade of Livy," in: *Classical Journal* 55 (1959) 81ff.

T.J. Cornell, "The Value of the Literary Tradition on Archaic Rome," in K.A. Raaflaub (ed.), *Social Struggles in Archaic Rome: New Perspectives on the Conflict of the Orders* (Berkeley - Los Angeles, 1986) 52ff.

J. von Ungern-Sternberg, "The Formation of the 'Annalistic Tradition': The Example of the Decemvirate," ibid. 77ff.

(for more literature on Roman historiography see below, class no.26)

Focus: Livy, Preface; I.16-18

Questions:

1. There are several categories of sources which historians use to reconstruct the course, character and significance of Rome. What can each of them teach us, and what are its limitations?

2. What can we learn about life in the early Roman community from the names of the festivals in the calendar which has been preserved on stone (LR no.9)?

3. Livy I.16-18 provides us with a good example of the historical message contained in archaic institutions. What can we learn from this example about early Roman kingship?

4. Livy's preface gives us a lot of information about intention, purpose, weaknesses and characteristics of Roman historiography. What are they? Combining this with the other sources quoted by LR on p.4, 6 and 7, you should be able to describe the difficulties faced by a modern historian in using literary sources on Roman history in general and for the reconstruction of the history of early Rome in particular.

3. **Tues., Sept. 11: Rome's cultural and political environment, I: Greeks, Italics, and Celts**

Sources:

HYW ch. I; II, 10-11 (pp.19-21); or CS ch. 1; 2; 3, 1
LR no. 1, 3, 14 (p.74), 16 (p.77), 17
Livy I.1-21 (pp.33-56)
Handout no.9

Recommended Reading:

M.I. Finley, *Early Greece, The Bronze and Archaic Ages* (New York, 1970, pb)
H.D.F. Kitto, *The Greeks* (Penguin, 1951)
J. Boardman, *The Greeks Overseas* (Penguin, 1964)
T.G.E. Powell, *The Celts* (London, 1958)
N. Chadwick, *The Celts* (Penguin, 1970)
E.T.A. Salmon, *Samnium and the Samnites* (Cambr., 1967)

Questions:

1. Look at the maps in your handout and on p.25 of HYW or p.32 of CS. Why was Rome an ideal spot for a settlement? Why did this spot have great potential and was it at the same time extremely dangerous? How would you describe the geopolitical situation of Rome?

2. What can the piece on the 'sacred bands of the Samnites' in Dionysius' Roman history (LR no.16) add to this picture?

3. Why did the Greeks settle in Southern Italy and Sicily at all? Why did they settle only in Southern Italy? In what ways was their presence crucial for Rome's cultural and political development?

4. Thur., Sept. 13: Rome's cultural and political environment, II: The Etruscans

Sources:

    HYW ch. II, 1-9 (pp.8-19) or CS ch. 3, 2-4
    LR no. 2, 6
    Livy I.22-41 (pp.56 bottom - 80)
    Handout no.10a-f

Recommended Reading:

    M. Pallottino, *The Etruscans* (Penguin, 6th ed., 1978)
    J. Heurgon, *Daily Life of the Etruscans* (New York, 1964)
    R. Bloch, *The Etruscans* (New York, 1958)
    E. Richardson, *The Etruscans, their Art and Civilization* (Chicago, 1964)
    C.F.C. Hawkes, "The Problem of the Origins of the Archaic Cultures in Etruria and
        its main Difficulties," in *Studi Etruschi* 27 (1959) 363ff.
    J. Heurgon, *The Rise of Rome* (London, 1973, with ample bibliogr.)
    H.H. Scullard, *The Etruscan Cities and Rome* (Ithaca, NY, 1967)
    W.V. Harris, *Rome in Etruria and Umbria* (Oxford, 1971)

Questions:

    1. Etruscan civilization and power emerged in surprising suddenness and speed in the eighth century B.C. What were the main preconditions of this development?
    2. The Etruscan cities were ruled by kings and aristocracies. What was the basis of their power? What was the situation of the other inhabitants of these communities? And what were the political consequences of the relationship between upper and lower classes?
    3. How can we explain the fact that the Etruscan predominance in northern and central Italy broke down rather rapidly in the 5th and 4th centuries?

5. Tues., Sept. 18: The Etruscans and Rome; the emergence of the city-state; king, council and assembly; the Latin League

Sources

    HYW ch. III or CS ch. 4; 5, 1-3 and 6-8
    LR no. 4, 5, 12, 27
    Livy I.42-60 (pp. 81-101)
    Handout no. 10g-i; 11a-c

Recommended Reading:

    Heurgon (as mentioned above)
    R. Bloch, *The Origins of Rome* (New York, 1960)
    J.C. Meyer, *Pre-republican Rome* (Odense, 1983)
    R.M. Ogilvie, *Early Rome and the Etruscans* (Fontana, pb 1976)
    H.H. Scullard, *A History of the Roman World, 753-146 B.C.* (London - New York, 4th
        ed. 1980)
    R. Thomsen, *King Servius Tullius. A Historical Synthesis* (Copenhagen, 1980)

A. Momigliano, "An Interim Report on the Origins of Rome," in *Journal of Roman Studies* 53 (1963) 95ff.

H. Last, "The Servian Reforms," in *Journal of Roman Studies* 35 (1945) 30ff.

A.M. Snodgrass, "The Hoplite Reform and History," in *Journal of Hellenic Studies* 85 (1965) 110ff.

J.-C. Richard, "Patricians and Plebeians: The Origin of a Social Dichotomy," in K.A. Raaflaub (ed.), *Social Struggles in Archaic Rome* (as cited above) 105ff.

Focus: Livy I. 34-35 (pp.72-74 middle); 39-41 (pp.77 middle - 80 bottom)
LR no. 27; Livy I.42-43 (pp.81-82)

Questions:

1. Rome was situated between Etruscans in the North and Greeks in the South. What social and political structures do these two peoples have in common that became decisive for Rome's further development? And where do they differ completely?

2. The Etruscan kings represent an era of Etruscan domination in Rome. What achievements were most important during their reign? How do we have to imagine this Etruscan domination? What was Rome's status during this period?

3. The name of Servius Tullius is connected with an important reform of the army and the popular assembly. Why was such a reform necessary, what was its purpose, and how did the system work?

4. Many scholars think that the centuriate system described by Livy and Dionysius is primarily a political, not a military system and that it emerged much later, after a long development. Why would that system be unsuitable for military purposes, and what would the original military system have looked like?

6. Thur., Sept. 20: Roman society and institutions: an introduction into structures and terminology

Sources
HYW ch. IV or CS ch. 5, 3-7; 11, 1-2
LR no.8, 10, 25, 26, 29, 30, 34, 36, 37, 43, 148, 155, 156, 159-161
Polybius VI.2-18 (pp. 302-318)
Livy II.1-22 (pp.105-129 top)
Handout no. 13-14

Focus: Polybius VI.11-18

Recommended Reading:
J. Heurgon, *The Rise of Rome* (London, 1973)
M. Gelzer, *The Roman Nobility* (Oxford, 1969)
E.S. Staveley, *Greek and Roman Voting and Elections* (Ithaca, NY, 1972)
H.J. Wolff, *Roman Law. An Historical Introduction* (pb, Norman, OK, 1951)
W. Kunkel, *An Introduction to Roman Legal and Constitutional History* (Oxford, 2nd ed., 1973)
F.F. Abbott, *A History and Description of Roman Political Institutions* (Boston, 3rd ed., 1901, repr. New York, 1963)
G.W. Botsford, *The Roman Assemblies from their Origin to the End of the Republic* (New York, 1909)
L.R. Taylor, *The Voting Districts of the Roman Republic. The Urban and Rural Tribes* (Rome, 1960)
L.R. Taylor, *Roman Voting Assemblies* (Ann Arbor, 1966)
R.E. Mitchell, "The Aristocracy of the Roman Republic," in F.C. Jaher (ed.), *The Rich, the*

Well-Born, and the Powerful: Elites and Upper Classes in History (Urbana, Illinois, 1974) 27ff.

C. Nicolet, *The World of the Citizen in Republican Rome* (London, 1980)

M.R. Lefkowitz - M.B. Fant (eds.), *Women's Life in Greece and Rome. A Source Book in Translation* (pb, Baltimore, 1982)

S.B. Pomeroy, *Goddesses, Whores, Wives, and Slaves: Women in Classical Antiquity* (New York, 1975, with bibliography)

S.B. Pomeroy, "Selected Bibliography on Women in Classical Antiquity," in J. Peradotto - J.P. Sullivan (eds.), *Women in the Ancient World : The Arethusa Papers* (Albany, NY, 1984) 315ff.

J.P.V.D. Balsdon, *Roman Women: Their History and Habits* (London, 1962)

Questions:

1. In a century long process the Romans developed a regular political career scheme. On the basis of your readings and of the diagram in the handout (no. 13), you should be able to describe in detail the career of an average Roman from his first public office to the very highest positions.

2. The members of the Roman elite in time became professional "politicians" (this term, however, is misleading: why?). Why was that possible and necessary? And what were its consequences?

3. To how many and what social and political units did a Roman citizen belong? Do you find an explanation for the strange institution of "group vote" (is it so strange?), and what did it mean for the distribution of power in Rome?

4. What is a client? Why is the institution of "clientela" so important?

5. You have read Polybius' analysis of the Roman constitution. What are its basic components and working principles? What are the major duties of assembly, senate and magistracies, how is the power distributed and how is it restricted and controlled? In what respects is this fundamentally different from most of our modern constitutions? What basic rules of behavior needed to be observed by everybody in order that such a constitution could function effectively?

PART II: FROM CITY-STATE TO WORLD-POWER

7. Tues., Sept. 25: From monarchy to republic; the outbreak of the "conflict of the orders"; the historical writing of Livy

Sources:
    HYW ch. V, 1-5 (pp.48-58) or CS ch.7
    LR no.23, 24, 28, 32 (tables I-IV, VII, X, XI)
    Livy II.23-65 (pp.129-180)
    Handout no.12

Focus: Livy I.57-60 (pp.97 bottom - 101); II.9-14 (pp.114-121) with Handout no.12
    Livy II.23-33 (pp.129-143 middle)
    Livy II.55-58 (pp.169 bottom - 173 middle)
    Optional: Livy II.9 (p.115 middle); II.34/5 (pp.143 bottom - 145 bottom); IV.12-16 (pp.169 bottom - 173 middle)

Recommended Reading:
    Heurgon, Bloch, Ogilvie, Scullard (as listed above)
    A. Alföldi, *Early Rome and the Latins* (Ann Arbor, 1965)

97

H. St.Jones - H. Last, "The Early Republic", in *Cambridge Ancient History*, Vol. VII (1928) 436ff.

A. Momigliano, "The Origins of the Roman Republic," in C. Singleton (ed.), *Interpretation: Theory and Practice* (Baltimore, 1969) 1ff.

A.W. Lintott, *Violence in Republican Rome* (Oxford, 1968)

A.W. Lintott, "The Tradition of Violence in the Annals of the Early Republic," in *Historia* 19 (1970) 12ff.

A.W. Lintott, "*Provocatio*. From the Struggle of the Orders to the Principate," in *Aufstieg und Niedergang der römischen Welt*, Vol. I.2 (1972) 226ff.

Ferenczy, Brunt (as listed below)

T. Frank, *An Economic History of Rome to the End of the Republic* (Baltimore, 1920)

T. Frank, *An Economic Survey of Ancient Rome*, Vol. I: *Rome and Italy of the Republic* (Baltimore, 1933, repr. New York, 1975)

M.I. Finley, "Debt-bondage and the problem of slavery," in id., *Economy and Society in Ancient Greece* (New York, 1981) 150ff.

A. Momigliano, "The Rise of the Plebs in the Archaic Age of Rome," in K.A. Raaflaub (ed.), *Social Struggles in Archaic Rome* (as cited above) 175ff.

K.A. Raaflaub, "From Protection and Defense to Offense and Participation: Stages in the Conflict of the Orders," ibid. 198ff.

T.J. Luce, *Livy*, and P.G. Walsh, *Livy* (as in no. 26 below)

Questions:

1. Our sources (Livy and Handout no.12) contain two contrasting versions about the expulsion of the king and Rome's war against Porsenna. As a historian, how do you interpret and reconcile these versions? How do you reconstruct the causes and the political context of the transition from monarchy to republic?

2. Livy's narrative of the fall of Tarquin reveals his views on historical causation. Do you find such an explanation of a major political revolt or even revolution satisfactory?

3. What is the "conflict of the orders"? What were its causes and its origins?

4. There is an important connection between the Roman military system of the early republic and the outbreak of the "conflict of the orders". What is the connection and what were its effects?

5. The first successes of the plebeians were the result of the famous *secessio plebis* to the sacred mountain outside Rome. Try to analyze in social and political terms (a) the nature of this event, and (b) its results.

6. The measures taken by the plebeians at that time were radical and violent. Why was this necessary and what does it tell us about the patricians?

8. Thurs., Sept. 27: The "conflict of the orders" (450 - 287 B.C.)

Sources:
HYW ch. V, 6 - end; VI, 1-5 (pp.58-72) or CS ch. 8 and 9
LR no.38-42
Livy III.1 - IV.8 (pp.183-279)

Recommended Reading:
A. Watson, *Rome of the XII Tables: Persons and Property* (Princeton, 1975)

E. Ferenczy, *From the Patrician State to the Patricio-Plebeian State* (Amsterdam, 1976)

H. St.Jones - H. Last, "The Making of a United State," in *Cambridge Ancient History*, Vol. VII (1928) 519ff.

P.A. Brunt, *Social Conflicts in the Roman Republic* (London, 1971, pb)

T.J. Cornell, "The Failure of the Plebs," in E. Gabba (ed.), *Tria Corda. Scritti in onore di A. Momigliano* (Como, 1983) 101ff.

K. von Fritz, "The Reorganization of the Roman Government in 366 B.C. and the
so-called Licinio-Sextian Laws," *Historia* 1 (1950) 3ff.

E.S. Staveley, "The Political Aims of Appius Claudius Caecus," *Historia* 8 (1959)
410ff.

W. Eder, "The Political Significance of the Codification of Law in Archaic Societies," in
Raaflaub (ed.), *Social Struggles in Archaic Rome* (as cited above) 262ff.

J. von Ungern-Sternberg, "The End of the Conflict of the Orders," ibid. 353ff.

Focus: LR no. 38, 39, 42
   Livy III.32-41 (pp.219-229)
   Livy IV.1-7 (pp.269-277)

Questions:

1. Why was the codification of law such an important issue? What was its political
significance? Livy presents it as a major victory of the plebeians; was it really one?
Could it possibly be described as a victory of the patricians as well?

2. What was at stake in the struggle about the ban on intermarriage? How do you
interpret and evaluate the religious arguments used in this debate?

3. The plebeians had demanded a solution for the problem of debts and the distribution
of land to the poor since the early 5th cent. When were these demands finally met,
why (and under what circumstances) then and not before?

4. It is possible to divide the conflict of the orders into two distinct phases, roughly
coinciding with the 5th and 4th centuries respectively. What are the characteristics of
each phase, what are the main differences, and what common elements exist in both
phases?

5. The political demands of an emerging plebeian elite or "aristocracy" played an
important part. Where did that elite come from, why and how was it distinguished
from the patrician aristocracy, and how did its gradual absorption into a new patricio-
plebeian elite effect the conflict of the orders?

6. The end of the conflict of the orders is usually dated in 287 B.C. because of the *lex
Hortensia*. Why would that law be particularly important? Do you consider this to be
a historically reasonable conclusion? If yes, if no: why?

**9. Tues., Oct. 2: Roman expansion I: the conquest and political organization of
Italy (450 - 270 B.C.)**

Sources:
   HYW ch. VI, 6-end (pp.72ff.) or CS ch. 10 and 11, 3-8
   LR no. 13, 15-22
   Livy V.32-55 (pp.378-402)
   Polybius I.1-28 (Introduction and beginning of First Punic War, pp.41-73)
   Handout no.15

Recommended Reading:
   E. Ferenczy, *From the Patrician State to the Patricio-Plebeian State* (Amsterdam, 1976)
   J. Heurgon, *The Rise of Rome* (London, 1973)
   W.V. Harris, *War and Imperialism in Republican Rome, 327 - 70 B.C.* (Oxford, 1979)
   E.T. Salmon, *Samnium and the Samnites* (Cambridge, 1967)
   E.T. Salmon, *Roman Colonization under the Republic* (Ithaca, NY, 1969)
   E.T. Salmon, *The Making of Roman Italy* (Ithaca, NY, 1981)
   A.N. Sherwin-White, *The Roman Citizenship* (Oxford, 2nd ed., 1973)
   C.G. Starr, *The Beginning of Imperial Rome: Rome in the Mid-Republic* (Ann Arbor,
1980)

Focus: LR no. 19-22

Questions:
1. What is described as the "conquest of Italy" by Rome was a long and difficult process which went through several different stages. Try to distinguish and characterize at least three such stages in Rome's relations to her neighbors. Where do you see decisive turning points, and why?
2. There were dozens of similar city-states and tribal communities in Italy. Can you describe some of the basic conditions that enabled Rome to become the master-city and not the subject of another?
3. After her victory in the Great Latin War, Rome carefully re-organized her relationship to her former allies. Similar principles were again used to organize Italy after the victories over the Etruscans, Samnites, Greeks, etc. What were these principles? What were their characteristics and advantages for Rome? How were they accepted by the former enemies, and why so?
4. What was the impact of the expansion on Roman society (upper and lower classes) and internal politics? To what extent did the external developments influence Rome's ability to solve her internal conflicts?

10. Thurs., Oct. 4: Roman expansion II: the Punic Wars (265 - 201 B.C.)

Sources:
HYW ch. VII - IX or CS ch. 12-13
LR no. 58, 59, 63, 64, 65, 67
Polybius I.29-64 (pp.73-110); II.24 (pp.135f.); VI.51f. (pp.344-46)

Recommended Reading:
R.M. Errington, *The Dawn of Empire* (London, 1971)
E. Badian, *Foreign Clientelae, 264-70 B.C.* (Oxford, 1958)
M.I. Finley, *A History of Sicily: Ancient Sicily to the Arab Conquest* (London, 1968)
B.H. Warmington, *Carthage* (London, 1964)
C. Picard, *Carthage* (London, 1964)
T.A. Dorey - D.R. Dudley, *Rome against Carthage* (London, 1971)
H.H. Scullard, *Scipio Africanus, Soldier and Politician* (London, 1970)
D. Hood, *The Rise of Rome: How to Explain It?* (Lexington, Mass, 1969)
J.F. Lazenby, *Hannibal's War: A Military History of the Second Punic War* (Westminster, 1978)

Focus: LR no. 58, 64, 65, 67; Polybius I. 7-12

Questions:
1. What were the causes of the First Punic War? Are there any analogies to the outbreak of the Second Punic War?
2. Compare the causes of those wars with their results as they are reflected in the peace-treaties with Carthage. What does that tell us about Rome's motives to go to war?
3. In dealing with the effects of their victories the Romans developed some new principles of organization and administration. Which ones? And why did they not repeat what had been so successful in Italy?
4. What does Polybius consider to be the main causes of war? How do you judge his assessment? Was war between Rome and Carthage inevitable? Although it is always dangerous to draw immediate parallels between history and the present, this might be

a moment to examine the relevance of history for our own times and problems.

11. Tues., Oct. 9: *First classroom exam*
Roman expansion III: The conquest of the Mediterranean (215 - c. 150 B.C.)

Sources:
> HYW ch. X and XI or CS ch. 14 (parts 1-4), 15 (parts 1-6), 16 (parts 1-3)
> LR no. 68-80, 120, 122
> Polybius VII.9 (pp.358f.), XVIII, XXIV, XXXVI (pp.494-520; 535-539)

Recommended Reading:
> F. Walbank, *The Hellenistic World* (Fontana/Harvard pb, 1982)
> M. Rostovtzeff, *A Social and Economic History of the Hellenistic World* (Oxford, 1941)
> E. Badian, *Roman Imperialism in the Late Republic* (Oxford, 1968; pb Ithaca, NY, 1971)
> C.H.V. Sutherland, *The Romans in Spain* (1939, rep. 1971)
> W.V. Harris, *War and Imperialism in Republican Rome* (Oxford, 1979)
> E.S. Gruen, *The Hellenistic World and the Coming of Rome*, 2 vols. (Berkeley and Los Angeles, 1984, with rich bibliogr.).
> A.N. Sherwin-White, *Roman Foreign Policy in the East, 168 B.C. - A.D. 1* (Norman, OK, 1984)
> E. Badian, "Rome and Antiochus the Great: A Study in Cold War," in *Classical Philology* 54 (1959) 81ff.
> E. Badian, *Titus Quinctius Flamininus, Philhellenism and Realpolitik* (Cincinnati, 1970)

Focus: LR no.68-71, 73; Polybius VII.9; XVIII.44-46; XXXVI.9

Questions:
> 1. In 197 the Romans established two provinces in Spain. Nevertheless, long and heavy fighting went on for almost another 200 years. Can you see reasons why the Romans should have had such difficulties in Spain rather than in other provinces?
> 2. Between the first Roman victories in any area of the Eastern Mediterranean and the establishment of a province in this same area there usually occurred a remarkable time gap. Can you explain this? What does it tell us about Roman attitudes toward conquest and rule of foreign territories?
> 3. The political situation and the Roman expansion in the East were in several important ways different from the previous wars against Carthage in the West. List such differences - and some obvious analogies - and try to explain them.
> 4. Was it necessary to destroy Carthage? Cato and many others thought so, but later the Romans themselves believed that Rome's moral decline had begun with the elimination of that formidable city. As a Roman senator, how would you have advised your colleagues?

12. Thurs., Oct. 11: Rome's rule in the Mediterranean: the organization of the conquered territories and the administration of the provinces

Sources:
> HYW ch. VII (parts 5-6, pp.93-95) and Handout no. 17 or CS ch. 14 (parts 5-7), 15 (parts 7-8), 16 (parts 4-5), 17
> LR no. 88-91, 125-126, 128-130, 132, 133 (pp.336f.), 136, 138-140, 145
> Polybius III.1-15, 17, 20-75

Handout no.16

Recommended Reading:
　W.T. Arnold, *The Roman System of Provincial Administration* (third ed., Oxford, 1914)
　G.H.T. Stevenson, *Roman Provincial Administration till the Age of the Antonines* (Oxford, 1939)
　E. Badian, *Publicans and Sinners* (Ithaca, NY, 1972)
　E. Badian, *Foreign Clientelae* (as listed in no.10 above)
　D. Magie, *Roman Rule in Asia Minor*, 2 vols. (Princeton, 1950)
　P.C. Sands, *The Client Princes of the Roman Empire Under the Republic* (Cambr., 1908)
　A.J.N. Wilson, *Emigration from Italy in the Republican Age of Rome* (Manchester, 1966)
　P.A. Brunt, "British and Roman Imperialism," in *Comparative Studies in Society and History* 7 (1964-65) 267ff.

Focus: LR no. 88, 89, 126, 132, 133, 136, 140, 145

Questions:
　1. Study the diagram (handout no. 16) which shows the structure of the Roman imperial administration and the various categories of statuses and relationships in Italy and the Mediterranean world around 140 B.C. Use it to describe to an outsider how the Romans ruled the world.
　2. What were the principles and characteristics, the advantages and disadvantages of the Roman way of governing and administrating an empire?
　3. One of the results of the emergence of the empire was an increasingly marked division of labor and responsibilities between senators and *equites*. Why would that be necessary and what political problems could it produce? Can you translate this aspect of the Roman system into our own time and thereby make the problems even more visible?

13. Tues., Oct. 16: *First take-home essay due*
Conclusion: explanations of Rome's conquest of the Mediterranean

Sources: Polybius III. 77-end; IX; X

PART III: THE CRISIS OF THE REPUBLIC AND THE EMERGENCE OF THE PRINCIPATE

14. Thurs., Oct. 18: Roman social and economic conditions after the Punic Wars

Sources:
　HYW ch. XII and XIII (part 1) or CS ch. 18, 19, 24 (part 4)
　LR no. 44, 94, 95, 165 - 173, 191
　Plutarch, *Tiberius Gracchus* (Handout no. 18)
　Appian, *Civil Wars*, Introduction (Handout no. 22)

Recommended Reading:
　M.I. Finley, *The Ancient Economy* (pb, Berkeley and Los Angeles, 1973)
　T. Frank (ed.), *An Economic Survey of Ancient Rome*, vol. I: *Rome and Italy of the*

Republic (1933, rep. 1975)

P.A. Brunt, *Italian Manpower, 225 B.C. - A.D. 14* (Oxford, 1971)

A.J. Toynbee, *Hannibal's Legacy*, 2 vols. (Oxford, 1965)

E.S. Gruen, *Roman Politics and the Criminal Courts, 149-78 B.C.* (Cambridge, Mass., 1968)

A.E. Astin, *The lex annalis before Sulla* (Brussels, 1958)

M.I. Finley (ed.), *Slavery in Classical Antiquity. Views and Controversies* (Cambridge, 1960)

M.I. Finley, *Ancient Slavery and Modern Ideology* (New York, 1980, pb)

Th. Wiedemann, *Greek and Roman Slavery* (Baltimore, 1981, source book)

J. Vogt, *Ancient Slavery and the Ideal of Man* (1975, Cambr., Mass, pb, contains a chapter on the structure of the slave wars)

W.L. Westermann, *The Slave Systems of Greek and Roman Antiquity* (Philadelphia, 1955)

P. Green, "The First Sicilian Slave War," in: *Past and Present* 20 (1960) 10ff.

Z. Rubinsohn, "Was the Bellum Spartacium a Slave Insurrection?," *Rivista di Filologia ed Istruzione Classica* 99 (1971) 290ff.

S. Treggiari, *Roman Freedman during the Late Republic* (Oxford, 1969)

Focus: LR no. 94-95, 168, 170

Questions:

1. The empire brought about tremendous changes and difficulties for every segment of Roman society. How were the upper classes affected?

2. The ancient authors linked the emergence of domestic troubles in Rome to the destruction of Carthage. What speaks for, what against this view?

3. The century between c. 150 and 50 B.C. is the century of the great slave revolts. Why only then? What are the characteristics of these revolts? What were the goals of the revolting slaves?

15. Tues., Oct 23: *Optimates and populares:* the agrarian crisis and the failure of the Gracchan reforms

Sources:
HYW ch. 14 or CS ch. 20
LR no. 96-102, 154, 157
Plutarch, *Gaius Gracchus* (Handout no.19)

Recommended Reading:
Gruen (as listed above)

P.A. Brunt, *Social Conflicts in the Roman Republic* (London, 1971, pb)

K.D. White, *Roman Farming* (Ithaca, NY, 1970)

M. Gelzer, *The Roman Nobility* (Oxford, 1969)

A.W. Lintott, *Violence in Republican Rome* (Oxford, 1968)

H.C. Boren, *The Gracchi* (New York, 1978)

D. Stockton, *The Gracchi* (Oxford, 1979)

D.C. Earl, *Tiberius Gracchus: A Study in Politics* (Brussels, 1963)

A.H. Bernstein, *Tiberius Sempronius Gracchus: Tradition and Apostasy* (Ithaca, NY, 1978)

E. Badian, "Tiberius Gracchus and the Beginning of the Roman Revolution," in *Aufstieg und Niedergang der römischen Welt*, vol. I.1 (1972) 668ff.

L.R. Taylor, "Forerunners of the Gracchi," *Journal of Roman Studies* 52 (1962) 19ff.

H.C. Boren, "The Urban Side of the Gracchan Economic Crisis," in *American*

Historical Review 63 (1957/58) 890ff.

P.A. Brunt, "The Equites in the Late Republic," in R. Seager (ed.), *The Crisis of the Roman Republic* (Cambridge - New York, 1969) 83ff.

J.P.V.D. Balsdon, "History of the Extortion Courts at Rome, 123-70 B.C.," in *Papers of the British School at Rome* 14 (1938) 98ff.

Focus: LR 96, 97, 98 (in each, the passage from Appian), 101 (pp.252ff.), 157
Plutarch, *Tiberius Gracchus* 8-9; *Gaius Gracchus* 5, 8-9

Questions:

1. What were the causes of the agrarian crisis? Why was this crisis a major concern for the Roman Senate, whose members, after all, did extremely well?

2. What were the aims of Tiberius Gracchus? Why was the Senate so fiercely opposed to his proposals?

3. What was new in the political methods used by the two Gracchi? What are the *optimates* and *populares*?

4. In the cases of both Gracchi the Senate finally used violence to eliminate dangerous tribunes. Out of this experience grew a new political or constitutional instrument: the "last decree of the Senate", an emergency decree. What was its legal and moral basis, how could it be defended? And why could it be declared to be illegal by the opposition against this method? What was at stake in the discussion about the "last decree of the Senate"?

16. Thur., Oct. 25: Marius and the new Roman army

Sources:

HYW ch XV, parts 1-12 (pp.167-177) or CS ch. 21
LR no.45, 163, 168
Sallust, *War against Jugurtha*
Plutarch, *Marius* (Penguin pp. 13ff.)
S.A. Handford, Introduction to *Sallust*

Recommended Reading:

Brunt, *Manpower* (as listed above)
M. Grant, *The Army of the Caesars* (New York, 1974)
R.E. Smith, *Service in the Post-Marian Roman Army* (Manchester, 1958)
E. Gabba, *Republican Rome, the Army and the Allies* (Berkeley and Los Angeles, 1976)
G.R. Watson, *The Roman Soldier* (Ithaca, NY, 1969)
P.A. Brunt, "The Army and the Land in the Roman Revolution", in *Journal of Roman Studies* 52 (1962) 69ff.
T.F. Carney, *A Biography of C. Marius* (2nd ed. 1970)

Focus: LR no.168
Sallust, *Jug. War* 39-42 (pp.75-79), 84-85 (ch. IX)
Plutarch, *Marius* ch. 7 and 9

Questions:

1. Marius is traditionally credited with the creation of a "professional army". Is that a correct assessment? What precisely did Marius change? Why had these changes become necessary?

2. How did Marius' changes affect the legal situation? What was the Senate's attitude towards the "new army"?

3. How did the civil and the military sphere relate to each other in Rome? Was there

that clear separation we are used to? Would it be correct to say that the civil government controlled (or occasionally lost control over) the military or the army?

4. What is the "army clientela"? What were the economic and political consequences of Marius' reforms? Why did the armies after Marius become a decisive political factor?

17. Tues., Oct. 30: The Italic Wars and the integration of the allies (95-87 B.C.)

Sources:

HYW ch. XV (parts 13-15, pp.177-180), XVI (parts 1-6, pp.181-184) or CS ch. 22
LR no. 103, 150-152, 162 (pp.417-428)
Plutarch, *Sulla* 1-25
Appian, *Civil Wars* I.5.34 - 6.53 (Handout no.20)

Recommended Reading:

E. Gabba, "The Origins of the Social War and Roman Politics after 89 B.C.," in Gabba, *Republican Rome* (as listed above) 70ff.

E. Badian, "Roman Politics and the Italians (133 - 91 B.C.)," in *Dialoghi di Archeologia* 4/5 (1970/71) 373ff.

T.J. Luce, "Marius and the Mithridatic Command," *Historia* 19 (1970) 161ff.

P.A. Brunt, "Italian Aims at the Time of the Social War," *Journal of Roman Studies* 55 (1965) 90-109

D.B. Nagle, "An Allied View of the Social War," *American Journal of Archaeology* 77 (1973) 367-78

E.T. Salmon, "The Cause of the Social War," *Phoenix* 16 (1962) 107-119

Focus: LR no.103; Appian, *Civil Wars* I.5.34-36; Plutarch, *Sulla* 7-12

Questions:

1. In the third century the allies had been happy to keep their local citizenship and to remain autonomous. Why was there a strong demand for Roman citizenship in the late second and early first centuries?

2. Why did the Romans not only firmly oppose this demand but treat with great hostility and violence the leaders of the movement to enfranchise the allies? What was so dangerous about the movement and the persons promoting it?

3. How did the extension of Roman citizenship over all of Italy change the nature and meaning of this citizenship? What was so unique about and what were the advantages of the Roman system of extending the citizenship?

4. In 88 for the first time a Roman general led an army against Rome to correct in his favor a previous political decision made by the constitutionally legitimate authorities in Rome. What caused Sulla to do that, and why did the army obey his orders? What is the political significance of this event?

18. Thur., Nov. 1: From Sulla to Pompey: generals against Senate and constitution

Sources:

HYW ch. XVI, parts 7-12; XVII, parts 1-14 (pp.185-202)
or CS ch. 23, 24 (parts 1-5), 25 (parts 1-4)
LR no.81-83, 104, 131, 141-44, 146-47
Plutarch, *Sulla* 26 - end; *Pompey* 1-42

Recommended Reading:

E.S. Gruen, *Roman Politics and the Criminal Courts,* 149-78 B.C. (Cambr., Mass., 1968)

E. Badian, *L. Sulla, the Deadly Reformer* (Sidney, 1970)

Gruen, *The Last Generation* (listed below)

C.M. Bulst, "Cinnanum Tempus," *Historia* 13 (1964) 307ff.

B. Frier, "Sulla's Propaganda. The Collapse of the Cinnan Republic," *American Journal of Philology* 92 (1971) 585ff.

J. Leach, *Pompey the Great* (London, 1978)

R. Seager, *Pompey, a Political Biography* (Oxford, 1979)

L. Hayne, "M. Lepidus (consul 78): a Reappraisal," *Historia* 21 (1972) 661ff.

Focus: LR no.81, 104, 141, 144

Plutarch, *Sulla* 25, 30-31; *Pompey* 6-8, 24-28

Questions:

1. Do you consider Sulla's restoration of senatorial government successful? Or was it doomed to fail from the beginning? If *we* think so, could the contemporaries know?

2. In what ways was Pompey's career exceptional? What problems did he create? Why was he at the same time very typical for the period after Sulla? Is it right to say that the Roman state could not do without, and at the same time could not afford, men like Pompey?

3. Use the example of the problems caused by the pirates and the war against Mithridates to analyze the deficiencies of the Roman system of government and imperial administration.

19. Tues., Nov. 6: *Second take-home essay due*
Cicero and Catiline: revolution or "crisis without alternative"?

Sources:

HYW ch. XVII, parts 15-end; XVII, parts 1-3 (pp.202-212) or CS ch. 24, parts 6-9

LR no. 106, 107, 158

Sallust, *Conspiracy of Catiline*

Plutarch, *Cicero* 1-34; *Caesar* 1-14; *Pompey* 43-49

Plutarch, *Cato* 26-29 (Handout no.21)

Recommended Reading:

E.S. Gruen, *The Last Generation of the Roman Republic* (Berkeley and Los Angeles, 1974)

A.M. Ward, *Marcus Crassus and the Late Roman Republic* (Columbia, MO, and London, 1977)

B.A. Marshall, *Crassus: A Political Biography* (Amsterdam, 1976)

R.E. Smith, *Cicero the Statesman* (Cambridge, 1966)

D. Stockton, *Cicero: A Political Biography* (London, 1971)

D.R. Shackleton Bailey, *Cicero* (New York, 1971)

A. Kaplan, *Catiline, the Man and his Role in the Roman Revolution* (New York, 1968)

L.R. Taylor, *Party Politics in the Age of Caesar* (Berkeley and Los Angeles, 1949, pb)

Z. Yavetz, "The Living Conditions of the Urban Plebs in Republican Rome," in *Latomus* 17 (1958) 500ff.

Z. Yavetz, "The Failure of Catiline's Conspiracy," *Historia* 12 (1963) 485ff.

K.H. Waters, "Cicero, Sallust and Catiline," *Historia* 19 (1970) 195ff.

Th.N. Mitchell, "Cicero, Pompey and the Rise of the First Triumvirate," in *Traditio* 29 (1973) 1ff.

E.J. Phillips, "The Prosecution of C. Rabirius in 63 B.C.," in *Klio* 56 (1974) 87ff.

Focus: LR no.106 and 107
Plutarch, *Pompey* 47-48; *Caesar* 13-14
Sallust, *Cat. Conspiracy*, ch. III and VI

Questions:

1. Give a concise analysis of causes and goals of the Catilinarian conspiracy.
2. Why was the Senate able to overcome this crisis without conceding extraordinary powers to a general and, in addition, to prevent other politicians from exploiting the crisis for their personal ends? How did this effect the distribution of power in Rome and future political decisions?
3. What was at stake in the confrontation between Cato and Caesar in the Senate in Dec. 63? Is it justified to establish a direct connection between the victory of the Senate in 63 and its disastrous humiliation and defeat in 59?
4. What precisely was the "First Triumvirate"? What were the goals of its members? Why did and could it not last?
5. Analyze critically the Senate's handling of Caesar's and Pompey's proposals and aspirations in 60/59 B.C. What was at stake? Why did the Senate leaders choose a hard line, and why did they think they could succeed with it? Given their situation, was there an alternative? As an aid to Cato (and not judging from hindsight), how would you advise him to proceed?

20. Thur., Nov. 8: Caesar: from the conquest of Gaul to military dictatorship

Sources:

HYW ch. XVIII, parts 4-end; XIX (pp.212-231) or CS ch. 26, 27
LR no.85, 108-113
Plutarch, *Caesar* 15-end
Appian, *Civil Wars* II.2-5 (Handout no.22)
Caesar, *Civil Wars* I.1-23 (Handout no.23)

Recommended Reading:

Caesar, *The Conquest of Gaul* (Penguin)
Caesar, *The Civil War* (Penguin)
Cicero, *Letters to Atticus* (Penguin), esp. books VII-X
Suetonius, *The Twelve Caesars* (Penguin): Life of Julius Caesar
Gruen, Taylor (as listed above)
M. Gelzer, *Caesar* (Cambr., Mass, 1968, pb)
R. Syme, *The Roman Revolution* (Oxford, 1939, pb)
J.P.V.D. Balsdon, *Julius Caesar and Rome* (London, 1967)
J.H. Collins, "Caesar as a Political Progagandist," in *Aufstieg und Niedergang der römischen Welt*, vol. I.1 (1972) 922ff.
Z. Yavetz, *Julius Caesar and his Public Image* (Ithaca, NY, 1983)
M. Cary, "The Land Legislation of Caesar's First Consulship," *Journ. of Philology* 35 (1920) 174ff.
R.E. Smith, "The Significance of Caesar's Consulship in 59 B.C.," *Phoenix* 18 (1964) 303ff.
P. Cuff, "The Terminal Date of Caesar's Gallic Command," *Historia* 7 (1958) 445ff.
R. Syme, "Caesar, the Senate and Italy," in *Papers of the British School at Rome* 14 (1938) 1ff.
J.P.V.D. Balsdon, "The Ides of March," *Historia* 7 (1958) 80ff.

Focus: LR no.107, 108, 110; Plutarch, *Caesar* 29-32, 46; Caesar, *Civil Wars* I.7, 9, 22

(Handout no.23)

Questions:
1. Why was Caesar so eager to conquer Gaul? Try to answer this question at least partly by comparing Caesar's and Pompey's careers.
2. Compare the reports about the outbreak of the Civil War in Caesar, Suetonius, Appian, Plutarch, and Cicero. Where do they agree; where and why do they disagree?
3. What was at stake in the civil war of 49? Why did it break out? What was the role of the Senate? A few days after the outbreak of the war, Cicero described in a letter to Atticus Caesar's rapid advance in northern Italy. After comparing Caesar with Hannibal he adds: "And he says he's doing all this for his honour's *(dignitas)* sake." How do you explain this remark of Caesar's?
4. To start and win a civil war is one thing; to be responsible for the clean-up and rebuilding after the end of the war, obviously is another. How do you judge Caesar's success in this last and greatest challenge of his life?

21. Tues., Nov. 13: *Second classroom exam*
From Caesar to Augustus; the emergence of monarchy

Sources:
HYW ch. XX and XXII, parts 1-4, or CS ch. 28 and 30, parts 1-2
LR no.114-118
Augustus, *Accomplishments* 1-13 (Handout no.25)
Suetonius, *Augustus* 1-22 (Handout no.28)

Recommended Reading:
R. Syme, *The Roman Revolution* ((Oxford, 1939, pb)
A.H.M. Jones, *Augustus* (London, 1970, pb)
A. Hadas, *Sextus Pompey* (New York, 1930)
J. Lindsay, *Cleopatra* (London, 1970)
F. Millar, "Triumvirate and Principate," *Journ. of Roman Studies* 63 (1973) 50ff.
K. Scott, "The Political Propaganda of 44-30 B.C.," in *Memoirs of the American Academy in Rome* 11 (1933) 7ff.
P.A. Brunt, "The Army and the Land in the Roman Revolution," *Journal of Roman Studies* 52 (1962) 69ff.
K.A. Raaflaub, "The Political Significance of Augustus' Military Reforms," in *Roman Frontier Studies 1979 (Brit. Archaeol. Reports,* Internat. Ser. 71, 1980) 1005ff.
H.C. Boren, "Rome: Republican Disintegration, Augustan Re-integration: Focus on the Army," in *Thought: Fordham University Quarterly* 55, no. 216 (1980) 51ff.
Ch.Wirszubski, *Libertas as a Political Idea during the Late Republic and the Early Principate* (Cambr., 1950)

Focus: LR no. 115; Augustus, *Accomplishments* ch. 1-2, 13 (Handout no.25)

Questions:
1. In Octavian's rise to power you find all the elements that were characteristic of the crisis of the Republic. List them and show in how many ways we find here the logical conclusion and climax of a development that began with the Scipios and the Gracchi.
2. Compare Augustus' and Caesar's rise to power. How far can such a comparison explain Augustus' final success? What additional reasons do you find for Augustus' success?
3. The Civil War against Antonius was presented by Octavian's propaganda as a war against the Queen of Egypt and the evil forces of the East. Why was this possible

108

and why was it successful?
4. What role did the armies play in Octavian's rise to power? What problems did this raise for him once he gained sole power? As an aide to Octavian, how would you advise him to deal with these problems?

22. Thur., Nov. 15: Augustus, the "restored Republic", and the pacification of the Empire

Sources:
 HYW ch. XX, parts 5-7; 23; 24, or CS 30, parts 3-7; 31
 Augustus, *Accomplishments* 14 - end (Handout no.25)
 Suetonius, *Augustus* 23 - end (Handout no.28)
 Tacitus, *Annals* 1.1-4, 9-10 (Handout no.26)
 Dio Cassius, *Roman Antiquities* 53, extracts (Handout no.27)

Recommended Reading:
 F.B. Marsh, *The Founding of the Roman Empire* (Oxford, 2nd ed. 1927)
 C. Wells, *The German Policy of Augustus. An Examination of the Archaeological Evidence* (Oxford, 1972)
 G.W. Bowersock, *Augustus and the Greek World* (Oxford, 1965)
 Z. Yavetz, *Plebs and Princeps* (Oxford, 1969)
 M. Hammond, "The Sincerity of Augustus," in *Harvard Studies in Classical Philology* 70 (1965) 139ff.
 M. Reinhold, *Marcus Agrippa. A Biography* (New York, 1933, rep. 1965)
 R. Syme, *The Roman Revolution,* and A.H.M. Jones, *Augustus* (as cited above)
 R. Syme, "Livy and Augustus," in *Harvard Studies in Class. Philology* 64 (1959) 27ff.
 J.K. Newman, *Augustus and the New Poetry* (Brussels, 1967)
 Articles by D.L. Stockton, Th.N. Mitchell, M. Reinhold, and T. Rufus Fears in *Thought: Fordham University Quarterly* 55, no.216 (1980)
 F. Millar - E. Segal (eds.), *Caesar Augustus, Seven Aspects* (Oxford, 1984, important articles)

Focus: Augustus, *Accomplishments* 34-35; Tacitus, *Dio* (as in sources)

Questions:
1. Augustus claimed to have restored the Republic. Was that merely propaganda (why?), did it contain some truth (how much, why?), and why was it necessary to present it that way?
2. Among scholars there is an old and intensive debate about the nature of the precise constitutional definition of Augustus' Principate. It is obviously not a simple problem. How would you define and describe it?
3. Judgment on Augustus' reign was split already among the Romans. Suetonius, Tacitus and Dio Cassius, both writing much later when monarchy had become more oppressive, give us some insight into the ongoing debate. How do you assess the achievement of Augustus and the historical significance of his reign?
4. Undeniably, Augustus succeeded in pacifying Roman society and the empire. How did he do it? What did the Romans have to sacrifice for it? And why were they willing to accept these sacrifices?

23a. Tues., Nov. 20: Conclusion: how to explain and interpret the transition from Republic to monarchy?

Question:
The problem of how to explain this transition has provoked one of the most intensive and profound discussions among ancient historians. Military, economic, political, even moral factors have been stressed in varying intensity and combinations. Write down your own assessment (c. 2 pp.).

PART IV: ASPECTS OF ROMAN CIVILIZATION IN THE REPUBLIC

23b. Tues., Nov. 20: Architecture, Engineering

Sources:
HYW ch. XIII, part 2; ch. XXI, part 13; XXV, part 4,
or CS ch. 11, part 6; 19, part 6; 29 part 5; 34, part 4

24. Tues., Nov. 27: Society and Religion

Sources:
HYW ch. IV, part 4; XIII, part 8; XXI, parts 1-7, 9-10, 12; XXIII, part 7 or
CS ch. 11, part 7; 19, parts 1-5, 9-10; 29, parts 1-4, 8-9; 34, part 8
LR no.46-56, 175-180; 171-172; 181-183; 191

Recommended Reading:
M. Grant, *Roman Myths* (New York, 1971)
J. Ferguson, *Greek and Roman Religion. A Source Book* (Park Ridge, NJ, 1980)
G. Dumézil, *Archaic Roman Religion*, 2 vols. (Chicago 1970)
H.H. Scullard, *Festivals and Ceremonies of the Roman Republic* (London, 1981)
H.J. Rose, *Ancient Roman Religion* (London, 1949)
R.M. Ogilvie, *The Romans and their Gods in the Age of Augustus* (London, 1969, pb)
R.J. Goar, *Cicero and the State Religion* (Amsterdam, 1972)
A. Wardman, *Religion and Statecraft among the Romans* (Baltimore, 1982)
G.J. Szemler, *The Priests of the Roman Republic. A Study of Interactions between Priesthoods and Magistrates* (Brussels, 1972)
Surveys of recent literature by H.J. Rose in: *Journal of Roman Studies* 50 (1960) 161ff. (to 1960) and R. Schilling, in *Aufstieg und Niedergang der römischen Welt*, vol. I.2 (1972) 317ff.

Focus: LR no.176, 178; Augustus, *Accomplishments* 19-21 (Handout no.25)

Questions:
1. Official Roman religion was characterized by remarkable tolerance. Why was the cult of Bacchus oppressed in 186 B.C.? Do you see any analogies with later Roman attitudes towards the Christians?
2. Why was Augustus so emphatically concerned with religious restoration?

25. Thur., Nov. 29: Economy and Law

Sources:
    HYW ch. XIII, parts 3, 7, 9; XXI, parts 8, 11, 14 - end; XXV, parts 5-15 or
    CS ch. 11, part 8; 19, parts 7-8; 29, parts 6-7; 34, parts 5-7
    LR no.32, 185-187

Recommended Reading:
    H. Julius Wolff, *Roman Law. An Historical Introduction* (Norman, OK, 1951)
    W. Kunkel, *An Introduction to Roman Legal and Constitutional History* (Oxford, 2nd
        ed. 1973)
    H.F. Jolowicz - B. Nicholas, *Historical Introduction to the Study of Roman Law* (Cam-
        bridge, 3rd ed. 1972)

26. Tues., Dec. 4: Literature and Historiography

Sources:
    Prefaces and Introductions of Livy (pp.33f.) and Polybius, book I (pp. 41-46), III
        (pp.178-183), VI (pp.302f.), IX (pp.386f.), XXIX (pp.540f.)
    Polybius, book XII (pp.429-451)
    Sallust, pref. to *Jug.* I (pp.35-38), *Cat.* I (pp.175-183)
    LR pp.3-16
    Materials from Handout about historiography (no.30-33)

Recommended Reading:
    R.M. Ogilvie, *Roman Literature and Society* (Brighton and Totowa, NJ, 1980, pb)
    W. Laistner, *Greater Roman Historians* (Berkeley and Los Angeles, 1947, pb)
    M. Grant, *Roman Literature* (Penguin 1958)
    J.W. Duff, *A Literary History of Rome* I: *From the Origins to the Close of the Golden
        Age* (London, 1909, pb)
    The Cambridge History of Classical Literature II: *Latin Literature* (Cambr., 1982)
    E. Rawson, Intellectual Life in the Late Roman Republic (Baltimore, 1985)
    T.A. Dorey (ed.), *Latin Historians* (London, 1966)
    T.A. Dorey (ed.), *Latin Biography* (New York, 1967)
    R. Syme, *Sallust* (Berkeley, 1964)
    T.J. Luce, *Livy: The Composition of his History* (Princeton, 1977)
    P.G. Walsh, *Livy: His Historical Aims and Methods* (Cambr., 1961)
    A. Wardman, *Plutarch's Lives* (London, 1974)
    R.H. Barrow, *Plutarch and his Times* (Bloomington, 1969)
    F.W. Walbank, *Polybius* (Berkeley, 1972)
    K. Sacks, *Polybius on the Writing of History* (Berkeley, 1981)

27. Thur., Dec. 6: *Third classroom exam*
    Political Thought

Sources:
    Polybius I.1-4, 63f.; III.4; VI.1-18, 53-57
    Handout no.29

Recommended Reading:
    K. von Fritz, *The Theory of Mixed Constitution in Antiquity: A Critical Analysis of
        Polybius' Political Ideas* (New York, 1954)

111

D. Kagan, *The Great Dialogue. History of Greek Political Thought from Homer to Polybius* (New York, 1965)

F.W. Walbank, "Polybius on the Roman Constitution," *Classical Quarterly* 37 (1943) 73ff.

F.W. Walbank, *Polybius* (Berkeley - Los Angeles, 1972)

F.W. Walbank, "Polybius and the Roman State", in *Greek, Roman, and Byzantine Studies* 5 (1963) 239ff.

W.W. How, "Cicero's Ideal in his De Republica," *Journal of Roman Studies* 20 (1930) 24ff.

F.R. Cowell, *Cicero and the Roman Republic* (Harmondsworth, 3rd. ed. 1964)

C.W. Keyes, "Original Elements in Cicero's Ideal Constitution," *Amer. Journ. of Philology* 42 (1921) 309ff.

W.K. Lacey and B.W.J.G. Witson, *Res Publica: Roman Politics and Society According to Cicero* (pb, Oxford, 1970)

D.C. Earl, *The Political Thought of Sallust* (Cambr., 1961)

H. Strasburger, "Poseidonius on the Problems of the Roman Empire," *Journal of Roman Studies* 55 (1965) 40ff.

Wirszubski (as listed in no.21 above)

28. Fri., Dec. 14: *Termpapers and take-home essays due*

E. ADDITIONAL COURSE MATERIALS (IN HANDOUT OR ON RESERVE)

1.	Map: the ancient and modern Mediterranean
2.	Map: the roads of the Roman Empire
3./4.	Maps of central Italy
5.a-c	Plans: the development of the city of Rome
6.a-b	Coins as historical sources
7.a-j	Inscriptions as historical sources
8.a-e	The historical value of archaeology: Cosa
9.	Map: the expansion of the Celts
10.a-i	The Etruscans (maps, drawings and texts) Dionysius of Halicarnassus, *Roman Antiquities* 1.26-30; Diodorus of Sicily 5.40.1-2; Dion. of Hal. 3.61, 67-70; 4.59-61
11.a-c	Texts concerning Servius Tullius/Mastarna *CIL* XIII.1668; Dion. of Hal. *Rom. Ant.* 3.65.3; Festus, p. 486.12; cf. for comparison Livy 1.39ff.
12.a-e	Texts concerning the origins of the Republic Pliny, *Natural History* 34.39.139; Tacitus, *Histories* 3.72; Dion. of Hal. *Rom. Ant.* 5.21, 22.3, 30-35, 65.3; 7.1-2; Extract from Greek chronicle from Cumae: Dion Hal. 7.3-6; 7.12; 5.36
13.	Diagram: Roman society and institutions
14.	The Roman assemblies
15.a-f	Maps: the Roman expansion in Italy
16.	Diagram: the structure of the Roman Empire
17.	The administration of the Roman Empire (summary)
18.	Plutarch: *The Life of Tiberius Gracchus*
19.	Plutarch: *The Life of Gaius Gracchus*
20.	Appian: the Social Wars *(Civil Wars* I.5.34 - 6.36)
21.	Plutarch: *Life of Cato the Younger* (ch.26-29)

22.   Appian: the age of the Civil Wars (*Civil Wars*, Introduction)
       Appian: the outbreak of Caesar's Civil War (*Civil Wars*, II.2 -5)
23.   Caesar: the beginning of the Civil War *(Civil Wars* I.1-23)
24.   Suetonius: the outbreak of the Civil War *(Life of Caesar*, ch. 27-33)
25.   The Accomplishments of Augustus *(Res Gestae)*
26.   Tacitus: assessment of Augustus *(Annals* I.1-4; 9-10)
27.   Dio Cassius: the power of Augustus *(Roman History* 53, ch.12-19)
28.   Suetonius: *Life of Augustus*
29.   Cicero: selections from *The Republic*
       (I.1-9, 17-31, 35, 39-40, 45-47; II.1-2, 8-17, 21-34, 38-39)
30.   Historiography I: passages from Herodotus (I.1-6, 177; II.123)
31.   Historiography II: passages from Thucydides (I.1-3, 20-23, 97; V.26)
32.   Historiography III: Diodorus of Sicily (I.1-5; V.1; XX.1-3)
33.   Historiography IV: Dion. of Halic. *Roman Antiquities* (I.1-13)

Individual and Class Visits to nearby Sites and Museums are part of this Course.

Donald Lateiner
Syracuse in Florence

Fall 1984
HIS 400.2

A SURVEY HISTORY OF ANCIENT ITALY
(esp. 500 BCE to 150 CE)

1. Introductory: Archaeological and Literary Sources
    Ancient Economy: Producers, Markets, Slavery, Law
    City, Town and Country

GRANT, A History of Rome 1, MacKENDRICK, Mute Stones Speak 1,
KAGAN, Problems in Ancient History: Rome –

2. Italic Pre-History: Villanovans, Etruscans, & Greeks   1000–509 BCE
    Earliest Rome and Etruscan Rome
    The Monarchy   G 2, M 2-3, K 1

3. The Republic: Roman Politics; Class Struggles   509–260
    Conquest of Central Italy
                                          G 3-4, M 4, K (2)-3

4. Phoenicians and Greeks in Italy and Sicily   –264–146
    Punic Wars, esp. Hannibal
                                          G5-7, M –, K 4

5. Imperial Expansion in the Eastern Mediterranean   280–146
    Administration of the Provinces
                                          G 8-9, M –, K 5

6. Consequences of Success in Italy   146–63
    The Gracchan Reforms
    Reaction: Social War; Civil War   G 10-11, M 5, K 6-(7)

7. The Crumbling of the Republican Oligarchy   63–44
    Cicero
    Caesar: Gallic Campaigns; Roman Army G 12, M 12, K –

8. Caesar's Dictatorship; his Heirs   44–27
    Octavian (Augustus) and Mark Antony
    A Generation of Civil War Again   G 13, M –, K 8

9. Augustus' New Order   27 BCE–14 CE
    Italy: the Revolution in Government
    Roman Empire: New Government, New Opportunities G –, M 6, K 9

10. The Julio-Claudian Principate   14–69
    Dynastic Rule
    Collapse: Italy's 4 Emperors (68-69) G 14, M 7, K 10

11. The Flavian Dynasty   69–96
    Pompeii or Life of the Ordinary
                                          G 15, M 8-9, K –

12. Non-Italian Autocrats: Trajan to M. Aurelius   96–161
    Religions of the Roman Empire
                                          G 16, M 10-11 &13, K 11 & pp. 421-23.

114

HISTORY OF THE ROMAN EMPIRE

Classics 103   MTWTh
Spring 1983
                                                Susan Treggiari

                                                Stanford University

A survey of the Roman empire from its beginnings under Augustus
through its consolidation and later crisis to its transformation
under Constantine into the Christian Roman Empire of the early
Middle Ages (ca. 30 B.C. - 330 A.D.).

Emphasis will be placed on the achievement of Augustus in establishing
a constitutional system, the Principate, which gave relative peace
and stability to the Roman world for 250 years, on the subsequent
history of the Julio-Claudian dynasty, on the life and culture of the
empire (Mediterranean lands and North-West Europe) during the first
two centuries A.D., on the crises and transformations of A.D. 235-
330 and on the enduring contribution of Rome to western civilisation
(e.g. in literature, architecture, law, the transmission of Judaeo-
Christian ideas).

Schedule:

March 29   Introductory

        30-31   44-30 B.C. Caesar's heir and civil wars

April 4-7   The establishment of the Principate. Octavian to
                    Augustus.

        11-14   Dynastic plans and the Roman upper class. The
                    conciliation of opinion. Vergil, Horace, Livy.

        18-21   The new socio-political system. Senators and equites.
                    Italy and the provinces.

        25-28   The Julio-Claudian dynasty.

May   2-4   Flavians and Five Good Emperors. Pax Romana.

        5   Pompeii.

        9-11   Urban workers and peasants. Civil servants. Slavery.

        12   Towns: Italy.

        16   Tacitus on women.

        17-18   2nd-century life and thought. Pliny. Philosophy
                    and religion.

        19   The provinces. Defense. Romanisation. Urbanisation.
                    Arena and circus.

        23   Early Christianity.

        24-25   Diocletian and Constantine. Decline and fall?

Suggested Essay Topics

1. 'I shall not fear rebellion nor violent death while Caesar rules the earth.'
    (ego nec tumultum / nec mori per vim metuam tenente / Caesare terras.
    Horace Odes iii.14. 14-16). What made it possible for Horace to write this?

2. 'As a mother dangerous to the state, as a stepmother dangerous to the family
    of the Caesars' (Tacitus Annals i. 10). Comment on the portrayal of Livia in
    the ancient sources.

3. If Suetonius and the Annals of Tacitus were our only sources, what would we
    know about the 'civil servants' of slave and freed status who worked in
    imperial administration under the Julio-Claudian and Flavian emperors?

Bibliographical suggestions to follow.
Please consult me if you want to design your own essay topic.
I shall talk to the group about how I would expect the above topics to be handled.

                                                        Susan Treggiari

CLASSICS 103 - Essay 1 - Bibliography

"I shall not fear rebellion nor violent death while Caesar rules the earth."
What made it possible for Horace to write this?

HORACE, ODES especially:

I. 2, 12, 14, 35, 37;

II. 1, 7, 16, 18;

III. 1-6, 14, 24, 29;

IV. 4, 5, 14, 15.

There are many translations.
For those with some Latin, commentaries will be useful. Nisbet & Hubbard on
Odes I and II give immense detail. Williams on III is succinct and up to date.
Wickham and Page on all the Odes are old but still useful.

Selection of discussions of Horace's political poems:

Steele COMMAGER, The Odes of Horace, (Bloomington, 1962) ch. IV, 'The political
Odes'.

Edward FRAENKEL, Horace, (Oxford, 1957), ch. I (life)
                             ch. V, section 5 "Odes concerned with
                                Augustus" (for those who can read
                                Latin).

Alfred NOYES, Portrait of Horace, (London, 1947) (a very readable and persuasive
account by a poet, not a professional scholar).

*Ronald SYME, The Roman Revolution, (Oxford, 1939), ch. 30.

Gordon WILLIAMS, Tradition and Originality in Roman Poetry, (Oxford, 1968), ch. VI:
"The poetry of institutions" pp. 366-8, 430-442, and see index for other poems.

_____, ed., The Third Book of Horace's Odes, (Oxford, 1969) pp. 1-10.

The Work of Augustus

The achievements of the Deified Augustus.

Earl, Millar, Rowell, Syme RR, (on main bibliography)

Thought. A review of culture and ideas. 55 (March 1980): Roman empire anniversary
issue. Especially for D.L. Stockton, "Augustus sub specie aeternitatis", 5-17.
(Classics library).

S.M. Treggiari

117

Classics 103 – Essay 2: The portrayal of Livia in the ancient sources.
Suggested Bibliography

Sources (selected)

Horace, Odes 3. 14. 5-6
Velleius II 75.2, 79.2, 94, 95.1, 130.4-5
Seneca, On Clemency/De Clementia 1. 9.6 (fiction)
Tacitus, Annals 1.3, 5, 6, 8, 10, 14, 73;
2.14, 34, 42, 43, 50, 72, 77;
3.3, 10, 15-17, 64;
4.8, 12, 37, 57, 71;
5.1-3;
6.5, 51.
Suetonius, Augustus 29.4; 40.3, 62.1, 63.1, 69.1, 84.2, 99.1, 101.2
Tiberius 4.3, 6.2, 14.1, 22, 50.2-3
Gaius 7, 10.1, 15.2, 23, 16.3
Claudius 1.1, 3.2, 4.3, 11.2
Galba 1.1, 5.2
Otho 1.1
Cassius Dio (very select list) 55.8.2, 55.10.10, 55.22.2, 57.12, 58.2-6

There are Loeb translations of all the above.

Moderns

R. Syme, Tacitus, ch. XL.
Barry Baldwin, 'Women in Tacitus', Prudentia 4.2 (1972), 83-102 (if you read Latin
J.P.V.D. Balsdon, Roman women : see index.

Classics 103 – Essay 3: Civil Servants

This essay is meant to be an original piece of research based on a close
reading of Suetonius and Tacitus. The commentaries of Furneaux and Goodyear
on the Annals and of Warmington or Bradley on Nero may be useful for
consultation. For background, consult Paul Weaver, Familia Caesaris, for a
mass of technical information on civil servants (largely drawn from inscriptions) or (more accessible) A.M. Duff, Freedmen in the early Roman empire
and R.H. Barrow, Slavery in the Roman empire. A.H.M. Jones, Studies in
Roman government and law has a useful chapter on sub-clerical grades. For
Claudius' alleged subjection to his freedmen, see Arnaldo Momigliano,
Claudius (index).

CLASSICS 103 - SPRING 1983

SELECT BIBLIOGRAPHY: THE EARLY ROMAN EMPIRE

Augustus to the Antonines c. 44 B.C. to A.D. 150

Brunt, P.A. 'Charges of provincial maladministration under the early Principate', Historia 10, 1961, 189 ff.

_____, 'Reflections on British and Roman imperialism', Comparative Studies in society and history 7, 1964/5, 267-288.

_____, 'Conscription and volunteering in the Roman imperial army', Scripta classical israelica 1, 1974, 90-115.

Cary, M. & Scullard, H.H., A History of Rome

*Earl, Donald C., The age of Augustus (London, Thames & Hudson, 1968)

*Garzetti, Albino, From Tiberius to the Antonines: a history of the Roman empire A.D. 14-192 (London: Methuen, 1974)

Levick, Barbara, Tiberius the politician (London: Thames and Hudson, 1976)

*Luttwak, E.N., The grand strategy of the Roman empire from the first century A.D. to the third (Baltimore: Johns Hopkins, 1976)

*MacMullen, Ramsay, Enemies of the Roman order: treason, unrest and alienation in the empire (Cambridge: Harvard U.P., 1966)

*Millar, Fergus, The Roman empire and its neighbours (London: Weidenfeld, 1967)

* _____, The emperor in the Roman world (31 B.C.-A.D. 337) (London: Duckworth, 1977)

Petit, Paul, La paix romaine (Paris: P.U.F., 1971), Pax Romana (Eng. tr.) useful for bibliography

Rowell, H.T., Rome in the Augustan Age (Norman: U. Oklahoma Press, 1962)

Seager, Robin, Tiberius (Berkeley: U. Cal, 1972)

Starr, C.G., Civilisation and the Caesars, (Ithaca: Cornell, 1954)

Sherwin-White, A.N., The letters of the younger Pliny (Oxford: Clarendon, 19): for introduction etc.

*Syme, Ronald, The Roman Revolution (Oxford: Clarendon, 1939)

_____, Tacitus (Oxford: Clarendon, 1958) 2 vols.

*Syme, Ronald, Roman papers (Oxford: Clarendon, 1979, two vols.)

_____, History in Ovid (Oxford: Clarendon Press, 1978)

*Wells, C.M., The German policy of Augustus (Oxford: Clarendon, 1972)

Wirszubski, Ch., Libertas as a political idea at Rome during the late Republic and early Principate (Cambridge: C.U.P., 1950)

*Yavetz, Z., Plebs and Princeps (Oxford: Clarendon, 1969)

Christianity and the period c. A.D. 150-330

Barnes, T.D., 'Legislation against the Christians', Journal of Roman Studies 58, 1968, 32-50.

_____, Constantine

*Brown, Peter, The world of late antiquity from Marcus Aurelius to Muhammad (London: Thames and Hudson, 1971)

*Kagan, Donald, Decline and Fall of the Roman Empire (New York: Heath, 1972)

MacMullen, R., Soldier and civilian in the later Roman Empire (Cambridge: Harvard, 1963)

*Ste. Croix, G.E.M. de, 'Why were the early Christians persecuted?' Past & Present 26, 1963, 6-38

_____, The class struggle in the Greek world

Walbank, F.W., The awful revolution: the decline of the Roman empire in the West (Liverpool: , 1969)

White, K.D., 'The fall of the Roman empire in the West: a process of elimination Nigeria and the Classics 13, 1971, 45-62

Social

*Balsdon, J.P.V.D., Roman women. Their history and habits (2nd ed. London: Bodley Head, 1974)

*_____, Life and Leisure in Ancient Rome (London: Bodley Head, 1969)

_____, Romans and aliens (London: Duckworth 1979)

*Crook, J.A., Law and life of Rome (London: Thames & Hudson, 1967)

*D'Arms, John, Commerce and social standing in ancient Rome (Cambridge, Mass.: Harvard, 1981)

Duncan-Jones, R., The economy of the Roman empire: quantitative studies (Cambridge: C.U.P., 1974, 2nd ed., 1981)

Finley, M.T., The ancient economy (Berkeley: UCal, 1973)

Friedlaender, Roman life and manners under the early empire (London: Routledge, 1908) 4 vols.

Garnsey, P.D.A., Social status and legal privilege in the Roman empire (Oxford: Clarendon, 1970)

_____, ed., Non-slave labour in the Greco-Roman world (Cambridge: Cambridge Philological Society, 1980)

*Hermansen, G., Ostia. Aspects of Roman city life (Edmonson: University of Alberta Press, 1982)

Jones, A.H.M., The Roman economy, ed. by P.A. Brunt (Oxford: Blackwell, 1974)

*MacMullen, R., Roman social relations 50 B.C. to A.D. 284 (New Haven: Yale, 1974)

*_____, Paganism in the Roman empire (New Haven: Yale, 1981)

Meiggs, R., Ostia (Oxford: Clarendon, 1960, 2nd ed. 1974)

Ogilvie, R.M., The Romans and their Gods (London: Chatto, 1969)

*Pomeroy, Sarah B., Goddesses, wives, whores and slaves (New York: Schocken, 1975)

Rickman, G., The corn supply of ancient Rome (Oxford: Clarendon, 1980)

Rostovtzeff, M., Social and economic history of the Roman empire (Oxford: Clarendon, 2nd ed., 1957, 2 vols.)

(Social continued)

Sherwin-White, A.N., Roman society and law in the New Testament (Oxford: O.U.P., 1963)

*_____, Racial prejudice in imperial Rome (Cambridge: C.U.P., 1967)

Treggiari, S., 'Domestic staff at Rome in the Julio-Claudian period, 27 B.C.- A.D. 68', Histoire sociale/Social History 6, 1973, 240-255.

_____, 'Roman social history: recent interpretations' Histoire sociale 8 1975, 149-164 (for bibliography)

_____, 'Lower-class women in the Roman economy', Florilegium 1, 1979, 65-86.

*Watson, Alan, The law of the ancient Romans (Dallas: S.M.U.P., 1970)

Weaver, Paul R.C., Familia Caesaris. A social study of the emperor's freedmen and slaves (Cambridge: C.U.P., 1972)

White, K.D., Roman farming (London: Thames & Hudson, 1970)

DEPARTMENT OF HISTORY
Fordham University

HS 20251 The Eastern Roman Empire, 300-800

Fr. Meyendorff   Fall 1980

Requirements:

In addition to normal class attendance and discussion or the
more important issues related to the course, the students will present
three short papers (maximum: 5 pages) based on the required readings.
The subjects of the papers will be announced a week in advance of the
dates at which they are due. The Final Examination will cover the entire
material of the course.

Required Reading:

Brand, Ch., Icon and Minaret: Sources of Byzantine and Islamic
    Civilization, Prentice-Hall.

Chadwick, H., The Early Church, Pelican.

Barker, J.W., Justinian and the Later Roman Empire, Univ. of Wisc.

Runciman, S., Byzantine Style and Civilization, Pelican.

Recommended Reading:

Ostrogorsky, G., History of the Byzantine State, Rev. ed.
    Rutgers Univ. Press, 1969

Jones, A.H.M., The Later Roman Empire, 284-602: A Social, Economic
    and Administrative Survey, Oxford, 1964

Coleman-Norton, Roman State and Christian Church

Stevenson, J., A New Eusebius

Meyendorff, J., Byzantine Theology, Fordham Univ. Press

Program of the course

Sept. 3-4 The Roman Empire and Christianity: the early church, Greek
           and Roman paganism; persecutions.
           Chadwick, 9-73, 116-124.

Sept. 8-11 Emperor Constantine and his "conversion".
            Chadwick, 125-132 (cf. also bibliography, 1, 292)
            Brand, 5-7; 14-22. Runciman, 1-44.

Sept. 15-18 Church and State in the fourth century: Emperor Julian, Emperor
             Theodosius I. Theological controversies. Monasticism.
             Chadwick, 133-183. Brand, 38-46.

Sept. 22-25 The beginnings of Christian civilization.
             Sept. 25: first paper due.

Sept. 29- Barbarian invasions in East and West: contrasts and similarities.
Oct. 2   The role of the Roman bishop in the West.
           Barker, 3-63. Chadwick, 247-257.

Oct. 6-9 The Eastern Empire and the controversies on the identity of
          Jesus Christ: Nestorianism, Monophysitism.
          Chadwick, 184-212. Meyendorff, 32-41.

Oct. 15-16 Justinian I, emperor. The ideal of universal unity.
            Ecclesiastical policies.
            Barker, 64-130. Runciman, 45-76.

Oct. 20-23 The reconquest of Africa and Italy.
            Barker, 131-166.

Oct. 27-30 The heritage of Justinian: The Code; St. Sophia; assessment
            of the reign.
            Barker, 166-210.

Nov. 3-6 Heraclius and the Persians. Monotheletism.
          Barker, 211-247.

Nov. 10-13 The rise of Islam: Mohamed and the Koran.
            Brand, 133-146.

Nov. 17-20 The Byzantine resistance: Constantine IV, Justinian II.
            Barker, 247-266.

Nov. 24-26 Iconoclasm: ideological war with Islam and internal crisis.
            Meyendorff, 42-53. Runciman, 77-124.

Dec. 1-4 The second council of Nicosa (787) and the Triumph of Orthodoxy,
          The coronation of Charlemagne.

Dec. 8 Conclusion: Byzantium and Europe.
        Runiciman, 125-212.

THE BYZANTINE EMPIRE
John Meyendorff
Fordham University

Requirements:
1. regular participation in class discussions.
2. two short papers (maximum 5 pages) on topics related to both class work and readings.
3. a longer paper on a topic agreed on with the instructor.
4. a final exam covering the work of the semester.

1. The Empire. The New Capital. The Roman State and the Christian Religion.

2. The Christian Church: doctrinal disputes and schisms. Byzantine Orthodoxy.
    Reading completed of: Ostrogorsky, 27-68 or
    Vasiliev 1, 43-128; Brand, 5-7.

3. Emperor Justinian and the Reconquest.
    Ostrogorsky, 68-86, or Vasiliev, 129-192.
    Barker, Justinian and the Later Empire

4. Emperor Heraclius and the Persians.
    Ostrogorsky, 92-109; Vasiliev, 193-233.
    Barker, Justinian

5. The Rise of Islam.
    Ostrogorsky, 110-146; Vasiliev, same as above.
    Brand, 135-180.

6. Iconoclasm in Byzantium: a crisis of civilization.
    Ostrogorsky, 147-209; Vasiliev, 234-299.

7. Charlemagne and Byzantium. The cultural and political separation between East and West.

8. The Conversion of the Slavs. Patriarch Plotius.
    Ostrogrosky, 210-269; Vasiliev, 301-351.

9. The Macedonian Dynasty: economic reforms and military conquests.
    Ostrogorsky, 270-320; Vasiliev, same as above.

10. The Schism between Rome and Byzantium. Crusades begin.
    Ostrogorsky, 320-375; Vasiliev, 351-412.

11. The Commenian Dynasty. The Fourth Crusade.
    Ostrogrosky, 374-417; Vasiliev, 412-505.

12. The Palaeologan Dynasty. Union negociations.
    Ostrogorsky, 418-533; Vasiliev, 506-629.

13. The Council of Florence. The Fall.
    Ostrogorsky, 533-572; Vasiliev, 629-722.

14. Byzantine Civilization. Art, architecture, literature.

REQUIRED READING:

    Brand, Ch., Icon and Minaret: Sources of Byzantine and Islamic
Civilization
    Ostrogorsky, G., History of the Byzantine State, rev. ed.,
1969.
    Barker, J. W., Justinian and the Later Roman Empire,
    Vasiliev, A. A., History of the Byzantine Empire, Vols. I & II.

RECOMMENDED READING:
    Jones, A. H. M., The Later Roman Empire, 284-602: A Social,
Economic and Administrative Survey, 1964.
    Meyendorff, J., Byzantine Theology, 1979.
    The Cambridge Medieval History, vol. IV. "The Byzantine Empire"
Part 1 & 2. ed. Hussey, 1967.
    Nicol, D. M., The Last Centuries of Byzantium, 1972.
    Dvornik, F., The Photian Schism: History and Legend, 1948.
    Runciman, S., The Eastern Schism: A Study of the Papacy and the
Eastern Churches during the XI and XII Centuries, 1955.
    Gill, J., The Council of Florence, 1959.
    Meyendorff, J., St. Gregory Palamas and Orthodox Spirituality,
1975.

TRANSLATED SOURCES:
    Barker, E., Social and Political Thought in Byzantium from
Justinian I to the Last Palaeologus, 1957.
    Psellus, M., Fourteen Byzantine Rulers: tr. Sewter, 1966.
    Procopius, The Secret History
    Comena, Anna, The Alexiad, tr. Sewter, 1969.
    Porplyrogenitus, Constantine, De Administrando Imperio, tr.
Moravczik and Jenkins.

CLASSICS 181

Susan M. Treggiari
Stanford University

ROMAN SOCIETY IN THE AGE OF CICERO AND AUGUSTUS

Tentative Programme - Autumn Quarter, 1982

Sept.	29	Introduction
Oct.	1	The nature of the evidence: Cicero's writings.
	4	Cicero's letters and how they came down to us.
	6	Other sources. Roman nomenclature.
8, 11, 13		Society: Cicero's life, background, family, career. Nobles and New Men
	15	Clientela and amicitia
	18	Economics: senatorial wealth.
	20	Villas.
22, 25		Household staff: slaves and freedmen.
27, 29		The lower classes: work and 'dependence'
Nov. 1, 3		Horace: freedman's son, army officer, civil servant and poet.
	5	Daily life.
8, 10		Marriage
	12	Augustus: marriage legislation and practice.
	15	'Familia Caesaris'
	17	Contubernium (quasi-marriage where one partner at least is a slave)
	19	Concubinage.
22, 24, 29		Students' presentations.
Dec. 1, 3		No class.
6, 8, 10		'Loose ends'
	13	Exam.

127

Susan Treggiari

History 100I: The City in the Greek, Roman, and Byzantine World.

Instructor: Mr. Hitchner   University of Virginia
Office hours: MW 11-12 TH 1:30-3:30 or by appt.
Office: Room 124 Randall Hall

The course will examine the nature and role of the city in the Greek,
Roman, and Byzantine world. We will consider such aspects as the
political concept of a city among the ancients, urban institutions,
and how cities were planned and developed. We will also explore the
relationship between city and country in antiquity. Readings for the
course include primary sources (ancient authors), important modern
studies of ancient urbanism, as well as archaeological reports,
numismatic evidence, maps, and slides.

General Information

Students should expect to discuss assigned readings and present at least
one oral report which will be expanded and submitted as a written paper
at the end of the semester. There will also be a final take-home examination.

The following books for the course will be found at both Newcomb Hall
and the Corner bookstores.

Aristotle, Politics (Penguin)
The Letters of the Younger Pliny (Penguin)
Pausanias, Guide to Greece, I (Penguin)
R. E. Wycherley, How the Greeks Built Cities (Norton)

Students should also attempt to purchase a copy of Homer, Iliad if at
all possible. Most of the additional readings will, however, be provided
by the instructor one week prior to the class in which they are to be
discussed. Reading assignments will be provided for all the books at
the same time.

SYLLABUS

HISTORY 100I

The City in the Greek, Roman and Byzantine World

Sept. 3   Introduction: What is a City?

Sept. 10   Cities in the Bronze Age and
                            Archaic period in Greece.

Sept. 17   The Greek City in the Classical
                            Period: Athens and Sparta.

Sept. 24   The Concept of the Polis

Oct. 1   Cities as Colonies: The Greek
                            and Phoenician models.

Oct. 8   Carthage.

Oct. 15   The Foundation of Rome: Myth
                            and Archaeology.

128

Oct. 22	Image and Reality: The City of Cicero and Juvenal./Topography.
Oct. 29	The Cities of the Roman Provinces.
Nov. 5	The Administration of Ancient Cities.
Nov. 12	City and country in Antiquity.
Nov. 19	The Cities of Late Antiquity: Change or Decline?
Nov. 26	The City in the Reign of Justinian.
Dec. 3	Epilogue and Summary.

California State University, Los Angeles

History 311   Classical Civilization
Dr. K. Pratt
Fall Quarter, 1985
KH 3014 (18292)

    Egypt, India, China, Japan, Mexico have all produced
civilizations that have influenced other peoples. In this course,
however, our work is in the Graeco-Roman--classical--tradition. Below
is a list of topics that will illustrate what I mean.   Part of the
time in our course, I will lecture and show slides; part of the time
we will organize some projects, and part of the time you will be able
to conduct the class individually or in groups.
    There is a mid-term examination (Th. Oct. 29) and a final (Dec.
10). These will be discussed at length in class so that you will have
the best possible preparation. In addition, part of your grade will
depend on your project, but I would rather that the project would be
more interesting and fun than preparing for an exam.

        Assignments: For the mid-term exam - Finley, Aspects of Antiquity

                              Pausanius, Guide to Greece
                              (mainly the section on
                              Olympia and the Olympics)

        Final examination - The Hippocratic Writings

                              Pliny, Letters
                              (which ones to be assigned)

The lectures will cover five main areas of classical influence:

    1. Architecture and City Planning.

    2. Sports

    3. Science and Medicine

    4. Political Theory

    5. Language

(There are many other subjects that we could use: eg. Religion,
psychology, law, the family, slavery, magic, coinage, myth, music and
dance, the theatre, food and drink, sculture, art and, of course,
literature, and rhetoric. Maybe one of these would interest you?)

130

Class schedule:

        Sept. 26 First meeting: Introduction to the course; the scheme of Helladic, Hellenic, and Hellenistic history

Week one

        Oct. 1 Introduction, cont. The outline of Roman history

        Oct. 3 Hellenic buildings and builders

Week two

        Oct. 8 Roman Architecture

        Oct. 10 Modern classical building

Week three

        Oct. 15 Hellenic-Hellenistic sports tradition; the Olympics

        Oct. 17 Roman sports; modern indebtedness and differences

Week four

        Oct. 22 Ancient political theory; the mixed constitution; Aristotle

        Oct. 24. Political theory then and now

Week five

        Oct. 29 Mid-term examination

        Oct. 31 Science: atomism, evolution and Aristotle

Week six

        Nov. 5 Medicine: the Hippocratic tradition of rational medicine; neurology

        Nov. 7 Medicine: get Galen off the road

Week seven

        Nov. 12 The Latin language and classical education

        Nov. 14 Reports (3?)

Week eight

    Nov. 19 The English language; the Romance languages

    Nov. 21 Reports

Week nine

    Nov. 26 Reports
        (holiday 28-30)

Week ten

    Dec. 3 The Romance languages, cont.

    Dec. 5 Reports

Introductory bibliography:

Aristotle, History of Animals (several translation of the Historia animalium)

R.H. Barrow, Slavery in the Roman Empire (1928)

C. Bailey, ed., The Legacy of Rome (1923)

Jessica Benjamin, "The Oedipal Riddle: Authority, Autonomy and the New Narcissism," in the Problem of Authority in America, ed., John Diggens, Mark Kahn (1982)

Stanley Bonner, Education in Ancient Rome (1977)

J. Bowen, A History of Western Education (1972)

John Bowle, Western Political Thought (1961. From the beginnings to Rousseau.

E.L. Butler, The Tyranny of Greece over Germany (1935)

E.B. Castle, Ancient Education and Today (1961)

Charles Cochrane, Christianity and the Classical Culture (1957)

Wayne Craven, Sculpture in America (1968)

R. Crossman, Plato Today (1959)

Simome duBeauvoir, The Second Sex (1970)

Bibliography cont.

Allen Debus, <u>Science, Medicine and Society in the Renaissance</u> (1972)

J.F. Dobson, <u>Ancient Education and Its Meaning to Us</u> (1932)

Francis Dvornik, <u>Early Christian and Byzantine Political Theory: Origins and Background</u> (1966)

Donald Earl, <u>The Moral and Political Tradition of Rome</u>

E. Edelstein & L. Edelstein, <u>Asclepius</u>, 2 vols. (1945)

L. Edelstein, <u>Ancient Medicine</u> (1967)

Galen, <u>On Anatomical Procedures</u> (1962)

idem, <u>On Medical Experience</u> (1944)

idem, <u>On the Usefulness of the Parts of the Body</u>, 2 vols. (1968)

E. Gardiner, <u>Athletics in the Ancient World</u> (1930)

H.A. Harris, <u>Sport in Greece and Rome</u> (1972)

Bill Henry, <u>An Approved History of the Olympic Games</u> (1984)

Moses Hadas, <u>Hellenistic Culture</u> (1972)

C.H. Haskins, <u>The Renaissance of the Twelfth Century</u> (1970)

Werner Hegeman, Albert Peets, <u>The American Vitruvious: an Architectural Handbook</u> (1922)

Gilbert Highet, <u>The Classical Tradition</u> (1957)

Walter C. Kidney, <u>The Architecture of Choice</u> (1974)

Evelyn Fox Keller, <u>Reflections of Gender and Science</u> (1985)
Especially ch. I: Love and Sex in Plato's epistemology

R. Klibansky, E. Panofsky & F. Saxl, <u>Saturn and Melancholy: Studies in the History of Natural Philosophy, Religion and Art</u> (1964)

Mary Lefjowitz & Maureen B. Fant, <u>Women's Life in Greece and Rome</u> (1982)

S. Lieberman, <u>Greek in Jewish Palestine</u> (1942)

R. Livinstone, ed., <u>The Legacy of Greece</u> (reprint, 1962)

J.A. Larrabee, <u>English Bards and Grecian Marbles</u> (1943)

Guido Majno, <u>The Healing Hand, Man and Wound in the Ancient Worl</u> (1975)

Christopher Morris, <u>Western Political Thought</u> I (1967)

<u>Our Debt to Greece and Rome</u>, 52 vols. (1922-1935)

H.T. Parker, <u>The Cult of Antiquity & the French Revolution</u> (1937)

E.D. Phillips, <u>Greek Medicine</u> (1973)

Sarah Pomeroy, <u>Goddesses, Whores, Wives and Slaves</u> (1975)

Charles H. Reilly, <u>McKim, Meade and White</u> (reprint, 1972). 3 classica architects.

John W. Reps, <u>Monumental Washington</u> (1967)

J.E. Sandys, <u>History of Classical Scholarship</u>, 3 vols. (1908-1921)

Geoffrey Scott, <u>The Architecture of Humanism</u> (1924)

John A. Scott, ed. and tr., <u>The Defense of Gracchus Babeuf before th</u> <u>High Court of Vendome</u> (1967)

H.O. Taylor, <u>The Classical Heritage of the Middle Ages</u> (1911)

Frank Lloyd Wright, <u>On Architecture</u> (1941)

Charles S. Singleton, ed., <u>Art, Science and History in the Renaissanc</u> (1967)

O. Temkin, <u>Galenism</u> (1973)

Charles Vereker, <u>The Development of Political Theory</u> (1965)

ANCIENT DREAMS AND DREAM INTERPRETATION

A Course Outline

J. Donald Hughes, Professor of History, University of Denver
Denver, CO 80208

A history of ancient attitudes toward dreams, and ancient methods of
dream interpretation. Ancient records of dreams in literature,
inscriptions, and other written sources. Dreams as divination,
methods of foreseeing the future, incubation and healing, dictation.
Comparison with modern psychological theories.

Subjects for reading, lecture, and discussion:

1. Introduction: Dreams and interpreters of dreams. The importance
    of dreams to the ancients and differences between ancient and
    modern attitudes.

2. How dreams began: Primal societies such as the Siberians,
    American Indians, Australian Aborigines, Senoi of Malaya, etc.

3. Ancient Egyptian dreams: Inscriptions, papyri, the god Bes,
    Thutmose IV, the Chester Beatty dreambook.

4. Mesopotamian dreams: The Epic of Gilgamesh, dreambooks, etc.

5. Dreams in Ancient Israel: The Old Testament dreams.

6. The Greeks: Dreams of heroic men and women (Homer).

7. Dreams reported by the Greek historians: Herodotus, Xenophon,
    Plutarch.

8. Dreams in lyric and dramatic literature.

9. The temples of dream healing: Incubation (enkoimesis) as a
    widespread practice.

10. Medicine and dreams: The teachings of "Hippocrates" in Regimen
    IV (On Dreams).

11. Philosophers interpret dreams: Plato, Aristotle's three books,
    Zeno.

12. The Dreams of Alexander the Great.

13. The Romans: Scepticism and credulity. Lucretius, Cicero.

14. The Early Christians and dreams: The New Testament; Synesius of
    Cyrene, etc.

15. Dream books from the ancient world: Artemidorus of Daldis,
    Macrobius, Aelius Aristides.

16. Ancient dreams and modern dreamers: The use of ancient thought
    by Freud, Jung, and modern psychology generally.

READINGS:

There is no single book that can easily serve as a text for this
course. The instructor has therefore assigned readings from ancient
and modern sources selected from the following list. Those
particularly useful are marked with an asterisk.

BIBLIOGRAPHY:

I. Ancient Texts.

* Aelius Aristides, Sacred Tales (tr. by C.A. Behr, Amsterdam:
    Hakkert, 1968).
* Aristotle, On Sleeping and Waking, On Dreams, On Divination by
    Dreams, Metaphysics 4.29, 1024b.
* Artemidorus, The Interpretation of Dreams (Oneirocritica) (tr. by
    R.J. White, Park Ridge, N.J.: Noyes, 1975).
  Bible: See the book by M.T. Kelsey listed below.
* Cicero, De Divinatione 39-62, 119-150; Dream of Scipio.
* Hippocrates Regimen IV (On Dreams).
* Homer, Iliad 1.62-64, 2.1-83, 5.148-51, 10.496-97, 22.199-200,
    23.62-107. Odyssey 4.795-841, 6.13-50, 11.206-22, 14.495-98,
    19.535-69, 20.83-90, 21.79, 24.12.
  Lucian, Somnium.
  Macrobius, Commentary on the Dream of Scipio (tr. by W.H. Stahl,
    N.Y.: Columbia, 1952).
* Plato, Republic 2.382, 9.571-72, Crito 44, Phaedo 60, Symposium
    203, Timaeus 71, Meno 99, Ion 533, Laws 738, 909, Theaetetus 155.
  Plutarch, Progress in Virtue 12 (Moralia 82F), Lives passim.
  Synesius of Cyrene, On Dreams (tr. by A. Fitzgerald in The Essays
    and Hymns of Synesius of Cyrene, Oxford, 1930).
  Tragedians: See the book by G. Devereux listed below.

It should be noted that it is difficult to find any ancient author
of importance who did not make some reference to dreams.
Thucydides is one outstanding exception.

II. Modern Works.

  Balsdon, J.P.V.D. Romans and Aliens. Chapel Hill: University of
    North Carolina Press, 1979. (Has a short section on dreams).

  Brenk, Frederick E. "The Dreams of Plutarch's Lives." Latomus:
    Revue d'Etudes Latines 34 (1975): 336-349.

  Brenk, Frederick E. In Mist Apparelled: Religious Themes in
    Plutarch's Moralia and Lives. Leyden: Brill, 1977.

  Buechsenschuetz, Albert Bernhard. Traum und Traumdeutung in
    Alterthume. Berlin: S. Calvary & Co., 1868.

  Clay, Diskin. "An Epicurean Interpretation of Dreams." American
    Journal of Philology 101 (1980): 342-365.

  Dambska, Izydora. "Le Probleme des Songes dans la Philosophie des
    Anciens Grecs." Revue Philosophique de la France et de
    l'Etranger 151 (1961): 11-24.

* Devereux, George. <u>Dreams in Greek Tragedy: An Ethno-Psycho-Analytical Study</u>. Berkeley: University of California Press, 1976.

Dodds, E.R. "Supernormal Phenomena in Classical Antiquity." Chapter 10 in <u>The Ancient Concept of Progress and Other Essays on Greek Literature and Belief</u>. Oxford: Clarendon Press, 1973.

* Dodds, E.R. <u>The Greeks and the Irrational</u>. Berkeley: University of California Press, 1951 (1973).

Edelstein, E.J. and L. <u>Asclepius: A Collection and Interpretation of the Testimonies</u>. Baltimore: Johns Hokins Press, 1945.

Engle, John D. "Dreams and Poetry: A Prelimiary Checklist." <u>Dreamworks</u> 1 (1980): 183-190.

Freud, Sigmund. <u>The Interpretation of Dreams</u>. Translated by James Strachey. London: Hogarth Press, 1953.

Gallop, David. "Dreaming and Waking in Plato." In <u>Essays in Ancient Greek Philosophy</u>, ed. by J.P. Anton and G.L. Kustas. Albany: State University of New York Press, 1971, pp. 187-201.

Gardiner, A.H. <u>Hieratic Papyri in the British Museum, Third Series: Chester Beatty Gift 1</u>. London, 1935: 9-23. (Chester Beatty Papyrus III is the earliest extant dreambook).

Hughes, J. Donald. "The Dreams of Alexander the Great." <u>Journal of Psychohistory</u> 12 (1984): 168-192.

Jung, C.G. <u>Memories, Dreams, Reflections</u>. Ed. by Aniella Jaffe. New York: Vintage, 1961.

* Jung, C.G., ed. <u>Man and His Symbols</u>. London: Aldus Books, 1964.

Jung, C.G. "Lecture IV, Tavistock Clinic, London, 1935." <u>Collected Works</u>, Vol. 18, pp. 102-123. Princeton: Princeton University Press, 1953.

* Kelsey, Morton T. <u>God, Dreams, and Revelation: A Christian Interpretation of Dreams</u>. Minneapolis: Augsburg Publishing House, (1968) 1974.

* Lang, A., Taylor, A.E., Sayce, A.H., Foucart, G., Phillpotts, B.S., and Bolling, G.M. "Dreams and Sleep." In <u>Encyclopaedia of Religion and Ethics</u>, ed. by James Hastings. New York: Charles Scribner's Sons, 1912.

* Lewis, Naphtali, ed. <u>The Interpretation of Dreams and Portents</u>. Toronto: Samuel Stevens, 1976. An excellent source collection.

Lincoln, Jackson Steward. <u>The Dream in Primitive Cultures</u>. New York: Cressett Press, 1935; New York: Johnson Reprint Corp., 1970.

* Meier, C.A. <u>Ancient Incubation and Modern Psychotherapy</u>. Translated by Monica Curtis. Evanston, Ill.: Northwestern University Press, 1967.

Messer, William Stuart. _The Dream in Homer and Greek Tragedy_. New York: Columbia University Press, 1918.

Misch, Georg. _A History of Autobiography in Antiquity_. 2 vols. Cambridge, Mass.: Harvard University Press, 1951. (Contains a study of Aelius Aristides).

Oberhelman, Steven M. "Galen, On Diagnosis from Dreams." _Journal of the History of Medicine and Allied Sciences_ 38 (1983): 36-47.

Oberhelman, Steven M. "Popular Dream-Interpretation in Ancient Greece and Freudian Psychoanalysis." _Journal of Popular Culture_ 11 (1977): 682-695.

Oberhelman, Steven M. "A Survey of Dreams in Ancient Greece." _Classical Bulletin_ 55 (1979): 36-40.

Oppenheim, A. Leo. "The Interpretation of Dreams in the Ancient Near East: With a Translation of an Assyrian Dream-Book." _Transactions of the American Philosophical Society_, n.s. 46 (1956): 179-373.

Roscher, Wilhelm Heinrich and Hillman, James. _Pan and the Nightmare_: Being the Only English Translation (from the German by A.V. O'Brien, M.D.) of "Ephialtes: A Pathological-Mythological Treatise on the Nightmare in Classical Antiquity" by Wilhelm Heinrich Roscher (1900) together with "An Essay on Pan: Serving as a Psychological Introduction to Roscher's _Ephialtes_" by James Hillman. Dallas, Texas: Spring Publications, 1979.

Rousselle, Robert. "Healing Cults in Antiquity: The Dream Cures of Asclepius of Epidaurus." _Journal of Psychohistory_ 12 (1985): 339-352.

Van Lieshout, R.G.A. "A Dream on a _Kairos_ of History: An Analysis of Herodotos _Hist_. VII 12-19; 47." _Mnemosyne_ 23 (1970): 225-249.

* Von Grunebaum, G.E., and Callois, Roger, eds. _The Dream and Human Societies_. Berkeley: University of California Press, 1966.

Woods, Ralph L., and Greenhouse, Herbert B. _The New World of Dreams: An Anthology_. New York: Macmillan, 1974.

John Scarborough
University of
Kentucky

ON TEACHING COURSES IN ANCIENT MEDICINE

One of our members (p. 2 above) has suggested that it would be "Most useful [to] share course outlines and books." The following listings will thus be the first in a 'continuing series,' as I would ask any members now teaching courses in ancient medicine to send me copies of their course-outlines and any supplementary materials so that I can reproduce them in future issues of the Newsletter. Course outlines will also answer (partially) another member's request for a "...pamphlet/book to serve as an introduction to the study of ancient medicine ...[and] what major topics and problems are of importance in the study of ancient medicine" (p. 2 above).

For the broader scope of history of medicine as a whole, one may now turn to Chester R. Burns, The Teaching of Medical History to College Undergraduates in the United States and Canada: Report of a Survey in 1977 (Galveston: For the Committee on Education of the American Association for the History of Medicine, 1978 [at this moment, copies can be obtained ($5.00) from Chester R. Burns, MD, Institute for the Medical Humanities, University of Texas Medical Branch, Galveston, Texas 77550 USA]). Within the "Selected Outlines and Reading Lists" of eighteen courses, generally of survey courses in the history of medicine, there are materials on 'early' medicine, that might be quite useful to members of the SAM as they ponder the broad problems in the history of medicine, which usually apply to the study of ancient medicine as well. Burns' listings do, however, emphasize medicine since the European Renaissance, and particularly medical history in the United States and Europe since c. 1700; it would appear from the listings that the great majority of courses in medical history consider "modern" history, with some background and synopsis of "Hippocratic" and "Galenic" heritages.

Fifth Century Greek Medicine   Ann Ellis Hanson (176 Western Way, Princeton, New Jersey 08540 USA)

Professor Hanson has sent me a copy of her Supplementary Readings for the Study of Hippocratic Medicine (Princeton, 1978; 232 pp. typescript), which is used to supplement readings taken from the Loeb Hippocrates and the new Lloyd collection of Hippocratic writings (for which see p. 13 below). A listing of the Hippocratic works in the four volumes of the Loeb edition, correlated with the selections in the Lloyd anthology, appears on p. v. There are eleven main selections:

I. Thucydides, Peloponnesian War, 2. 47-55 (trans. Rex Warner)
II. Hippocrates, Generating Seed/Nature of the Child (trans. T. U. H. Ellinger)
III. Hippocrates, Diseases of Young Girls (Littré, VIII, 466-470; trans. Hanson)
IV. Hippocrates, Diseases of Women, I [selections] (Chs. 1, 2, 6, 7, 10, 11, 21, 25, 33, 35, 62; trans. Hanson [see also p. 13 below])
V. Soranus, Gynecology, I, 1-47, 60-65; II, 9-16, 19-20; III, 1-16, 26-29 (trans. Owsei Temkin)
VI. Hippocrates, Oath (trans. Ludwig Edelstein, with "Interpretation," "The Ethical Code," "The Covenant," "The Unity of the Document," "Date and Purpose of the Oath," and "Conclusion," as in Edelstein's The Hippocratic Oath [Bulletin of the History of Medicine, Supplement 1], without notes)
VII. Herodotus, The Persian Wars, 3. 129-137: Democedes the Physician (trans. George Rawlinson)
VIII. Soranus, Ancestry and Life of Hippocrates (Ilberg, CMG, IV, pp. 175-178; trans. Hanson)
IX. Suda, "Hippocrates" entries (ed. Adler, entries Nos. 564-569; trans. Hanson)
X. Galen, Prognosis (Kühn, XIV, 599-673; trans. Hanson)
XI. Aelius Aristides, Sacred Tales, II (trans. C. A. Behr)

SYLLABUS   Greek and Roman Medicine   John Scarborough
                History 504   Professor
                                             Ancient History/History
                                             of Medicine & Pharmacy
ASSIGNED BOOKS   University of Kentucky

Arthur John Brock, trans., Greek Medicine: Being Extracts Illustrative of Medical
    Writers from Hippocrates to Galen. New York: AMS, 1977 [rpt. of London 1929 ed.
    [paperback]
G. E. R. Lloyd, Early Greek Science: Thales to Aristotle. New York: Norton, 1973
    [paperback]
G. E. R. Lloyd, Greek Science After Aristotle. New York: Norton, 1973 [paperback]
G. E. R. Lloyd, ed., Hippocratic Writings. New York: Viking/Penguin, 1978 [paperback]
E. D. Phillips, Aspects of Greek Medicine. New York: St. Martin's Press, 1973
    [British edition titled Greek Medicine (London: Thames & Hudson, 1973)]
John Scarborough, Roman Medicine. Ithaca, New York: Cornell University Press, 1969;
    rptd. with corr., 1976 [British edition (1969) Thames & Hudson]
Wesley D. Smith, The Hippocratic Tradition. Ithaca, New York: Cornell University
    Press, 1979
from the Loeb Classical Library (Cambridge, Mass.: Harvard University Press):
    No. 292: W. G. Spencer, ed. and trans., Celsus: De medicina, Vol. I
    No. 71: Arthur John Brock, ed. and trans., Galen: On the Natural Faculties
from the Bobbs-Merrill Reprint Series in the History of Science (Indianapolis:
    Bobbs-Merrill):
    No. HS-8: Marshall Clagett, "Science in Late Antiquity"
       HS-17: Ludwig Edelstein, "Recent Trends in the Interpretation of Ancient
            Science"
       HS-73: Owsei Temkin, "Greek Medicine as Science and Craft"
       HS-82: L. G. Wilson, "Erasistratus, Galen, and the Pneuma"

Extra reading can be drawn from: [Library Reserve]
Thomas W. Africa, Science and the State in Greece and Rome. New York: Wiley, 1961
T. Clifford Allbutt, Greek Medicine in Rome. New York: Blom, 1970; rpt. of 1921 ed.
Frank N. Egerton, ed., Edward Lee Greene: Landmarks of Botanical History. 2 vols.
    Stanford, California: Stanford University Press, 1983
Paul Ghalioungui, The House of Life: Per Ankh. Magic and Medical Science in Ancient
    Egypt, 2nd ed. Amsterdam: B. M. Israël, 1973
C. R. S. Harris, The Heart and the Vascular System in Ancient Greek Medicine. Oxford:
    Clarendon Press, 1973
Edwin B. Levine, Hippocrates. New York: Twayne, 1971
G. E. R. Lloyd, Magic. Reason and Experience: Studies in the Origins and Development
    of Greek Science. Cambridge: University Press, 1979
G. E. R. Lloyd, Science. Folklore and Ideology: Studies in the Life Sciences in
    Ancient Greece. Cambridge: University Press, 1983
Guido Majno, The Healing Hand: Man and Wound in the Ancient World. Cambridge, Mass.:
    Harvard University Press, 1975
John Stewart Milne, Surgical Instruments in Greek and Roman Times. Chicago: Ares
    Press, 1976; rpt. of 1907 ed.
Vivian Nutton, ed., Galen: Problems and Prospects...the 1979 Cambridge Conference.
    London: Wellcome Institute for the History of Medicine, 1981
John M. Riddle, Herbs. Rocks and Animals: Dioscorides and Medicine. Austin, Texas:
    University of Texas Press, 1984
John Scarborough, ed., Byzantine Medicine. Washington, D.C.: Dumbarton Oaks, 1984
    [Dumbarton Oaks Papers, Vol. 38]
Henry E. Sigerist, A History of Medicine, Vol. I: Primitive and Archaic Medicine.
    New York: Oxford University Press, 1951; paprback rpt. 1967
Henry E. Sigerist, A History of Medicine, Vol. II: Early Greek, Hindu, and Persian
    Medicine. New York: Oxford University Press, 1961
Bennett Simon, Mind and Madness in Ancient Greece. Ithaca, New York: Cornell Univer-
    sity Press, 1978
William H. Stahl, Roman Science. Madison, Wisconsin: Univ. Wisconsin Press, 1962

Owsei Temkin, The Double Face of Janus and Other Essays in the History of Medicine.
    Baltimore: Johns Hopkins Press, 1977
Owsei Temkin, The Falling Sickness, 2nd ed. Baltimore: Johns Hopkins Press, 1971
Oswei Temkin, Galenism. Ithaca, New York: Cornell University Press, 1973
Owsei Temkin and C. Lilian Temkin, eds., Ancient Medicine: Selected Papers of
    Ludwig Edelstein. Baltimore: Johns Hopkins Press, 1967
R. E. Walker, Roman Veterinary Medicine, appendix in J. M. C. Toynbee, Animals
    in Roman Life and Art. Ithaca, New York: Cornell University Press, 1973
R. Walzer, Galen on Jews and Christians. London: Oxford University Press, 1949
Gilbert Watson, Theriac and Mithridatium. London: Wellcome Historical Medical
    Library, 1966

[the following is designed for a semester of 15 weeks]

I. The Study of Medical History: Introduction. Common Themes. Smith, pp. 13-44
II. The Background of the Ancient Near East. Egypt and Mesopotamia. Lloyd, Early
    Greek Science, introd. and ch. 1
III. Egypt and Mesopotamia Continued. The Comparative Technique in Medical History:
    Honey and the Egyptians, and the Biochemistry of Honey. Garlic. [assignments
    from Ghalioungui or Majno]
IV. Greece: The Beginnings. Pre-Socratics and Concepts of Nature. Lloyd, Early Greek
    Science, chs. 2-4
V. Greek Philosophy and Greek Medicine. Temkin, "Greek Medicine as Science and Craft."
    Lloyd, Early Greek Science, ch. 6. Lloyd, ed., Hippocratic Writings, introduc-
    tions (pp. 9-66).
VI. The Hippocratics and the Hippocratic corpus. Lloyd, Early Greek Science, ch. 5.
    Phillips, Greek Medicine, chs. 3 and 4. Lloyd, ed., Hippocratic Writings,
    "The Oath," "The Canon," "Tradition in Medicine," "Epidemics I and III,"
    "Airs Waters Places," "The Sacred Disease," "The Nature of Man," "Fractures,"
    and "The Heart"
VII. Aristotle, Diocles, Praxagoras and post-Hippocratic Medicine. Botany and Theo-
    phrastus. Lloyd, Early Greek Science, chs. 7-9. Phillips, Greek Medicine, ch.
    5. Lloyd ed., Hippocratic Writings, "The Science of Medicine," "Prognosis,"
    "Aphorisms," "Dreams," "The Seed [and] the Nature of the Child" and "Regimen
    in Acute Diseases." Brock, trans., "Aristotle: Biological Extracts" in Greek
    Medicine: Being Extracts Illustrative of Medical Writers
VIII. Hellenistic Medicine and the Museum of the Ptolemies. Phillips, Greek Medicine,
    ch. 6. Scarborough, Roman Medicine, ch. 2. Lloyd, After Aristotle, chs. 1-2, 6.
IX. The Heritage of Alexandria. Rumors and Dissection. Medical Theories. Wilson,
    "Erasistratus, Galen and the Pneuma"
X. Early Roman Medicine. Italic Traditions. The Etruscans. Scarborough, Roman Medicine,
    ch. 1
XI. Hellenistic Medicine and the Romans. Contacts and Interminglings. A Greek carnifex.
    Temple medicine: Asclepius/Aesculapius. Scarborough, Roman Medicine, ch. 3.
    Phillips, Greek Medicine, ch. 7 and Appendix: The Cult of Asclepius. Smith,
    Hippocratic Tradition, pp. 177-203.
XII. The Late Roman Republic. The Roman Synthesis: Cato, Asclepiades, and Celsus.
    Scarborough, Roman Medicine, ch. 4. Spencer, trans., Celsus: De medicina,
    Prooemium, and Books I and II.
XIII. Roman Imperial Medicine to Galen. Dioscorides and Pharmacology. Soranus and
    Gynecology. Rufus and Aretaeus. Scarborough, Roman Medicine, chs. 5-10.
    Phillips, Greek Medicine, ch. 9. Brock, trans., "Rufus of Ephesus: On the
    Interrogation of the Patient" and "Anatomical Nomenclature."
XIV. Galen and the 'Encapsulation' of Medicine. Brock, trans., Galen: Natural Facul-
    ties, introduction and Book I. Smith, Hippocratic Tradition, pp. 61-178 and
    204-246. Lloyd, After Aristotle, ch. 9. Brock, trans., "Galen: On the Medical
    Sects, for Beginners," "Atomist and Vitalist Schools," "Galen's Religion,"

"Junction of the Optic Nerves," "Why Arteries are Joined to Veins," "On
Anatomical Procedures," "On Prognosis," "How to Detect Malingerers," and
"That the Mental Faculties Follow the Bodily Constitution."

XV. Roman Pharmacology. "Galenism" and Byzantine Medicine. The Western Links.
Edelstein, "Recent Trends in the Interpretation of Ancient Science."
Clagett, "Science in Late Antiquity." Lloyd, After Aristotle, chs. 8 and
10. Brock, trans., "Galen: Search for the Lemnian Seals," and "On Antidotes,"
and "Aetius: Aneurysms" and Fatty Tumours" in Greek Medicine: Being Extracts
Illustrative of Medical Writers...

Further Sources for Greek and Roman Medicine can be found listed in:

Helmut Leitner, Bibliography to the Ancient Medical Authors. Bern/Stuttgart/Vienna:
Hans Huber, 1973
John Scarborough, ed., Society for Ancient Medicine Newsletter, Nos. 3-11 (September,
1978-September, 1983) (Lexington, Kentucky: Society for Ancient Medicine/Univer-
sity of Kentucky [generally biannual]). Each issue has "Publications in Ancient
Medicine" (recent books and articles) and "Supplements to Leitner" (recent published texts and translations of Greek, Roman, and Byzantine medical and related
authors, as well as 'filling in' the holes in the original Leitner [viz. veterinary medicine, medical botany, papyri, Arabic translations of Greek and Roman
authors in medicine, etc.])

Byzantine Medicine   History 595-B   John Scarborough
One semester; offered every sixth semester   Dept. History
                                             University of Kentucky

Books:

J. M. Hussey, ed., _The Cambridge Medieval History_, Vol. IV: _The Byzantine Empire_, Part 2: _Government, Church and Civilisation_. Cambridge: University Press, 1967

Manfred Ullmann, _Islamic Medicine_. Edinburgh: University Press, 1978

Stanley Rubin, _Medieval English Medicine_. New York: Barnes and Noble, 1974

Copies of the following provided as appropriate:

[selections from] Francis Adams, trans., _The Seven Books of Paulus Aegineta_. 3 vols. London: The Sydenham Society, 1844-1847

Robert Renehan, ed. and trans., _Leo the Physician: Epitome on the Nature of Man_. Berlin: Akademie Verlag, 1969 [English translation only]

Georgina Buckler, _Anna Comnena_ (Oxford: Clarendon Press, 1929), ch. 32: "Art and Science"

Pan S. Codellas, "The Case of Smallpox of Theodorus Prodromus," _Bulletin of the History of Medicine_, 20 (1946), 207-215

Demetrios J. Constantelos, _Byzantine Philanthropy and Social Welfare_ (New Brunswick, New Jersey: Rutgers University Press, 1968), ch. 11: "Hospitals"

A. Z. Iskandar, "An Attempted Reconstruction of the Late Alexandrian Medical Curriculum," _Medical History_, 20 (1976), 235-258

Zoltán Kádár, _Survivals of Greek Zoological Illuminations in Byzantine Manuscripts_, trans. by Timothy Wilkinson (Budapest: Akadémiai Kiadó, 1978), Part I, ch. 2: "The Byzantine Heritage of Greek Zoological Literature"

Mary Emily Keenan, "St. Gregory of Nazianzus and Early Byzantine Medicine," _Bulletin of the History of Medicine_, 9 (1941), 8-30

Mary Emily Keenan, "St. Gregory of Nyssa and the Medical Profession," _Bulletin of the History of Medicine_, 15 (1944), 150-161

Georg Ostrogorsky, "Agrarian Conditions in the Byzantine Empire," in M. M. Postan, ed., _Cambridge Economic History of Europe_, Vol. I: _The Agrarian Life of the Middle Ages_ (Cambridge: University Press, 1966), 204-234

Evelyne Patlagean, "Birth Control in the Early Byzantine Empire," in R. Forster and O. Ranum, eds., _Biology of Man in History: Selections from the Annales. Économies Sociétés Civilisations_, trans. by E. Forster and P. N. Ranum (Baltimore: Johns Hopkins Press, 1975), 1-22

Jerry Stannard, "Byzantine Botanical Lexicography," _Episteme_, 5 (1971), 168-187

Owsei Temkin, "Medicine and Greco-Arabic Alchemy," _Bulletin of the History of Medicine_, 29 (1955), 134-153

Owsei Temkin, _Galenism_ (Ithaca, New York: Cornell University Press, 1973), ch. 2: "The Rise of Galenism as a Medical Philosophy"

Owsei Temkin, _The Double Face of Janus and Other Essays in the History of Medicine_ (Baltimore: Johns Hopkins Press, 1977) [various articles reprtd.]

   12: "Studies on Late Alexandrian Medicine, I: Alexandrian Commentaries on Galen's _De sectis ad Introducendos_," _Bulletin of the History of Medicine_, 3 (1935), 405-430

   13: "The Byzantine   Origin of the Names for the Basilic and Cephalic Veins," _XVIIe Congrès International d'Histoire de la Médecine_, Vol. I: _Communications_ (Athens, 1961), 336-339

   14: "Byzantine Medicine: Tradition and Empiricism," _Dumbarton Oaks Papers_, 16 (1962), 97-115

I. Introduction. A Survey of the 'State of Research' in Byzantine Medicine. The Sources. Manuscript Holdings. Language Problems. Ancient, _Koine_, Roman, and Medieval 'Byzantine' Greek. Why Study Byzantine Medicine? Gibbon's _dicta_. Some Western Prejudices and their Origins.

II. The Background and Some Heritages. Galen and Oribasius. The Later Roman Empire.
Christian Education.
   Vogel, "Byzantine Science" (in Hussey, ed., CAMBRIDGE MEDIEVAL HISTORY, IV,
       part 2)
III. Oribasius and his Era. Julian. The "Medical Handbook." Purposes. Some Addi-
tional Sources for Medicine and Zoology in the 4th and 5th centuries. The
Medical backround of the Geoponica and other agricultural/zoological/veteri-
nary sources
   Kadar, "Byzantine Heritage of Greek Zoological Literature"
   Ostrogorsky, "Agrarian Conditions in the Byzantine Empire"
IV. Fifth and Sixth Centuries: Alexander of Tralles, Aetius of Amida, Paul of
Aegina. Medical Practice and Court Life.
   Adams, trans., SEVEN BOOKS OF PAULUS AEGINETA [selections]
V. On the Eve of the Arab Outburst. Alexandria's 'Last Gasp.'
   Temkin, "Studies in Late Alexandrian Medicine, I"
   Iskandar, "Late Alexandrian Medical Curriculum"
VI. Some Military Medicine. Surgery. Procopius. The Veterinarians. Vegetius and
Others.
VII. Byzantine Medicine and the Orthodox Church. Social Implications
   Keenan, "St. Gregory of Nazianzus"
   Keenan, "St. Gregory of Nyssa"
   Patlagean, "Birth Control in the Early Byzantine Empire"
VIII. Medical Theory. Galen Again.
   Temkin, "The Rise of Galenism as a Medical Philosophy" from GALENISM
IX. The Other Side: Islamic Medicine. Translators: ibn-Ishaq and others. Looking
Back to Sergius of Resaina. Christian minorities and Syriac versions.
   Ullmann, MEDICINE, chs. 1-4
X. Islamic Medicine, Astrology, and Alchemy. Drug Lore. The Puzzle of why so little
Indian influence compared with the Byzantine. at-Tabari and The Paradise of
Wisdom. The Inner Reaction: Tibb an-Nabi, "Medicine of the Prophet". The
Mixture of Traditions: Astrology, Alchemy, etc. al-Kindī. Istafan ibn Basīl
and Dioscorides. Toxicology. ibn Wahshīya and his Kitāb al-Sumūm, "Book of
Poisons." Various 'Listings.' al-Kindī and his Aqrabadhīn, "Medical Formu-
lary." Synonymic lists: Moses Maimonides. The Western Linkages.
   Ullmann, MEDICINE, chs. 5-8
   Temkin, "Medicine and Greco-Arabic Alchemy"
XI. Byzantine Medical Botany. Anatomy. What shall we Call It? Nomenclature.
   Stannard, "Byzantine Botanical Lexicography"
   Temkin, "Byzantine...Names for Basilic and Cephalic Veins"
XII. Institutionalized Health Care: Hospitals
   Codellas, "Pantocrator"
   Constantelos, "Hospitals," from BYZANTINE PHILANTHROPY
XIII. 'Saving the Classics:' Constantine Porphyrogenitus. Byzantium and the Cru-
sades. Medical Theory and Practice in the Age of Alexius Comnenus. Medical
Compilations. Corpus hippiatricorum Graecorum and others.
   Buckler, "Art and Science" from ANNA COMNENA
   Codellas, "Case of Smallpox"
   Renehan, trans., LEO THE PHYSICIAN
XIV. Comparative Techniques: Medicine in the Medieval West
   Rubin, ENGLISH MEDICINE, chs. 2-7
XV. The Connections. Byzantine Medicine and the Renaissance. Symeon Seth.
   Temkin, "Byzantine Medicine: Tradition and Empiricism"

CLASSICS 22: GREEK AND ROMAN ATHLETICS   PROFESSOR T. SCANLON
(PHYSICAL EDUCATION 22)   Department of Literatures and
MWF 10:10-11 am   Languages
HUMANITIES 1132   Humanities 3338, office
                                  787-3709
                                  Office Hours: M, W 11-12 or
                                  by appointment

REQUIRED TEXTS:
Gardiner, E.N. Athletics of the Ancient World. (Ares, Chicago: 1980).
Robinson, R.S. Sources for the History of Greek Athletics. (Ares, Chicago: 1979).

OBJECTIVES:
We will survey the origin, development, and techniques of Ancient Greek and Roman athletics in their social and cultural contexts. We will also examine certain topics of ancient athletics with special contemporary relevance, e.g. professionalism, women's role, and politics and sports. Ancient views of competition, the Greek agonistic spirit, and professional vs. amateur interests will be thematic in our study. By close examination of the literary and archaeological evidence, students will better understand athletics as the true mirror of the spirit of a people.

PROCEDURE:
Lectures will draw primarily upon the original sources such as literature, vase paintings, inscriptions, and archaeology of the ancient sites. Slides will often augment these lectures. Class discussion and questions are encouraged.

ASSIGNMENTS:
Required readings as indicated on the Syllabus should be completed before the lecture date for which they are assigned in order to better understand the background and evidence.
Two Quizzes (objective format) will be given: Monday, April 12 and Monday, May 17. The lower (or missed) one will be dropped; no make-ups.
The Midterm exam (Monday, May 3) and the Final (Tuesday, June 8) are required for all. The format will be mostly essay with some objective questions. The Final will be comprehensive.
Those wishing to write a term paper in lieu of a final may do so. Recommended length is 15 pages. Students choosing this option must consult with the professor soon after the midterm, but no later than May 17. Papers will be due on the last day of class, June 4th.

GRADING: % of Final Course Grade
QUIZ (best one of two)... 10%
MIDTERM 30%
FINAL EXAM OR PAPER...... 60%

BOOKS ON RESERVE IN MAIN LIBRARY:
Buchanan, David. Greek Athletics (London)
Buchanan, David. Roman Sport and Entertainment (London, 1976).
Drees, Ludwig. Olympia: gods, artists and athletes (NY/ Washington, 1968).
Finley, Moses, and Pleket, H.W. The Olympic Games: the first thousand years (London, 1976)
Gardiner, E.N. Athletics of the Ancient World (Ox.,1930;repr.Chicago, 1978).
_____. Greek Athletic Sports and Festivals (Oxford, 1910).
Harris, H.A. Greek Athletes and Athletics (Bloomington, 1966).
Harris, H.A. Sport in Greece and Rome (Ithaca, 1972).
Miller, Stephen. Arete: ancient writers, papyri, and inscriptions on the history and ideals of Greek athletics and games (Chicago, 1979)
Robinson, R.S. Sources for the History of Greek Athletics (Chicago, 1979).

CLASSICS 22/PHYSICAL EDUCATION 22   T. SCANLON, INSTRUCTOR
SYLLABUS   SPRING QUARTER, 1982

WEEK.	DATE.	LECTURE TOPIC.	REQUIRED READINGS (G=Gardiner, _AAW_; R=Robinson, _SHGA_)
I.Mar.	29	1. Introduction	
	31	2. The Importance of Sport in Ancient and Modern Societies	G.I.
Apr.	2	3. Sources and Chronology	G.II.
II.	5	4. The Spread of Greek Athletics	R.III.A,B,C,D,I; R.IV.F.
	7	5. Athletics and the Epics	G.III; R.I.A,B,C,D.
	9	6. Footraces	G.IX.
III.	12	7. QUIZ I; Jumping	G.X.
	14	8. Discus and Javeling Throwing	G.XI & XII.
	16	9. Wrestling and Pentathlon	G.XIII & XIV.
IV.	19	10.Boxing and Pancration	G.XV & XVI; R,VII.H & R.III.E.
	21	11.Athletes as Heroes	R.III.G & IV.B.
	23	12.Were Athletes Professionals?	G.VII; R.VII.D & J; R.VIII.D,E,F.
V.	26	13.Stadia, Gymnasia, and Palaestrae	G.IX; R.VI.G.
	28	14.Management and Spectators	R.V.D, VI.E, & VII,I,J,K.
	30	15.Education, Training, and Diets	G.VI; R.VIII.B &IX (esp. sec's.14-58).
VI.May	3	MIDTERM	
	5	16.The Olympic Games, I.	G.XVII; R.II (all).
	7	17. The Olympic Games, II.	
VII.	10	18.Other Panhellenic and Local Festivals	G.IV.
	12	19.Athletics and Politics	R.IV.C sec.6 & IV,D.2.
	14	20.Women and Athletics	R.IV.C sec.3, V.C sec.2 & VII.F.
VIII.	17	21. QUIZ II; Athletics in Art and Literature	G.V
	19	22. Greek Chariot Races and the Hippodrome	
	21	23. Roman Athletics and Society	
IX.	24	24. The Roman Circus	
	26	25. Gladiators and Beast Games	
	28	26. The Colosseum and other Amphitheaters	
X.	31	27. The Roman Bath	
June	2	28. Greek and Roman Athletics Compared	
	4	29. The Modern Olympics and 'Olympism'	

FINAL EXAMINATION June 8th, 11:30-2:30 pm.

146

BIBLIOGRAPHY

I. Books

A. Greek Athletics

1. Drees, L. Olympia: Gods, Artists, and Athletes. N.Y., 1968.

2. Finley, M.I. and Pleket, H.W. The Olympic Games: The First
   Thousand Years. N.Y., 1976.

3. Forbes, C.A. Greek Physical Education. N.Y. 1970 reprint of
   1929.

4. Gardiner, E.N. Greek Athletic Sports and Festivals. Dubuque,
   Iowa, 1970 reprint of 1910 .

5. _____. Olympia: Its History and Remains. Washington,
   D.C., 1973 reprint of 1925.

6. _____. Athletics of the Ancient World. Chicago, 1979
   reprint of 1930.

7. Harris, H.A. Greek Athletes and Athletics. Bloomington, Indiana,
   1966.

8. _____. Sport in Greece and Rome. Ithaca, N.Y., 1972.

9. Juethner, J. Die athletischen Leibesuebungen der Griechen.
   F. Brein, ed. 2 vols. Vienna, 1965.

10. Weiler, I. Der Sport bei den Voelker der alten Welt. Darm-
    stadt, 1981.

11. Weiler, I. Der Agon im Mythos. Darmstadt, 1974.

12. Yalouris, N. The Eternal Olympics. N.Y., 1979 (also appeared
    as The Olympic Games through the Ages with the inclusion of
    chapters on the modern Olympics).

147

I.A. Greek Athletics (cont.)

13. Young, D. The Myth of Greek Amateurism. Chicago, 1983.

B. Roman Athletics

1. Auguet, R. Cruelty and Civilization: The Roman Games. London,
   1972.

2. Bonner, S.F. Education in Ancient Rome. Berkeley and L.A., 1977.

3. Buchannan, D. Roman Sport and Entertainment. London, 1976.

4. Friedlaender, L. Roman Life and Manners under the Early Empire.
   London, 1908-1913.

5. Grant, M. Gladiators. London, 1967.

6. Maehl, E. Gymnastik und Athletik im Denken der Roemer.
   Amsterdam, 1974.

7. Pearson, J. Arena: The Story of the Colosseum. N.Y., 1973.

8. Quinnell, P. Colosseum. N.Y., 1971.

9. Robert, L. Gladiateurs dans l'Orient grec. Paris, 1940.

C. Sourcebooks

1. Berger, M. and Moussat, E. Anthologie des textes sportifs
   de l' antiquité. Paris, 1927.

2. Miller, S.G. Arete: Ancient Writers, Papyri, and Inscriptions
   on the History and Ideals of Greek Athletics and Games.
   Chicago, 1979.

I. C. Sourcebooks (cont.)

3. Piernavija del Pozo, M. "El deporte en la literatura latina (Antalogía)." Citius Altius Fortius 2 (1960):417ff.

4. Robinson, R.S. Sources for the History of Greek Athletics. Chicago, 1979 reprint og 1955.

D. General

1. Huizinga, J. Homo Ludens: A Study of the Play-Element in Culture. Boston, 1955.

2. Marrou, H.I. A History of Education in Antiquity. N.Y., 1956.

II. Articles

1. Ariete, J.A. "Nudity in Greek Athletics." CW 68 (1975):431-436.

2. Booth, A. D. "Roman Attitudes to Physical Educaiion." Échos du Monde Classique. Classical News and Views. 19(1975):27-34.

3. Briggs, W.W. "Augustan Athletics and the Games of Aeneid 5." Arena (=Stadion) 1(1975):267-283.

4. Crowther, N.B. "Weightlifting in Antiquity. Achievement and Training." G&R 24(1977):111-120.

5. Fontenrose, J. "The Hero as Athlete." CSCA 1(1968):73-104.

6. Forbes, C.A. "Crime and Punishment in Greek Athletics." CJ 41(1951/52):169ff.

7. _____. "Accidents and Fatalities in Greek Athletics." Pp.50-59 in Classical Studies in Honor of W.A. Oldfather. Urbana, 1943

II. Articles (cont.)

8. Lucas, J.A. "A History of the Marathon Race, 490 B.C.
     to A.D. 1975." Journal of Sport History 3(1976):120-138.

9. Matthews, V.J. "The Hemerodromoi. Ultra Long-Distance
     Running in Antiquity." CW 68(1974):161-169.

10. Montogomery, H.C. "The Controversy about the Origins of
     the Olympic Games." CW 29(1936):169-174.

11. Pleket, H.W. "Games, Prizes, and Ideology. Some Aspects
     of the History of Sport in the Greco-Roman World." Arena
     (=Stadion) 1(1975):19-89.

12. Willis, W.H. "Athletic Contests in the Epic." TAPA 72
     (1941):392-417.

SELECTED LATIN PASSAGES ON ATHLETICS

1. Virgil _Aeneid_ 5.104-603.

2. Statius _Thebaid_ 6.

3. Lucan _Pharsalia_ 4.590ff.

4. Plautus _Mostellaria_ 149-156.

5. Horace _Carmina_ 3.24.51ff: _Sermones_ 2.2.10ff.

6. Propertius _Carmina_ 3.14.

7. Juvenal _Satira_ 3.68; 6.264, 356, 421.

8. Seneca _Epistulae_ 13, 15, 78, and 80.

9. Tacitus _Annales_ 14.20; _Dialogus_ 10.5.

10. Quintilian _Institutiones oratoriae_ 2.8.

11. Tertullian _De spectaculis_.

Ancient Athletics   Dr.T.Scanlon
Chronology for Greek and Roman Athletics

Dates of Historical Importance   ·   Athletic Dates

GREEK

B.C.

I. Bronze Age, 3rd-2nd millenium
II. Minoan Civilization flourishes   Minoan Bull-leaping
      on Crete, 2200-1450
III. Mycenaean Civilization flourishes, 1400-1120   ·   Funeral Games for Heroes
      "Fall of Troy", 1250 (historical)
                    1184 (traditional)
IV. "Dorian Invasion", 1100-1000 ·
V. Dark Ages 1100-750   Aristocratic Competitions,1100-750
                                                 (hero-,funeral-,victory-games)
   Homer, ca. 750-700   First Olympic Games, 776
VI. Colonization, 750-550 (Croton ca.710)
VII. Archaic Greece 750-479
   "Age of Tyranny",7th-6th c.   Lyric Poetry flourished 6th c.
                                                 (Sappho, Solon, Xenophanes, et al.)
   Peisistratus,560-527   Black-figure pottery, 600-530
                                              Eleans win control of Games from Pisatans,
                                                 c. 570
   Aeschylus, 524-456   Pythagoras born, c.570 (530 to Croton)
   Cleisthenes and democracy,508   Pisistratus founds Panathenaia (quadrennial;
                                                 games, poetry)
                                              "Golden Age of Athletics",550-450
   Ionian Revolt, 499-494   Red-figure pottery, 530-400
   Sophocles, 496-406   Pindar born, 518
   Pericles, 495-429
   Euripides,'485-406
   Greek Persian Wars:
       Marathon, 490
       Salamis, 480
       Plataea, 479
VIII. Classical Greece, 479-399
   Delian League Formed, 477
   Socrates, 469-399
   Ephialtes' Reform of Areopagus, 462
   Temple of Zeus at Olympia, ca.460   Olympia Pedimental Sculpture: Chariot Race
                                                 and Apollo scenes
   Athenian Empire begins, 448   Pindar dies, 438
   "Golden Age of Athens", 450-404   Alcibiades wins at Olympia, 416
                                              Elis invaded by Sparta, 400
                                              First Olympic Bribes, 388
IX. Hellenistic Age, 399-31   Arcadia Invades Elis, 365-364 ·
   Reign of Alexander the Great, 336-323   Aristotle dies, 322
   Roman Flaminius "liberates" Greece
       at Isthmia, 196   First Professional Association of Athletes, c.
   Peloponnesus made a Roman Province, 27

Historical Dates   Athletic Dates

ROMAN

B.C.

I. Roman Regal Period, 753-509   Influence of Etruscan Athletics
Founding of Rome , 753
Etruscans, 650-500
II. Early Roman Republic: Italy united,
     509-264
1st and 2nd Punic Wars, Macedonian Wars,
     264-164
III. Middle Roman Republic: Mediterranean
     Expansion, 264-133
IV. Fall of the Republic, 133-31   Games and Circuses (Ludi et Circenses)
Marius, Sulla, Pompey, and Italic Wars, ca. 120-48
Julius Caesar, 101-44

                                          Herod Presides at Olympia, 12
A.D: V. Republic Ends, Empire Begins with
          Augustus, Julio-Claudians, 31 B.C.-A.D.68
                                          Augustan Games at Naples, A.D. 2
Augustus (1st Emperor) dies, A.D.14   Three Sister Athletes (Delphi), 41-47
Nero Dies, 68   Capitoline Games at Rome
VI. Flavian and Antonine Emperors,
          A.D. 69-192   "Athletic Renaissance" in Roman Empire, 2nd c.
Trajan, 117
Hadrian, 138   Pausanias at Olympia, 160-170
VII. Collapse and Recovery of Rome,
          AD. 193-330   Galen dies, post 200
VIII. Constantinople Est. by Constantine,
          330   Philostratus dies, 245
"Edict of Theodosius", 393   Last Regular Olympics, 261

                                          Phidias' Workshop converted into Church,
                                            c. 400

SAMPLE LECTURE OUTLINES
Lecture .: The Spread of Greek Athletics, Minoan Crete to the Fifth Century B.C.

I. Minoan Civilization on Crete, 2200-1450 B.C.
1. Knossos-palace and main city. King Minos. Minotaur=bull-man.
   Bull in Cretan Myth: Heracles & Cretan Bull, Theseus & Minotaur. King=bull?

2. Evidence for bull sports: bull-leap fresco, Hagia Triad rhyton (=vase with
   4 bands showing boxers and bull-leapers).

3. Boy boxers- Thera (island)fresco.

4. Crete and the Mainland: "Androgeos, son·of Minos, brought athletics to Athens".
   Plato and Aristotle report that nakedness in athletics began with the Cretans.

II. Mycenae. Mycenaean Civilization 1450-1100 T.C.
1. Palace at Mycenae.

2. Chariots.

3. Games: Funeral games
           Marriage competitions
           Competition for succession

4. Religion and social structure: patriarchy

III. Dark Ages: 1100-750. 'Dorian Invasion'
1. Aristocratic competitions: hero-, funeral-, victory-games.

2. Hero worship (Hera- female fertility goddess)

IV. Colonization: 750-550. Colonial and agonal (competitive) man.
    Greeks spread to Asia Minor, Sicily, and Italy.

1. Homer, Iliad book 23, Odyssey book   .
   Il.chariot racing, boxing, wrestling, footrace, javelin, armed combat,
      weight throwing, archery.
   Od.discus, boxing, running, jumping, archery.
Panhellenic games

2. Olympia.
Pelops vs. king of Elis (Oenomaus) to win Hippodameia.
Heracles establishes site. Founds games to Zeus.
Truce of Iphitus(776) of Elis.
Spartan 50 year'dynasty.'
Many victors from colonies; 6 of 12 treasuries at Olympia built by colonial cities.
Games every 4 yrs, in honor of Zeus; prize is olive leaf crown.

3. Pythian Games, at Delphi, N.Greece; est. 582 B.C., to Apollo;quadrennial; laurel crown.

4. Isthmian Games near Corinth & the isthmus, 582, to Poseidon, every 2 yrs.; pine crown.

5. Nemean Games at Nemea, Peloponnesus, 573 est., to Nemean Zeus, every 2 yrs.,parseley cro
   'Circuit Games'- the Big Four or Crown Games. Greatest honor to win all four.

6. Solon, c. 594 B.C. (Rob. p.59f.)- makes law of 500 drachma reward to Oly. winners.
   Solon has dialogue with Anacharsis of Scythia, c. 560, on pros and cons
      of Greek athletics (Rob. 62-78)(source is Lucian of Syria, 125-180 A.D.).

7. C.598-2 B.C. Eleans visit Egyptian King Psammis, discuss Oly. rules (Rob.60-61).

Lecture -

IV. (cont.)
8. Xenophanes denounces athletics as unworthy profession, c. 550–500.
   (Rob. 90.).

9. Local Festivals.
   Prize Games for value prizes: oil, cash, tripods, etc.
   Athens held Panathenaea (All-Athenian) festival on grand scale every
four years. Established 566 B.C. to honor Athena. Prize was vase (amphora)
containing olive oil (6 to 60 per victor; each worth about 6 days wages).
Program had variety: athletics, chariot races, music, poetry contests, torch race,
dance contests, regatta, and a beauty contest.

   Boys began to be included in the 6th century, 17–20 years at Olympia.
'Beardless' category at Nemea, Isthmia, Panathenaea, 12-16 year category.

V. Fifth Century: Classical Greece

1. 'Super Games' of 476 B.C., highpoint of Greek nationalism after 480 defeat of
Persians. Five victory odes by Pindar for the occasion. Greatest Athenian
general, Themistocles, attended. Victors came from all over Greece, Asia Minor,
and Sicily and Italy.

LECTURE : ATHLETICS AND THE EPICS

Primary Sources: Homer's Iliad book 23, and Odyssey, book 8.. (Robinson, ch.I).

I. Occasions: Funeral Games (for Achilles friend, Patroclus). Iliad.
              Fun and Entertainment (arrival of a guest-friend Odysseus). Odyssey.
              Marriage Contest
              Contest for Succession of the King.   In other literature & myths.
              Victory Celebration.
II. The Events: reflect Mycenaean or Homeric times? (1450-1100 or 750 B.C.?)
    Iliad 23: chariot race   Odyssey 8: footrace
              boxing   wrestling
              wrestling   jumping
              footrace   discus throwing
              armed combat   boxing
              discus throwing
              archery
              javelin throwing

III. Procedure of Games
1. Informal gathering of nobles. Achilles presides; challenge made, prizes offered.
   Wise old Nestor advises on strategy. Spectators bet on chariots.

2. Was 'fair play' observed? Note reckless Antilochus vs. Menelaus in chariot race.
   Gods aid or hinder men. Note Ajax caused to slip by Athena in footrace (Il.23).
   Cunning (Odysseus) vs Strength (Ajax) in wrestling.
   Ideals of HONOR: note especially giving of prizes in Iliad chariot race
(Antilochus yields to Menelaus who in turn gives prize back to Antilochus.
Achilles gives old Nestor cup.) In javelin throwing Agamemnon, leader of Greeks,
is given prize out of respect for status.

IV. The Homeric Athlete: ARETE= Greek EXCELLENCE.
Excellence in individuals or races may vary (some specialization):
        Odysseus better in discus, javelin, etc. (upper body strength). More 'Mycenaean'.
        Islànd peoples, Phaiakians, sponsors of games in Od.16, excell in running and
        agility, like Minoans.

Ideal of excellence is same for all: "desire to be best always and excell others"
(Il.6.208;11.784). Competitive spirit is at the basis of Greek excellence.

Achievement in action is essential to win Honor and Glory:
"There is no greater glory than what a man does by hands and feet" (Od.8 .).
Excellence must be proven in deeds.

I. OLYMPIAN DYNASTIES. After Sparta's First Messenian War (735-715)
Messenian 'dominance' ends; 1 victory only 720-369 BC.
Spartan dominance at Olympia, 720-576 BC: 30 victors(672-576), but 9(572-47
"Western Greek" (Italy & Sicily) victories, 648 on.
Athenian victors appear during 7th & late 6th-early 5th c BC.
Rhodes (E. Medit.) strong in 5th c. BC.
Elis intermittently strong. Alexandria (Egypt) strong 1st and 2nd c AD.

II. Importance of Individual Victors. Honor to self, family, city.
Heroization of historical athletes seen in stories about: divine
birth or patronage, remarkable feats as children, impressive
athletic victories, leadership in war, remarkable statues.
Illustrates importance of athletics in politics, war, and religion.

Croton. Famed for victors 596-476 BC. "The last of the Crotoniates
was the first of all the other Greeks." "More healthful than Croton".
Pythagoras- founded city & school of philosophy; religious sect.
MILO- friend of Pythagoras; 7 Ol. wrestling victories (6 Pythian,
10 Isthmian, 9 Nemean). Gustatory feats with chugging wine, eating
bread and meat, carrying and eating ox. Feats of strength: stood
on greased discus, burst headband, grasped pomegranate (all fr.statue?).
"This is the statue of Milo, best among the best, who conquered 7 times
at Olympia without bending a knee." As a soldier led vs. Sybarites
(S. It.) dressed as Herakles.
PHAYLLUS- 3 Pythian victories (482,478);none at Olympia. Fought
with Greeks vs. Persians at Salamis (480), forsaking 480 ol. games.
Honored by Alexander the Great, 150 yrs. later.
ASTYLOS of Croton. 3 Ol. victories, 488-480 (484 &480 as Syracusan).
Dishonored by Croton.

Rhodes (Island in E. Medit.). Family of Diagoras.
DIAGORAS- (Pind. Ol. 7 Ode). Son of Hermes (?). "Immense"(7'4+").
Won Ol. boxing 464 (+ 2 at Nemea, 4 at Isthmia). Statue at Olympia.
DORIEUS (youngest & most famous of 3 sons)-3 pancration at Ol. (432-424)
(8 isth., 7 Pythian).
Diagoras watched sons Acusilaus and Damigetus win in 448 Olympics:
"Long live Diagoras." "Die now Diagoras. There is nothing left for
you but to ascend to Olympus." Dorieus fought for Sparta vs. Athens;
captured by Athens; killed by Spartans.
Sons or Diagoras' daughters also famous: Eucles, Ol. boxing 396,
Peisirodus, boy boxing Ol.388.

THEOGENES of Thasos (Rob.p.105). Ol. boxing 480;lost pancration &
fined for trying. Total 1400 (!) victories. (9Nem., 10 Isthm.).
As boy stole statue, replaced it. Own statue tried for manslaughter,
dropped in sea, fished out, worshipped. Theogenes ("god born")-
son of Heracles (?).
POLYDAMAS of Scotussa-"largest of all human beings, except for heroes
and whatever race existed before heroes"- Pausanias. Won Ol. 408 pancration.
Many athla-"feats" of strength: killed lion near Mt. Olympus;
pulled bull's leg from socket; stopped racing chariot; killed Persian
bodyguards ("The Immortals"); saved companions in cave collapse.
Other notables: GLAUCUS of Carystus (Rob.84). PRAXIDAMUS of Aegina.
HERODORUS of Megara (trumpeter, Ol.328-292, 10 successive);aided
Demetrios Poliorcetes capture Argos. Elite Multiple Victors: Caprus
of Elis (212 Ol. pancr.& wrest.), Aristomenes (Ol.156 box.&panc.),
Leonidas of Rhodes(triple- 4 times: Ol. 164-152:stade, diaul., hoplite).

Olympian "Dynasties" ·   T. Scanlon

City-states which fared well or "dominated" in the Olympic
games at various periods. This list is based on the in-
complete lists of Olympic victors handed down by various
ancient authors. See L. Moretti, <u>Olympionikai</u> and N. Yalouris, ed., <u>The Eternal Olympics</u>, pp.289-296. It is therefore not 100% historically accurate, but does accurately
represent trends in the victories of certain states.

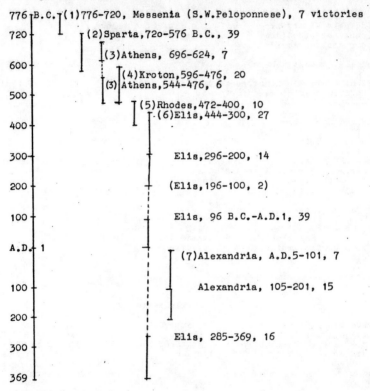

776 B.C. (1)776-720, Messenia (S.W.Peloponnese), 7 victories

720   (2)Sparta,72o-576 B.C., 39

        (3)Athens, 696-624, 7

600   (4)Kroton,596-476, 20
        (3)Athens,544-476, 6

500

        (5)Rhodes,472-400, 10
400   (6)Elis,444-300, 27

300   Elis,296-200, 14

200   (Elis,196-100, 2)

100   Elis, 96 B.C.-A.D.1, 39

A.D. 1

        (7)Alexandria, A.D.5-101, 7

100   Alexandria, 105-201, 15

200

        Elis, 285-369, 16
300

369

157

LEGENDARY ORIGINS OF THE OLYMPIC GAMES
(See Robinson Chapter II for sources)

ELEAN VERSION (Pindar;Strabo;Pausanias)   PISATAN VERSION
                                                            (Phlegon)
1. Zeus vs. Cronos (Olympians in Victory Games)   Zeus
      Zeus + Protogeneia

2. Aëthlius ("sir Sport")   Cretan Heracles of Ida   Peisos of Pisa
. Robinson's 1st Era (1370-1104)(Curetes hold Leisure   (namesake)
                                       Games)

3. ENDYMION of Elis
      (defeats Clymenus──────────── Clymenus of Pisa (1380)
      (sons hold footrace-   (Games for Cr.Heracles)
       succession games)

4. Aetolus (Aetolian Race)   Oenomaus of Pisa

   ┌PELOPS of Lydia (As.Minor) defeats┐ ─ ─ ─ ─ ─ ─ ₤ ─ ─ ─ ─ PELOPS of Lydia
    OENOMAUS in chariot race for daut.   (holds funeral games
   └HIPPODAMEIA: Victory Games to Zeus┘   for Oenomaus)

5. ELEIUS (namesake of ELIS)

6. AUGEAS of Elis

7. HERACLES of Argos (son of Zeus & _ _ _ _ _ _ _ _ _ _ HERACLES of Argos
      Alcemene; cleans Augean stables;   (funeral games for
      conquers Augeas; games to Zeus-   Pelops)
      Victory Games, c. 1230 BC)

   Trojan War, c. 1186 BC

8. OXYLUS (1150 BC) invades Elis with
      "Sons of Heracles"(Dorian Invasion?),
      "Founder of Olympics"-Strabo, by oracle
      rules Elis; Games to Zeus; Elis Neutral.

I. Robinson's 2nd Era of Dark Ages, games lapse
       (late 11th to 10th c BC)

II. Robinson's 3rd Era, Revival or Reorganization.

9. Truce of Iphitus (alone or with Lycurgus   CLEOSTHENES of Pisa
      of Sparta); oracle to avoid plague;   makes SACRED TRUCE
      884 reorganization, 776 1st recorded   WITH IPHITUS of Elis and
      victor (Coroebus) in 28th Olympiad   LYCURGUS of Sparta,
                                                 776 BC (Phlegon)
                                                 -no wreath (apple) 776-
                                                 756 BC: 1st wreat to
                                                 Daicles of Messenia, 752 BC

OTHER PANHELLENIC AND LOCAL FESTIVALS

PYTHIA 1) Python dragon slain by Apollo. Apollo god of light,
reason, music, art.
2) Musical and artistic cotests get special attention: choral
dance, singing, lyre and cithara (stringed instruments), and
flute playing. Muses lived nearby on Mt. Parnassus.
3.) Before 582, every 8 years as music festival.
In 582, reoganized as Panhellenic games, quadrennial with
Olympic program. Local league of 12 tribes took Delphi as
a center and selected tribal reprentatives (hieromnemones)
to organize festival: maintenance, preparations, program,
invitations, etc., like Olympic Hellenodikai.

4) Program- bay leaves crown.
Musical origins seen in festival focus: central competition
was shging hymn to Apollo; other hymn on slaying Python.
Horse and chariot races 2nd in import. Held in Plain of Crisa;
alluded to in Sophocles' Electra (Rob.113-115). Delphi
near horse breeding centers in Thessaly, Macedonia. Bronze
charioteer statue (475BC) at Delphi; 4 horse victory of Polyzalos(?).
Men and boys events in: stade, diaulos, dolichos, pentathlon,
wrestling, boxing, pancration; men only,hoplitodromos.
Musical events first, gymnastic (boys first) second, horse events last.

5) Site: Pre 5th c. all in Plain of Crisa; late 5th c. stadium
above temple of Apollo--remodelled by Herodes Atticus in 2nd c.AD.

ISTHMIA 1) Funeral games for Melicertes by Sisyphos. In honor
of Poseidon (sea god) since 8th c.BC.
2) Location near Corinth "the market of Greece and Asia".
3) Program:crown pine to wild parsely in 5th c BC, to pine in
2nd c BC. Horse events importané, Poseidon "horse breaker".
Horse and chariot racers reverent to"The Benefactor":hippios
diaulos imp. here (4 stades-not at Oly.).
Most varied panhellenic program: women and boys by 1st c AD.
Competitors mostly local. Ship race; painting contest.
Diogenes the Cynic on spectators (Rob.p.138).
Less rigorous program: Solon gave 100 drachmas (vs 500 for Oly. victor).
Athens boycotted during 5th c. due to Corinth-Spartan ties.
4) Political Import: 196 BC "Freedom for Greece"-Flaminimus.
146BC Corinth destroyed; J.Caesar restored games.
Nero competed, proclaimed "freedom" again, proposed a canal.

NEMEA 1)Reorganized 573 BC as Panhellenic games; biennial, July.
Originated from Funeral Games for Opheltes; Heracles vs. Lion there.
Sponsor was town of Cleonai to 460 BC, then Argos.
In honor of Zeus.
2) Program mostly gymnastic: races, 3 heavy events, chariot;
musical and others added later after 300 BC.
Women included by 1st c AD (also at Delphi, Isthmia, Athens).

PANATHENAIC GAMES (at Athens; not Panhellenic)
Began in mid 500's BC by tyrant Peidistratos.
Program widely varied: 25 events by Roman times. Pericles supported.
Classes of competitors: tribal leaders, knights, citizens, "all others".
OTHER LOCAL CONTESTS: at least 20 by Pindar's day (early 5th c);
140 by Roman times in Greek lands. Most modelled on Panhellenic.

THE ROMAN CIRCUS AND CHARIOT RACING

CIRCUS- "circle"; Circus Maximus near Palatine Hill, 329 BC(650 x250 yds);
  Circus of Flamininus in Campus Martius, 221 BC; Circus of Maxentius, 4th c AD
  on Appian Way (530 x 52 yds).
SPINA-"spine", dividing strip; meta- turning post (3 gilded by Claudius in CM).
CARCERES- "cells",starting gates; 1st 429 BC at Rome (cp. aphesis at Olympia).
BREAK LINE- described by Cassiodorus, 6th c AD Xtian writer; to avoid early
convergence.
Lap counters on spina: 7 eggs at CMax. from 174 BC; 33 BC 7 bronzed dolphins.

EVENTS: 2 or 4 horse chariots usual; sometimes 3,6,8, or 10.
Program: 7 laps per race; up to 24 races per day.
First race(pompa) for experienced only; others for novice horses.
Special events: "On foot from the chariot"(pedibus a quadriga)one of 2 riders exits.
    "barback vaulters" (equi desultores)known at Caesar's 46BC games-last lap on foot.
TWELVE CHARIOTS per race, 2 or 4 colors with 2 or 3 chariots each.
THE RACE- Praetor or consul drops napkin to start. Gates pour open.
Turn trickiest. "Fans" (hortatores-"supporters") on foot shouted nika (win!).
Home stretch- "seventh lap" (septima spatio)
PRIZES up to 60,000 sestertii ($15,000), usually 20,000."100 x lawyer's salary"(Juvenal).
Magical incantations used. Curses forbidden in AD 389.
Awards given at end with palms.

ORGANIZATION -"Lords" directed parternerships of FACTIONS (known by color).
Staff maintained stables. Drivers recruited usually from non-citizens.
This was organization under empire, 1st c AD and later.
Earlier, under EARLY REPUBLIC (pre 100 BC) wealthy elite gave games as gifts (munera)
asto the people to gain prestige.
under LATE REPUBLIC (1st c BC) both politicians and wealthy sponsored games
with stables, each with loyal fans.
FACTIONS (factiones) teams known by colors- REDS and WHITES at first (3rd c BC?);
GREENS AND BLUES added 1st c AD. (Domitian added short lived Golds and
Purples late 1st c AD); Blues absorbed Reds, and Greens took over Whites in
mid-2nd c AD. Greens most popular, Blues 2nd in mid 1st c AD.

CHARIOTEERS- monuments of early Xtian era (5th c AD on) have career details.
Gaius Appuleius DIOCLES- known from 2nd c AD inscription: from Spain, career
began in 122 AD for Whites; 128 for Greens; 131 for Reds until 146 retirement.
Drove 4 horse chariot (quadriga): 4257 starts, placed 2900; 1462 fursts;
861 seconds; 576 thirds; one fourth; unplaced 1351 times.
Of his wins: 1064 in singularum; 347 with team of two; 51 with team of 3.
PRIZE MONEY- 1st prizes from 30,000-60,000 sestertii per race; 35,863,120
aggregate ($9 million).
TACTICS and qualities included: "came from rear and won"; "held lead and won";
"won in stretch".

HORSES-best from Spain and Africa, brought on "horse transports" (hippago)
Lists of horses come at end of inscriptions to charioteers: 46 of 74 of Diocles'
are African; best is horse "Olympus" (152 wins). Over 30 adjectives for
horse color names; many horses anmed after mythical heroes(Ajax, Daedalus);
some for character or appearance(Spotty, Bright One, Petulant, Laughing);
some from hppes of owner(victor, Palm-bearer, Flier, Arrow)

Drivers from provinces, mostly slaves and freedmen, but heroes to people.
Drivers bought and traded by faction owners. Successful ones set free.
Most had monuments set up by widows (many accidents- knives in belt).

Sarah B. Pomeroy
Hunter College and the
Graduate School, C.U.N.Y.

The following syllabus has been prepared for the use of students.
Instructors are invited to write to Prof. Sarah B. Pomeroy, Department
of Classical and Oriental Languages, Box 1264, Hunter College, 695 Park Ave.,
New York, N.Y.10021 for free copies of <u>Women in Classical Antiquity:</u>
<u>Four Curricular Modules</u> (Archaic, Classical, Hellenistic, and Roman).
These curricular modules were prepared collaboratively by a Humanities
Institute funded by NEH grant EH 20215-82. The modules are interdisciplinary.
They include suggestions for teaching approaches, films and slides, and
for bibliographic resources.

GREEK WOMEN

INTRODUCTION
  Sources of our knowledge of women in antiquity
    Male orientation of Greek and Roman literature, art, and
    historical data
  The need for interdisciplinary and non-traditional approaches to
  the study of women in antiquity
  Chronological parameters of course .
    Problems with evidence from prehistoric and Bronze Age Greece

ARCHAIC GREECE
  Goddesses in literature and visual arts
    Chthonic and Olympian
    Mother goddesses
    Virginity
  Definitions
    Matriarchy, Patriarchy
    Matriliny, Patriliny
    Monogamy, Polygamy
  Myths of Matriarchy
    Amazons
  Anthropological and historical theories on gender hierarchy
    Historical materialism - Engels
    Myth as history - Bachofen
    Sociobiology
      Dominance/Subordination
    Structural Anthropology
      Nature/Culture
      Domestic/Public
      Incest, Exchange of women
    Theory of "Muted Groups"
  Homeric Epic
    Chronological setting, oral tradition
      Structure of "Homeric society"
    Heroes, heroines
  Homeric Hymn to Demeter
  Hesiod
    Misogyny
    Pandora
    Women in an agricultural society
    Influence of slavery on status of free women
  Iambic poetry
    Semonides
    Archilochus
  Archaic Lyric
    Poets and audience
      Autobiography and lyric tradition

Sappho
    Sappho
        Women's beauty .
Archaic sculpture
    Korai
        Female body as "sign"
Spartan Women
    Sources of our knowledge of Sparta
        Sparta as the "other," as utopia
    Dorian women
        The Code of Gortyn
    Class structure of Spartan women: women in an aristocracy
    Education of Spartan women
    Alcman, Partheneion
        Women's beauty
        Athletics
        Rites of passage
Students' assignments
Homer, Ody. sel., Il. 6
Homeric Hymn to Demeter
Selections from Hesiod, Semonides, Archilochus, Sappho, Alcman
Plut., Lyc. sel.

CLASSICAL ATHENS
    The Status of Women: establishing appropriate criteria
    Political, legal, social, and economic aspects
        Wives, concubines, hetairas, slaves
        Women in a democratic polis
    Private lives
        Demographic data
            Infanticide
    Public Lives
        Religion
            Festivals: Eleusinian Mysteries, Thesmophoria, Panathenaea,
                        Artemis at Brauron
            Priestesses
                Maenadism
            Theater Attendance
    Images of Women in Literature and the Visual Arts
            Psychoanalytic interpretations
        Relationship of images to historical reality
            Impact of Peloponnesian War on women's roles
        Dramatic Literature
        Hippocratic writings on obstetrics and gynecology
        Vase painting and sculpture
Students' assignments
    Plut., Solon sel.
    (Demos.) 59, sel.
    Xen., Oec. sel.
    Lysias, I, sel.
    Aristoph., Lys., Aes., Soph., Eur., sel.
Hippocratic corpus, Diseases of Women, I, Diseases of Young Girls,
On the Nature of the Child, On Seed, sel.

162

WOMEN IN THE FOURTH CENTURY AND IN THE HELLENISTIC WORLD

Public roles
        Queens: Spartan, Macedonian and Ptolemaic
        Non royal women, expanding legal capacities
                Marriage contracts
        Religion: cult of Isis
Private lives
        Cosmopolites
                Alexandrians: women in a monarchy
        Women's Education
                Women in the professions and liberal arts
Women in Litèrature
        Women poets
        Heroines of Novels
        Philosophy, Plato and Aristotle
        Medicine
Women in the Vusual Arts
        Nudity, sexuality
        The artistic canon
Students' assignments
        Papyri and inscriptions, sel.
        Theocritus, Idyll 2 and 15
        Plato, Rep. 5
        Arist., sel. from Pol., Gen. An., Eth Nic.,
        Apollonius of Rhodes, Arg.
        Erinna, Distaff and sel. from other women poets
        Apuleius, Golden Ass. sel.

UNIVERSITY OF OTTAWA HIS 3492: WOMEN IN HISTORY 1981/2

S. Treggiari
D. Angers
A. Lévesque

September 16: Discussion meeting

September 14 and September 21 to November 2: Roman period
(Treggiari)

November 4 to end of January: Middle Ages (Angers)

February - April: Modern period (Lévesque)

1.   Introduction & Roman social structures.

     THEMES

2.   "Patriarchy": _patria_ _potestas,_ _manus_ etc.

3.   Ideas on marriage. The stereotypes of women.

4.   Marriage: who, when, how and what?

     CHRONOLOGICAL SURVEY - I THE REPUBLIC

5.   Changes in the status of women in the 2nd and 1st
     centuries B.C.

6.   Case study 1: Clodia Metelli.

7.   Case study 2: Terentia Ciceronis and Tullia
                    Ciceronis filia.

                    II THE PRINCIPATE

8.   Transition to the Principate. Augustus' legislation:
     the Julian law on adultery and the Julian and Papio-
     Poppaean laws on marriage.

9.   Women of the imperial and aristocratic families.

10-11. Women of other classes. Alternatives to Roman marriage.
        Work and women.

12. Christianisation of the empire and consequent reforms.
     Jesus, Paul, Constantine, Justinian.

UNIVERSITÉ D'OTTAWA UNIVERSITY OF OTTAWA

OTTAWA ONTARIO
CANADA

1981/2

HIS 3492 ROMAN WOMEN - PROVISIONAL PROGRAMME

Monday, Sept. 14: Introduction & Roman social structures.

THEMES

Monday, Sept. 21: "Patriarchy": patria potestas, manus etc.

Monday, Sept. 23: Ideas on marriage. The stereotypes of women.

Wednesday, Sept. 28: Marriage: who, when, how and what?

CHRONOLOGICAL SURVEY - I THE REPUBLIC

 Monday, Oct. 5: Changes in the status of women in the 2nd and 1st
                   centuries B.C.

Wednesday, Oct. 7: Case study 1: Clodia Metelli.

(Monday, Oct. 12: Thanksgiving holiday)

Wednesday, Oct. 14: Case study 2: Terentia Ciceronis and Tullia
                      Ciceronis filia.

II THE PRINCIPATE

Monday, Oct. 20: Transition to the Principate. Augustus' legislation:
                  the Julian law on adultery and the Julian and
                  Papio-Poppaean laws on marriage.

Wednesday, Oct. 22: Women of the imperial and aristocratic families.

Monday, Oct. 26 and
Wednesday, Oct. 28: Women of other classes. Alternatives to Roman
                     marriage. Work and women.

Monday, Nov. 2: Christianisation of the empire and consequent reforms.
                 Jesus, Paul, Constantine, Justinian.

Wednesday, Nov. 11: Short test on the Roman period (10%).

165

UNIVERSITÉ D'OTTAWA UNIVERSITY OF OTTAWA

OTTAWA ONTARIO
CANADA

1981/2

HIS 3492 WOMEN IN HISTORY - ROMAN PERIOD ESSAYS

Write an essay (about 10 typed pages) on one of the following topics:

1) How much power could be exercised by an exceptional woman in Rome?

2) Analyse, with reference to several literary works, the double standard of Roman sexual morality.

3) Would you rather have been Tullia daughter of Cicero, or a slave hairdresser on the staff of a lady of the Julio-Claudian family?

Bibliographical suggestions for beginning research:

1) Balsdon, Pomeroy, Rutland.

2) Cicero, Pro Caelio (On behalf of Caelius), R.I. Frank, Hopkins Population Studies 18, Townend.
c.f. Keith Thomas 'The Double Standard' (Journal of the History of Ideas 20 (1959) 195

3) On Tullia: Balsdon, Oxford Classical Dictionary, Cicero's letters passim. On working women and slaves: Pomeroy; Rawson; Treggiari, 'Domestic staff at Rome in the Julio-Claudian period' (Social History/ Histoire sociale 6 (1973) 240-255; 'Jobs in the household of Livia' (Papers of the British School at Rome 43 (1975) 48-77; 'Jobs for women' (American Journal of Ancient History 1 (1976) 76-104.

166

THE ENVIRONMENTAL HISTORY OF THE ANCIENT MEDITERRANEAN WORLD

Course Outline

J. Donald Hughes, Professor of History, University of Denver
Denver, CO 80208

The relationship of human beings to the natural environment of the earth from the
earliest times to the fall of the Roman Empire. The influences of environment on
civilizations; human impact on the ecological balance of the earth; changing
attitudes toward nature; understanding of ecological processes.

Subjects for Reading, Lecture, and Discussion:

1. The general subject of the relationship of environment with civilization.
    Definition of ecology. Differences between the ancient and modern worlds.

2. The ecosystems of the Mediterranean. Climate and climatic change, geology,
    hydrology, animals and plants, life zones.

3. Early prehistory. The evolution of human beings. Hunting as a way of life;
    the ethos of the hunter. Gathering; fishing. Evidence from art and
    comparative anthropology of early attitudes toward the environment.

4. Later prehistory. The origins of agriculture and pastoralism. Domestication.
    Attitudes of neolithic farming people, and their impacts on the environment.

5. The rise of civilization in Mesopotamia. Impacts of larger concentrations of
    population. New attitudes: the conquest of nature; imposition of order on
    chaos. Gilgamesh and Enkidu: city and wilderness; the Cedars of Lebanon.

6. Egypt and the natural environment. Hydraulic civilization. The gods and
    nature. Naturalism in art; celebration of nature in literature.

7. Persia. The sacredness of the elements. Why did a nation with an "ecological"
    religion still ruin its environment?

8. Ancient Israel. Old Testament attitudes to the natural world. Ecology and
    the religious law. The meaning of "dominion."

9. Early Greek religious attitudes toward the natural environment. Gods of nature.
    Sacred groves and other sacred places. Reciprocity and environmental ethics.

10. Greek attitudes to nature. Poetic and artistic treatments. The natural
    philosophers and the rational treatment of nature. Hippocrates and
    environmental determinism.

11. Pythagoras and reverence for life. An organic, cyclical view of the world.
    The divorce of soul and body/nature.

12. Plato, Aristotle, and Theophrastus. The debate over _telos_ and the human place
    in nature. Theophrastus' ecological philosophy.

13. The impact of Greek civilization on the natural environment. Deforestation, erosion. Hunting. Mining. Grazing, agriculture. City planning. War.

14. Roman traditional attitudes to nature. Love of the land; religion. Celebrations of natural beauty. .

15. Roman philosophical views. Stoics, Epicureans. Cicero. Pragmatism.

16. The impact of Roman civilization on the natural environment. Technology. The arena and extinctions. Hunting as a sport. Mining, forestry. Agriculture. Architecture and city planning. The military influence.

17. Ecological reasons for the fall of Rome. Climate, plague. Exhaustion of forests, soils, metals. Lead poisoning. Pollution. "Triumphalism."

18. The end of the ancient world. Christian attitudes: stewardship and the desacralization of nature. Dominion. Love of nature. Creation and creator.

19. The onset of the middle ages. Monasticism and world-denial. Lynn White's "The Historical Roots of Our Ecologic Crisis." St. Francis of Assisi and St. Benedict of Nursia.

20. The ancient roots of our ecological crisis. What can the modern world learn from the ancient experience?

READINGS:

The instructor has written the only book that covers exactly this subject and period. This is J. Donald Hughes, Ecology in Ancient Civilizations (Albuquerque: University of New Mexico Press, 1975). Supplementary studies can be found in his "The Environmental Ethics of the Pythagoreans," Environmental Ethics 3 (1980): 195-213, and "Gaia: Environmental Problems in Chthonic Perspective," Environmental Review 6 (1982): 92-104.

Also very helpful, but out of print, is Ellen Churchill Semple, The Geography of the Mediterranean Region: Its Relation to Ancient History (New York: Henry Holt, 1931). On ancient attitudes to nature, one should consult the early chapters of Clarence J. Glacken, Traces on the Rhodian Shore (Berkeley: University of California Press, 1967). Also Henry Rushton Fairclough, Love of Nature among the Greeks and Romans (New York: Longmans Green, 1930).

Following is a selected list of books that elucidate particular subjects within ancient environmental history or which, while more general, contain sections that deal with the subject.

BIBLIOGRAPHY

I. Ancient Texts.

Aelian, De Natura Animalium
Aristotle, Historia Animalium, Meteorologica, Politics
Cato, De Agricultura
Columella, De Re Rustica
Dio Chrysostom, Euboean Discourse
Hesiod, Works and Days
Hippocrates, Airs, Waters, Places
Hymn, Homeric, to Aphrodite, to Earth
Hymns, Orphic
Pausanias
Plato, Critias 111B-D
Pliny the Elder, Natural History
Plutarch, Moralia, Gryllus: Whether Beasts are Rational, Whether Land or Sea
    Animals are Cleverer
Strabo
Theophrastus, De Causis Plantarum, Historia Plantarum
Varro, De Re Rustica
Vergil, Georgics
Vitruvius, De Architectura
Xenophon, Cynegeticus, Oeconomicus

II. Modern Works.

Angel, J. Lawrence. "Ecology and Population in the Eastern Mediterranean."
    World Archaeology 4, 1 (June 1972): 88-105.

Bradford, John. Ancient Landscapes in Europe and Asia. London: G. Bell
    and Sons, 1957.

Cary, Max. The Geographic Background of Greek and Roman History. Oxford:
    Clarendon, 1949.

Davies, Oliver. Roman Mines in Europe. Oxford: U. Press, 1935.

Drewitt, Bruce. "Ecological Factors in the Rise of Civilization." Kroeber
    Anthropological Society Papers, No. 27 (Fall 1962): 1-26.

Goulandris, Niki A., and Goulimis, C.M. Wild Flowers of Greece. Ed. by
    W.T. Stearn, Kifissia, Greece: Goulandria Natural History Museum, 1968;
    reprint ed., New York: Academic Press, 1969.

Hughes, J. Donald. "Deforestation, Erosion, and Forest Management in Ancient
    Greece and Rome," in collaboration with J.V. Thirgood, Journal of Forest
    History 26 (April 1982): 60-72.

Hughes, J. Donald. "Early Greek and Roman Environmentalists." The Ecologist 11
    (January 1981): 24-35.

Levine, Louis D., ed. <u>Man in Nature: Historical Perspectives on Man in His Environment</u>. Toronto: Royal Ontario Museum, 1975.

Lowry, S.T. "The Classical Greek Theory of Natural Resource Economics." <u>Land Economics</u>. Vol. 41, No. 2 (August 1965): 292-98.

Meiggs, Russell. <u>Trees and Timber in the Ancient Mediterranean World</u>. Oxford: Clarendon Press, 1982.

Mikesell, Marwin W. "The Deforestation of Mt. Lebanon." <u>Geographic Review</u> 59 (1969): 1-28.

Moule, C.F.D. <u>Man and Nature in the New Testament</u>. London: Athlone, 1964.

Pollard, John. <u>Birds in Greek Life and Myth</u>. London: Thames and Hudson, 1977.

Polunin, Oleg and Huxley, Anthony. <u>Flowers of the Mediterranean</u>. Boston: Houghton Mifflin, 1966.

Rostovtzeff, Michael. <u>The Social and Economic History of the Hellenistic World</u>. 3 vols. Oxford: Clarendon Press, 1941.

Rostovtzeff, Michael. <u>The Social and Economic History of the Roman Empire</u>. 2nd ed., 2 vols. Oxford: Clarendon Press, 1957.

Scully, Vincent. <u>Earth, the Temple, and the Gods: The Greek Sacred Architecture</u>. New Haven: Yale, 1968.

Smith, Catherine Delano. <u>Western Mediterranean Europe: A Historical Geography of Italy, Spain, and Southern France Since the Neolithic</u>. New York: Academic Press, 1979.

Soutar, George. <u>Nature in Greek Poetry: Studies Partly Comparative</u>. London: Oxford University Press, 1939.

Thirgood, James V. <u>Man and the Mediterranean Forest: A History of Resource Depletion</u>. New York: Academic Press, 1981.

Thomas, William L., Jr., ed. <u>Man's Role in Changing the Face of the Earth</u>. Chicago: University of Chicago Press, 1956.

Tozer, Henry Fanshawe. <u>A History of Ancient Geography</u>. 2nd ed. Cambridge: Cambridge University Press, 1897; reprint ed., New York: Biblo & Tannen, 1964.

Ward-Perkins, J.B. <u>Cities of Ancient Greece and Italy: Planning in Classical Antiquity</u>. New York: Braziller, 1974.

Vita-Finzi, Claudio. "Roman Dams in Tripolitania." <u>Antiquity</u> 35 (1961): 77-95.

R. Sealey   University of California,Berkeley   Winter 1979

History 280A: Sparta from the beginnings until 371

The class will meet once a week for about two hours each time to discuss the topics in the following list. No papers will be presented on the first two topics; each participant should write papers on two of the remaining topics.

1. Early accounts of Sparta

Herodotus 1. 65-68; 6. 56-60; 7. 204; 8. 131
Thucydides 1. 18. 1; compare Herodotus 1. 65-66
Xenophon: Constitution of the Lacedaemonians; with 1. 7-9 compare
    Polybius 12. 6b. 8
Aristotle: Politics 2. 9. 1269b29 - 1271b19
Aristophanes: Lysistrata 74-253
Plato: Laws 3. 682e-694a

  On artistic work attention is drawn to R. M. Cook: "Spartan History and Archaeology," CQ. NS. 12 (1962) 156-158

"Early" means before the reformers of the third century B.C. corrupted the tradition. A question worth bearing in mind is, how did the Athenians picture the Spartans ?

2. The conquests of Laconia and Messenia

Tyrtaeus fr. 4 (Diehl, third edition)
Pausanias 2. 24. 7; 3. 2; 3. 3; 3. 7. 4; 4. 4-23
Plutarch, Moralia 194b = regum et imperatorum apophthegmata 23
G. H. Huxley: Early Sparta (London 1962) 13-36, 53-60
W. G. Forrest: A History of Sparta 950-192 B.C. (London 1968) 28-39, 69-78
H. T. Wade-Gery: Cambridge Ancient History 3. 537-538
H. T. Wade-Gery: "The Rhianos-Hypothesis'," Ancient Society and Institutions = Studies presented to Victor Ehrenberg (ed. E. Badian) 289-302
F. Jacoby: Die Fragmente der griechischen Historiker III a (Kommentar) 112-119
T. Kelly: "Did the Argives defeat the Spartans at Hysiae in 669 B.C.?" American Journal of Philology 91 (1970) 31-42

3. The "Great Rhetra": authenticity and intent

Plutarch: Life of Lycurgus, especially 6-7
H. T. Wade-Gery: "The Spartan Rhetra in Plutarch, Lycurgus VI," CQ. 37 (1943) 62-72; 38 (1944) 1-9, 115-123 = Essays in Greek History (Oxford: Blackwell 1958) 37-85
A. Andrewes: Probouleusis (Inaugural Lecture, Oxford 1954), or idem: The Greek Tyrants (London 1956) 66-77
L. H. Jeffery: Historia 10 (1961) 145-147
W. G. Forrest: The Date of the Lykourgan Reforms at Sparta, Phoenix 17 (1963) 157-179
W. G. Forrest: A History of Sparta 40-68
G. L. Huxley: Early Sparta 37-52
N. G. L. Hammond: "The Lycurgean Reform at Sparta," Journal of Hellenic Studies 70 (1950) 42-64 = Studies in Greek History (Oxford 1973) 47-103
A. M. Snodgrass: "The Hoplite Reform and History," JHS. 85 (1965) 110-122
J. Salmon:"Political Hoplites ?" JHS 97 (1977) 84 - 101

It is suggested that questions about tribes and obes be avoided.

. The origins of the Peloponnesian League

Herodotus 1. 65–70; 1. 82; 1. 141; 1. 152–153; 3. 39–59; 5. 90–93
Thucydides 1. 18 .1; 2. 9
Pausanias 7. 1. 8
Plutarch: On the Malignity of Herodotus 21 = Moralia 859c–d
H. T. Wade-Gery: CAH. 3. 565–569
J. A. O. Larsen: "Sparta and the Ionian Revolt," Classical Philology
    27 (1932) 136–150
idem: "The Constitution of the Peloponnesian League," CP. 28 (1933)
    257–276; 29 (1934) 1–19
D. M. Leahy:The Bones of Tisamenus," Historia 4 (1955) 26–38`
G. E. M. de Ste. Croix: The Origins of the Peloponnesian War (Ithaca 1972)
    105–123

5. Cleomenes I and policy towards Persia

Herodotus 1. 141; 1. 152–153; 3. 39–56; 4. 148; 5. 49–51; 5. 62–96;
    6. 49–51; 6. 61–82; 6. 84; 6. 106; 6. 108; 6. 120; 7. 133–137
J. Wells: "The Chronology of the Reign of Cleomenes I," JHS. 25 (1905)
    193–203 = Studies in Herodotus (Oxford: Blackwell 1923) 74–94
D.   Hereward: "Herodotus vi. 74," Classical Review, NS. 1 (1951) 146
W. P. Wallace: "Kleomenes, Marathon, the Helots, and Arkadia," JHS.
    74 (1954) 32–35
K. J. Beloch. Griechische Geschichte II (second edition), 1 (Strassburg
    1914) 40 note 6
W. G. Forrest: A History of Sparta 85–93
G. L. Huxley: Early Sparta 77–96

6. Spartan dealings with other Peloponnesian states ca. 478–456

Herodotus 6. 75–83; 9. 35
Aristotle: Politics 5. 1303a6–8
Diodorus 11. 54. 1; 11. 65
Thucydides 1. 101–103; 1. 128–138; 2. 27; 3. 54; 4. 70
Xenophon: Hellenica 5. 2. 3
Plutarch: Kimon 16–17
Strabo 8. 3. 2. 336–337
W. P. Wallace: as for topic 5
A. Andrewes: "Sparta and Arcadia in the Early Fifth Century," Phoenix
    6 (1952) 1–5
W. G. Forrest: "Themistokles and Argos," CQ. NS. 10 (1960) 221–241
A. W. Gomme: A Historical Commentary on Thucydides I (Oxford 1945) 401–408
D. M. Lewis: "Ithome Again," Historia 2 (1953–54) 412–418
D. W. Reece: "The Date of the Fall of Ithome," JHS. 82 (1962) 111–120
G. A. Papantoniou: "Once or Twice ?" AJP. 72 (1951) 176–181

7. The powers of the kings, the Gerousia and the assembly

Herodotus 5. 39–40; 5. 74–75; 6. 49–73
Thucydides 1. 67–87; 1. 118–125; 1. 128–134
Xenophon: Hellenica 3. 3; 5. 2. 11–24
A. Andrewes: "The Government of Classical Sparta," Studies presented
    to Victor Ehrenberg 1–20
G. E. M. de Ste. Croix: The Origins of the Peloponnesian War 126–131
U. Kahrstedt: Griechisches Staatsrecht I: Sparta und seine Symmachie
    (Göttingen 1922) 119–143
C. G. Thomas: "On the Role of the Spartan Kings," Historia 23 (1974)
    257–270
G. Dickens: "The Growth of Spartan Policy," JHS. 32 (1912) 1–42

8. The Spartan share in the outbreak of the Peloponnesian War

Thucydides 1; 7. 18
D. W. Kagan: The Outbreak of the Peloponnesian War (Ithaca 1969) 345-374
G. E. M. de Ste. Croix: The Origins of the Peloponnesian War 1-5, 50-63, 180-210, 290-292
C. Fornara: "Plutarch and the Megarian Decree," Yale Classical Studies 24 (1975) 213-228
T. E. Wick: "Thucydides and the Megarian Decree," L' Antiquité Classique 46 (1977) 74-99

9. The navarchy and Spartan naval enterprise in the Peloponnesian War

Thucydides 2. 66; 2. 80-94; 3. 15-16; 3. 26-33; 3. 69; 3. 76-81; 4. 2; 4. 8. 2; 4. 11. 2; 8. 1-20; 8. 29; 8. 31-33; 8. 38-44; 8. 78; 8. 83-85
Xenophon: Hellenica 1. 1. 1-26; 1. 1. 32; 1. 5; 1. 6; 2. 1
K. J. Beloch: "Die Nauarchie in Sparta," Rheinisches Museum 34 (1879) 117-130
idem: Griechische Geschichte II (second edition) 2 (Strassburg 1916) 269-289
G. Busolt and H. Swoboda: Griechische Staatskunde II (München 1926) 715-716
W. Judeich: Kleinasiatische Studien (Marburg 1892) 107-112
L. Pareti: "Ricerche sulla potenza marittima degli Spartani e sulla cronologia dei Navarchi," Memorie della Reale Accademia di Torino, Serie seconda, Tomo 59 (1909), Scienze morali, storiche e filologiche 83-95

It is advisable not to take the study beyond 404.

10. Spartan politics and policies 405-371

Xenophon: Hellenica 2. 4. 24-43; 3. 1. 1 – 3. 3. 4; 3. 4. 1 – 3. 5. 25; 4; 5; 6. 1. 1 – 6. 4. 19
C. D. Hamilton: "Spartan Politics and Policy, 405-401 B.C.," AJP. 91 (1970) 294-314
D. G. Rice: "Agesilaus, Agesipolis, and Spartan Politics, 386-379 B.C.," Historia 23 (1974) 164-182
G. L. Cawkwell: "Agesilaus and Sparta," CQ. NS. 26 (1976) 62-84
R. E. Smith: "The Opposition to Agesilaus' Foreign Policy," Historia 2 (1953-54) 274-288
H. W. Parke: "The Development of the Second Spartan Empire," JHS. 50 (1930) 37-79

Kurt A. Raaflaub
Department of Classics, Box 1935
Brown University, Providence, RI 02912

CLASSICS 136 (HISTORY 104)

THE DISCOVERY OF FREEDOM IN ANCIENT GREECE

A. COURSE DESCRIPTION

M.I. Finley reminded us of an often neglected fact: "Freedom...is a concept which had no meaning and no existence for most of human history; it had to be invented finally, and that invention was possible only under very special circumstances." We shall take this statement as a point of departure and try to follow and understand the emergence and development of one of the most important and influential, most highly praised and widely abused political concepts of western civilization. Especially in the United States and in view of the historical developments in our century and even the last decades, the significance of the subject does hardly need further justification. However, there does, at present, not exist a satisfactory modern scholarly work on this subject in the English language. The course will therefore offer a fascinating "discovery trip" into new territory, where the participants, by using the ancient sources, can find their own answers to our common questions and check their validity in our common discussions. It will be a combination of a lecture course and a seminar, the success of which will depend heavily on the regular and careful preparation and the active participation of every single student.

The course will deal mainly with the following range of questions: Why did the Near-Eastern and Aegean societies of the third, second and early first millenium B.C. not know the concept of political freedom -- despite their high degree of organization and their developed civilization? What general conditions made it possible to develop such a concept in Greece; when and under what specific circumstances was it finally developed? How, why and when was the concept, once it was discovered, differenciated and further developed? What was the range of meanings, what was the significance of and were the limitations on the concept, how was it used and how did it relate to other political concepts, when it finally entered the unbroken tradition of western political thought?

Accordingly, after the discussion of methodological and theoretical questions, we shall take a close look at the conditions that prevented a high estimation of freedom in archaic Greece. We shall then focus on the fifth century B.C. during which most of the important terminological developments occurred. We shall, on one hand, study the discovery of the concept of "external freedom", i.e. the freedom of the political community from the rule of another power, and the emergence of related concepts, such as "autonomy" and "self-sufficiency". We shall, on the other hand, investigate how the Greeks discovered and defined the freedom of the citizen within his community as opposed to the oppression by a tyrant or an oligarchy, how they linked this concept with democracy, and what aspects became especially important there (e.g. "freedom of speech"). Furthermore, it will be of special interest to follow the development of freedom from a term of highest value (which it in some ways always remained) to a slogan of political propaganda and ideology which could be almost depleted of its original content and used for the justification of its opposite: oppression and enslavement.

On the side of practical politics, a natural terminal point for these developments can be

174

found in the Peloponnesian War at the end of the fifth century B.C., or in the battle of Chaeronea in the second half of the fourth century; on the side of political theory and philosophy, in Plato's major works and especially in Aristotle's *Politics*. At the end of the course, we shall briefly look at the way these two authors deal with the problem of freedom, trace some important aspects of the development of our concept in the 4th century, and compare the results of our investigation with the meaning and function of freedom in Republican and Imperial Rome. Such a comparison will help to understand even more clearly the specific characteristics of the Greek concept and bring out some additional aspects which became very important in the later development of the concept in western (including Christian) thought.

The methodology to be used in the course is based on recent theoretical and methodological discussion among modern historians of political concepts and ideas (especially in Germany where it is called *Begriffsgeschichte* and has emerged as a historical discipline of its own right). The theory which is by now widely accepted at least as a fruitful and in many cases very successful working hypothesis, says that significant changes in the social and political structure and experience of a given society are mirrored in significant changes in the ways in which this society thinks and expresses itself. This leads to changes and adaptations in the political and social terminology which, in turn, can again influence the thought, political and social behaviour and structure of this society. There is, accordingly, a clear and recognizable interaction between the development of terminology and society; to grasp the exact meaning of words in their contemporary setting not only depends on a clear understanding of the social and political context but, in turn, also contributes to the study of social and political conditions. The investigation of social and political terms, therefore, is an integral part of social and political history.

The course will, therefore, try to understand the development of the terminology in the area of political freedom (i.e. of the main term *eleutheros, eleutheria* and of a broad range of related, opposed and supplementary terms which help to define and limit the meaning of freedom) entirely on the basis of the contemporary evidence and in close connection with their social and political background. The course will be devoted mainly to discussion and historical interpretation of those writings (or passages in writings) of ancient authors which contain the relevant terms or deal with problems that are important for their understanding. Herodotus, Thucydides, some tragedies of Aeschylus and and Euripides, a few comedies of Aristophanes, Pseudo-Xenophon's and Aristotle's *Constitution of the Athenians* and the latter's *Politics,* supplemented by a handout with a large collection of excerpts from Homer through lyric and tragic poetry to Xenophon, the Attic orators and philosophers of the fourth century, will form the main bulk of the assigned readings. On the basis of the evidence found in these sources, we shall discuss the most important problems and the answers found by the participants in their own preparation. In order to facilitate your preparation the course syllabus contains not only the list of required readings but also a number of questions: these will help you to focus on, and think about, essential problems that will be discussed in class.

This is not a course on Greek history in general; rather, it follows one important problem through Greek history. It is essential, therefore, that the students be familiar from the beginning with the main events, institutions, terms and names of Greek history; otherwise they will not be able to participate properly in our discussions. Students who do not have such knowledge of Greek history are requested to acquire it by themselves by studying the textbook; at the beginning of the course and of each part of the program a discussion section will be scheduled to answer questions and discuss matters of general importance.

The following *list of topics* will be covered by the course:

175

I.   Historical, theoretical and methodological foundations

II. Homer, Hesiod and early archaic society: a world lacking the concept of political free-
     dom

III. The crisis of the archaic world and the discovery of political "slavery"
        a) Solon, the problem of debt-slavery and the codification of law
        b) Tyranny, the crisis of aristocracy and the emergence of a new society

IV. The Persian Wars and the discovery of the concept of political freedom
        a) The Persian empire, the Greek cities and the discovery of freedom
        b) The breakdown of tyranny and the emergence of freedom of the citizen
        c) Religion and politics: the cult of Zeus the Liberator

V.   The Athenian empire, the power-struggle between Greek cities, and the abuse of an
     ideal
        a) From confederate freedom to imperial tyranny: Athens' rule in the Aegean
        b) The discovery of the concept of "political autonomy"
        c) The freedom of the imperial city: "No one is free but Zeus"
        d) The propagandistic abuse of an ideal: domination for the sake of freedom and
           liberation for the sake of domination

VI. Freedom and democracy
        a) Freedom, democracy and oligarchy
        b) Democratic freedom: content, meaning and reality
        c) "Freedom of speech": the discovery of a human right

VII. Outlook: Freedom in political life and political philosophy of the fourth century B.C.
     and beyond
        a) Common peace and the last struggle for freedom
        b) Plato's and Aristotle's views on political freedom
        c) Freedom as a political idea at Rome: a comparison with the Greek concept

B. REQUIRED READING AND BIBLIOGRAPHY

Ancient Sources:

Aeschylus, *Prometheus Bound and other Plays* (including *Suppliant Women, Seven Against
        Thebes, Persians:* Penguin)
Aristotle, *The Politics* (Penguin, rev. ed. 1981)
Aristotle, *The Athenian Constitution* (Penguin)
Euripides, *Orestes and Other Plays* (incl. *Children of Heracles, Andromache, Suppliants,
        Phoenician Women, Iphigenia in Aulis:* Penguin)
Herodotus, *The Persian Wars* (Modern Library)
Hesiod,   *Theogony; Works and Days* (Johns Hopkins)
Plato, *The Republic*
Plutarch, *The Rise and Fall of Athens* (incl. the Lives of Solon, Themistocles, Aristides,
        Cimon, Pericles, Lysander: Penguin)
Thucydides, *The Peloponnesian War* (Penguin)
Handout: Selections from Homer through the 4th cent. (see part E below)

Textbook: M. Rostovtzeff, *Greece* (ed. E. J. Bickerman)

176

BIBLIOGRAPHY

A.W.H. Adkins, *Moral Values and Political Behaviour in Ancient Greece*, 1972 (pb)
--------------, *Merit and Responsibility. A Study in Greek Values*, 1960 (repr. 1975, pb)
M. Amit, *Great and Small Poleis. A Study in the Relations between the Great Powers and the Small Cities in Ancient Greece*, 1973
M. Austin and P. Vidal-Naquet, *Economic and Social History of Ancient Greece: An Introduction*, 1977 (pb)
J.M. Balcer, *The Athenian Regulations for Chalkis. Studies in Athenian Imperial Law*, 1978
-----------, Sparda by the Bitter Sea. Imperial Interaction in Western Anatolia, 1984.
A.R. Burn, *Persia and the Greeks: The Defense of the West*, 1962
---------, The Lyric Age of Greece, 1960 (pb, 1968)
W.R. Connor, *The New Politicians of Fifth-Century Athens*, 1971
W. Donlan, *The Aristocratic Ideal in Ancient Greece*, 1980
V. Ehrenberg, *The Greek State*, 1960
M.I. Finley, *Early Greece: The Bronze and Archaic Ages*, 1970 (pb)
-----------, *The World of Odysseus*, 2nd ed. 1977 (pb)
-----------, *The Ancient Economy*, 1973 (pb)
-----------, *Ancient Slavery and Modern Ideology*, 1980 (pb)
-----------, *Economy and Society in Ancient Greece*, 1980 (pb)
-----------, *Politics in the Ancient World*, 1983 (pb)
W.G. Forrest, *The Emergence of Greek Democracy 800 - 400 B.C.* (pb)
H. Frankfort (ed.), *The Intellectual Adventure of Ancient Man*, 1946 (pb)
S.C. Humphreys, *Anthropology and the Greeks*, 1978
A.H.M. Jones, *Athenian Democracy*, 1957 (pb)
D. Kagan, *The Outbreak of the Peloponnesian War*, 1969
P. Karavites, *Capitulations and Greek Interstate Relations. The Reflection of Humanistic Ideals in Political Events*, 1982
D.M. Lewis, *Sparta and Persia*, 1977
A. Lintott, *Violence, Civil Strife and Revolution in the Classical City*, 1981
R. Meiggs, *The Athenian Empire*, 1972 (pb)
O. Murray, *Early Greece*, 1983 (pb)
M. Ostwald, *Nomos and the Beginnings of the Athenian Democracy*, 1969
---------, *Autonomia. Its Genesis and Early History*, 1982 (pb)
T.T.B. Ryder, *Koine Eirene, General Peace and Local Independence in Ancient Greece*, 1965
G.E.M. de Ste. Croix, *The Origins of the Peloponnesian War*, 1972
--------------------, *The Class Struggle in the Ancient Greek World*, 1981
A. Snodgrass, *Archaic Greece*, 1984 (pb)
C.G. Starr, *The Economic and Social Growth of Early Greece, 800-500 B.C.*, 1977 (pb)
D. Whitehead, *The Ideology of the Athenian Metic*, 1977
C. Wirszubski, *Libertas as a Political Idea at Rome during the Late Republic and Early Principate*, 1950

C. EXAMS AND PAPERS

2 short papers: c. 5 pp. each;
Termpaper (topic of free choice) or final paper (selection of given topics): c. 10-15 pp.
Occasionally written homework assignments

177

D. SYLLABUS

1. HISTORICAL AND METHODOLOGICAL INTRODUCTION
Purpose and organization of the course
Requirements, demands, exams, history section
The sources
Definitions and terminology
Historical foundation

I. EARLY ARCHAIC SOCIETY: A WORLD LACKING THE CONCEPT OF POLITICAL FREEDOM

2. I.1. The heroic world of the Iliad

Readings: Handout no.1, 3-5, 7-9, 11-15, 18, (72)
Rostovtzeff, Greece, *16-71*

Questions: 1. In what form, when and concerning whom does the idea of freedom occur? What is the content of freedom; what does its loss mean to those affected by it?
2. What is the character of wars, for what do people fight wars, what is the result for the winners and the losers? In what ways is freedom concerned here? Is the concept of "freedom of the community" developed at all?
3. What is the value system of this society? What are the foundations of social prestige? What role could freedom play in this system?

NOTE: History section (time to be determined)

3. I.2. The domestic world of the Odyssey

Readings: Handout no. 2, 6, 10, 16-17, 19-25
Theognis (Handout no. 39, 41)
Questions: 1. What are the origins of slavery in this society? What is the position of a slave in the oikos (household) and his relationship to its free members?
2. What are the characteristics of a slave, i.e., how is he typologically distinguished from a free man?
3. Analyse the meetings of assembly and council that you find described in the *Iliad* and the *Odyssey:* Who participates? Who speaks? How do the main characters deal with each other? What is the role of the king, the aristocrats, the people? What is the purpose of such meetings? What stage in the development of political institutions do they represent? How far is the political community developed? Why is such an analysis of political assemblies important for the investigation of the concept of political freedom?

178

4. I.3. The world of Hesiod

Readings: Hesiod, *Theogony:* Invocation (1-104); Children of the Night (211-232); Hymn to Hekate (411-452); The offspring of Zeus and Themis (901-06); *Works and Days*

Questions: 1. The world of Hesiod is the world of simple, poor farmers, separated, it seems, by a wide gap from the world of Achilles and Odysseus. What are the main problems and values of the Hesiodic farmer? What is Hesiod's opinion about the political community, social and political life? How does this compare with Homer's view?
2. Apart from a few references to slaves, freedom and slavery as problems or concepts are conspicuously absent from Hesiod's world and vocabulary. In what contexts (passages) of his works would they most likely occur if they had been current and familiar values? How can we explain the absence of such terms and concepts?

5. I.4. Conclusion: Why did the early archaic society not know a concept of political freedom?

Readings: Th. Jacobsen, "Mesopotamia: The Good Life," in H. Frankfort (ed.), *The Intellectual Adventure of Ancient Man* (Chicago-London, 1946) pp. 202-18 (handout)
Rostovtzeff, *Greece*, pp. 81-97

Questions: 1. Overlooking the society of the early archaic period (as represented in Homer and Hesiod) as a whole, we can try to answer the following questions: Why did this society not develop a concept of political freedom? What changes needed to occur (in one or several areas of life) in order to make it possible to develop such a concept? Answer this question in a written statement of not more than 2 pages.
2. Looking ever farther back to Mesopotamia in the 2nd millenium BC, what was it that prevented such a highly developed civilization from recognizing the value of freedom (let alone political freedom), and how does that compare to archaic Greece?
3. The administration of subject territories and communities (as opposed to the incorporation of conquered territories into the own community of the conqueror) presupposes a certain structural and institutional development. How can we define these conditions? In other words: Why is the type of warfare we observed in Homer structurally necessary for Homeric society? What has to change and develop to make a different exploitation of military victory possible?

II. THE CRISIS OF THE ARCHAIC WORLD AND THE DISCOVERY OF POLITICAL "SLAVERY"

6. II.1. Solon, the problem of debt-bondage and the codification of law

Readings: Plutarch, *Solon* 1-28 (p. 43-72)
Aristotle, *Constitution of the Athenians*, ch. 5-12
Handout no. 26-29, 32-33, 43-45
Rostovtzeff, *Greece*, pp. 98-120

Questions: 1. The time of Solon witnessed an acute social crisis. Who or what was responsible for it, what were the main problems, demands and solutions? Whom does Solon himself blame? What is his view of the role of aristocrats and commoners in the community?

2. What role did the problem of freedom play in this crisis and in the reforms of Solon? What kind of freedom was this and how far did it effect the development of the idea of political freedom?

3. In many places attempts to solve the crisis included the codification of law. Again: how was the question of freedom (and what kind of freedom?) involved in such codifications?

NOTE: History section (time to be determined); topics of first short paper announced

7. II.2. Tyranny, the crisis of aristocracy and the emergence of a new society

Readings: Plutarch, *Solon*, 29-31 (p. 72-75)
Aristotle, *Constitution of the Athenians*, ch. 13-22
Herodotus I.59-64; III.80-82, 142f.; V.55f., 62-65, 67f., 78, 90-94
Handout no. 29-32, 34-38, 40, 46
Aristotle, *Politics* V.10-12 (p. 332-56)

Questions: 1. What kind of regime is the tyranny? Who is most (and in what ways) affected by the rule of the tyrant? What would the aristocrats' attitude towards tyranny be before (see no.32) and during a tyranny? How would the lower classes react? And how did all this look like in the case of the tyranny of Peisistratus and his sons?

2. Considering the regime which is ousted by the tyrant: what slogans would most likely be used in the fight against tyranny?

3. How does Solon (no. 26, 31, 30) describe the situation of the city under the tyrant? Are we justified in assuming that for him non-tyranny was equal to freedom?

III. THE PERSIAN WARS AND THE DISCOVERY OF "POLITICAL FREEDOM"

8. III.1. Greek interstate relations and dependencies in the archaic period and the new experience of the Ionian Greeks

Readings: Wars: Handout no. 47; Herodotus I.18, 65-68, 82, 150; V.74, 77-90, 94f.; VII.9; Thucydides I.15-16
Colony and Mother-City: Herodotus VI.145-160; Thucydides I.31-43
Protective Alliance: Herodotus VI.108; Thucydides III.55, 61, 63
The Ionians and the Eastern Empires: Herodotus I.1-6, 14-22, 25-28, 46-56, 69-91, 141-64, 168-70
Rostovtzeff, *Greece*, pp. 72-80 (Sparta); 121-125.

Questions: 1. The conquest of Messenia by Sparta undoubtedly is one important example of a military subjection and enslavement. In the 7th cent. there was a great Messenian revolt, followed by new conquest and subjection. We could expect that freedom, even political freedom, played a role here. Is the type of control and rule exercized by the Spartans over the subject population likely to give room to such a concept? And what about the communities of the *perioikoi*?

2. The relationship of colonies to mother-cities and of weak cities to their allies and protectors (like Plataea to Athens) provides another example of existing dependencies. Why were they not perceived and denoted as such (i.e. why was the term "slavery" not used for them)?

3. Earlier, we studied the aims and types of warfare in early archaic society (as described in the Homeric poems). Herodotus tells a number of stories on warfare between Greek cities before the Persian Wars. How does this evidence compare with that in Homer? Define the purposes of wars between Greek cities before the intervention of Lydians and Persians. Is the "independence of cities" an issue in such wars? If not, what has to change in order for "independence" to become an issue?

4. Read Herodotus' report of the subjection of the Ionians and other Greeks in Asia Minor by the Lydians and Persians very carefully. How is it presented? What are the characteristic patterns of behaving and reacting to this danger?

NOTE: History section to be scheduled. Short paper I due!

9. III.2.a. The Persian Empire and the Ionian Greeks

Readings: The Greek View of the Persian Empire: Handout no. 58, 59, 67; Herodotus 7.96, 101-104, 134-136. Aeschylus, *Persians* 1-248 (pp. 122-130, top).
The Ionian Revolt: Herodotus V.23-VI.42; cf. IV.97f., 133, 136-42.
Rostovtzeff, *Greece*, pp. 125-135

Questions: 1. How did the Greeks understand the rule of the Persian Great King over his subjects and the status of these subjects? What was the closest analogy to this relationship they could think of in their own experience? What fundamental misunderstanding does their judgment show to us?

2. What does "subjection by the Persians" or "Persian rule" mean? How is it realized, what are the instruments of ruling, what are the obligations of the subjects? Considering their own experience and background (as determined by questions 1-3 last time), to what extent was the confrontation with the Persians a new experience for the Greeks?

3. What were the motives of the Ionians in revolting against the Persians? What motives does Herodotus explicitly mention and what additional reasons can you infer from Aristagoras' actions at the very beginning of the revolt (particularly if you take into consideration what we are told in book IV of the Ionian tyrants' behavior during the Scythian campaign)?

4. To what extent, then, was the Ionian Revolt a struggle for freedom? Looking back from the middle of the 5th century, it probably appeared like that; but did it to the contemporaries, too? How do you reconcile with such an interpretation the episode concerning the exiles from Naxos that led to the revolt, and the failure of many Greek cities to support the revolt or to fight all the way to the end?

10. III.2.b. The confrontation with the Persians and the discovery of freedom

Readings: Handout, no. 42, 48-55, 56-57, 61, 63-64, 68, 73, 104 (chs. 20-47)
Aeschylus, *Persians; Seven Against Thebes* (prayer of Eteocles, p. 90 bottom; Chorus, p. 91-93; Chorus, p. 97-99)
Herodotus, book VII

Questions: 1. How were the Greek victories over the Persians and the Athenian contribution to these victories presented:
(a) in Lysias' *Funeral Oration* (Handout no.104, chs. 20-47: early 4th cent.)
(b) in Herodotus (i.e. in the second half of the 5th cent.);
(c) in Aeschylus' Persians (472) and Pindar's Pythian 1 (Handout no.61: 470);
(d) in the contemporary documents (Handout 48-55, 63-64, 73; 56 and 57 are not authentic)?
How does this presentation change over the decades?
2. What did the Athenians fighting on the fleet at Salamis exactly mean when they asked the gods to "liberate their city" (Aeschylus, *Persians* 402-5: p. 134; cf. Handout no. 68)? Compare the impression the approach of the Persians must have made on the Greeks (as it is described in Herodotus) with what Aeschylus says in the *Persians* and the *Seven*.
3. Among the contemporary documents, you will find a marked difference in emphasis and outlook between no. 42, 48-53, 73 on the one hand, and no. 54-57, 61, 63-64 (and Aeschylus' *Persians*) on the other. What could have caused this change within less than ten years?
4. What role, then, did "freedom" play in the Persian Wars and how, in conclusion, do you explain this?

11. III.3. The discovery of the concept of "internal freedom" (freedom of the citizen within the community)

Readings: Handout no. 61, 66-67, 69
Herodotus III.142f.; V.55f., 62-66, 69-78; Book VIII
Aeschylus, *Prometheus Bound*

Questions: 1. When and how does the concept of "internal freedom" appear in our sources? What is the content of such freedom? What is it directed against?
2. If, despite the existence of tyrannies, such a concept was not developed in the 6th cent. (as we concluded earlier in the semester), why now? What has happened to the values which prevailed in the 6th cent.? And why are the values which are expressed by "freedom", suddenly important now?
3. More specifically: what role did tyrants play in the wars against the Persians in Ionia and in Greece? Why could the struggle against the Persians at the same time be perceived as a struggle against tyranny? Would that apply only to the Ionians or to the Athenians as well? And how would all this affect the development of the concept of freedom?
4. Collect the elements of the typology of a tyrant or absolute monarch in Aeschylus' *Persians* and *Prometheus Bound*. What was it that made the Greeks identify the Great King of Persia with a tyrant? And how did this identification stimulate the emergence of such a typology?

182

12. III.4. Religion and politics: the cults of "Zeus the Savior" and "Zeus the Liberator"

Readings: Handout, no. 62, 69-71 (and look back to no. 4, 11 and 13)
Herodotus III.142f.
Thucydides II.71; III.58
Herodotus, Book IX. 1-98
Plutarch, *Aristides* 11-20

Questions: 1. Looking at the documents for the emergence of a cult of "Zeus the Liberator", can you discover a pattern concerning time and causes? More specifically: when, where, and for what reasons was such a cult established?
2. The cult of "Zeus the Liberator" is closely related to the cult of "Zeus the Savior". How and why?
3. Why is it obvious and natural that the cult of the Savior-God is older than that of the Liberator-God?
4. According to Herodotus (III.142f.), a cult of "Zeus the Liberator" was established at Samos after the death of the tyrant Polycrates (i.e. in 522 B.C.). I believe that this piece of information is not historically accurate. After comparing this case with the pattern emerging from all the other cases, do you agree or disagree with me, and why? Prepare a brief written response to this question.

13. III.5. Conclusion: the Persian Wars and the concept of freedom; the foundation of the Delian League

Readings: Herodotus IX. 99-122
Thucydides I.1; 13-23; 89-117
Rostovtzeff, *Greece*, 136-150

Questions: 1. Last time we analyzed the emergence of cults connected with "freedom". How does this evidence fit in with our conclusions concerning the origins of the concept of freedom? How can we define the relations between religion and politics at that time?
2. Sum up the reasons why it is plausible to assume that the concept of political freedom was discovered by the Greeks during the Persian Wars, and why this concept covered both the independence of the community and the freedom of the citizen within his community.
3. 478/77 the Athenians and a number of other cities founded a new alliance, the Delian League. How was this league organized, what was the status of the allies and the relationship between leader and allies? How did the foundation of this new league affect politics and the balance of power among the Greek city-states?
4. Due to this new league, the war against the Persians was continued, mostly in Asia Minor. How would this have affected the concept of freedom?

NOTE: History section (to be scheduled); topics for short paper II announced

183

IV.   THE ATHENIAN EMPIRE, THE POWER-STRUGGLE BETWEEN GREEK
      CITIES, AND THE ABUSE OF A RECENT IDEAL

14. IV.1.   From confederate freedom to imperial tyranny: Athens' rule in the
            Aegean and the definition of "elements of freedom"

Readings: Pseudo-Xenophon I.14-18; II.1-8; 11-16
            Thucydides I.1, 13-23; 66-88; 118-125; 139-146; II. 59-65; III.1-50;
            V.84-116
            Aristotle, *Constitution of the Athenians* 23-24
            Plutarch, *Aristides* 23-25; *Cimon* 6-13; *Pericles* 11-12
            Handout no. 74-77, 83, 87

Questions: 1. Why and how did the Athenian Empire in the Aegean develop? What
            was its origin? What was new and different for the Greek cities affected by it?
         2. More specifically: how did the Athenians treat those cities that revolted or did
            not want to join the alliance at all (look particularly at Thuc. 1.98, 100, 105, 108;
            Handout, no. 74-76)? What other reasons do the ancient authors cite for the shift
            of power in favor of Athens (Thuc. 1.99; Plutarch, *Cimon* 11)?
         3. Most allies were (after c.450 B.C.) considered to be subjects and frequently called
            "slaves" of the Athenians. What defines their status as "slavery"? What are the
            "elements of slavery" of a city? What are, conversely, the "elements of freedom"
            of a city?
         4. The rule of the Athenians was occasionally compared to a tyranny (so by the
            Corinthians in Thuc. I.123, 124; by Pericles: II.63; by Cleon: III.37). On the
            basis of the speeches of the Athenian ambassadors in Sparta (I.72ff., esp. 76f.),
            of Pericles (esp. I. 140f.) and of the Mytileneans (III.9-11), and considering the
            observations of Thuc. I.99: what are the main criteria to define the rule of a city
            as a tyranny? Who would use such a comparison and why?

15. IV.2. The emergence of the concept of autonomy

Readings: Handout, no. 78-87, 95, 97, 98
            Hippocrates, *Airs, Waters, Places* 16, 23
            Herodotus *I.95-96; VIII.140-144*
            Thucydides *IV.75-88; 102-116; V.13-24; 40-51; 76-79.* For the differ-
            ence between *eleutheria* and *autonomia* the following passages are
            important (translators usually say "freedom" or "liberty" for *eleuthe-
            ria,* "independence" or "self-government" for *autonomia):* I.67, 69, 76,
            108, 113, 124, 139-146; *II.71f.; III.10-13,* 39, 46; IV. 95; VI.77,
            84-85, 88; *VII.57;* VIII.21 (passages in italics are particularly impor-
            tant).

Questions: 1. On the basis of question 4 last time (criteria to define the rule of a
            city as tyranny), try to figure out in what ways the Greeks tried to cope with
            those specific problems in interstate relations and treaties? How were statuses
            and rights of partners defined and why were they defined in that specific way?
         2. Even though unfortunately our translations are very unprecise: can you figure
            out a difference between the use of *eleutheria* and *autonomia* in our sources? Look
            especially at the passages in Herodotus and at Thuc. I.139 *(autonomia)* with II.8
            (eleutheria) or IV.86 (both). What determines the use of one or the other in each
            case?
         3. What is the difference between the various categories of Athenian allies whom

184

Thuc. mentions in VI.85 and VII.57? Why would certain allies be called autonomous one time, free another? Why are Samos, Lesbos, Chios regularly referred to as autonomous (cf. also Aristotle, *Constitution of the Athenians* 24)?

4. The term *autonomia* seems to have been created shortly before 450 B.C. Why then and why was it needed at all? In other words: what did it express that *eleutheria* could not express?

5. In the early 4th century a new formula *("eleutheros* and *autonomos")* was frequently used in treaties. Why was that necessary? What do the regulations in the "Decree of Aristoteles" (the invitation to join a new Athenian League) reveal about the shortcomings of the first one (the Delian League) and the meaning of *autonomia?*

16. IV.3. The freedom of the imperial city: "No one is free but Zeus"

Readings:
a) *Absolute Sovereignty:* Thucydides I.89-94, 139-141; II.61; VI.82
Euripides, *Heraclidae* (esp. pp. 109-121); *Suppliants* (p. 193-212, esp. pp. 208-212)

b) *Absolute Self-Sufficiency* (voluntary): Thucydides I.37; II.36-41, 51
Herodotus I.32
Pseudo-Xenophon II.7
Aristotle, *Politics* I.2, 8; II.2 (1261b 6ff); IV.4; VII.4, 8
Handout no. 93 (a-g), 94, 101-103

c) *Absolute Freedom:* Aeschylus, *Prometheus* 49f. (p. 22 upper half)
Herodotus VII. 135; IX.122; VI.109; I.170
Thucydides II.63.f.; III.45; IV.95; VI.89; VII.69; VIII.68, 71
Euripides, *Phoenician Women* 499-553 (p. 253-255)
Handout no. 90-92, 96

Questions: 1. After the Persian Wars the Spartans tried to prevent the rebuilding of the Athenian walls, but, because of Themistocles' tricks, they did not succeed. The debate about this event (Thuc. I.89ff.) contains the core of an important political doctrine which became extremely consequential in the last years of Pericles. What is this doctrine, and how is it expressed in Pericles' first speech in Thucydides and in Euripides' *Heraclidae?*

2. Compare Herodotus VIII.135 with Handout no.96. The two passages are separated by about forty years (and Athens' defeat in 404). What has changed in outlook and values?

3. In Thuc. VI.89 and VII.69 two Athenians call their city the greatest and the freest. What do they mean by that?

4. To put the same question in a more complex framework: The Athenian politicians developed a concept of superior freedom with which they explained and justified the power and rule of their city. What are the elements of this freedom, how is it formulated, and what is its historical and intellectual background?

NOTE: Short paper II due!

185

17. IV.4. The propagandistic and political abuse of a recent ideal: domination for the sake of freedom

Readings: Herodotus IV.135-142; VI.11-17; VII.139; VIII. 140-144; IX.27
    Thucydides I.72-78, 124, 140-141; II.37, 40f.; III.37, 40f., 61-63; V.89-91; VI.76-87; VIII.18, 37, 43.
    Euripides, *Iphigenia in Aulis* 1255ff. (p.412 bottom - 413 top), 1374ff. (p.418 - 419 middle)
    Aristotle, *Politics* VII.14
    Handout no. 89, 97, 100, 104 (chs. 44-60)

Questions: 1. "Freedom" and "liberation" were used by the Athenians generously and systematically to explain and justify their leadership and later their rule over a large part of the Greek world. *Eleutheria* became, within fifty years of its discovery as a political concept, a model of the propagandistic use and abuse of an important concept (if not "ideal"). We have to piece together this propaganda from a number of scattered sources. How did the Athenians use "freedom" to justify their power? What are the main focuses of this use of *eleutheria*?
2. In what contexts do we find such justifications? What is the immediate purpose of such justification? How representative and realistic are these contexts? Think of modern parallels and differences.
3. Since good propaganda always contains a blend of truth and distortion: what is the ratio here? Since good propaganda is meant to be convincing: what does this kind of propaganda tell us about political mentalities and expectations?
4. As Herodotus and Thucydides show, there prevailed in the late fifth century a clear prejudice against the Ionians who were often presented as not deserving of freedom. What was this prejudice based upon, and how was it exploited politically?
5. In *Politics* VII.14 (p. 430) Aristotle defines the conditions in which he considers the rule of one city over another justified. How do these conditions compare with the claims of Athenian propaganda?

18. IV.5. The Spartan side: liberation for the sake of domination

Readings: Thucydides I.66-88; II.8, 67, 72-74; III.32, 52-68; IV.75-88, 102-134; V.3, 12-39; VIII.1, 4-18, 37, 43, 46, 52, 58, 84
    Plutarch, *Life of Lysander* 13
    Handout no. 84, 88, 95

Questions: 1. While the propagandistic abuse of "freedom" by the Athenians and its condemnation by Thucydides are generally well known, most scholars and textbooks still believe in the honesty and fairness of the Spartan slogan of "liberation of the Greeks". Is this view right, does it need to be modified, or is it simply wrong?
2. More specifically: what does Thucydides think and say (especially in his description of the preliminaries and the outbreak of the war: I.66-68, 118-125, 139-146) about the Spartan motives to go to war?
3. During the Peace of Nikias and in the last part of (as well as after) the war, Sparta's relationship to her allies changed dramatically. How and why? What were the causes of this "Spartan imperialism"? And what role did concepts like *eleutheria* and especially *autonomia* play in this development?
4. The existence of the two competing power blocks created a difficult situation for many small cities that were too weak to maintain their independence without

186

outside support. It became obvious then more than ever before that the basic ideal of independence of the city was restricted in many ways. What are these factors? In other words: how far could "freedom" be an absolute value, and how far was it bound to be a relative value?

V. FREEDOM AND DEMOCRACY

19. V.1. Equality, democracy and the freedom of the citizen

Readings:
Rostovtzeff, *Greece* 162-202
Aristotle, *Constitution of the Athenians* 23-28.

a) *Freedom against tyranny: the persistence of an obsolete opposition:*
Handout no. 112, 115, 117-120
Herodotus I.95f.; III.83f.; V.78, 90-92; VI.109
Thucydides VI.27-29, 53-61

b) *From democratic equality to democratic freedom*
Handout no. 61 (second stanza), 65
Aeschylus, *Suppliant Women*
Euripides, *Suppliants* (esp. 297-597: pp. 202-212)
Plutarch, *Pericles* 11-12
Pseudo-Xenophon I.6-9
Herodotus III.80-84, 142f.; IV.137; V.37; VI.43
Thucydides IV.85-87; VI.38-40

Questions: 1. Tyrannies were eliminated in the Greek world after the Persian Wars at the latest. Except for some remote areas, tyranny was no real danger, no concrete problem. Nevertheless, the Athenians continued to fear tyranny and to use this fear as a political weapon. This tendency even increased in the course of the Peloponnesian War. Why? What does this phenomenon tell us about the outlook and psychological-political stability of democracy?

2. While the concept of "internal freedom" (the freedom of the citizen within his city) was familiar to the Greeks at least since the late seventies (Pindar, Handout no. 61: 470 B.C.), it was directly linked with "democracy" only much later. It is important to know when this happened. Try to narrow the dates down by using Aeschylus' *Suppliants* (463), Herodotus' Constitutional Debate (c.450), the bulk of Herodotus' work as represented by the other passages mentioned under (b) (430's and early 420's), Pseudo-Xenophon (431-424) and Euripides' *Suppliants* (424).

3. In Aeschylus' *Suppliants* (in the meeting of the "democratic" king and the chorus of suppliants: esp. 359ff.: pp. 65-70 top) two totally different views of decision-making in a city are contrasted to each other: which? The presentation of the main characteristics of democracy in the *Suppliants* has close analogies in Herodotus' (III.80) and Euripides' *(Suppliants:* p. 204 bottom, p. 206 bott.-207 bott.) discussion of the advantages of democracy, but is strongly opposed by Pseudo-Xenophon. How do these authors perceive the "rule of the people" and what do they mean by "people"?

4. The word "democracy" was -- like all the political and constitutional terms we are studying -- created in a specific period under the impression of specific experiences and conditions. Democracy existed before the word. There are strong indications that the "proto-democratic" constitution was called *isonomia* (equality of political participation). Use especially Pseudo-Xenophon (I.6-9), Thucydides (IV.85-87 and VI.38-40) and Plutarch *(Pericles* 11f.) to find out what changes,

circumstances and experiences forced the Athenians to create a new and very different term for the "rule of the people". When would such a term most likely have come up?

20. V.2. Democratic freedom: content, meaning, reality

Readings: Handout no. 128-129, 133-138
Euripides, *Suppliants* 297-597 (pp.202-212)
Herodotus I.96-101; VII.102-104, 135, 139
Thucydides II.36-43; IV. 86; VI.89; VII.69; VIII.68, 71
Plato, *Republic* VIII. 555b-573c (Handout no.158)
Aristotle, *Politics* III.12f.; IV.4; V.9; VI.2
Pseudo-Xenophon I.1-9, 10-12

Questions: 1. What does "democratic freedom" mean and consist of? How was it judged by advocates and opponents of democracy?
2. What about the problem of ideal (or "ideology") and reality?
3. Among the elements of democratic freedom are some basic social or anthropological components which seem to be closer to the status distinction between free and slave than to the specific political rights of a citizen. Why were these social aspects emphasized that much?
4. Is there anything comparable to modern "civil rights"? If yes or not (or just very little): why?

21. V.3. "Freedom of speech": the discovery of a civil right

Readings:
a) *eleutheros legein* (to speak freely, speak like a free man):
Aeschylus, *Persians* 591-94 (p.139); *Suppliants* 937-50 (p.82); *Prometheus* 180f. (p. 26 middle: Chorus)
Handout no. 117

b) *isegoria* (equality of speech)
Herodotus 5, 78 (in content related to Hipprocates, *Airs, Waters, Places* 16)
Pseudo-Xenophon I.10-12
Euripides, *Suppliants* 429-41 (p. 207: Theseus)
Handout no. 116, 126

c) *parrhesia* (freedom to say all, to say what you wish, freedom of speech)
Handout no. 110, 111, 119, 121-125, 128, 130, 135

d) *the democratic right to address the assembly:*
Thucydides II.40; III.37f., 42f.
Euripides, *Suppliants* 409-62 (pp. 206-208 middle); *Orestes* 855-956 (pp.330 bottom - 334 top)
Handout no. 127, 131, 132, 171

e) *the prehistory of this right:*
Handout no. 1-2, 6-7, 10, 16-17 for Homeric assemblies
Aristotle, *Constitution of the Athenians* 21 for Cleisthenes

Questions: 1. The Athenians used three different terms to describe the citizens' right of speech: a-c above. These terms focus on different aspects, they were prominent in different stages of the constitutional development and used in different contexts. Nevertheless, they continued to exist side by side, and their meanings and uses overlap considerably. How and when are they used?

2. *Parrhesia* appears in our sources for the first time in 428 (Euripides, *Hippolytus*). It does not seem to have existed (or at least been important) long before then. How does the use of *parrhesia* and *isegoria* compare? Why would it be necessary to create such a new term at all, and what does its creation tell us about changes in the political situation and outlook around 430?

3. What is the position of this specific right among the elements of democratic freedom? What is its importance in democratic theory? And what role does it play in reality, how is it judged by contemporaries?

4. How did the "right of speech" develop from Homeric to democratic society? What are the major historical turning points in this development? Describe this development in a short essay (2 pages).

22. V.4. Democratic freedom against aristocratic will to power

Readings: Handout no. 99, 104 (ch.61-68), 129, 139-140, 156-157
Aristotle, *Constitution of the Athenians* 29-33
Pseudo-Xenophon I.1-9; II.20; III.11
Thucydides IV.85-87, 105f.; VI.32-41, 88-93; VIII.45-98
Herodotus III.80-82
Euripides, *Suppliants* 409ff. (p.207 top)

Questions: 1. While for the democrats "freedom" became the most important political slogan, the centre of their propaganda and ideology, the opposition to democracy (aristocrats or oligarchs) did not adopt the word for their own positive self-representation. Why not?

2. What were the main points of criticism brought forward by the opposition against democracy?

3. What were the claims, the main values and ideals of aristocrats or oligarchs? How did they present themselves and their constitution (and what did they oppose to the democratic "ideology of freedom")? Try to answer these questions on the basis of both the theoretical discussions in our sources and of the reality as it appeared in the rule of the oligarchs in 411 and 404 B.C.

4. As it turned out in 411 and 404, the oligarchs differed from the democrats not only in their constitutional views but also in their opinions about the Athenian empire, the power and independence of their city and its relations to other cities and powers. Try to define the views of the two groups or "parties". Why were they logical and necessary under the prevailing conditions? How did they influence the content, meaning and significance of democratic freedom?

23. V.5. The aristocrats' response: the nobleman's superior freedom

Readings:
a) *eleutherios = noble, generous, "liberal"*
Handout no. 144, 152-155

b) *eleutherios paideia = "liberal education"*
Handout no. 147-150, 159
Aristotle, *Politics* VII.5;. VIII.1-3

189

c) *eleutherios techne = "free occupation"*
Handout no. 141-143, 146, 151
Aristotle, *Politics* III.4-5; VII.12

Questions: 1. Try to define as precisely as possible the three concepts of *eleutherios* (the sources for which are listed above) in their positive orientation and in their opposites (i.e., for example: what, exactly, is a "free occupation" and what is an "unfree occupation"?)
2. What exactly is the connection between these concepts and the basic meaning of "free"? How did such concepts develop?
3. What is the political significance of these concepts? Where do they fit in our picture? In what ways (if any) can they be understood as a response to the democrats' exclusive claim to freedom? What aspects of the democratic concept of freedom do they attack? And in what respects is this a typical aristocratic reaction or solution?

VI. THE FOURTH CENTURY AND AFTER

24. VI.1. The significance of "freedom" during the crisis of the polis (4th cent. B.C.) and the Hellenistic period

Readings:
a) *The philosophical side*
"Freedom from the city": Handout no. 162; Aristotle, *Politics* VII.2-3
The ideal of complete personal independence, self-control and "internal freedom": Handout no. 160,161; Euripides, *Children of Heracles*, p. 119 middle (Makaria) - 124 top; *Iphigenia in Aulis* 923ff. (p. 401 bottom - 403 top: speech of Achilles)

b) *The political side*
Independence of the city: Handout no. 87, 100 (ch. 115-128), 163-173; Aristotle, *Politics* VII.7
Democratic Freedom: Handout no. 129, 134, 168

c) *Political Theory and Democratic Freedom*
Handout no. 174
Plato, *Republic* VIII.555B - 573C (Handout no. 158)
Aristotle, *Politics* III.1 - V.5; V.9; VI.2

25. VI.2. Freedom as a political idea at Rome

Readings: on a special handout

Final discussion

E. LIST OF SOURCES COLLECTED IN THE COURSE HANDOUT

Translations of documents are taken from:

C.W.Fornara, *Archaic Times to the End of the Peloponnesian War*[2] (Cambridge, 1983)
J. Wickersham and G. Verbrugghe, *Greek Historical Documents: The Fourth Century B.C.* (Toronto, 1973)
R.E. Wycherly, *Literary and Epigraphical Testimonia*, The Athenian Agora III (Princeton, 1957)

I. HOMER, THE *ILIAD* AND THE *ODYSSEY*; HESIOD

NO.	SOURCE	CONTENT
1.	*Iliad* 1. 1-305	The struggle between Achilles and Agamemnon
2.	*Iliad* 2. 1-401	Agamemnon's temptation of the Athenians; The Thersites episode
3.	*Iliad* 6. 144-211	Values and privileges of the nobles
4.	*Iliad* 6. 390-528	Hektor, the protector of Troy; Hektor and Andromache; women's plight in war; "the day of freedom"
5.	*Iliad* 7. 303-312	Surviving in combat
6.	*Iliad* 9. 9-105	Council of the nobles
7.	*Iliad* 9. 441-43	The qualities of the nobleman
8.	*Iliad* 9. 529-99	The Meleagros story (war between cities)
9.	*Iliad* 11. 669-760	Nestor recalls his youth (war between Pylos and Elis)
10.	*Iliad* 14. 103-34	The nobleman's pride and ancestry
11.	*Iliad* 15. 484-99	Fighting for family and *oikos*
12.	*Iliad* 16. 816-37	The "day of liberty"
13.	*Iliad* 17. 215-28	The purpose of fighting
14.	*Iliad* 18. 478-540	The shield of Achilles
15.	*Iliad* 20. 174-98	The "day of liberty"
16.	*Odyssey* 2. 1-258	Assembly in Ithaca
17.	*Odyssey* 8. 385-99	Leaders of the Phaeacians
18.	*Odyssey* 8. 521-30	The misery of war
19.	*Odyssey* 11. 488-91	The king and the *thes*
20.	*Odyssey* 14. 191-359	Odysseus' fictitious story of his life
21.	*Odyssey* 15. 351-484	The story of Eumaeus' life
22.	*Odyssey* 17. 300-27	The impact of slavery on man
23.	*Odyssey* 18. 357-65	The labor of a ·*thes*
24.	*Odyssey* 21. 203-16	The faithful servants rewarded
25.	*Odyssey* 24. 205-55	The typology of slave and free man

II. SOURCES OF THE ARCHAIC PERIOD

26.	Solon, *fragm.* 3D	The aristocrats' lack of responsibility, civil strife and tyranny, good order
27.	Solon, *fragm.* 4D	The aristocrats' greed and ambition
28.	Solon, *fragm.* 5D	Solon, the mediator; the role of the people
29.	Solon, *fragm.* 24D	Solon's achievement; the liberation of the debt-bondsmen
30.	Solon, *fragm.* 8D	The people and the tyrant
31.	Solon, *fragm.* 10D	Cause and inevitability of tyranny
32.	Solon, *fragm.* 23D	Solon's assessment of his role and of tyranny
33.	Solon, *fragm.* 25D	Solon reproaches the citizens
34.	Alcaeus	Testimonia
35.	Alcaeus, *fragm.* 70LP	Tyranny destroys the city
36.	Alcaeus, *fragm.* 129LP	The betrayal of Pittacus
37.	Alcaeus, *fragm.* 130LP	The exile yearning to participate in politics
38.	Alcaeus, *fragm.* 348LP	Pittacus as an "elected tyrant"
39.	Theognis 529f.; 535-38	Typology of slave and free man
40.	Theognis 847-50	Contempt for the demos
41.	Theognis 903-30	"Free man's food"
42.	Theognis 773-82	Prayer for protection against the Persians
43.	Law Code of Gortyn (excerpts from col. I and II	The significance of legal status: free, slave (tr. Willetts)
44.	Aeschines, *or.* 1.138f.	Law of Solon concerning slaves
45.	Demosthenes, *or.* 23.53	Law of Solon concerning slaves
46.	*Schol. Anonym.* 893-96P	The "Harmodios Song" (Fornara, No.39)
47.	Aeschines, *or.* 3.107-9	The Sacred War

III. SOURCES ON THE PERSIAN WARS AND RELATED EVENTS

48-57.		*Monuments from the Persian Wars*
48.	*GHI* No.25	Athenian Portico at Delphi (Fornara, No. 43)
49.	*GHI* No.19	Athenian thank-offering for Marathon at Delphi (Fornara, No. 50)
50.	*IG* I^2 927	Memorial of the Corinthians
51.	*IG* I^2 609	Memorial of Kallimachos, the polemarch at Marathon (Fornara, No. 49)
52.	*GHI* No. 28	Gelon's thank-offering for Himera (Fornara, No. 54)
53.	*GHI* No. 27	Inscription on the "Serpent Column" (Fornara, No. 59)
54.	*IG* I^2 763	Athenian epigram on the Persian Wars (Fornara, No. 51)
55.	*GHI* No. 20	Memorial of the Megarians (Fornara, No. 60)
56.	*GHI* No. 23	The "Themistocles Decree" (Fornara, No. 55)
57.	*GHI* II No. 204	The "Oath of Plataea" (Fornara, No. 57)
58.	Fornara, No. 34	List of Persian Satrapies under Dareios
59.	*GHI* No.12	Letter of Dareios to his satrap (Fornara, No.35)
60.	Pindar, *Olympian* 13.3-8	*Eunomia* in Corinth
61.	Pindar, *Olympian* 1.60-80	Hieron's contribution to the liberty of the Greeks
62.	Pindar, *Olympian* 12.1-6	Tyche Soteira, daughter of Zeus Eleutherios
63.	Pindar, *Isthmian* 8.1-16	The salvation of Greece's liberty
64.	Pindar, Fr. 76, 77Sn.	Praise of Athens' merits in the Persian Wars
65.	Pindar, *Pythian* 2.81-88	The three constitutions

66.	Aeschylus, *Libation Bearers* 807-11; 855-68; 1044-47	Liberation from tyranny
67.	Euripides, *Helen* 269-75	The Persian King as ruler over slaves
68.	Demosthenes, *or.* 14.31f.	What is at stake in a war against barbarians
69.	Diodorus of Sicily XI.72	The cult of Zeus Eleutherios in Syracuse
70.		*The cult of Zeus Eleutherios in Athens*
	a. *Inscr. Agora* I.2483	Boundary stone from the Agora (Wycherly, No.39)
	b. *IG* II² 43, lines 56f.	Decree of Aristoteles 377.B.C. (Wych., No.41)
	c. Xenophon, *Oeconomicus* 7.1	(Wycherly, No.36)
	d. Harpocration, s.v. *Eleutherios Zeus*	(Wycherly, No.27)
	e. Aristophanes, *Plutus* 1174f. with Scholion to 1175	(Wycherly, No. 24)
	f. Hesychius, s.v. *Eleutherios Zeus*	(Wycherly, No. 28)
	g. *Etymologicon Magnum*, s.v. *Eleutherios Zeus*	(Wycherly, No. 26)
	h. *IG* II² 680, lines 5ff.	Inscription from Delphi (supplementary evidence for Zeus Soter)
71.	Pausanias 9.2.5-7	The cult of Zeus Eleutherios and the "Liberty Games" at Plataea
72.	Anacreon, *fragm.* 419 P	Salvation from slavery
73.	Simonides, *fragm.* 531 P	Ode commemorating those who died at Thermopylae

IV. SOURCES ON THE ATHENIAN EMPIRE AND RELATED DEVELOPMENTS

74.	*IG* I² 10	The Erythrae Decree (Fornara, No.71)
75.	*IG* I² 39	Athenian Regulations for Chalkis (Fornara, No. 103)
76.	*GHI* No.56	Athenian Treaty with Samos (Fornara, No.115)
77.	Pindar, *Pythian* 8.95-100	The liberty of Aegina
78.	*IG* I² 60, lines 12f.	Decree from 427/6 B.C. granting autonomy to the Mytilenians
79.	*GHI*, No. 94	Honorary decree from 405 B.C. granting autonomy to the Samians (Fornara, No.166)
80.	*IG* I² 116, lines 10-12	Treaty from 409/8 B.C. granting autonomy to the Selybrians
81.	Sophocles, *Antigone* 817-22	Antigone as an autonomous person
82.	I. Bekker, *Anecdota Graeca* I (1814) 466	Definition of autonomy
83.	Andocides, *or.* 3.10-14	On the peace with Sparta: freedom and autonomy of Athens
84.		The King's Peace, 387/6 B.C.
	a. Xenophon, *Hellenica* 5.1.31; Diodorus Siculus 14.110.3	Decree of the Persian King Artaxerxes
	b. Xenophon, *Hellenica* 5.1.35f.	Execution of the terms
85.	*GHI* No. 118	Alliance of Athens and Chios, 384 B.C. (Wickersham-Verbrugghe No.17)
86.	*GHI* No. 124	Alliance of Athens and Chalkis, 377 B.C. (Wickersham-Verbrugghe No. 23)
87.	*GHI* No. 123	Decree of Aristoteles, 377 B.C. (Wickersham-Verbrugghe No. 22)

88.	*IG* XII.9	Eretria honors Hegelochus of Tarentum
89.	Xenophon, *Hellenica* 2.2.1-23	The fall of Athens
90.	Lysias, *or.* 25.32	Freedom and greatness of Athens
91.	Lysias, *or.* 28.14	Same
92.	Pseudo-Andocides, *or.* 4.1	Same
93.	References to self-sufficiency *(autarkeia)*	

    a. Aeschylus, *Libation Bearers* 755/57
    b. Sophocles, *Oedipus at Colonus* 1057
    c. Euripides, *Fragm.* 29N
    d. Democritus, *Fragm.* B 176 DK
    e. Xenophon, *Memorabilia* 1.2.14
    f. Isocrates, *or.* 4.42
    g. Demosthenes, *or.* 3.14

94.	Hermippus, *Fr.* 63 Edm.	Athens as the center of world trade
95.	Xenophon, *Hellenica* 3.2.21-31	Sparta promotes autonomy in the Peloponnese
96.	Xenophon, *Hellenica* 4.1.34-36	Agesilaus and Pharnabazus: freedom and power guarantee happiness
97.	Xenophon, *Hellenica* 5.2.11-14	*Autopolites*
98.	Xenophon, *Hellenica* 7.1.12-14	Equality in an alliance
99.	Andocides, *or.* 2.27f.	Democracy and empire
100.	Isocrates, *or.* 4.96-121	Defense of the 5th cent. Athenian empire
101.	Aristotle, *Nicomachean Ethics* 1.7.6-8	Self-sufficiency
102.	Aristotle, ibid., 9.9.1-3	Self-sufficiency
103.	Aristotle, ibid., 10.7.1-4	Self-sufficiency
104.	Lysias, *or.* 2	Funeral oration

V. SOURCES PERTAINING TO ATHENIAN DEMOCRACY AND RELATED MATTERS

110.	Euripides, *Ion* 668-76	Freedom of speech
111.	Euripides, *Hippolytus* 418-25	Freedom of speech
112.	Sophocles, *Electra* 957-85	Liberation from the tyrant's rule
113.	Sophocles, *Electra* 1253-57	Freedom of speech
114.	Sophocles, *Electra* 1296-1300	Liberation from the tyrant's rule
115.	Sophocles, *Electra* 1508-10	Liberation from the tyrant's rule
116.	Sophocles, *Oed. Tyr.* 400-10	Right of speech
117.	Sophocles, *Fragm.* 192 P	Right of speech
118.	Sophocles, *Fragm.* 873 P	Slavery under a tyrant
119.	Nicostratus Com., *Frag.* 29 Edm.	Freedom of speech
120.	Euripides, *Fragm.* 275 N	Freedom from tyranny or oligarchy
121.	Euripides, *Electra* 1049-56	Freedom of speech
122.	Euripides, *Bacchae* 665-71	Freedom of speech
123.	Democritus, *Fragm.* B226 DK	Freedom of speech
124.	Demosthenes, *Fragm.* 21S	Freedom of speech
125.	Aristoph. *Thesm.* 540-43	Freedom of speech
126.	Xenophon, *Cyropaedia* 1.3.10	Freedom of speech
127.	Xenophon, *Memorabilia* 3.7.1-9	Speaking in the assembly
128.	Demosthenes, *or.* 9.3f.	Freedom of speech
129.	Demosthenes, *or.* 20.107f.	Equality and freedom
130.	Demosthenes, *or.* 21, 123f.	Freedom of speech
131.	Aeschines, *or.* 1.17-32	Those prohibited from speaking in the assembly
132.	Plato, *Protagoras* 319A-D	Speaking in the assembly

133.	Aristotle, *Rhetoric* 1.8.3-5	Democracy and freedom
134.	Xenophon, *Cyropaedia* 8.1.3f.	Obedience to magistrates
135.	Isocrates, *or.* 7.20f.	The ideal democracy of old
136.	Strabo, *Geography* 10.4.16	Liberty and the protection of property
137.	Andocides, *or.* 4.16-19	Democracy and the protection of the person
138.	Demosthenes, *or.* 24.160-69	Democracy and the protection of one's house
139.	Lysias, *or.* 12.92-98	Liberation from the tyranny of the Thirty
140.	Lysias, *or.* 18.24-27	Liberation from the tyranny of the Thirty
141.	Xenophon, *Cyropaedia* 1.2.3f.	The "free citizens"
142.	Xenophon, *Memorabilia* 2.7.1-14	The gentleman, "liberal education" and "free occupation"
143.	Xenophon, *Mem.* 2.8.1-6	Same
144.	Xenophon, *Mem.* 3.10.4-5	*Eleutherios*, noble
145.	Xenophon, *Constitution of the Lacedaemonians* 8.1-2	Obedience to laws and magistrates
146.	Xenophon, *Oeconomicus* 4.1-4	Illiberal occupations
147.	Isocrates, *or.* 4.48-50	Liberal education
148.	Isocrates, *or.* 7.43	Liberal education
149.	Plato, *Protagoras* 312B	Liberal education
150.	Plato, *Laws* I.643D-644B	Liberal education
151.	Plato, *Laws* XI.919B-920A	Liberal occupations
152.	Aristotle, *Rhetoric* 1.5-7	"Liberal property"
153.	Aristotle, *Nicomachean Ethics* 1.13-20	Liberality
154.	Aristotle, *Nic. Eth.* 2.7.1-5	Liberality
155.	Aristotle, *Nic. Eth.* 4.8.1-10	*Eleutherios:* a gentleman
156.	Xenophon, *Hellenica* 2.3.11-56	The "Thirty" in Athens
157.	Xenophon, *Hellenica* 2.4.1-43	The Fall of the "Thirty"
158.	Plato, *Republic* 8.555b-573c	Democracy and freedom

VI. SOURCES ON DEVELOPMENTS IN THE 4TH CENTURY.

159.	Plato, *Republic* 3.395 b-c	Liberal education
160.	Xenophon, *Memorabilia* 1.2.5f.	The philosopher's independence
161.	Xenophon, *Memorabilia* 1.5.1-6	The philosopher's self-control
162.	Xenophon, *Memorabilia* 2.1.1-20	Freedom from the community
163.	Isocrates, *or.* 8.41-44	Freedom of cities
164.	Demosthenes, *or.* 6.23-25	Greek liberty threatened by Philip of Macedon
165.	Demosthenes, *or.* 8.38-47	Same
166.	Demosthenes, *or.* 10.4f.	Oligarchs ready to yield to Philip
167.	Demosthenes, *or.* 19.259-62	Same
168.	Demosthenes, *or.* 15	For the liberty of the Rhodians
169.	Demosthenes, *or.* 18.45f.	Lack of resistance against Philip
170.	Demosthenes, *or.* 18.65-68	The last struggle for freedom
171.	Demosthenes, *or.* 18.168-72	Same
172.	Demosthenes, *or.* 18.180-87	Same
173.	Demosthenes, *or.* 18.206-8	Same
174.	Plato, *Laws* 3.691A-702A	Democratic freedom

F. FURTHER READINGS SUGGESTED TO THE TEACHER

This course is based on my own research on the origins and development of the concept of political freedom. A comprehensive and systematic survey of the sources from Homer to Aristotle is available in Raaflaub, "Zum Freiheitsbegriff der Griechen: Materialien und Untersuchungen zur Bedeutungsentwicklung von *eleutheros/eleutheria* in der archaischen und klassischen Zeit," in E.C. Welskopf (ed.), *Soziale Typenbegriffe im alten Griechenland* IV (Berlin, 1981): 180-405. For the historical analysis see now Raaflaub, *Die Endeckung der Freiheit: Zur historischen Semantik und Gesellschaftsgeschichte eines politischen Grundbegriffes der Griechen*, Vestigia vol. 37 (Munich, 1985). The latter volume also contains a large international bibliography. The following survey is confined to literature in English.

At present, no adequate study of the Greek concept of political freedom exists in English. H.T. Muller, *Freedom in the Ancient World* (London, 1961) pursues a line of inquiry radically different from ours: "My main concern is the living tradition of freedom: what has entered the broad stream leading to the consciousness of modern man, and lately to the almost universal acceptance in theory of the once-revolutionary principle of "human rights" or the rights of man... While I have of course tried to understand the mentality of ancient peoples, I have not sought primarily to present them as they saw themselves... In effect I have dwelt rather on their contributions to *us*, and their shortcomings by *our* standards" (xvi). Nothing is wrong with such a goal, but it is precisely what Muller does *not* intend to do, that we try to do here. The following articles may serve as a general introduction: A.W. Gomme, "Concepts of Freedom," in id., *More Essays in Greek History and Literature* (Oxford, 1962): 139-55; J.A.O. Larsen, "Freedom and its Obstacles in Ancient Greece," *Class. Philol.* 57 (1962): 230-34; C. B. Welles, Greek Liberty, Journ. Jur. Pap. 15 (1965): 29-47; M. van Straaten, "What Did the Greeks Mean by Liberty?" *Theta-Pi* 1 (1972) 105-27; V. Ehrenberg, "Freedom - Ideal and Reality," in id., *Man, State and Deity* (London, 1974): 19-34; M.I. Finley, "The Freedom of the Citizen in the Greek World," in id., *Economy and Society in Ancient Greece* (New York, 1981): 77-94.

For related terms see, e.g., on slavery and servile statuses: W.L. Westermann, *The Slave Systems of Greek and Roman Antiquity* (Philadelphia, 1955); id., "Slavery and the Elements of Freedom in Ancient Greece," in M.I. Finley (ed.), *Slavery in Classical Antiquity* (Cambridge, 1960): 1-32; A.R.W. Harrison, The Law of Athens I (Oxford, 1968) 166-80; M.I.Finley, "Between Slavery and Freedom," in id., *Economy and Society in Ancient Greece* (New York, 1981): 116-32; id., "The Servile Statuses of Ancient Greece," ibid., 133-49; id., "Debt-bondage and the Problem of Slavery," ibid., 150-66. On status categories among the free population: Harrison, loc. cit. 1-86 (freedmen), 187-99 (metics); D. Whitehead, *The Ideology of the Athenian Metic* (Cambridge, 1977). On *eunomia:* A. Andrewes, *"Eunomia," Classical Quarterly* 32 (1938): 89-102; V. Ehrenberg, *Aspects of the Ancient World* (Oxford, 1946): 70-93; M. Ostwald, *Nomos and the Beginnings of the Athenian Democracy* (Oxford, 1969): 62-95 (also on *dysnomia* and *anomia*). On *isonomia:* G. Vlastos, "Isonomia," *Am. Journ. of Philol.* (1953): 337-66; id., *"Isonomia politike,"* in J. Mau and E.G. Schmidt (eds.), *Isonomia: Studien zur Gleichheitsvorstellung im griechischen Denken* (Berlin, 1964): 1-35; V. Ehrenberg, *Polis und Imperium* (Zurich and Stuttgart, 1965): 279-86); Ostwald, loc. cit. 96-136, 137-60; H.W. Pleket, "Isonomia and Cleisthenes: A Note," *Talanta* 4 (1972): 63-81. On *isegoria:* G.T. Griffith, "Isegoria in the Assembly at Athens," in *Ancient Society and Institutions: Studies... V. Ehrenberg* (Oxford, 1966): 115-138; A.G. Woodhead, *"Isegoria* and the Council of 500," *Historia* 16 (1967): 129-40; J.D. Lewis, "Isegoria at Athens: When did it begin?" *Historia* 20 (1971): 129-40. On *isokratia:* M. Ostwald, "Isokratia as a Political Concept (Herodotus 5.92a.1)," in *Islamic Philosophy and the Classical Tradition: Essays... R. Walzer* (1973): 277-91. On *parrhesia* nothing exists in English; see Raaflaub, *Entdeckung* 277-83, and id., "Des freien Bürgers Recht der freien Rede," in W. Eck, H. Galsterer and H. Wolff (eds.), *Studien zur antiken Sozialgeschichte* (Cologne and Vienna, 1980): 7-57 (also on *isegoria*). On equality, see furthermore F.D. Harvey, "Two Kinds of Equality," *Classica et Medievalia* 26 (1965) 101-46. On *autonomia:* M. Ostwald, *Autonomia: Its Genesis and Early History,* Amer. Classical Studies 11 (1982); a contrasting view in Raaflaub, *Entdeckung* 189-207. On *autarkeia* (self-sufficiency): M. Wheeler, "Self-Sufficiency and the Greek City," *Journ. of the History of Ideas* 16 (1955): 416-20; on the origins and the political use of the term: Raaflaub, *Entdeckung* 237-41. On *demos* and *demokratia:* W. Donlan, "Changes and Shifts in the Meaning of *demos* in the Literature of the Archaic Period," *La Parola del passato* 25 (1970): 381-95; V. Ehrenberg, "Origins of Democracy," *Historia* 1 (1950) 515-48, repr. in id., *Polis und Imperium* (1965): 264-97; R. Sealey, "The Origins of *Demokratia,*" *Calif. Stud. in Class. Ant.* 6 (1974): 283-95. On *eleutherios* in the sense of "noble, generous": Raaflaub, "Democracy, Oligarchy, and the Concept of the 'Free Citizen' in Late Fifth-Century Athens," *Political Theory* 11 (1983): 517-44.

Foundations of Athenian Democracy

Virginia Hunter
1984-85

York University

Sept. 11-13   Introduction

A. Andrewes, Greek Society, Chapters 4 and 8.

Sept. 18-20   Politics: population and participation

Andrewes, Chapter 1, "Geography and Climate."

S. Isager and M. H. Hansen, Aspects of Athenian Society in
    the Fourth Century B. C., Odense, 1975, "Athenian
    Foreign Trade," pp. 11-52 (handout).

Recommended: M. I. Finley, Politics in the Ancient World,
              Cambridge, 1983, Chapters 1 and 2.

              H. H. Hansen, "The Athenian Ecclesia and the
              Assembly-Place on the Pnyx," GRBS 23 (1982)
              pp. 241-49.

Tutorial: Aristotle, Constitution of Athens, Chapters 42-62
           (handout).

           deme map from J. S. Traill, The Political Organization
           of Attica, Princeton, 1975.

Sept. 25   Politics: power and process

Andrewes, Chapter 9, "Government and Law-Courts."

Isager and Hansen, "Private Process," pp. 107-23.

Recommended: Finley, Politics, Chapters 3 and 4.

Tutorial: Aristotle, Constitution, Chapters 63-69.

           Lysias 12, "On the Execution without Trial of
           Polemarchus" (handout).

Oct. 2-4   Politics: issues and conflict

Andrewes, Chapters 5 and 10.

Thucydides, Book 6, Chapters 1-26.

Recommended: Finley, Politics, Chapters 5 and 6.

Tutorial: Aristotle, Constitution, Chapters 42-62.

           Thucydides (as above).

198

Oct. 9-11   A region of Attica: deme, village, and house

A. Burford-Cooper, "The Family Farm in Greece,"
CJ 73 (1977-78) pp. 162-75.

J. Pecirka, "Homestead Farms in Classical and
Hellenistic Hellas," in Problèmes de la
Terre en Grèce ancienne, edited by M. I.
Finley, Paris, 1973, pp. 113-29 and 133-37
(handout).

Recommended: C. W. J. Eliot, Coastal Demes of Attika,
Toronto, 1962, Chapter 4, "Anagyrous."

S. C. Humphreys, "Archaeology and the Social
and Economic History of Classical Greece,"
in Anthropology and the Greeks, London, 1978,
pp. 109-29.

Tutorial: Lysias 1, "On the Killing of Eratosthenes the
Seducer" (handout).

Oct. 16-18   Agriculture and agronomy, ancient and modern

Andrewes, Chapter 6.

H. A. Forbes, "The 'Thrice-Ploughed Field':
Cultivation Techniques in Ancient and
Modern Greece," Expedition 19 (1976)
pp. 5-11 (handout).

M. H. Jameson, "Agriculture and Slavery in
Classical Athens," CJ 73 (1977-78) pp. 122-45
(handout).

Recommended: Virginia Hunter, "Classics and Anthropology," Phoenix 35 (1981) pp. 145-55.

Tutorial: Demosthenes 55, "Damage to a Farm" (handout).

Xenophon, Economics, Chapters 16-20.

Oct. 23-25   Lectures to be announced

          Tutorial: J. Le Goff, "The Historian and the Ordinary Man" in
                    Time, Work, and Culture in the Middle Ages, Chicago,
                    1980, pp. 225-36 (handout).

Oct. 30-Nov. 1   Reading Week for preparation of first assignment (which
                should include readings from the following:)

                J. du Boulay, Portrait of a Greek Mountain Village,
                Oxford, 1974.

                E. Friedl, Vasilika. A Village in Modern Greece, New York,
                1962, Chapters 1 and 2.

                K. D. White, Country Life in Classical Times, Ithaca, 1977,
                Selections.

                Xenophon, Economics.

Nov. 6-8   The Family in Classical Athens

                J. K. Davies, Athenian Propertied Families, 600-300 B. C.,
                London, 1971, Introduction.

                W. K. Lacey, The Family in Classical Greece, London, 1968,
                Chapter 5.

                S. Pomeroy, Goddesses, Whores, Wives, and Slaves. Women in
                Classical Antiquity, New York, 1975, Chapters 4 and 5.

        Recommended: L. Stone, "Family History in the 1980's," JIH 12 (1981)
                51-87.

          Tutorial: Selections from Davies, Diodotus (.3885-pp. 151-54) and
                Ciron (#8443-pp. 312-16).

Nov. 13-15   Family Structures: kinship and household

                S. Isager, "The Marriage Pattern in Classical Athens. Men
                and Women in Isaios," C&M 33 (1981-82) pp. 81-96.

                D. M. MacDowell, The Law in Classical Athens, Ithaca, 1978,
                Chapter 6 (handout).

                Isaeus and Lysias as below.

          Tutorial: Isaeus 8, "Claim to a Legacy" and Lysias 32, "Embezzlement
                of Trust Funds" (handout).

Nov. 20–22   The Family: sentiment/mentality

E. Friedl, Vasilika, Chapters 3 and 4.

J. Gould, "Law, Custom and Myth: aspects of the social position of women in classical Athens," JHS 100 (1980) pp. 38–59.

Demosthenes and Xenophon as below

Recommended: K. J. Dover, "Classical Greek Attitudes to Sexual Behaviour," Arethusa 6 (1975) pp. 59–73.

Cf. Dover's Greek Homosexuality, Cambridge, Mass., 1978, Part 2, "The Prosecution of Timarkhos."

Tutorial: Demosthenes 59, "An Illegal Union" (handout).

Xenophon, Economics, Chapters 7–10.

Nov. 27–29   The Family: household economy

J. K. Davies, "Athenian Citizenship: The Descent Group and the Alternatives," CJ 73 (1977–78) pp. 105–21.

B. Denich, "Sex and Power in the Balkans," in Woman, Culture, and Society, edited by M. Z. Rosaldo and L. Lamphere, Stanford, 1974 (handout).

D. M. Schaps, Economic Rights of Women in Ancient Greece, Edinburgh, 1979, Chapter 6, "The Dowry" pp. 74–88.

Tutorial: Demosthenes 59.

Dec. 4–6   The Polis: state and preindustrial city

Davies, "Athenian Citizenship."

M. I. Finley, "The Freedom of the Citizen in the Greek World," in Economy and Society in Ancient Greece, New York, 1981, pp. 77–94.

R. E. Wycherley, The Stones of Athens, Princeton, 1978, Chapter 3, "The Market" and Chapter 10, "Houses, Streets, Water Supply" (handout).

Recommended: M. I. Finley, "The Ancient City: From Fustel de Coulanges to Max Weber and Beyond," in Economy and Society, pp. 3–23.

Wycherley, The Stones, Chapter 2, "The Agora" or How the Greeks Built Cities, New York, 1962, Chapter 4.

Tutorial: Lysias 23 and 24, "A Claim to Citizen Rights" and "Defence of a State Pension" (handout).

HISTORY 3120   Winter Term
                                        1984-85

Jan. 15-17   Slavery in classical Athens

                M. I. Finley, Ancient Slavery and Modern Ideology,
                    New York, 1980, Chapter 1.

Jan. 22-24   The slave condition and the function of slavery

                Finley, Chapter 2.

                T. Wiedemann, Greek and Roman Slavery, Baltimore and London,
                    1981, Introductory Outline, and peruse.

        Recommended: G. E. M. de Ste. Croix, The Class Struggle in the
                         Ancient Greek World, Ithaca, 1981, Chapter 3, pp. 133-47.

            Tutorial: Demosthenes 27, Against Aphobus.
                       Xenophon, Economics, Chapters 3, 9, and 13.
                       AVN 50 and 51, "The two types of slavery" and
                           AVN 75, "The slaves of the metic Kephisodorus."

                       (AVN - M. M. Austin and P. Vidal-Naquet, Economic
                       and Social History of Ancient Greece, London, 1977)

Jan. 29-31   The slave's life and the ideology of slavery

                Finley, Chapter 3.

                O. Patterson, Slavery and Social Death. A Comparative Study,
                    Harvard, 1982, Chapter 8, "Manumission, Its Meaning
                    and Modes."

        Recommended: R. L. Sargent, "The Use of Slaves by the Athenians
                         in Warfare," Parts 1 and 2, CP 22 (1927) pp. 201-12
                         and 264-79.

            Tutorial: Aeschines 1, Against Timarchus, Chapters 54-66 and 97.
                       Aristotle, Economics, Book 1.
                       Aristotle's will.
                       Demosthenes 48, Against Evergus, Chapters 52-67.
                       Lysias 4, "Quarrel over a Slave-girl."

Feb. 5-7   The Athenian economy: class and status

                Andrewes, Chapter 7, esp. pp. 142 ff.

                K. Polanyi, "The Economy Embedded in Society," from
                    The Livelihood of Man, New York, 1977 (handout).

Recommended: M. I. Finley, The Ancient Economy, London, 1973, Chapter 2, "Orders and Status."

G. E. M. de Ste. Croix, "Class in the Ancient World," New Left Review 146 (1984) pp. 94-111.

Tutorial: Demosthenes 36, For Phormio.

Feb. 12-14   The Athenian economy: the "industrial" sector

M. I. Finley, "Technical Innovation and Economic Progress in the Ancient World," in Economy and Society in Ancient Greece, pp. 176-95 (handout).

R. J. Hopper, Trade and Industry in Classical Greece, London, 1979, Chapter 6, and one of Chapters 4, 7, or 9.

Recommended: A. Burford, Craftsmen in Greek and Roman Society, London, 1972.

Tutorial: Demosthenes 32, Against Zenothemis.
AVN 95, "The silver mines of Laurion" and
AVN 121, "A written contract for a bottomry loan."

History 3120

Virginia Hunter
1984-85

Feb. 26-28   Thucydides, historian of the Peloponnesian War

                    Thucydides, Book 1.

          Recommended: E. A. Havelock, "The Preliteracy of the Greeks"
                        in The Literate Revolution in Greece and its
                        Cultural Consequences. Princeton, 1982.

                        V. J. Hunter, Past and Process in Herodotus
                        AND Thucydides. Princeton, 1982, Chapter 3.

          Tutorial: Thucydides 1.1-23.

Mar. 5-7   War as social history

                    Thucydides, Book 2.1-65.

                    Y. Garlan, War in the Ancient World: A Social History,
                        London, 1975, Chapter 3, pp. 134-45 (handout).

          Tutorial: Thucydides, 2.34-65.

Mar. 12-14   Empire, war, and stasis

                    Thucydides, Book 3.1-85.

                    M. I. Finley, "The Athenian Empire: A Balance Sheet"
                        in Economy and Society, pp. 41-61 (handout).

                    documents from N. Lewis, The Fifth Century B. C.,
                        Toronto, 1971 (handout).

          Tutorial: Thucydides, 3.36-50 and 69-84.

Mar. 19-21   The challenge of the Sophists

                    Thucydides, Books 4.1-41 and 5.1-26.

                    G. B. Kerferd, The Sophistic Movement, Cambridge,
                        1981, Chapters 1, 3, and part of 5 (handout).

          Tutorial: Thucydides, 5.84-116 and 6.1-32.

204

Mar. 26-28   Medicine and systematic research

                    Hippocratic Writings, edited by G. E. R. Lloyd,
                        Introduction and Epidemics, pp. 87-107 and
                        The Nature of Man.

        Recommended: G. E. R. Lloyd, Magic, Reason and Experience,
                     Cambridge, 1979, Chapter 3, "The Development
                     of Empirical Research," pp. 126-69.

        Tutorial: Hippocrates, Tradition in Medicine and Airs, Waters,
                  Places.

Apr. 2-4   Historiography and the Presocratic tradition

                    Thucydides, Book 7.

        Recommended: one of:

                    F   F. M. Cornford, Thucydides Mythistoricus,
                         London, 1907, Chapters 10 and 11.

                         J. H. Finley, Thucydides, Cambridge, Mass., 1942,
                         Chapter 8.

                         Hunter, Past and Process, Chapter 6.

        Tutorial: Thucydides, 7.59 to end.

Apr. 9-11   Euripides, psychodramatist or traditionalist?

                    Euripides, Hecuba and Andromache.

        Tutorial: Trojan Women.

                                                    Feb. 26, 1985

History 3120

Virginia Hunter
1984-85

Suggested essay topics:

1. A study of self-help and community control in the Attic orators.

2. What alternatives were there to the ideal monogamous marriage in classical
    Athens, and who chose them?

3. Consider the family in Menander's new comedy. How far do his plays
    reflect new attitudes?

4. How great a role did the state play in the economy and society of Athens,
    including her cultural life?

5. The women of Aristophanes seem to contradict all that the orators indicate
    about women's role and behaviour. Discuss.

6. How much can we learn about Athenian Slavery from Aristophanes' comedies?

7. Consider the treatment of slaves in Classical Athens, using Genovese's first
    two categories, living conditions and conditions of life.

8. Who were the freedmen in classical Athens and what did they do?

9. Estimate the cost of living in the fourth century.

10. Many, perhaps most, Athenians aspired to a rentier existence. What possibilities
    were there for investments (including investments in slaves) in the
    classical period, and what kind of income could be derived from them?

11. Trace the career of Pasio the banker (and his successor Phormio) as rare
    examples of upward nobility in Athenian society.

12. What role did metics play in Athenian society, as indicated in the Attic
    orations?

13. Consider Thucydides' History as a source for the social history of war.

        Length: 20 pages
        Due date: April 11, 1985
        % of marks: 30-35

                                                        February 7, 1985

Virginia Hunter
1984-85

More essay topics:

14. Were Athenian women literate in the fifth century? A study based on art.

15. A study of the oral aspects of Athenian Society in the fourth century.

16. Athens power as a city depended on the Peiraieus. Discuss.

17. How did the Athenians transport building materials, goods, and people overland?

18. Thucydides' <u>History</u> is a close study of Collective psychology. Discuss.

University of California, Berkeley

Fall Semester 1985
R. Sealey

History 275A: Greek history 478-338 B.C.

This course is intended primarily to prepare participants for written and oral examinations. To a lesser extent it is intended to prepare them for History 285A, which will be given in spring 1986 and is called "research seminar," whatever that may mean. The class will meet once a week, probably on Tuesday afternoons, for about two hours each time. The first meeting will be held Tuesday, August 27, at 2 p.m. in the instructor's office, 2317 Dwinelle, and if any change in the time of the weekly meetings is needed, it can be negotiated then.

Each of the weekly meetings will be devoted to one of the topics stated in the list below. Each participant is required to take responsibility for three of the topics. "Responsibility" means that, when the class meets on a scheduled topic, the responsible participant will be expected to give an account of the topic and of the problems arising within it; ideally his account should offer his own solution. Each such account should be full, in that it should expound all issues arising within the topic, but most participants will be well advised to aim at brevity. The account given orally to the meeting may be delivered from notes, provided that exposition is clear and consequential, but usually it is wise to speak from a fully written script. A finished version of the treatment of the topic should be handed as a paper to the instructor about a week after the account was delivered orally. The last paper of the semester should be handed in not later than Friday, December 6. Papers in legible handwriting are preferred to typewritten papers. Participants are advised to guard against devoting excessive time to the three papers; each should embody about one week's work.

Most of the material to be read can be found in the Art History/Classics Graduate Service of the Main Library. The main sources to be studied are:

    Thucydides: Historiae (ed. Jones and Powell, Oxford)
    Xenophon: Opera I, Historia Graeca (alias Hellenica, ed. Marchant, Oxford)
    Demosthenes: Orationes I (ed. Butcher, Oxford)

Ed Hunolt's Berkeley Book Store has been asked to provide copies of the above in the "recommended" category.

Participants should familiarize themselves with the following works of reference:

1. J.K. Davies: Athenian Propertied Families 600-300 B.C. (Oxford 1971)
2. J. Kirchner: Prosopographia Attica (Berlin 1901 and 1903)
3. G.F. Hill: Sources for Greek History between the Persian and Peloponnesian Wars (new edition, revised by R. Meiggs and A. Andrewes, Oxford 1951)

4. R. Meiggs and D. Lewis: A Selection of Greek Historical Inscriptions
   to the end of the fifth century B.C. (Oxford 1969)
5. M.N. Tod: A Selection of Greek Historical Inscriptions, volume II,
   from 403 to 323 B.C. (Oxford 1948)
6. A.G. Woodhead: The Study of Greek Inscriptions (Cambridge 1967)
7. P.J. Rhodes: A Commentary on the Aristotelian Athenaion Politeia
   (Oxford 1981)

Topics

1. The origin of the Delian League

   Herodotus 8.2-3; 9.106
   Thucydides 1.89-102; 1.128-138; 3.8-14; 4.102; 6.75-76
   Aristotle: Athenaion Politeia 23
   Aristotle: Politics 3.128 4a 38-41
   Plutarch: Life of Kimon 9
   scholion to Aischines 2.31, accessible in Hill-s Sources page 3
   J.A.O. Larsen, "The constitution and original purpose of the Delian
      League," Harvard Studies in Classical Philology 51 (1940) 175-213
   K. Raaflaub, "Beute, Vergeltung, Freiheit? Zur Zielsetzung des
      delisch-attischen Seebundes," Chiron 9 (1979) 1-22
   N.D. Robertson, "The true nature of the Delian League of 478-461
      B.C.," American Journal of Ancient History 5 (1980) 64-96 and
      110-133

   further reading, if desired:
   B.D. Meritt, H.T. Wade-Gery, M.F. McGregor: The Athenian Tribute
      Lists III, 94-224

   In what circumstances was the Delian League formed, and what was its
   purpose?

2. The activities of Ephialtes

   Aristotle: Athenaion Politeia 23-28
   Plutarch: Kimon 14-17
   Andokides 1.83-84
   H.T. Wade-Gery, "The judicial treaty with Phaselis and the history of
      the Athenian courts," Essays in Greek History (Oxford, Blackwell
      1958) 180-200
   P.J. Rhodes: The Athenian Boule (Oxford 1972) 144-207
   E. Ruschenbusch, "Ephialtes," Historia 15 (1966) 369-376
   J. Martin, "Von Kleisthenes zu Ephialtes," Chiron 4 (1974) 5-42

   further reading, if desired:
   E. Ruschenbusch: Athenische Innenpolitik in 5. Jahrhundert v. Chr.
      (Bamberg 1979) 57-65
   J.R. Cole, "Cimon's dismissal, Ephialtes' revolution and the
      Peloponnesian Wars," Greek Roman and Byzantine Studies 15 (1974)
      369-385

further reading, (con't)
R.W. Wallace, "Ephialtes and the Areopagos," GRBS. 15 (1974) 259-269

Did Ephialtes undertake a comprehensive reform for doctrinaire
reasons or precise correction of a specific abuse?

3. The missing tribute-quota-list

Thucydides 1.89-118
H.T. Wade-Gery, "The question of tribute in 449/8," Hesperia 14
(1945) 212-229
B.D. Meritt and H.T. Wade-Gery, "Athenian resources in 449 and 431
B.C.," Hesperia 26 (1957) 163-197
W.K. Pritchett, "The height of the lapis primus," Historia 13 (1964)
129-134
W.K. Pritchett, "The top of the lapis primus," GRBS. 7 (1966)
123-129
B.D. Meritt, "The top of the first tribute stele," Hesperia 35 (1966)
134-140
W.K. Pritchett, "The location of the lapis primus," GRBS. 8 (1967)
113-119
R. Meiggs: The Athenian Empire (Oxford 1972) 152-174

Participants should familiarize themselves with
B.D. Meritt, H.T. Wade-Gery, M.F. McGregor: The Athenian Tribute
Lists I-IV

Was there a year when no tribute was collected? If so, which year
was it?

4. The hypothesis of class-struggle in the Athenian Empire

Thucydides 2.8; 3.1-51; 4.78-88; 4.102-116; 4.120-135; 5.84-116;
8.21; 8.73
G.E.M. de Ste. Croix, "The character of the Athenian Empire,"
Historia 3 (1954-55) 1-41
D.W. Bradeen, "The Popularity of the Athenian Empire," Historia 9
(1960) 257-269
C.W. Fornara, "I. G. I^2, 39.52-57 and the popularity of the Athenian
Empire," Californian Studies in Classicial Antiquity 10 (1977)
39-55

further reading, if desired:
H.W. Pleket, "Thasos and the popularity of the Athenian Empire,"
Historia 12 (1963) 70-77
T.J. Quinn, "Thucydides and the unpopularity of the Athenian Empire,"
Historia 13 (1964) 257-266
J. de Romilly, "Thucydides and the cities of the Athenian Empire,"
Bulletin of the Institute of Classical Studies 13 (1966) 1-12

further reading (con't)
T.J. Quinn, "Political groups at Chios: 412 B.C.," Historia 18 (1969)
  22-30
R.P. Legon, "Samos in the Delian League," Historia 21 (1972) 145-158

Were political struggles in the Athenian Empire due to a constant
conflict between rich and poor or to other causes?

5. The Athenian decree or decrees concerning Megara

    Thucydides 1
    Plutarch: Perikles 29-33
    Meiggs/Lewis Nos. 61, 63, 64
    W.R. Connor, "Charinus' Megarian Decree," American Journal of
      Philology 83 (1962) 225-246
    G.L. Cawkwell, "Anthemocritus and the Megarians and the decree of
      Charinus," Revue des Etudes Grecques 82 (1969) 327-335
    G.E.M. de Ste. Croix: The Origins of the Peloponnesian War (Ithaca
      1972) 225-289, especially 252-289
    T.E. Wick, "Thucydides and the Megarian decree," L' Antiquite
      Classique 46 (1977) 74-79

    What policy did the Athenians pursue towards Megara? How did this
    policy bear on the outbreak of the Archidamian War?

6. The constitution of the 5000

    Thucydides 8.45-98
    [Lysias] 20
    Aristotle: Athenaion Politeia 29-33
    G.E.M. de Ste. Croix, "The constitution of the five thousand,"
      Historia 5 (1956) 1-23
    P.J. Rhodes, "The five thousand in the Athenian revolutions of 411
      B.C.," JHS. 92 (1972) 115-127
    C. Hignett: A History of the Athenian Constitution (Oxford 1952)
      356-362
    A. Andrewes in Gomme, Andrewes, Dover: Historical Commentary on
      Thucydides 5.323-328
    E. Ruschenbusch: Athenische Innenpolitik im 5. Jahrhundert v. Chr.
      (Bamberg 1979) 94-109

    What two views can be held about the intermediate regime? How does
    this question bear on the causes of the revolution?

7. The codification of the laws and nomothesia

    Thucydides 8.97
    Andokides 1.17; 1.22; 1.82-89; 1.95-96
    Demosthenes 24.20-33; 24.138
    Aischines 3.38-39
    Aristotle: Ethics 5.1137a31-1138a2

[Plato]: Definitions 415b
Supplementum Epigraphicum Graecum 26.72 = R.S. Stroud, Hesperia 43
    (1974) 158-188
Lysias 6.10
Lysias 30
Aristophanes: Thesmophoriazousai 361
Herodotos 1.29
Xenophon: Memorabilia 1.2.42
U. Kahrstedt, "Untersuchungen zu athenischen Behorden II: Die
    Nomotheten und die Legislative in Athen," Klio 31 (1938) 1-32
M.H. Hansen, "Nomos and psephisma in fourth-century Athens," GRBS. 19
    (1978) 315-350
M.H. Hansen, "Did the Athenian ecclesia legislate after 403/2 B.C.?"
    GRBS. 20 (1979) 27-53

further reading, if desired:
S. Dow, "The Athenian calendar of sacrifices: the chronology of
    Nikomakhos' second term," Historia 9 (1960) 270-293

What was the difference between a law and a decree in the fourth
century, and how far back can the distinction be traced?

8. Athenian politics during the Corinthian War

Xenophon: Hellenica 3.1-5.1, especially 3.5 and 4.8
Hellenica Oxyrhynchia 6-7, 16-18
M.N. Tod: Greek Historical Inscriptions II, Nos. 107 and 116
Andokides 3
Lysias 28 and 29
R. Seager, "Thrasybulus, Conon and Athenian imperialism," JHS. 87
    (1967) 95-115
G.L. Cawkwell, "The imperialism of Thrasybulus," Classical Quarterly,
    New Series 26 (1976) 270-277
P. Funke: Homonoia and Arche - Historia Einzelschriften 37 (1980)
    1-16 and 162-167

further reading, if desire:
S. Perlman, "Athenian democracy and the revival of imperialistic
    expansion at the beginning of the fourth century B.C.," Classical
    Philology 63 (1968) 257-267
S. Perlman, "The causes and outbreak of the Corinthian War," CQ. NS.
    14 (1964) 64-81

Were political groupings in Athens programmatic or personal or
non-existent?

9. The foundation of the Second Athenian League

Xenophon: Hellenica 5.2-7.1
Diodoros 15.25-33, 38, 45-47, 50
Deinarchos 1.37-40

Tod II, Nos. 118, 121, 122, 123
A.P. Burnett, "Thebes and the expansion of the Second Athenian
  Confederacy," Historia 11 (1962) 1-17
G.L. Cawkwell, "The foundation of the Second Athenian Confederacy,"
  CQ. NS. 23 (1973) 47-60
D.G. Rice, "Xenophon, Diodorus and the year 379/8 B.C.,
  reconstruction and reappraisal," Yale Classical Studies 24 (1975)
  95-130

further reading, if desired:
J. Cargill: The Second Athenian League 51-82

Can stages be traced and explained in the foundation of the League?

10. Athenian operations in the North Aegean from 368

Xenophon: Hellenica 6.3-7.1
Demosthenes 9.16; 19.137; 19.253
[Demosthenes] 7.29
Aischines 2.32
Demosthenes 23.100-180
S. Accame: La lega ateniese del secolo IV. a. C. (Roma 1941)
  155-157, 165-167
G.L. Cawkwell, "The common peace of 366/5 B.C.," CQ. NS 11 (1961)
  80-86
T.T.B. Ryder: Koine Eirene: General Peace and Local Independence in
  Ancient Greece (Oxford 1965) 137-139
A. Hock, "Das Odrysenreich in Thrakien im funften und vierten
  Jahrhundert v. Chr.," Hermes 26 (1891) 76-117, especially 89-117
L. Kallet, "Iphikrates, Timotheos, and Athens 371-360 B.C.," GRBS.
  24 (1983) 239-252

When were the Athenian claims to Amphipolis and the Chersonese
recognized, and how serious were the Athenians in prosecuting those
claims?

11. Euboulos

Diodoros 16.7; 16.21-22
Isokrates 8 (On Peace)
Xenophon: Poroi
Demosthenes 20.127; 22.48-49; 24.11
A. Schaefer: Demosthenes und seine Zeit (Leipzig, first edition
  1856) 158-191
G.L. Cawkwell, "Eubulus," JHS. 83 (1963) 47-67
G.L. Cawkwell, "Notes on the Social War," Classica et Mediaevalia 23
  (1962) 34-49

Did Euboulos have a distinctive policy?

12. Athens and the Olynthian War

Demosthenes 1, 2, 3, 4
Demosthenes 5.5
Plutarch: Phokion 12-14
I.G. II², 207
G.L. Cawkwell, "The Defence of Olynthus," CQ. NS. 12 (1962) 122-140
M.J. Osborne, "Athens and Orontes," Annual of the British School at
   Athens 66 (1971) 297-321
Philochoros, F. Gr. Hist. III B 328 F 49, 50, 51, 156

What were the merits and defects of the Athenian strategy?

13. The peace of Philokrates

Aischines 2.12-80, 94-129; 3.58-78
Demosthenes 5; 19.9-60, 150-176, 234-235; 18.17-41
R. Sealey, "Proxenos and the peace of Philocrates," Wiener Studien
   68 (1955) 145-152
G.L. Cawkwell, "Aeschines and the peace of Philocrates," REG. 73
   (1960) 416-438
G.L. Cawkwell, "Aeschines an the ruin of Phocis in 346," REG. 75
   (1962) 453-459
M.M. Markle, "The strategy of Philip in 346 B.C.," CQ. NS. 24 (1974)
   253-268
G.L. Cawkwell, "The peace of Philocrates again," CQ. NS. 18 (1978)
   93-104

Why were the Athenians distressed after peace was concluded?

14. Philip's negotiations with Athens 344-342

Demosthenes 6
[Demosthenes] 7
Didymos 8.7-31, including Philochoros F 157
Aischines 3.89-105
F.R. Wust: Philipp II. von Makedonien und Griechenland in den jahren
   von 346 bis 338, 54-101
F. Jacoby: Die Fragments der griechischen Historiker III b
   (Supplement) I, 531-533
G.L. Cawkwell, "Demosthenes' policy after the peace of Philocrates,"
   CQ. NS. 13 (1963) 120-138 and 200-213
P.A. Brunt, "Euboea in the time of Philip II," CQ. NS. 19 (1969)
   245-265

What aims did each party pursue in the negotiations?

214

15. Transmission of the Demosthenic text

    C. Fuhr: introduction to volume I of the Teubner text of 1914
    S.H. Butcher: introduction to volume I of the Oxford text (note two
      misprints:
      on page xvii, in the account of S, "xxxii-xxxiv" should be
      "xxxii-xxxv"
      on page xviii, in the account of A, "xvi, xv, xviii, li" should be
      "xvi, xv, xvii, li")
    Dionysios of Halikarnassos: First Letter to Ammaios
    [Plutarch]: Lives of the Ten Orators 847
    F. Blass: Die attische Beredsamkeit III, 1 (Leipzig, second edition
      1893) 50-60
    E. Drerup, "Antike Demosthenesausgaben," Philologus Supplementband 7
      (1899) 531-551

    For general information on the transmission of classical texts one
    may consult
      L.D. Reynolds and N.G. Wilson: Scribes and Scholars (Oxford,
      second edition 1974), especially 1-37

    Are the preserved texts what was spoken?

16. Didymos

    H. Diels and W. Schubart: Didymos Kommentar zu Demosthenes -
      Berliner Klassikertexte 1 (Berlin 1904) IX-LIII
    P. Foucart: Etude sur Didymos. Memoires de l' Institut National de
      France. Academie des Inscriptions et Belles-Lettres 38 (1909)
      25-52
    Plutarch: Demosthenes 11, 15
    Dionysios of Halikarnassos: Demosthenes 13
    F. Blass: Die attische Beredsamkeit III, 1 (Leipzig, second edition
      1893) 49-50
    K. J. Dover: Lysias and the Corpus Lysiacum (California 1968) 1-27

    Was Didymos a pioneer in the study of Demosthenes or did he draw on
    earlier commentaries? Was the Demosthenic Corpus known to him
    similar in content to the Corpus now extant? Where did it come
    from?

17. Demosthenes and the tribrach

    F. Blass: Die attische Beredsamkeit III, 1 (Leipzig, second edition
      1893) 105-112
    C.D. Adams, "Demosthenes' avoidance of Breves," CP. 12 (1917)
      271-294
    F. Vogel, "Die Kurzenmeidung in der griechischen Prosa," Hermes 58
      (1923) 87-108
    Does presence of tribrachs show that a speech is not be Demosthenes?
    Does avoidance of tribrachs show that it is by Demosthenes?

18. The Fourth Philippic

Demosthenes 8 and 10
A. Korte, "Zu Didymos' Demosthenes-Commentar," Rheinisches Museum 60
   (1905) 388-410
C.D. ADams, "Speeches VIII and X of the Demosthenic Corpus," CP. 33
   (1938) 129-144
S.G. Daitz, "The relationship of the De Chersoneso and the
   Philippica quarta of Demosthenes," CP. 52 (1957) 145-162
R.M. Errington, "Review-Discussion: Four Interpretations of Philip
   II," AJAH. 6 (1981) 79-80
G.L. Cawkwell, "Demosthenes' policy after the peace of Philocrates
   I," CQ. NS. 13 (1963) 134-136

Is the speech authentic? If so, what was its original form and when
was it delivered?

R.Sealey   University of California, Berkeley   Fall Semester 1984

History 280A: The Constitution and Society of Athens

The constitutional history of Athens has often been regarded as a series of catastrophic changes, associated with the names of Solon, Peisistratos, Kleisthenes, and Ephialtes. The present course will try to understand Athenian development by attending to continuity. As far as possible, each social or political institution will be studied first in its mature form and then traced back to its origin.

The class will meet once a week for two hours, probably on Tuesdays at 2-4 p.m. The first meeting will be held on Tuesday, August 28, at 2 p.m. in the instructor's office, 2317 Dwinelle, and that will be the occasion to arrange a different time of the week, if necessary. Each participant will be required to report to the class on three topics in the following list. After addressing the class and receiving comments, one should hand in the final version of one's essay to the instructor a week later. But the last paper of the semester should be handed in on Friday, December 7.

1. The population of Attica

    Athenaios 6.272b
    Plutarch: Life of Phokion 28.7
    Diodoros 18.18.4
    [Demosthenes] 25.50-51
    [Plutarch]: Lives of the Ten Orators 843d
    Plato: Kritias 112d
    Hypereides fr. 29 (Kenyon)
    Thucydides 2.13.6-8; 7.27.5; 8.65.3; 8.97.1
    [Lysias] 20.13

    P. J. Rhodes: "Ephebi, Bouleutai and the Population of Athens," Zeitschrift für Papyrologie und Epigraphik 38 (1980) 191-201
    E. Ruschenbusch: "Epheben, Buleuten und die Bürgerzahl von Athen," ZPE 41 (1981) 103-05
    E. Ruschenbusch: "Noch einmal die Bürgerzahl Athens um 330 v. Chr.," ZPE 44 (1981) 110-12
    E. Ruschenbusch: Athenische Innenpolitik im 5. Jahrhundert v. Chr. (Bamberg 1979) 133-52

    Further reading, if desired:

    D. Whitehead: The Ideology of the Athenian Metic (Cambridge Philological Society, Supplementary Volume 4 [1977]) 7-10, 97-98, 159-63.
    M. I. Finley: The Ancient Economy (California 1973) 24
    A. H. M. Jones: Athenian Democracy (Oxford, Blackwell 1957) 8-10, 76-79.
    A. W. Gomme: The Population of Athens in the Fifth and Fourth Centuries B.C. (Oxford, Blackwell 1933) 1-35
    K. J. Beloch: Die Bevölkerung der griechisch-römischen Welt (Leipzig 1886) 57-60, 84-99

2. Phratries and gene

    IG II^2, 1237
    IG I^3, 104 = R. Meiggs and D. Lewis: A Selection of Greek Historical Inscriptions (Oxford 1969), No. 86

A. Andrewes: "Philochoros on Phratries," Journal of Hellenic Studies 81 (1961) 1-15
A. Andrewes: "Phratries in Homer," Hermes 89 (1961) 129-40
C. Hignett: A History of the Athenian Constitution (Oxford 1952) 55-57, 313-15, 390-91
H. T. Wade-Gery: "Studies in the Structure of Attic Society: I. Demotionidae," Classical Quarterly 25 (1931) 129-43 = Essays in Greek History (Oxford, Blackwell 1958) 116-34

3. Marriage, succession, citizenship I: the sons of Mantias

Demosthenes 39
[Demosthenes] 40

J. Rudjardt: "La reconnaissance de la paternité: sa nature et sa portée dans la société athénienne," Museum Helveticum 19 (1962) 39-64
J. K. Davies: Athenian Propertied Families (Oxford 1971) 364-68
H. J. Wolff: "Marriage Law and Family Organization in Ancient Athens. A Study on the Interrelation of Public and Private Law in the Greek City," Traditio 2 (1944) 43-95

4. Marriage, succession, citizenship II: concubines and bastards

Demosthenes 23.53-55
Herodotos 2.92,1
Isaios 3
Isaios 6.18-24
[Demosthenes] 46.18
Aristotle: Athenaion Politeia 26.4; 42.1-2

A. R. W. Harrison: The Law of Athens I: The Family and Property (Oxford 1968) 1-15, 61-68
D. M. MacDowell: "Bastards as Athenian Citizens," CQ. NS. 26 (1976) 88-91
P. J. Rhodes: "Bastards as Athenian Citizens," CQ. NS. 28 (1978) 89-92

Further reading, if desired:

S. C. Humphreys: "The Nothoi of Kynosarges," JHS.94 (1974) 88-95
A. Ledl: "Das attische Bürgerrecht und die Frauen," Wiener Studien 29 (1907) 173-227; 30 (1908) 1-46, 173-230

5. Revisions of the list of citizens

Aristotle, AP. 13.5; 26.4
Aischines 1.77-78; 1.86; 2.182
Demosthenes 57
Androtion: F. Gr. Hist. III B 324 F 52
Philochoros: 328 F 52; F 119
Plut. Per. 37.4
[Demosthenes] 59.16 and 52
Isaios 6.47; 8.43
Athen. 13.555d-556a, 557b-c
Scholiast to Aischines 1.39
Diogenes Laertios 2.26
Aulus Gellius 15.20.6

F. Jacoby: Die Fragmente der griechischen Historiker III b (Supplement) I
(Leiden 1954) 158-61
J. Day and M. Chambers: Aristotle's History of Athenian Democracy (Califor-
nia 1962) 118
P. J. Rhodes: A Commentary of the Aristotelian Athenaion Politeia (Oxford
1981) 188
J. K. Davies: "Athenian Citizenship: The Descent Group and the Alterna-
tives," Classical Journal 73 (1977-78) 105-21
E. Ruschenbusch: Athenische Innenpolitik 83-87

6. The age for attaining majority

Aristotle, AP. 42; 53
Demosthenes 27, 28, 29, 30, 31

J. M. Carter: "Eighteen Years Old?" Bulletin of the Institute of Classical
Studies (University of London) 14 (1967) 51-57
Davies: APF. 123-26
M. Golden: "Demosthenes and the Age of Majority at Athens," Phoenix 33
(1979) 25-38

Further reading, if desired:

W. Dittenberger: De ephebis atticis (Göttingen 1863) 22-23
Ch. Pélékidis: Histoire de l'ephébie attique des origines à 31 avant
Jésus-Christ (Paris 1962) 215

7. Atimia

Demosthenes 9.44
Aristotle, AP. 16.10
Solon F 70 = Plut. Sol. 19.4 (E. Ruschenbusch: Solonos Nomoi. Die Frag-
mente des solonischen Gesetzeswerkes mit einer Test -- und Ueberliefe-
rungsgeschichte = Historia Einzelschriften Heft 9 [Wiesbaden 1966])
Andokides 1.73-79, 107-08

E. Ruschenbusch: Untersuchungen zur Geschichte des athenischen Strafrechts
(Köln and Graz 1968) 11-21
M. H. Hansen: Apagoge, Endeixis and Ephegesis against Kakourgoi, Atimoi and
Pheugontes. A Study in the Athenian Administration of Justice in the
Fourth Century B.C. (Odense University Classical Studies, volume 8
[1976]) 54-66, 75-82
U. Kahrstedt: Staatsgebiet und Staatsangehörige in Athen. Studien zum
öffentlichen Recht Athens, Teil I (Stuttgart and Berlin 1934) 109-10

8. The origin of citizens and metics

Solon F 75 = Plut. Sol. 24.4
Iliad 9.432-95; 23.83-92
Odyssey 6.207-08; 13.256-86
Herodotos 1.35
Aischylos: Pers. 319; Seven 548; Suppl. 609, 994; Agam. 57; Cho. 971; Eum.
1018,
IG I^3, 244C line 8

P. A. L. Greenhalgh: "The Homeric Therapon and Opaon and Their Historical Implications," BICS 29 (1982) 81-90
D. Whitehead: The Ideology of the Athenian Metic 140-47
E. Grace: "Status Distinctions in the Draconian Law," Eirene 11 (1973) 5-30

9. Homicide

Aristotle, AP. 57
Demosthenes 23.22-99
IG I³, 104 = Meiggs/Lewis No. 86

E. Ruschenbusch: "Phonos. Zum Recht Drakons und seiner Bedeutung für das Werden des athenischen Staates," Historia 9 (1960) 129-54
M. Gagarin: Drakon and Early Athenian Homicide Law (New Haven and London 1981) 96-110
A. R. W. Harrison: The Law of Athens II: Procedure (Oxford 1971) 36-43
F. Jacoby: Fragmente IIIb (Supplement) I, 22-25

10. From heliaia to dikasterion

Aristotle, AP. 3.5; 9.1; 42.1; 45.3; 53.2; 55.2
Demosthenes 23.28, 97; 24.105-14
Lysias 10.16
IG I³, 40 = Meiggs/Lewis No. 52, line 75
Antiphon 6.21-24
Pollux 8.62
[Demosthenes] 34.21

H. T. Wade-Gery: "Themistokles' Archonship," Annual of the British School at Athens 37 (1936-37) 263-70 = Essays 171-79
H. T. Wade-Gery: "The Judicial Treaty with Phaselis and the History of the Athenian Courts," Essays 180-200
E. Ruschenbusch: "Ephesis. Ein Beitrag zur grieshischen Rechtsterminologie," Zeitschrift der Savigny-Stiftung für Rechtsgeschichte 78 (1961), Romanistische Abteilung 386-90
E. Ruschenbusch: "Heliaia. Die Tradition über das solonische Volksgericht," Historia 14 (1965) 381-84
M. H. Hansen: "The Athenian Heliaia from Solon to Aristotle," Classica et Mediaevalia 33 (1981-82) 9-47
M. H. Hansen: "Demos, Ecclesia and Dicasterion in Classical Athens," Greek, Roman and Byzantine Studies 19 (1978) 127-46

11. The origin of judicial litigation

Iliad 18.497-508; 23.566-613
Demosthenes 23.53
Lysias 1
Solon F 28
[Demosthenes] 59.66

H. J. Wolff: "The Origin of Judicial Litigation among the Greeks," Traditio 4 (1946) 31-87
L. Gernet: "Sur l'exécution capitale," Revue des Etudes Grecques 37 (1924) 261-93
E. Ruschenbusch: "Der Ursprung des gerichtlichen Rechtsstreits bei den Griechen," Symposion 1977 (Köln and Wien 1982) 1-8

12. **Eisangelia**

Hypereides: For Euxenippos 1-8
Aristotle, AP. 4.4; 8.4; 45.2; 59.2-4
Lexikon Rhetoricum Cantabrigiense, s.v. eisangelia, quoted by Harrison, infra 51, note 1
Krateros F. Gr. Hist. 342 F 11
Herodotus 6.104
[Demosthenes] 47.43

A. R. W. Harrison: The Law of Athens II: Procedure 50-59
P. J. Rhodes: The Athenian Boule (Oxford 1972) 162-64
M. H. Hansen: Eisangelia. The Sovereignty of the People's Court in the Fourth Century B.C. and the Impeachment of Generals and Politicians (Odense University Classical Studies, volume 6 [1975]) 12-28
G. M. Calhoun: The Growth of the Criminal Law in Ancient Greece (Berkeley 1927) 57-62
P. J. Rhodes: "Eisangelia in Athens," JHS. 99 (1979) 103-14
M. H. Hansen: "Eisangelia in Athens: A Reply," JHS. 100 (1980) 89-95

13. **Nomos and psephisma in the fourth century**

Aristotle: Ethics 5.1137a31-1138a2
[Plato]: Definitions 415b
Demosthenes 24.20-33, 138
Aischines 3.38-39
Demosthenes 20.89-99
Supplementum Epigraphicum Graecum 26.72 = Stroud, Hesperia 43 (1974) 158-88

U. Kahrstedt: "Untersuchungen zu athenischen Behörden II: Die Nomotheten und die Legislative in Athen," Klio 31 (1938) 1-32
L. M. MacDowell: "Law-Making at Athens in the Fourth Century B.C.," JHS. 95 (1975) 62-74
M. H Hansen: "Athenian Nomothesia in the Fourth Century B.C. and Demosthenes's Speech against Leptines," Classica et Mediaevalia 32 (1980) 87-104
M. H. Hansen: "Did the Athenian Ecclesia Legislate after 403/2 B.C.?" GRBS. 20 (1979) 27-53
M. H. Hansen: "Nomos and Psephisma in Fourth-Century Athens," GRBS. 19 (1978) 315-30

14. **Nomos and psephisma before the fourth century**

Thucydides 8.97
Andokides 1.82-89, 95-96
IG I^3, 104 = Meiggs/Lewis No. 86
Lysias 6.10
Xenophon: Memorabilia 1.2.42
Herodotos 1.29
Andokides 1.17 and 22
Thucydides 8.67
Xenophon: Hellenica 1.7.12-13
[Demosthenes] 59.4-5
Aristophanes: Thesmophoriazousai 361

S. Dow: "The Athenian Calendar of Sacrifices: The Chronology of
Nikomakhos' Second Term," Historia 9 (1960) 270-93
S. Dow: "The Walls Inscribed with Nikomakhos' Law Code," Hesperia 30
(1961) 58-73
K.J. Dover: "Anapsephisis in Fifth-Century Athens," JHS. 75 (1955) 17-20

Further Reading, if desired:

H.J. Wolff: "Normenkontrolle und Gesetzesbegriff in der Attischen Demokratie"
(Sitzungsberichte der Heidelberger Akademie der Wissenschaften,
Philosophische-historische Klasse, [1970]) 15-22, 47-48, 78-80.

University of California, Berkeley

Spring semester 1985
R. Sealey

History 107A: The History of Ancient Athenian Law

The lectures will study legal phenomena, as they were in the fully
developed conditions of the fourth century B.C., and will try to work
back to their origins. The emphasis will be on procedural law.

Bookstores

Ed Hunolt's Berkeley Book Store has been asked to provide copies of the
following:

J.M. Moore: Aristotle and Xenophon on Democracy and Oligarchy.

Reserve-list

Moffitt Library has been asked to put the following on reserve:

I   texts in the series "Loeb Classical Library" for one-day reserve:

1. Demosthenes, 7 volumes

2. Homer: Iliad, 2 volumes

3. Isaeus

4. Lysias

5. Minor Attic Orators, 2 volumes. Volume 1 includes Antiphon and
   Andocides.

II   other books:

6. R.J. Bonner and G. Smith: The Administration of Justice from Homer
   to Aristotle, 2 volumes (one-day reserve)

7. C.W. Fornara: Archaic Times to the End of the Peloponnesian War
   (Translated Documents of Greece and Rome, volume 1)
   (two-hour reserve)

8. M. Gagarin: Drakon and Early Athenian Homicide Law (two-hour
   reserve)

9. A.R.W. Harrison: The Law of Athens, 2 volumes (one-day reserve)

10. D.M. MacDowell: Athenian Homicide Law in the Age of the Orators
    (two-hour reserve)

11. J.M. Moore: Aristotle and Xenophon on Democracy and Oligarchy
    (one-day reserve)

12. R.S. Stroud: Drakon's Law on Homicide (two-hour reserve)

13. H.T. Wade-Gery: Essays in Greek History (one-day reserve)

III   photocopies of the following articles:

14. M.H. Hansen: "Demos, Ecclesia and Dicasterion in classical Athens," Greek Roman and Byzantine Studies 19 (1978) 127-146

15. M.H. Hansen: "Did the Athenian Ecclesia legislate after 403/2 B.C.?" GRBS. 20 (1979) 27-53

16. H.J. Wolff: "The Origin of Judicial Litigation among the Greeks," Traditio 4 (1946) 31-87

Program of lectures and readings

1. Significance of the subject (about half a week)

   recommended reading:
   participants should make preliminary acquaintance with Aristotle: Constitution of Athens 42-62, accessible in J.M. Moore: Aristotle and Xenophon on Democracy and Oligarchy 183-202

2. Periods of Athenian history (about half a week)

3. Historical sources for Athenian legal development (about one week)

   recommended reading:
   Iliad 2. 48-399; 9. 9-174; 18. 497-508
   Herodotus 1. 29
   participants in the course should make preliminary acquaintance with the following works:
       Antiphon: speeches 1, 5, 6
       Lysias: speech 30
       Demosthenes: speeches 23, 24

4. Types of action available to the Athenian litigant (about one week)

   recommended reading:
   Aristotle: Constitution of Athens 3, 22, 52-53, 55-59, 68, accessible in Moore 147-149, 165-166, 192-193, 195-200, 207-207
   Antiphon 5 and 6

5. The sources of law (about two weeks)

   recommended reading:
   Demosthenes 24. 20-33; 20. 89-99
   Lysias 30
   Andocides 1. 17; 1. 22; 1. 82-89; 1. 95-96
   M.H. Hansen: "Did the Athenian Ecclesia legislate after 403/2 B.C.?"
   Greek Roman and Byzantine Studies 20 (1979) 27-53

224

6. The development of the popular court (about one and a half weeks)

recommended reading:
Lysias 10. 16
Demosthenes 24. 105-114; 23. 97
Aristotle: Constitution of Athens 3, 9, 42, 53, 55, accessible in
Moore 147-149, 153, 183-185, 192-193, 195-196
C.W. Fornara: Translated Documents of Greece and Rome, volume 1,
No. 103 (Athenian regulations for Chalkis)
H.T. Wade-Gery: Essays in Greek History 171-200
M.H. Hansen: "Demos, Ecclesia and Dicasterion in classical
Athens,"
Greek Roman and Byzantine Studies 19 (1978) 127-146

7. Homicide (about three weeks)

recommended reading:
Aristotle: Constitution of Athens 57, accessible in Moore 198-199
Demosthenes 23. 22-99
Fornara: Documents No. 15 (Drakon's Law on Homicide)
Antiphon 1
Lysias 1
M. Gagarin: Drakon and Early Athenian Homicide Law 22-26, 31-37,
96-110, 135-137
D.M. MacDowell: Athenian Homicide Law in the Age of the Orators
52-57

8. Eisangelia (about one and a half weeks)

recommended reading:
Hypereides: For Euxenippos, accessible in Minor Attic
Orators, volume 2
Aristotle: Constitution of Athens 4.4; 8. 4; 45. 2; 59. 2-4
[Demosthenes] 47. 35-44
Herodotus 6. 21; 6. 104; 6. 136
P.J. Rhodes: "Eisangelia at Athens," Journal of Hellenic Studies
99 (1979) 103-114

9. The origin of judicial litigation among the Greeks (about one week)

recommended reading:
Iliad 18. 497-508
Hesiod: Works and Days
[Demosthenes] 59. 64-70
H.J. Wolff: "The Origin of Judicial Litigation among the Greeks,"
Traditio 4 (1946) 31-87

10. The law of citizenship and marriage (about three and a half weeks)

recommended reading:
Aristotle: Constitution of Athens 26. 4; 42
Demosthenes 57. 30

10.   (cont.)

    Demosthenes 39
    [Demosthenes] 40
    Isaeus 3
    Isaeus 6. 18-24
    Isaeus 10. 10
    Plutarch: Solon 24. 4
    H.T. Wade-Gery: "Demotionidai," Classical Quarterly 25 (1931)
    129-143
    =Essays in Greek History 116-134

Paper

Each participant in the course is required to write one paper. The
subject should be chosen from the following list; anyone wishing to write
on a subject other than these should consult the instructor. Papers
should be handed in no later than Wednesday, March 27; it is important to
meet this deadline. No limit of length is specified for the paper, but
usually brevity is a good exercise. Legibly hand-written papers are
preferred to typewritten papers.

1.   A critical examination of M. Gagarin's theory about the law of
      Drakon

      C.W. Fornara: Translated Documents of Greece and Rome, volume 1,
      No. 15 (Drakon's Law on Homicide)
      R.S. Stroud: Drakon's Law on Homicide 34-40, 66-70
      M. Gagarin: Drakon and Early Athenian Homicide Law 31-37, 80-110

      further reading, if desired:
      D.M. MacDowell: Athenian Homicide Law in the Age of the Orators
      W.T. Loomis: "The Nature of Premeditation in Athenian Homicide
      Law," Journal of Hellenic Studies 92 (1972) 86-95

2.   Was legitimate birth requisite for Athenian citizenship?

      Isaeus 3
      Demosthenes 39
      [Demosthenes] 40; 59. 16 and 122
      A.R.W. Harrison: The Law of Athens 1. 63-65
      D.M. MacDowell: "Bastards as Athenian Citizens," Classical
      Quarterly, New Series 26 (1976) 88-91
      P.J. Rhodes: "Bastards as Athenian Citizens," CQ. NS. 28 (1978)
      89-92

3.   Did the court-action for declaring a law invalid necessarily bring
      an alternative law into force?

      Demosthenes 20. 89-90
      Demosthenes 24. 20-33

3.   (cont)

D.M. MacDowell: "Law-Making at Athens in the Fourth Century B.C.,"
JHS. 95 (1975) 62-74
M.H. Hansen: "Athenian Nomothesia in the fourth century and
Demosthenes' speech against Leptines," Classica et Mediaevalia 32
(1980) 87-104
M.H. Hansen: "Did the Athenian Ecclesia legislate after 403/2
B.C.?" Greek Roman and Byzantine Studies 20 (1979) 27-53

4.   The authenticity of the tetralogies ascribed to Antiphon

Antiphon speeches 2, 3, 4 = tetralogies 1, 2, 3
M. Gagarin: "The Proh bition of Just and Unjust Homicide in
Antiphon's Tetralogies," GRBS. 19 (1978) 291-306
K.J. Dover: "The Chronology of Antiphon's Speeches," Classical
Quarterly 44 (1950) 44-60
G. Zuntz: "Once again the Antiphontean Tetralogies," Museum
Helveticum 6 (1949) 100-103
P. von der Muhll: "Zür Unechtheit der antiphontischen
Tetralogien," Museum Helveticum 5 (1948) 1-5

5.   The age for attaining majority at Athens

Aristotle: Constitution of Athens 42
Demosthenes 27, 28, 29, 30, 31
J.M. Carter: "Eighteen Years Old?" Bulletin of the Institute of
Classical Studies (University of London) 14 (1967) 51-57
J.K. Davies: Athenian Propertied Families (Oxford 1971) 123-126
M. Golden: "Demosthenes and the age of majority at Athens,"
Phoenix 33 (1979) 25-38.

THE AMERICAN UNIVERSITY
Department of History

29.300/600.01 ANCIENT STUDIES: Valerie French
     ALEXANDER THE GREAT   McCabe 106
                                          885-2405

I. PURPOSE AND SCOPE OF COURSE

Not often can we point to a single individual and say, "This
person changed the world." Alexander III, the Great, probably merits
such an assessment. During the semester we will investigate the world
into which he was born, examine his life, and evaluate his impact on
the ancient Eastern Mediterranean.

II. FORMAT OF COURSE

We will conduct the course as a seminar. Controversies abound in
current scholarship, and many questions about Alexander are still to
be answered. Some may never be answered definitively. Because almost
all the primary sources still extant have been translated into English
and because so many of the scholars now working on Alexander write in
English, even the novice student of Alexander can quickly familiarize
him or herself with the issues at stake; even the novice can suggest
new solutions to the puzzles about Alexander's life. Thus Alexander
makes a marvelous subject for lively discussion and debate, for
formulating new (even novel) hypotheses, for working as a group on the
problems of his life and career.

In order to give our class discussion focus, each student will
write a series of brief reports on special and narrowly defined
topics; these reports (about 4-5 pages, typed, double-spaced) will
provide the basis for classroom work. The reports are to be working
papers rather than finely polished essays. However, even working
papers must be clearly organized and literately written.

The reports will be circulated to all students for several days
prior to the class session in which they are to be presented. Reading
the reports is part of each session's core reading assignment. You
should put at least two copies of your report in the "A the G" box (in
the bookcase next to the faculty mailboxes in the history department)
and put a third copy in my mailbox; keep another copy for yourself.
For reports scheduled to be presented on a Monday, copies should be
available by the preceding Thursday morning; for reports scheduled to
be presented on Thursday, copies should be available on the preceding
Monday afternoon.

We will usually cover some three to four reports in one seventy-
five minute class meeting; each student should expect to do three to
four reports over the semester.

III. REQUIREMENTS OF COURSE

A. Regular class attendance; core reading assignments (including student reports) done on time; informed participation in class discussion   15%

B. Three to four reports (see above); assignments for particular topics will be made in class   35%

C. One medium length paper (about twelve to fifteen pages, including endnotes, typed, double-spaced, finely polished and crafted) on a topic mutually agreeable to you and me. The topic must be approved by Thursday, March 25th; a brief description (about one page) of the paper and a bibliography is due on Thursday, April 1st; the paper is due on Monday, April 26th.   25%

D. Final examination   25%

N.B. In order to receive a passing grade for this course, students must complete all requirements.

Graduate students should consult with me soon about additional reading and about your major paper (which will be longer than that described above).

IV. CRITERIA FOR EVALUATION OF STUDENT PERFORMANCE

In general, I consider a grade of "C" to connote competent work. This entails a sound basic grasp of the historical and the historiographical issues: literate presentation of research (i.e., standard English usage, coherent organization, correct spelling and punctuation, proper endnote and bibliographic format, etc.); assignments completed on time; informed contribution to class discussion. A "B" connotes work that is considerably better than competent--a more detailed knowledge of the subject matter and writing that is not only clear and correct but also persuasive. An "A" connotes work that is distinguished by originality and/or exceptional intellectual vigor and by graceful writing.

Please feel free to consult with me at any time about the quality of your work.

V. READINGS AND BOOKS

A. Books to be Purchased: The following books are required and are available in the AU Bookstore.

Arrian, The Campaigns of Alexander, trans. A. de Selincourt (Baltimore: Penguin, 1971).
Borza, Eugene, ed.,The Impact of Alexander the Great (Hillsdale: Dryden, 1974).
Curtius, Quintus, The History of Alexander, trans. W. Heckel (Baltimore: Penguin, 1984).

229

Hamilton, J.R., _Alexander the Great_ (Pittsburgh: Univ. of
  Pittsburgh Press, 1974).
Plutarch, _The Age of Alexander_, trans. I. Scott-Kilvert
  (Baltimore: Penguin, 1973).
Wilcken, Ulrich, _Alexander the Great_, trans. G. C. Richards
  (New York: Norton, 1967).

The following book is recommended and available in the AU
Bookstore:

Renault, Mary, _Fire From Heaven_ (New York: Vintage, 1969).

    You might also enjoy reading the other two novels in
Renault's Alexander triology, _The Persian Boy_ and
Funeral Games.

  B. _Reserve Readings_

    Many of the books you will be using over the semester are on
two-hour reserve. A list of reserve items is appended to the
syllabus.

  C. _Additional Bibliography_

    An extensive bibliography is appended to the syllabus.

VI. SUMMARY OF CLASS SCHEDULE AND CORE READING ASSIGNMENTS

Week # 1   INTRODUCTION TO COURSE

    Thursday, January 14   The "Problem" of Alexander the Great

Week # 2   THE WORLD ALEXANDER INHERITED

    Monday, January 18   Macedonia and Greece in the Fifth
                            Century (Lecture)

    Thursday, January 21   Macedonia and Greece in the Fourth
                            Century (Lecture)

      Core Reading: Wilcken, Chapter 1
                    Plutarch, _Demosthenes_ and _Alexander_

Week # 3   THE SOURCES: LITERARY AND PATERNAL

    Monday, January 25   The Ancient Sources for the Life of
                            Alexander (Lecture and discussion)

      Core Reading: Arrian, "Introduction"
                    Curtius, "Introduction"
                    Hamilton, Chapter 1

Pearson, <u>The Lost Histories of Alexander
the Great</u> (on reserve; I expect you to
peruse this book)

Come to class prepared to discuss which ones of the
<u>extant</u> sources are likely to be the most reliable.

Thursday, January 28   Philip II of Macedon

Core Reading: Wilcken, Chapter 2
               Hamilton, Chapter 2

Reports: 1. Philip's Youth: Hostage to Thebes with Few
                  Prospects for the Throne
               2. The New Macedonian Army
               3. Philip's Conquests: Did He Have A Grand
                  Objective?
               4. Philip's Tomb?

Week # 4   THE YOUNG ALEXANDER

Core Reading for the Week:
               Plutarch, <u>Alexander</u>, 1 - 8
               Curtius, Book I (summary)
               Hamilton, Chapter 3
               Wilcken, Chapter 3
               Renault, <u>Fire From heaven</u> (optional, but well
                  worth the time)

Monday, February 1

Reports: 1. The Family Tree: A Dynasty of Death and
                  Divisiveness
               2. Olympias: What did the World Look Like
                  Through Her Eyes?
               3. Lanike and Leonidas: Surrogate Parents?
               4. Philip As Father

Thursday, February 4

Reports: 1. Alexander's Siblings: Where Did He Stand
                  Among His Father's Children?
               2. Child Prodigy? Any Early Evidence of Genius?
               3. Boyhood Friends: Who Were They?
               4. Aristotle and Formal Education

WEEK # 5   ADOLESCENT AND YOUNG ADULT

Monday, February 8   Alexander as Crown Prince

Core Reading: Hamilton, Chapter 4

Reports: 1. Alexander as Regent
                  2. The Wedding of Philip and Cleopatra; Exile
                  3. The Pixodaros Affair
                  4. The Assassination of Philip II

Thursday, February 11   Alexander Takes the Throne

   Core Reading: Arrian, Book I. 1-11
                  Curtius, Book II (summary)
                  Hamilton, Chapter 5
                  Wilcken, Chapter 4

   Reports: 1. Who Supported Alexander?
                  2. Campaigns on the Danube and in Illyria
                  3. Thebes and Athens

WEEK # 6   GREECE AND THE EAST

   Monday, February 15   Persia   479 - 334   (Lecture)

   Thursday, February 18   Preparation For Invasion

   Core Reading: Hamilton, 52-56
                  Wilcken, 78-82

   Reports: 1. Isocrates and the Panhellenic Crusade
                  2. The Corinthian League and the Greek
                     Attitude to the Campaign
                  3. Parmenio and Attalus in Asia Minor

WEEK # 7   ACROSS THE HELLESPONT

   Monday, February 22   The First Stage of the Conquest

   Core Reading: Arrian, I. 11 - II. 4
                  Hamilton, Chapter 6
                  Wilcken, 83-89

   Reports: 1. The Strength and Strategy of Alexander vs.
                     The Strength and Strategy of the Persians
                  2. The Battle of the Granicus River
                  3. Alexander and the Ionian Greeks

   Thursday, February 25   Catch-Up Day

WEEK # 8   ANATOLIA TO EGYPT   (333-331)

   Monday, March 1   Alexander vs. Darius,   Phase I

   Core Reading: Arrian, II. 5 - 27
                  Curtius, III. 1 - IV. 6
                  Hamilton, 64-74
                  Wilcken, 99-112

232

Reports: 1. The Battle of Issus
                  2. The Siege of Tyre
                  3. Why Not Peace? Alexander's Answer to Darius

Thursday, March 4   Alexander Becomes Pharaoh

Core Reading: Arrian, III. 1-5
                  Curtius, IV. 7-8
                  Plutarch, 26-27
                  Hamilton, 74-79
                  Wilcken, 112-131
                  Borza, Impact, Part II

Reports: 1. Alexander as Pharaoh
                  2. The Visit to the Oracle of Siwah
                  3. Alexandria

WEEK # 9 SPRING VACATION

WEEK # 10 ACROSS THE MIDDLE EAST (331-326)

Monday, March 15   Alexander vs. Darius, Phase II

Core Reading: Arrian, III. 6-30
                  Curtius, IV. 9 - VII. 5
                  Hamilton, Chapter 8
                  Wilcken, 131-163

Reports: 1. The Battle of Gaugamela
                  2. "Flames Over Persepolis"--Accident or Policy?
                  3. The "Conspiracy of Philotas" and the Murder
                     of Parmenio
                  4. Bessus: Why So Brutal?

Thursday, March 18   On to India

Core Reading: Arrian, IV. 1-22
                  Curtius, VII. 6 - VIII. 8
                  Hamilton, Chapters 9 and 10
                  Wilcken, 163-181

Reports: 1. Campaigning in the East: Organized Conquest?
                     Raiding Expedition? Sight-seeing?
                  2. Cleitus the Black: Was Alexander Just Drunk?
                  3. Roxane and Marriage: An Affair of the Heart
                     or of State?
                  4. Proskynesis and the Pages' Conspiracy

WEEK # 11 TO THE "END" OF THE WORLD AND BACK (326-324)

Monday, March 22   Porus and the Return

Core Reading: Arrian, IV. 22 - VI. 30

Curtius, VIII. 9 - IX. 10
Hamilton, 109-128
Wilcken, 181-206

Reports: 1. The Battle of the River Hydaspes
             2. The Army Mutinies: Why?
             3. The Awful Trek: Was It Necessary?

Thursday, March 25   Reorganization and Reconstitution

Core Reading: Arrian, VII. 1-8
               Curtius, X. 1-4
               Hamilton, 128-135
               Wilcken, 207-218

Reports: 1. Executions of Generals and Satraps
             2. The Harpalus Affair
             3. Mass Marriages

N.B. Term paper topic must be approved today.

WEEK # 12 THE LAST YEAR (324-323)

Core Reading for the week:

               Arrian, VII. 8-30
               Curtius, X. 5-6
               Hamilton, Chapters 13-15
               Wilcken, 218-238

Monday, March 29   Reconciliations and Losses

Reports: 1. The Exiles Decree and Affairs in Greece
             2. The Banquet at Opis: Mutiny, Feast, Dismissal
             3. The Request for Deification

Thursday, April 1   Dreams and Death

Reports: 1. The Death of Hephestion
             2. Alexander's Plans
             3. Death: Fever? Poison? Exhaustion? Drink?

N.B. Brief description and bibliography for term paper due today.

WEEKS # 13-15 UNDERSTANDING AND INTERPRETING ALEXANDER

Pick two (2) of the following issues and come to class prepared
(i.e., with working notes, references to both primary and secondary
sources, etc.) to offer and defend your interpretation.

Core Reading: Hamilton, Chapter 16
               Wilcken, 239-326

234

Alexander the Great, page 8

Badian, "Some Recent Interpretations of Alexander" (on reserve)

Monday, April 5   Alexander as a Military Man

Thursday, April 8   Alexander as an Administrator of an Empire

Monday, April 12   Alexander as a Person: Son, Friend, Male

Thusday, April 15   Alexander's Self-Image

Monday, April 19   Alexander's Legacy: Did He Change the World?

Thursday, April 22   Catch-Up

WEEK # 16 SUMMATION AND STUDY

Monday, April 26   Why Have/Do We Still Study Alexander?

We will have a general discussion about what each of us has
learned about Alexander and perhaps also about ourselves. We
will also devote some time to preparation for the final
examination.

N.B. Term papers are due today.

Thursday, April 29   No class: Study Day

WEEK # 17 FINAL EXAMINATION

The final examination will take place on Thursday, May 6th,
8:30-11:00 a.m.

ALEXANDER THE GREAT: BOOKS ON RESERVE

For complete, correct bibliographic citations, see Bibliography.

1. Adams, W. L. and E. N. Borza, Philip II, Alexander the Great and the Macedonian Heritage.

2. Atkinson, J. E., A Commentary on Q. Curtius Rufus' "Historiae Alexandri Magni," Books Three and Four.

3. Berve, H., Das Alexanderreich.

4. Bosworth, A. B., Historical Commentary on Arrian's History of Alexander.

5. Cawkwell, G., Philip of Macedon.

6. Diodorus Siculus, Books 16 and 17.

7. Ellis, J. R., Philip II and Macedonian Imperialism.

8. Engels, D. W., Alexander the Great and the Logistics of the Macedonian Army.

9. Fox, R. L., Alexander the Great.

10. Fuller, J. F. C., The Generalship of Alexander the Great.

11. Green, P., Alexander the Great.

12. Green, P., Alexander of Macedon.

13. Griffith, G. T., Alexander the Great: The Main Problems.

14. Hamilton, J. R., Plutarch Alexander A Commentary

15. Hammond, N. G. L., Three Historians of Alexander the Great

16. Hammond, N. G. L., Alexander the Great.

17. Justin/Pompeius Trogus, Books VII – XIII.1

18. Lipsius, F., Alexander the Great.

19. Milns, R. D., Alexander the Great.

20. Olmstead, A. T., History of the Persian Empire.

21. Pearson, L., The Lost Histories of Alexander the Great.

22. Renault, M., The Nature of Alexander.

23. Tarn, W. W., Alexander the Great, 2 vols.

236

THE AMERICAN UNIVERSITY
Department of History

29.300/600 ALEXANDER THE GREAT

BIBLIOGRAPHY

What follows is by no means an exhaustive listing of books and articles on Alexander, but it is a large enough selection to allow you to gain a sense of the kinds of work being done. I have copies of most of the articles: you are free to borrow them.

Adams, W. L., "Cassander and the Crossing of the Hellespont. Diodoros 17.7.4," Ancient World 2 (1979) 111-115.

Adams, W.L., "The Royal Macedonian Tomb at Vergina: An Historical Interpretation," Ancient World 3 (1980) 67-72.

Adams, W. Lindsay and Eugene N. Borza, eds., Philip II, Alexander the Great and the Macedonian Heritage (Washington, D.C.: Univ. Press of America, 1982).

Anderson, A. R., "Bucephalus and His Legend," American Journal of Philology 51 (1930) 1-21.

Andronikos, Manolis, "The Royal Tombs at Aigai," in Philip of Macedon, M.B. Hatzopoulos and L. Loukopoulos, eds. (Caratzas, 1981), 188-231.

Anson, Edward M., "Alexander's Hypaspists and the Argyraspids," Historia 30 (1981) 117-120.

Anson, Edward M., "The Meaning of the Term Macedones," Ancient World 12 (1985) 67-68.

Atkinson, J. E., A Commentary on Q. Curtius Rufus' "Historiae Alexandri Magni," Books Three and Four (Atlantic Highlands, N.J.: Humanities Press, 1980).

Badian. E., "The Eunuch Bagoas," Classical Quarterly 8 (1958) 144-157.

Badian. E., "Alexander the Great and the Unity of Mankind," Historia 7 (1958) 425-433.

Badian. E., "The Death of Parmenio," TAPA 91 (1960) 324-338.

Badian, E., "The First Flight of Harpalus," Historia 9 (1960) 245-246.

Badian, E., "Harpalus," Journal of Hellenic Studies 81 (1961) 16-43.

Badian, E., "The Death of Philip II," Phoenix 17 (1963) 244-250.

Badian, E., "Alexander the Great and the Loneliness of Power," in Studies in Greek and Roman History (Oxford, 1965).

Badian, E., "The Administration of the Empire," Greece and Rome 12 (1965) 166-181.

Badian, E., "The Date of Cleitarchus," Proceedings of the African Classical Association 8 (1965) 5-11.

Badian, E., "Alexander the Great and the Greeks of Asia," in Ancient Societies and Institutions, E. Badian, ed. (Oxford, 1966) 37-69.

Badian, E., "Alexander the Great, 1948-1967," Classical World 65 (1971) 37-83.

Badian, E., "Nearchus the Cretan," Yale Classical Studies 24 (1975) 147-170.

Badian, E., "Some Recent Interpreations of Alexander," in Alexandre le grand Image et realite, ed. E. Badian, Entretiens sur l'antiquite classique 22 (1975) 279-303.

Badian, E., "The Battle of the Granicus: A New Look," in Ancient Macedonia (Thessaloniki: Institute for Balkan Studies, 1977) 271-293.

Badian, E., "The Deification of Alexander the Great," Ancient Macedonian Studies in Honor of Charles F. Edson (Thessaloniki: Institute for Balkan Studies, 1981) 27-71.

Badian, E., "Greeks and Macedonians," in Studies in the History of Art, vol. 10 (Washington, D.C.: National Gallery of Art, 1982) 33-51.

Badian, E., "Eurydice," in Philip II, Alexander the Great, and the Macedonian Heritage. W. L. Adams and E. N. Borza, eds. (Washington D.C.: University Press of America, 1982) 99-110.

Bagnall, R.S., "The Date of the Foundation of Alexandria," American Journal of Ancient History 4 (1979) 46-49.

Balcer, J.M., "Alexander's Burning of Persepolis," Iranica Antiqua 13 (1978) 119-133.

Balsdon, J.P.V.D., "The Divinity of Alexander," Historia 1 (1950) 363-388.

Bamm, P., Alexander the Great: Power as Destiny (New York: McGraw-Hill, 1968).

Beare, Rhona, "Ptolemy's Daimon and Ruler Cult," Klio 62 (1980) 327-330.

Berve, Helmut, Das Alexanderreich auf prosopographischer Grundlage (Munich, 1926).

Bickerman, E.J., "Apropos d'un passage de Chares de Mytilene," La Parola del Passato 18 (1963) 241-255. [on proskynesis]

Bieber, Margaret, "The Portraits of Alexander," Greece and Rome 12 (1965) 183-188.

238

Bliquez, Lawrence, "Philip II and Abdera," _Eranos_ 79 (1981) 65-79.

Borza, E.N., "Alexander and the Return from Siwah," _Historia_ 16 (1967) 369.

Borza, E. N., "Cleitarchus and Diodorus' Account of Alexander," _Proceedings of the African Classical Association_ 11 (1968) 25-45.

Borza, E.N., "Fire From Heaven: Alexander at Persepolis," _Classical Philology_ 67 (1972) 233-245.

Borza, E.N., "Alexander's Communications," in _Ancient Macedonia_ (Thessaloniki, Institute for Balkan Studies. 1977) 295-303.

Bosworth, A.B., "The Death of Alexander the Great: Rumor and Propaganda," _Classical Quarterly_ 21 (1971) 112-136.

Bosworth, A. B., "Philip II and Upper Macedonia," _Classical Quarterly_ 21 (1971) 93-105.

Bosworth, A. B., "Arrian and the Alexander Vulgate," in _Alexandre le grand Image et realite_, ed. E. Badian, _Entretiens sur l'antiquite classique_ 22 (1975) 1-46.

Bosworth, A. B., "Errors in Arrian," _Classical Quarterly_ 26 (1976) 117-39. [on Siwah and A's pursuit of Darius]

Bosworth, A. B., "Alexander and Ammon," in _Greece and the Eastern Mediterranean in Ancient History and Prehistory_, ed. K. H. Kinzl (Berlin: de Gruyter, 1977) 51-77.

Bosworth, A. B., _Historical Commentary on Arrian's History of Alexander_, vol. 1, Books 1-3 (Oxford: Clarendon, 1980).

Bosworth, A. B., "Alexander and the Iranians," _Journal of Hellenic Studies_ 100 (1980) 1-21.

Bosworth, A. B., "A Missing Year in the History of Alexander the Great," _Journal of Hellenic Studies_ 101 (1981) 17-39.

Bosworth, A. B., "The Location of Alexander's Campaign Against the Illyrians in 335 B.C.," in _Studies in the History of Art_, vol. 10 (Washington, D.C.: National Gallery of Art, 1982) 75-84.

Bosworth, A. B., "History and Rhetoric in Curtius Rufus," _Classical Philology_ 78 (1983) 150-161 [review article].

Brandes, M. A., "Alexander der Grosse in Babylon," _Antike Kunst_ 22 (1979) 87-98.

Brown, T. S., "Callisthenes and Alexander," _American Journal of Philology_ 70 (1949) 225-248.

Brown, T.S., _Onesicritus_ (Berkeley and Los Angeles: Univ. of California Press, 1949).

Brown. T.S., "Clitarchus." <u>American Journal of Philology</u> 70 (1950) 134-155.

Brown, T. S., "Alexander's Book Order (Plu. <u>Alex</u>. 8)," <u>Historia</u> 16 (1967) 359-368.

Brunt. P. A., "Alexander's Macedonian Cavalry." <u>Journal of Hellenic Studies</u> 83 (1963) 27-46.

Brunt, P. A., "The Aims of Alexander," <u>Greece and Rome</u> 12 (1965) 205-215.

Brunt, P. A., "Notes on Aristobulus of Cassandria," <u>Classical Quarterly</u> 24 (1974) 65-69.

Brunt, P. A., "Alexander, Barsine, and Heracles," <u>Rivista di filologia classica</u> 103 (1975) 22-34.

Brunt, P. A., Introduction and Appendices in Loeb edition of Arrian's <u>Anabasis</u> and <u>Indica</u> (Cambridge: Harvard/Loeb, 1976 and 1983).

Burn, A. R., "The Generalship of Alexander," <u>Greece and Rome</u> 12 (1965) 140-153.

Burstein, Stanley M., "The Tomb of Philip II and the Succession of Alexander the Great," <u>Classical Views</u> 26 (1982).

Carney, E., "Alexander the Lyncestian: the Disloyal Opposition," <u>Greek, Roman, and Byzantine Studies</u> 21 (1980) 23-33.

Carney, E., "The Death of Clitus," <u>Greek, Roman, and Byzantine Studies</u> 22 (1981) 149-160.

Carney, E., "The Conspiracy of Hermolaus," <u>Classical Journal</u> 76 (1981) 223-231.

Carney, E., "The First Flight of Harpalus Again," <u>Classical Journal</u> 77 (1981) 9-11.

Cawkwell, G., <u>Philip of Macedon</u> (Boston: Faber & Faber, 1978).

Cawkwell, G., "Philip and Athens," in <u>Philip of Macedon</u>, eds. M. B. Hatzopoulos and L. Loukopoulos (Caratzas, 1981) 100-111.

Crossland, John, <u>Macedonian Greece</u> (New York: Norton, 1982).

Davis, E. W., "The Persian Battle Plan at the Granicus," <u>Laudatores Temporis Acti, James Sprunt Studies</u> 46 (1964) 34-44.

Dell, Harry, "Philip and Macedonia's Northern Neighbors," in <u>Philip of Macedon</u>, eds. M. B. Hatzopoulos and L. Loukopoulos (Caratzas, 1981) 90-99.

Develin. R., "The Murder of Philip II," <u>Antichthon</u> 15 (1981) 86-99.

Devine, A., "Grand Tactics at Gaugamela," <u>Phoenix</u> 29 (1975) 374-385.

Devine, A. M., "The Strategies of Alexander the Great and Darius III in the Issus Campaign," *Ancient World* 12 (1985) 25-38.

Devine, A. M., "Grand Tactics at the Battle of Issus," *Ancient World* 12 (1985) 39-59.

Edmunds, L., "The Religiosity of Alexander," *Greek, Roman, and Byzantine Studies* 12 (1971) 363-391.

Edmunds, L., "Alexander and the Calendar (Plu. *Alex.* 16.2)," *Historia* 28 (1979) 112-117.

Edson, Charles, "Early Macedonia," in *Philip of Macedon*, eds. M. B. Hatzopoulos and L. Loukopoulos (Caratzas, 1981) 10-35.

Eggermont, P. H. L., "Alexander's Campaigns in Gandhara and Ptolemy's List of Indo-Scythian Towns," *Orientalia Lovaniensia Periodica* 1 (1970) 63-123.

Ehrenberg, Victor, *Alexander and the Greeks* (Oxford, 1938).

Ellis, J.R., "Amyntas Perdikka, Philip II and Alexander the Great," *Journal of Hellenic Studies* 91 (1971) 15-24.

Ellis, J. R., "Alexander's Hypaspists Again," *Historia* 24 (1975) 617-618.

Ellis, J. R., *Philip II and Macedonian Imperialism* (London: Thames & Hudson, 1976).

Ellis, J. R., "Macedonia Under Philip," in *Philip of Macedon*, eds. M. B. Hatzopoulos and L. Loukopoulos (Caratzas, 1981) 146-165.

Ellis, J. R., "The Assassination of Philip II," *Ancient Macedonian Studies in Honor of Charles F. Edson* (Thessaloniki: Institute for Balkan Studies, 1981) 99-137.

Ellis, J. R., "The First Months of Alexander's Reign," in *Studies in the History of Art*, vol. 10 (Washington, D.C.: National Gallery of Art, 1982) 69-73.

Engels, Donald, *Alexander the Great and the Logistics of the Macedonian Army* (Berkeley and Los Angeles: Univ. of California Press, 1978).

Engels, D., "A Note on Alexander's Death," *Classical Philology* 73 (1978) 224-228.

Engels, D., "Alexander's Intelligence System," *Classical Quarterly* 30 (1980) 327-340.

Errington, R. M., "Bias in Ptolemy's History of Alexander," *Classical Quarterly* 19 (1969) 233-242.

Errington, R. M., "The Nature of the Macedonian State under the Monarchy," *Chiron* 8 (1978) 77-133.

Errington, R. M., "Review Discussion: Four Interpretations of Philip II," *American Journal of Ancient History* 6 (1981) 69-88.

Fears, J.R., "Pausanias, Assassin of Philip II, " *Athenaeum* 53 (1975) 111-135.

Fox. R. L., *Alexander the Great* (New York: Dial, 1973).

Foss, Clive, "The Battle of the Granicus: A New Look," in *Ancient Macedonia* (Thessaloniki: Institute for Balkan Studies, 1977) 493-502.

Fredricksmeyer, E. A., "Divine Honors for Philip II," *TAPA* 109 (1979) 39-61.

Fredricksmeyer, E. A., "Three Notes on Alexander's Deification," *American Journal of Ancient History* 4 (1979) 1-9.

Fredricksmeyer, E. A., "Again the So-called Tomb of Philip II," *American Journal of Archaeology* 85 (1981) 330-334.

Fredricksmeyer, E. A., "On the Final Aims of Philip II," in *Philip II, Alexander the Great and the Macedonian Heritage*, W. L. Adams and E. N. Borza, eds. (Washington, D.C.: Univ. Press of America, 1982) 85-98.

Fuller, J. F. C., *The Generalship of Alexander the Great* (New York: Minerva, 1960).

Green, Peter, *Alexander of Macedon* (Harmondsworth, 1974).

Green, Peter, *Alexander the Great* (New York: Praeger, 1970).

Green, Peter, "The Royal Tombs of Vergina: A Historical Analysis," in *Philip II, Alexander the Great and the Macedonian Heritage*, eds. W. L. Adams and E. N. Borza (Washington, D.C.: Univ. Press of America, 1982) 129-151.

Greenwalt, W. S., "The Search for Arrhidaeus," *Ancient World* 12 (1985) 69-77.

Griffith, G. T., "Alexander's Generalship at Gaugamela," *Journal of Hellenic Studies* 67 (1947) 77-89.

Griffith, G. T., "A Note on the Hipparchies of Alexander," *Journal of Hellenic Studies* 83 (1963) 68-74.

Griffith, G. T., "The Macedonian Background," *Greece and Rome* 12 (1965) 126-139.

Griffith, G. T., "Alexander and Antipater in 323," *Proceedings of the African Classical Association* 8 (1965) 12-17.

Griffith, G. T., *Alexander the Great: The Main Problems* (New York: Barnes and Noble, 1966).

Griffith, G. T., "Philip as General and the Macedonian Army," in Philip of Macedon, eds. M. B. Hatzopoulos and L. Loukopoulos (Caratzas, 1981) 58-77.

Hamilton, J. R., "Alexander and His So-Called Father," Classical Quarterly 3 (1953) 151-157.

Hamilton, J. R., "The Cavalry Battle at the Hydaspes," Journal of Hellenic Studies 76 (1956) 26-31.

Hamilton, J. R. "Cleitarchus and Aristobulus," Historia 10 (1961) 448-458.

Hamilton, J.R., "The Letters in Plutarch's Alexander," Proceedings of the African Classical Association 4 (1961) 9-20.

Hamilton, J. R., "Alexander's Early Life," Greece and Rome 12 (1965) 117-124.

Hamilton, J. R., Plutarch: Alexander   A Commentary (Oxford: Clarendon, 1969).

Hamilton, J. R., Alexander the Great (Pittsburgh: Univ. of Pittsburgh Press, 1974).

Hamilton, J.R., "Cleitarchus and Diodorus 17," in Greece and the Eastern Mediterranean in History and Prehistory, K. Kinzl, ed. (New York: deGruyter, 1975) 126-146.

Hammond, N.G.L., "Alexander's Campaign in Illyria," Journal of Hellenic Studies 94 (1974) 67-87.

Hammond, N.G.L., "The Campaign of Alexander Against Cleitus and Glaucias," in Ancient Macedonia (Thessaloniki: Institute for Balkan Studies, 1977) 503-509.

Hammond, N. G. L., "Philip's Tomb in Historical Context," Greek, Roman, and Byzantine Studies 19 (1978) 331-350.

Hammond, N.G.L and G. T. Griffith, A History of Macedonia, vol. 2 (Oxford: Clarendon, 1979).

Hammond, N.G.L., "The Battle of the Granicus River," Journal of Hellenic Studies 100 (1980) 73-88.

Hammond, N.G.L., Alexander the Great: King, Commander and Statesman (Park Ridge, N.J.: Noyes, 1981).

Hammond, N.G.L., "The End of Philip," in Philip of Macedon, eds. M. B. Hatzopoulos and L. Loukopoulos (Caratzas, 1981) 166-175.

Hammond, N. G. L., Three Historians of Alexander the Great (Cambridge: Cambridge University Press, 1983).

Hammond, N. G. L., "The Text and Meaning of Arrian vii 6.2-5," Journal of Hellenic Studies 103 (1983) 139-144.

Harris, R. I., "The Dilemma of Alexander the Great," <u>Proceedings of the African Classical Association</u> 11 (1968) 46-54.

Hatzopoulos, M. B., "A Reconsideration of the Pixodaros Affair," in <u>Studies in the History of Art</u>, vol. 10 (Washington, D.C.: National Gallery of Art, 1982) 59-66.

Hatzopoulos, M. B., "The Oleveni Inscription and the Dates of Philip II's Reign," in <u>Philip II, Alexander the Great and the Macedonian Heritage</u>, W. L. Adams and E. N. Borza, eds. (Washington, D.C.: University Press of America, 1982) 21-42.

Hauben, Hans, "The Expansion of Macedonian Sea-Power Under Alexander the Great," <u>Ancient Society</u> 7 (1976) 79-105.

Heckel, W., "The Flight of Harpalus and Tauriskos," <u>Classical Philology</u> 72 (1977) 133-135.

Heckel, W., "The Conspiracy Against Philotas," <u>Phoenix</u> 31 (1977) 9-21.

Heckel, W., "Leonnatos, Polyperchon and the Introduction of Proskynesis," <u>American Journal of Philology</u> 99 (1978) 459-461.

Heckel, W., "The Somatophylakes of Alexander the Great: Some Thoughts," <u>Historia</u> 27 (1978) 224-228.

Heckel, W., "Kleopatra or Eurydike?" <u>Phoenix</u> 32 (1978) 155-158.

Heckel, W., "Philip II, Kleopatra, and Karanos," <u>Rivista di filologia classica</u> 107 (1979) 385-393.

Heckel, W., "Polyxena, the Mother of Alexander the Great," <u>Chiron</u> 11 (1981) 79-86.

Hessierer, A. J., <u>Alexander the Great and the Greeks</u> (Norman: Oklahoma Univ. Press, 1980).

Higgins, W. E., "Aspects of Alexander's Imperial Administration: Some Modern Methods and Views Reviewed," <u>Athenaeum</u> 58 (1980) 129-152.

Holt, Frank, "The Hyphasis 'Mutiny': A Source Study," <u>Ancient World</u> 5 (1982) 33-59.

Hughes, J. Donald, "The Dreams of Alexander the Great," <u>Journal of Psychohistory</u> 12 (1984) 168-192.

Jouget, Pierre, <u>Alexander the Great and the Hellenistic World: Macedonian Imperialism and the Hellenization of the East</u> (Chicago: Ares, 1978).

Langer, Patricia, "Alexander the Great at Siwah," <u>Ancient World</u> 4 (1981) 109-127.

Lehmann, P. W., "The So-Called Tomb of Philip II: A Different Interpretation," <u>American Journal of Archaeology</u> 84 (1980) 527-531.

Leveque, Pierre, "Philip's Personality," in Philip of Macedon, eds. M. B. Hatzopoulos and L. Loukopoulos (Caratzas, 1981) 176-187.

Lipsius, Frank, Alexander the Great (New York: Saturday Review Press, 1974).

Lock, R., "The Macedonian Army Assembly in the Time of Alexander the Great," Classical Philology 72 (1977) 91-107.

Markle, M., "Use of Sarissa by Philip and Alexander of Macedon," American Journal of Archaeology 82 (1978) 483-497.

Markle, Minor, "Macedonian Arms and Tactics under Alexander the Great," in Studies in the History of Art, vol. 10 (Washington, D.C.: National Gallery of Art, 1982) 87-111.

Marsden, E. W., "Macedonian Military Machinery and its Designers under Philip and Alexander," Ancient Macedonia (Thessaloniki: Institute for Balkan Studies, 1977) 211-223.

Martin, Thomas R., "Diodorus on Philip II and Thessaly in the 350's B.C.," Classical Philology 76 (1981) 188-201.

Martin, Thomas R., "A Phantom Fragment of Theopompus and Philip II's First Campaign in Thessaly," Harvard Studies in Classical Philology 86 (1982) 55-78.

Merlan, P., "Isocrates, Aristotle, and Alexander the Great," Historia 3 (1953) 60-81.

Miller, Harvey F., "The Practical and Economic Background to the Greek Mercenary Explosion," Greece & Rome 31 (1984) 153-159.

Miller, S. G., "Drinking Uncut-Wine. . .to Death: Unpublished Greek Epigram for a Youth from Ephesus," Ancient World 2 (1979) 29-30.

Milns, R. D., "Alexander's Seventh Phalanx Battalion," Greek, Roman, and Byzantine Studies 7 (1966) 159-166.

Milns, R. D., Alexander the Great (New York: Pegasus, 1968).

Milns, R. D., "The Hypaspists of Alexander III--Some Problems," Historia 20 (1971) 186-195.

Milns, R. D., "The Army of Alexander the Great," in Alexandre le grand Image et realite, ed. E. Badian, Entretiens sur l'antiquite classique 22 (1975) 87-136.

Milns, R. D., "Arrian's Accuracy in Troop Details," Historia 27 (1978) 374-378.

Mitchel, F., "Athens in the Age of Alexander," Greece & Rome 12 (1965) 189-204.

Montgomery, Hugo, The Way to Chaeronea (New York: Columbia University Press, 1983).

Narain, A. K., "Alexander and India," Greece and Rome 12 (1965) 155-165.

Nikolitsis, N. T., The Battle of the Granicus (Stockholm: Swedish Institute At Athens, 1974).

Nock, A. D., "Notes on Ruler Cult, I-IV. Alexander and Dionysus," Journal of Hellenic Studies 48 (1928) 21-30.

O'Brien, John M., "The Enigma of Alexander: The Alcohol Factor," Annals of Scholarship 1 (1980) 31-46.

O'Brien, John M., "Alexander and Dionysus: the Invisible Enemy," Annals of Scholarship 1 (1980) 83-105.

Oikonomides, Al. N., "The Deification of Alexander in Bactria and India," Ancient World 12 (1985) 69-71.

Olmstead, A. T., History of the Persian Empire (Chicago: Univ. of Chicago Press, 1959).

Parsons, P. J., "The Burial of Philip II?" American Journal of Ancient History 4 (1981) 97-101.

Pearson, L., "The Diary and Letters of Alexander the Great," Historia 3 (1955) 429-455.

Pearson, Lionel, The Lost Histories of Alexander the Great (American Philological Association, 1960).

Prag, A. J. N. W., J. H. Musgrave, and R. A. H. Neave, "The Skull from Tomb II at Vergina: King Philip II of Macedon," Journal of Hellenic Studies 94 (1984) 60-78.

Pribichevich, Stoyan, Macedonia: Its People and History (University Park, Pa.: Pennsylvania State University Press, 1982).

Rahe, Paul, "The Annhilation of the Sacred Band at Chaeronea," American Journal of Archaeology 85 (1981) 84-87.

Renard, M. and J. Servais, "A propos du mariage d'Alexandre et de Roxane," L'antiquite classique 24 (1955) 29-50.

Renault, M., The Nature of Alexander (New York: Pantheon, 1975).

Robinson, C. A., The Ephemerides of Alexander's Expedition (Providence: Brown Univ. Press, 1932).

Robinson, C. A., "Alexander's Plans," American Journal of Philology 61 (1940) 402-412.

Robinson, C. A., "Alexander's Brutality," American Journal of Archaeology 56 (1952) 169-170.

246

Robinson, C. A., "The Extraordinary Ideas of Alexander the Great," _American Historical Review_ 62 (1957) 326-344.

Robinson, C.A., _Alexander the Great_ (Watts, 1963).

Roebuck, C., "The Settlements of Philip II with the Greek States in 338 B.C.," _Classical Philology_ 43 (1948) 73-92.

Rubinsohn, Zeev, "The 'Philotas Affair'--A Reconsideration," in _Ancient Macedonia_ (Thessaloniki: Institute for Balkan Studies, 1977) 409-420.

Sakellariou, M .B., "Panhellenism: From Concept to Policy," in _Philip of Macedon_, eds. M. B. Hatzopoulos and L. Loukopoulos (Caratzas, 1981) 128-145.

Samuel, Alan, "Alexander's Royal Journals," _Historia_ 14 (1965) 1-12.

Schachermeyr, F., _Alexander der Grosse   Das Problem seiner Personlichkeit und seines Wirken_ (Vienna, 1973).

Tarn, W. W., "Alexander's Plans," _Journal of Hellenic Studies_ 59 (1939) 124-135.

Tarn, W. W., _Alexander the Great_, 2 vols (Cambridge: Cambridge University Press, 1948).

Thomas, C. G., "Alexander's Garrisons: A Clue to His Administrative Plans?" _Antichthon_ 8 (1974) 11-20.

Tronson, Adrian, "Satyrus the Peripatetic and the Marriages of Philip II," _Journal of Hellenic Studies_ 94 (1984) 116-126.

Wardman, A. E., "Plutarch and Alexander," _Classical Quarterly_ 5 (1969) 96-107.

Wells, C. B., "Alexander's Historical Achievement," _Greece and Rome_ 12 (1965) 216-228.

Wells, C. B., _Alexander and the Hellenistic World_ (Toronto: Hakkert, 1970).

Wilcken, Ulrich, _Alexander the Great_, transl. G. C. Richards (New York: Norton, 1967).

Worthington, Ian, "The First Flight of Harpalus Reconsidered," _Greece & Rome_ 31 (1984) 161-169.

THE AMERICAN UNIVERSITY
Department of History

29.300/600 ANCIENT STUDIES   Valerie French
    CAUSES OF WAR IN ANTIQUITY   McCabe 106
    Spring 1985   885-2405

I. PURPOSE AND SCOPE OF COURSE

In the ancient world, people assumed that war was an inevitable, though
horrible, part of life. And indeed, the history of classical antiquity is
literally littered with armed conflict. However, both Greeks and Romans
recognized that individual wars had their own particular causes, and both
ancient and modern historians have struggled to try to understand why these
wars came about.

Over the semester, we will examine in detail the causes of the Persian,
Peloponnesian, Punic, and Roman Civil Wars. We will also examine carefully
the question of causality itself. Analysis of these four major ancient wars
will reveal something about why warfare was so characteristic of the ancient
world--and, perhaps by extension, of our own.

II. FORMAT OF COURSE

We will conduct this course as a seminar. That means that a large
measure of the responsibility for lively, stimulating, and challenging class
sessions rest on the students. I cannot seminar by myself.

Most class sessions will revolve around short papers written by
students. These papers will lay out questions and controversies and will
report on the various positions historians have taken on these issues.
Please feel free to stake out your own position and to critique arguments
offered by others. The reports will be more like working drafts rather than
finely polished essays. However, even working papers must be clearly
organized and literately written.

In order to avoid having students simply read their short papers in
class (this tends to use up too much time), papers are to be submitted four
days before the class meeting at which they will be discussed. Please put
two copies of your paper in the box labeled "Causes of War" in the History
Department (in the bookcase next to the mailboxes in the hallway of McCabe),
and put another copy of your paper in my mailbox; keep another copy for
yourself. Part of everyone's weekly assignment is to stop by the department
and read the papers that are to be discussed. We will all be familiar with
the issues and questions and can get right to a discussion of the historical
problems and interpretations.

III. REQUIREMENTS OF COURSE

A. Regular class attendance; core reading assignments done on time; informed participation in class discussion (15%).

B. Four to five short papers (about five pages, double-spaced, typewritten) on specific and well-defined topics. Assignments for these papers will be made in class (30%).

C. One medium-length paper (about 8-12 pages, double-spaced, typewritten, carefully edited and polished) on a topic mutually agreeable to you and me (25%).

D. Final examination (30%).

N.B. In order to receive a passing grade for this course, students must complete all assignments.

Graduate students should consult with me about additional reading and about your major paper (which will be longer than that described above).

IV. CRITERIA FOR EVALUATION OF STUDENT PERFORMANCE

In general, I consider a grade of "C" to connote competent work. This entails a sound basic grasp of the historical and the historiographical issues; literate presentation of research (i.e., standard English usage, coherent organization, correct spelling and punctuation, proper endnote and bibliographic format, etc.); assignments completed on time; informed contribution to class discussion. A "B" connotes work that is considerably better than competent—a more detailed knowledge of the subject matter and writing that is not only clear and correct but also persuasive. An "A" connotes work that is distinguished by originality and/or exceptional intellectual vigor and by graceful writing.

Please feel free to consult with me about the quality of your work.

V. READINGS AND BOOKS

A. Books to be Purchased: The following books are required and are available in the AU Bookstore.

Burn, A. R., The Pelican History of Greece (Baltimore: Penguin, 1965).
Herodotus, The Histories, trans. Aubrey de Selincourt (Baltimore: Penguin, 1954).
Livy, The War with Hannibal, trans. Aubrey de Selincourt (Baltimore: Penguin, 1965).
Plutarch, The Fall of the Roman Republic, trans. Rex Warner (Baltimore: Penguin, 1972).
Polybius, The Rise of the Roman Empire, trans. Ian Scott-Kilvert (Baltimore: Penguin, 1979).
Thucydides, The Peloponnesian War, trans. Rex Warner (Baltimore: Penguin, 1954).

B. Reserve Readings

Many of the books you will be using over the semester are on two-hour reserve in the library. A list of these books is appended to this syllabus.

C. Additional Bibliography

I have a rather extensive collection of copies of articles. Please consult the "Special Periodical Literature Supplement" for each section of the course. You are free to use these articles. I will bring them to class each week or you may stop by my office to get the ones you'll need.

ALL COPIES OF ARTICLES ARE TO BE RETURNED TO ME AS SOON AS YOU ARE FINISHED WITH THEM. OTHER STUDENTS ARE LIKELY TO WANT TO USE THEM TOO!

VII. OVERVIEW OF COURSE SCHEDULE

Week No.	Dates	Topic
1	Jan. 23	Introduction to Course and to Causal Analysis
2-4	Jan. 30 - Feb. 13	The Persian Wars
5-7	Feb. 20 - Mar. 6	The Peloponnesian War
8	Mar. 13	Causality: A Model
9	Mar. 20	Spring Vacation
10	Mar. 27	The Peloponnesian War: A Simulation
11-12	Apr. 3 - 10	The Second Punic War
13-15	Apr. 7 - May 1	The Roman Civil War
16	May 8	Study Day/Optional Review Class
17	May 15	Final Examination

VIII. WEEKLY COURSE AGENDA AND ASSIGNMENTS

Each week, everyone will do the "core reading" assingment and read the student papers scheduled for discussion.

Week # 1   January 10

Introduction to Course and to Causal Analysis

THE PERSIAN WARS

Reporters should routinely consult A. R. Burn, _Persia and the Greeks_; C. Hignett, _Xerxes' Invasion of Greece_; and A. T. Olmstead, _History of the Persian Empire_. For particular passages of Herodotus, be sure to consult How and Wells, _A Commentary on Herodotus_. You should also consult the "Special Periodical Literature Supplement" for articles that pertain to your topic.

Week # 2   January 30   BACKGROUND AND THE IONIAN REVOLT

Core Reading: Herodotus, Books 1, 5, and 6.1-93
              Burn, pp. 83 - 157

Reports:

    1. Croesus, Lydia, and the Greeks
    2. The Strength of Ionia in ca. 500 B.C.
    3. The Strength of Persia in ca. 500 B.C.
    4. The Causes of the Ionian Revolt
    5. The Athenian Reaction to the Ionian Revolt
    6. The Spartan Reaction to the Ionian Revolt

Week # 3   February 6   MARATHON AND THE TEN YEAR WAIT

Core Reading: Herodotus, 6.93 to end
              Burn, pp. 157 - 166

Reports:

    1. The Persian Reaction to the Ionian Revolt
    2. The Invasion at Marathon. Why Did Darius Invade Greece at All?
       Why Did Darius Invade Greece Where He Did~
    3. The Invasion at Marathon. Why Did Athens Stand Alone?
    4. The Decade of Waiting. Was Renewal of the War Inevitable?

        a. Persia 490 - 480
        b. Greece 490 - 480

    5. The Medizers. Why Did Some States Go Over to Xerxes?

Week # 4   February 13   XERXES' INVASION

Core Reading: Burn, pp. 167-192
              Sealey, "Thucydides, Herodotus, and the Causes of
                  War" (article on reserve)

Reports:

    1. Why Did Xerxes Invade in 480? Why Did He Invade As He Did?
    2. Who Lead the Greek Resistence?

In addition to these two reports, we will have a general discussion of three key issues: (1) What does Herodotus see as the cause(s) of the conflict between Persia and the Greeks? (2) How far does modern scholarship accept the Herodotean judgment? (3) Do you concur with Herodotus' views?

Come to class with notes for discussing these three questions. Be able to identify passages in Herodotus that support your conclusions.

THE PELOPONNESIAN WAR

Reporters should rely heavily on Kagan, <u>Outbreak of the Peloponnesian War</u>; de Ste. Croix, <u>Origins of the Peloponnesian War</u>; Meiggs, <u>The Athenian Empire</u>; and Gomme, <u>Historical Commentary on Thucydides</u>. In addition, consult the "Special Periodical Literature Supplement: Peloponnesian War" for articles pertaining to your topic. There is a useful compendium of the most important ancient sources in Kagan, <u>Problems in Ancient History</u>, vol. 1.

Week # 5   February 20   A BACKGROUND OF STRIFE: THE PENTEKONTAETIA

Core Reading: Thucydides, "Introduction" by Finley and I. 1-23 and
              I.89-117.
              Burn, pp. 193 - 257.
              Either, Kagan, <u>Outbreak</u>, 131-202, or de Ste. Croix,
              <u>Origins</u>, 89 - 224.

Reports:

1. The First Peloponnesian War. What were the issues that precipitated the conflict? Could the problems have been resolved without armed conflict?

2. The First Peloponnesian War. What was the outcome? Were the issues that provoked the war resolved? Did any new issues arise during the course of the war? Were they resolved? How solid was the Peace of 446?

3. The Attitude of Athens towards her Empire, 449-435. What did Athens want from her empire? Was there a unified Athenian attitude towards empire and appropriate imperial behavior?

4. The Internal Politics of Sparta, 446-435. Were there factions among the Spartans? If so, what were their aims and goals?

5. The Samian Revolt and War. Why did Sparta and Corinth pursue the policies they did? What alternative policies might Sparta and Corinth have adopted?

252

Week # 6   February 27   THE IMMEDIATE CAUSES: 435 - 432

    Core Reading: Thucydides, I.24 - II.17.
                  Burn, pp. 258 - 279.
                  Plutarch, Pericles

    Reports:

        1. The Epidamnian-Corcyrean Affair. What were the policy choices
        open to Athens? to Corinth? to Sparta? Why did each follow the
        policy it did?

        2. The Potidaean Affair. What were the policy choices open to
        Athens? to Corinth? to Potidaea? to Sparta? Why did each follow
        the policy it did?

        3. The Megarian Decrees. What were they? How many? When? What
        was the purpose of the decrees? What was the effect? Why the
        difference between Plutarch and Thucydides on the importance of
        the decrees?

        4. What could Athens reasonably expect her allies/empire to do in
        the event of a war with Sparta? Remain loyal? Defect to Sparta?
        Adopt a posture of neutrality? Would it matter what the allies
        did?

        5. What could Athens and Sparta reasonably expect Persia to do in
        the event of a general war in Greece? How far did the "Persian
        Question" enter into Spartan and Athenian policy formulation?

Week # 7   March 6   THE CAUSES OF THE WAR

    Assignment for Everyone: Choose at least five of the modern historians
    who have written on the causes of the Peloponnesian War and come to
    class prepared to (1) describe in considerable detail their arguments
    and (2) debate the strengths and weaknesses of their arguments. For
    bibliography, see "Supplement."

        You should also prepare an outline of your own position on the
    causes of the Peloponnesian War.

Week # 8   March 13   CAUSALITY: A MODEL

    Core Reading: Lichtman and French, Historians and the Living Past,
                  Chapter 3 (on reserve).

        During this class, Allan Lichtman will lay out for you the
    basic causal model described in Historians, and you will apply it to
    what we have learned so far about the causes of the Persian and
    Peloponnesian Wars.

253

Week # 9   March 20   SPRING VACATION   NO CLASS

Week # 10   March 27   THE WINTER OF 432/1: A SIMULATION

Core Reading: Review your previous assignments.

Reports: Each of you will sign up for one of three teams; you can be an
    Athenian, a Spartan, or a Corinthian. As a team, you should work
    out   answers to the following questions.   Try to catapult
    yourselves back into the late autumn and winter of 432/1 and see
    how the world looked from the point of view of your city-state.
    As the Athenians, Spartans, and Corinthians looked into their
    futures, what did they see?   This is the perspective you should
    try to achieve.

    1. What are your long-range objectives, both foreign and domestic?

    2. What is the biggest immediate problem facing you? What is the
    best way to solve the immediate problem?   Is this solution
    consonant with your long-range goals?

    3. What can you reasonably expect your adversaries to do? What do
    you think your adversaries want?   What will happen to you if they
    get what they want?

    4. What can you reasonably expect your friends and allies to do?
    Will they support your long-range goals? your short-term policies?
    If they do not support you, what will happen to you?

    5. Are there questions of honor at stake?   For you?   For your
    adversaries?   For your allies and friends?   What will honor call
    you to do?

        After you have wrestled with these questions, examine the
    ancient sources carefully to see if there is any evidence that
    people in your city were asking the same kinds of questions.   If
    they were, did they arrive at the same kinds of answers? If they
    were not, what questions did seem to guide their decisions?

    In class, we will pick up the action among these three states in
October 432 and "act out" their respective decisions through March 431;
as each state makes a decision and takes action, it will explain why it
came to its decisions in terms of the questions posed above; the other
states will have an opportunity to question the motives and reasoning
behind each major decision.

254

THE PUNIC WARS

Reporters should consult the following: Dorey and Dudley, <u>Rome Against Carthage</u>; Harris, <u>War and Imperialism</u>; Lazenby, <u>Hannibal's War</u>; Starr, <u>Emergence of Rome</u>; Walbank, <u>Historical Commentary</u>; Walbank, <u>Polybius</u>; and Warmington, <u>Carthage</u>. All are on reserve. In addition, see the "Special Periodical Literature Supplement: Punic Wars."

Week # 11 April 3   ANOTHER BACKGROUND OF STRIFE

<u>Core Reading</u>: Livy, "Introduction" and Book XXI
            Polybius, "Introduction" and Books I and VI

<u>Reports</u>:

1. The First Punic War--the Roman Side. What was Rome's objective? Did Rome achieve it?

2. The First Punic War--the Carthaginian Side. What was Carthage's objective? Did Carthage achieve it?

3. The First Punic War--Outcome. Were the issues that precipitated the war resolved? Did new issues arise during the course of the war? Were they resolved?

4. The Roman Empire in 220 B.C. What were its strengths? What were its weaknesses?

5. Carthage in 220 B.C. Who was in power? What were the objectives of Punic foreign policy?

6. The Barca Family. Was its influence disproportionate to its real power? What were its objectives for itself? for Carthage? Did the Barca's have a separate foreign policy?

Week # 12 April 10   FROM SPAIN TO ITALY: HANNIBAL ATTACKS

<u>Core Reading</u>: Review Livy and Polybius

(See also "Assignment for Everyone" on next page.)

<u>Reports</u>:

1. Sardinia. A real bone of contention? Why or why not?

2. The Ebro River Treaty. What were its purposes? Was it constructed so as to fulfill them?

3. The Affair at Saguntum. Why did Hannibal attack? Why did Rome respond as it did?

255

4. Hannibal's Invasion. Why did Hannibal choose this military strategy? Was Rome prepared for this eventuality? If not, why not?

Assignment for Everyone: Select three modern historians who have written on the causes of the Hannibalic War, particularly on Polybius' explanation of this war. Come to class prepared to (1) describe in some detail their arguments and (2) debate the strengths and weaknesses of their arguments.

Using the causal model from Historians, model Polybius' explanation of the Hannibalic War. Bring your model to class.

THE ROMAN CIVIL WAR

Reporters should consult the following: Gruen, Last Generation; Lintott, Violence; Marsh, History; and Syme, Revolution. All are on reserve. In addition, consult the "Special Periodical Literature Supplement: Roman Civil War."

Week # 13 April 17   EMPIRE AND DOMESTIC POLITICS: 60 - 56 BC

Core Reading: Marsh, History, pp. 177 - 213 (on reserve).
              Plutarch, Cicero, Pompey, Crassus, and Caesar

Reports:

1. The First Triumvirate. Who Got What?

2. Caesar as Consul. What were his main objectives? Did he accomplish them? At what cost? Does Caesar's career seem at all extraordinary at this point?

3. Clodius and Cicero. What were Clodius' objectives? What were Cicero's objectives? How well was what they did calculated to achieve their objectives?

4. Crassus and Pompey, 58 - 56. What did each of them want? What might each of them have feared?

5. The Conference at Luca. Who got what?

Week # 14 April 24   BREAKDOWN OF THE REPUBLIC: 55 - 49 BC

Core Reading: Marsh, History, pp. 213 - 228 and 387 - 399.
              Review Plutarch

Reports:

1. The Consulship of Pompey and Crassus

256

2. Violence Run Amuck: Clodius, Milo, and the Senate's Response

3. The Rechtsfrage/When Did Caesar's Command End?

    a. The Case for Caesar
    b. The Case for Pompey and the Senate

Week # 15 May 1   WAS CIVIL WAR INEVITABLE?

Core Reading: Review your reading and class notes.

Assignment for Everyone: Come to class prepared to discuss the following questions.

1. Was a civil war the only way to resolve the conflict between Caesar and Pompey and the Senate?

2. What or who caused this war? Prepare a causal model.

3. Who was to blame for this war? Is there a difference between assigning a cause and assessing blame?

4. What positions do modern historians take on these questions? Be prepared to describe the views of at least three historians and to critically evaluate their credibility.

Week # 16 May 8   STUDY DAY/OPTIONAL REVIEW CLASS

I will conduct a review session during the regular class time. Your attendance is optional.

N.B. YOUR MEDIUM LENGTH PAPER IS DUE AT CLASSTIME TODAY.

Week # 17 May 15   FINAL EXAMINATION

29.300/600 CAUSES OF WAR IN ANTIQUITY

RESERVE BOOKS

I. Persian Wars

Burn, A. R., Persia and the Greeks (New York: St. Martin's, 1962).

de Selincourt, Aubrey, The World of Herodotus (Boston: Little Brown, 1963).

Drews, Robert, Greek Accounts of Eastern History (Washington, D.C.: Center for Hellenic Studies, 1973).

Evans, J. A. S., Herodotus (New York: Twayne, 1982).

Fornara, Charles, Herodotus: An Interpretative Essay (Oxford: Clarendon, 1971).

Frost, Frank J., Themistocles. A Historical Commentary (Princeton: Princeton University Press, 1980).

Green, Peter, The Year of Salamis (London: Weidenfield & Nicholson, 1970).

Grundy, G.B., The Great Persian War and Its Preliminaries (London: J. Murray, 1901).

Hart, John, Herodotus and Greek History (New York: St. Martin's, 1982).

Hignett, Charles, Xerxes' Invasion of Greece (Oxford: Clarendon, 1963).

How, W. W., and J. Wells, A Commentary on Herodotus (Oxford: Clarendon, 1912).

Hunter, Virginia, Past and Process in Herodotus and Thucydides (Princeton: Princeton Univ. Press, 1982).

Olmstead, A. T., A History of the Persian Empire (Chicago: Univ. of Chicago Press, 1959).

Waters, K.H., Herodotos the Historian. His Problems, Methods and Originality (Norman: University of Oklahoma Press, 1985).

II. Peloponnesian Wars

Cogan, Marc, The Human Thing: The Speeches and Principles of Thucydides' History (Chicago: Univ. of Chicago Press, 1981).

Cornford, F. M., Thucydides Mythistoricus (London: E. Arnold, 1907).

Demand, Nancy, Thebes in the Fifth Century: Heracles Resurgent (London: Routledge & Kegan Paul, 1983).

258

Edmunds, Lowell, Chance and Intelligence in Thucydides (Cambridge: Harvard, 1975).

Fliess, Peter J., Thucydides and the Politics of Bipolarity (Baton Rouge: Louisiana State Univ. Press, 1966).

Gomme, A. W., A Historical Commentary on Thucydides, vol. 1 (Oxford: Clarendon, 1944).

Henderson, B. W., The Great War Between Athens and Sparta (London: Macmillan, 1927.

Hooker, J. T., The Ancient Spartans (Totowa: Biblio Distribution Center, 1980).

Hunter, Virginia, Thucydides: The Artful Reporter (Toronto: Hakkert, 1973).

Kagan, Donald, The Outbreak of the Peloponnesian War (Ithaca: Cornell University Press, 1969).

Kagan, Donald, Problems in Ancient History, vol. 1 (New York: Macmillan, 1975) Section X.

Meiggs, Russell, The Athenian Empire (Oxford: Clarendon, 1972).

Pouncy, Peter R., The Necessities of War: A Study of Thucydides' Pessimism (New York: Columbia Univ. Press, 1980).

Proctor, Dennis, The Experience of Thucydides (Warminster: Aris & Phillips, 1980).

de Romilly, Jacqueline, Thucydides and Athenian Imperialism, trans. Philip Thody (New York: Barnes & Noble, 1963).

Salmon, J., Wealthy Corinth: A History of the City to 338 B.C. (Oxford: Clarendon, 1984).

de Ste. Croix, G. E. M., The Origins of the Peloponnesian War (Ithaca: Cornell University Press, 1972).

III. Punic Wars

Dorey, T. A., and D. R. Dudley, Rome Against Carthage (New York: Doubleday, 1972).

Errington, R. M., The Dawn of Empire: Rome's Rise to World Power (Ithaca: Cornell Univ. Press, 1972).

Harris, W. V., War and Imperialism in Republican Rome 327 - 70 BC (New York: Oxford Univ. Press, 1979).

Kagan, Donald, Problems in Ancient History, vol. 2 (New York: Macmillan, 1975) Section IV.

Lazenby, J. F., Hannibal's War: A Military History of the Second Punic War (Warminster: Aris & Phillips, 1978).

Sacks, Kenneth, Polybius on the Writing of History (Berkeley & Los Angeles: Univ. of California Press, 1981).

Starr, Chester G., The Emergency of Rome as the Ruler of the Western World (Ithaca: Cornell Univ. Press, 1953).

Walbank, Frank W., Historical Commentary on Polybius, 2 vols. (Oxford: Clarendon, 1957, 1967).

Walbank, Frank W., Polybius (Berkely and Los Angeles: Univ. of California Press, 1972).

Warmington, B. H., Carthage (London: R. Hale, 1969).

IV. Roman Civil War

Badian, E., Roman Imperialism in the Late Republic (Ithaca: Cornell University Press, 1968).

Balsdon, J. P. V. D., Julius Caesar: A Political Biography (New York: Athenaeum, 1967).

Beard, Mary and Charles Crawford, Rome in the Late Republic, Problems and Interpretations (Ithaca: Cornell University Press, 1985).

Bradford, Ernle, Julius Caesar: The Pursuit of Power (London: Hamilton, 1984).

Brunt, P. A., social Conflicts in the Roman Republic (New York: Norton, 1971).

Fuller, J. F. C., Julius Caesar: Man, Soldier, and Tyrant (New Brunswick: Rutgers Univ. Press, 1965).

Gelzer, Mathias, Caesar: Politician and Statesman (Oxford: Blackwell, 1969).

Green, Peter. Caesar (Chicago: Follett, 1974).

Greenhalgh, P. A. L., Pompey, the Republican Prince (London: Weidenfield & Nicholson, 1981).

Greenidge, A. H. J., Roman Public Life (New York: Macmillan, 1901).

Gruen, Erich, The Last Generation of the Roman Republic (Berkeley and Los Angeles: Univ. of California Press, 1974).

Hill, Herbert, The Roman Middle Class in the Republican Period (Westport: Greenwood, 1952/1974).

Holmes, T. R., *The Roman Republic and the Founder of the Roman Empire* (Oxford: Clarendon, 1923).

Kagan. Donald, *Problems in Ancient History*, vol. 2 (New York: Macmillan, 1975) Section VIII.

Keaveney, Arthur, *Sulla: the Last Republican* (London: Croom Helm, 1982).

Lacey, W. K., *Cicero and the End of the Roman Republic* (New York: Barnes & Noble, 1978).

Leach, J., *Pompey the Great* (Totowa, N. J.: Rowman & Littlefield, 1978).

Lintott, A. W., *Violence in Republican Rome* (Oxford: Clarendon, 1968).

Marsh, F. B., *A History of the Roman World, 146 - 30 BC* (London: Methuen, 1963).

Perowne, Stewart, *The Death of the Roman Republic* (Garden City: Doubleday, 1968).

Rawson, Beryl, *The Politics of Friendship: Cicero and Pompey* (Sydney: Sydney Univ. Press, 1978).

Rawson, Elizabeth, *Cicero: A Portrait*, 2nd ed. (Ithaca: Cornell Univ. Press, 1983).

Seager, Robin, *Pompey: A Political Biography* (Berkeley & Los Angeles: Univ. of California Press, 1979).

Sherwin-White, A. N., *Roman Foreign Policy in the East, 168 B.C. to A. D. 1* (London: Duckworth, 1984).

Smith, R. E., *The Failure of the Roman Republic* (Cambridge: Cambridge University Press, 1955).

Stockton, David, *Cicero: A Political Biography* (London: Oxford Univ. Press, 1971).

Syme, Sir Ronald, *The Roman Revolution* (Oxford: Clarendon, 1939).

Taylor, Lily Ross, *Party Politics in the Age of Caesar* (Berkeley and Los Angeles: Univ. of California Press, 1949).

Ward, Allen, *Marcus Crassus and the Late Roman Republic* (Columbia: Univ. of Missouri Press, 1977).

Yavetz, Zwi, *Julius Caesar and His Public Image* (Ithaca: Cornell Univ. Press, 1983).

261

SPECIAL PERIODICAL LITERATURE SUPPLEMENT

THE PERSIAN WARS

Armavor, O. Kimball, "Herodotus' Catalogues of the Persian Empire in the Light of the Monuments and the Greek Literary Tradition," _TAPA_ 108 (1978) 1-9.

Avery, Harry C., "The Number of Persian Dead at Marathon," _Historia_ 22 (1973) 757.

Balcer, Jack Martin, "The Greeks and the Persians: The Process of Acculturation," _Historia_ 32 (1983) 257-267.

Ball, R., "Generation Dating in Herodotus," _Classical Quarterly_ 29 (1979) 276-281.

Brunt, P.A., "The Hellenic League Against Persia," _Historia_ 2 (1953/54) 135-63. (Addendum B discusses Thessalian Medism.)

Chambers, Mortimer, "The Authenticity of the Themistocles Decree," _American Historical Review_ 67 (1962) 306-316.

Donlan, Walter & Thompson, James, " The Charge at Marathon: Herodotus 6.112," _Classical Journal_ 71 (1976) 339-343.

Donlan, Walter & Thompson, James, "The Charge at Marathon Again," _Classical World_ 72 (1979) 419-20.

Evans, J.A.S., "Histiaeus and Aristagoras: Notes on the Ionian Revolt," _American Journal of Philology_ 84 (1963) 113-128.

Evans, J. A. S., "Herodotus and the Ionian Revolt," _Historia_ 25 (1976) 31f.

Evans, J. A. S., "Herodotus and Athens: The Evidence of the Encomium," _Acta Classica_ 48 (1979) 112-118.

Evans. J. A. S., "The Oracle of the 'Wooden Wall'," _Classical Journal_ 78 (1982) 24-29.

Ferrill, Arthur, "Herodotus and the Strategy and Tactics of the Invasion of Xerxes," _American Historical Review_ 72 (1966) 102-115.

Flory, Stewart, "Who Read Herodotus' Histories?" _American Journal of Philology_ 101 (1980) 12-28.

French, Valerie, "Herodotus: Revisionist Historian," in _Panhellenica_, eds. Stanley M. Burstein and Louis A. Okin (Lawrence, Kan.: Coronado, 1980) 31-42.

Frost, F. J., "The Athenian Military Before Cleisthenes," _Historia_ 33 (1984) 283-294.

Gomme. A.W., "Herodotus and Marathon," _Phoenix_ 6 (1952) 77-83.

Haas. Christopher, "Athenian Naval Power Before Themistocles," _Historia_ 35 (1985) 29-46.

Immerwahr, H. R., "Aspects of Historical Causation in Herodotus," _TAPA_ 87 (1956) 241f.

Lang, Mabel, "Herodotus and the Ionian Revolt," _Historia_ 17 (1968) 24-36.

Larsen, J.A.O., "Sparta and the Ionian Revolt," _Classical Philology_ 27 (1932) 136-149.

Lateiner, Donald, "The Failure of the Ionian Revolt," _Historia_ 31 (1982) 129-160.

Manville, P. B., "Aristagoras and Histiaios: The Leadership Struggle in the Ionian Revolt," _Classical Quarterly_ 27 (1977) 80f.

Maurice, F. D., "The Size of the Army of Xerxes," _Journal of Hellenic Studies_ 50 (1930) 210f.

McGregor, M.F., "The Pro-Persian Party at Athens from 510-480 BC," _Harvard Studies in Classical Philology_ Supp. Vol. I (1940) 71-95.

Momigliano, Arnaldo, "The Place of Herodotus in the History of Historiography," in _Studies in Historiography_ (New York: Harper & Row, 1966) 127-142.

Neville, J., "Was There an Ionian Revolt?" _Classical Quarterly_ 29 (1979) 268-275.

Roebuck, Carl, "The Early Ionian League," _Classical Philology_ 50 (1955) 26-40.

Sealey, R., "Thucydides, Herodotus, and the Causes of War," _Classical Quarterly_ 7 (1957) 1-12.

Shrimpton, Gordon, "The Persian Cavalry at Marathon," _Phoenix_ 34 (1980) 20-37.

Wardman, A. E., "Herodotus on the Cause of the Greco-Persian Wars," _American Journal of Philology_ 82 (1961) 133f.

Waters, K.H., "Herodotus and the Ionian Revolt," _Historia_ 19 (1970) 504-08.

Whatley, N., "On the Possibility of Reconstructing Marathon and Other Ancient Battles," _Journal of Hellenic Studies_ 84 (1964) 119-139.

Williams, G.M.E., "The Image of the Alcmeonidae Between 490 and 487/6 BC," _Historia_ 29 (1980) 106-110.

Williams, G. M. E., "Athenian Politics 508/7-480 B.C.: A Reappraisal," _Athenaeum_ 60 (1982) 521-544.

SPECIAL PERIODICAL LITERATURE SUPPLEMENT

THE PELOPONNESIAN WARS

I. Causes of the War: General

Andrewes, A., "Thucydides on the Causes of the War," CQ 9 (1959) 223-239.

Creed, J.L., "Moral Values in the Age of Thucydides," CQ 23 (1973) 213-231.

Hoffman, R.J., "Perdikkas and the Outbreak of the Peloponnesian War," GRBS 16 (1975) 359-377.

Huxley, G. L., "Thucydides on the Growth of Athenian Power," Proc. Roy. Irish Acad. 83 (1983) 191-204.

Powell, C.A., "Athens' Difficulty, Sparta's Opportunity: Causation and the Peloponnesian War," Antiq. Class. 49 (1980) 87-114.

Sealey, R., "Thucydides, Herodotus, and the Causes of War," CQ 7 (1957) 1-12.

Sealey, R., "The Causes of the Peloponnesian War," CP 70 (1975) 89-109.

Tannenbaum, R. F., "Who Started the Peloponnesian War?" Arion 2 (1975) 533-546.

II. Thucydides as Historian

Chambers, Mortimer, "Thucydides and Pericles," HSCP 62 (1957) 79-92.

Dover, Kenneth J., "Thucydides 'As History' and 'As Literature'," History and Theory 22 (1983) 54-63.

Hunter, Virginia J., "Thucydides and the Historical Fact," CJ 66 (1971) 14-19.

MacLeod, C.W., "Thucydides on Faction," Proc. Camb. Phil. Soc. 25 (1979) 52-68.

Mittlestadt, Michael C., "Thucydidean Psychology and Moral Value Judgment in the History," R. Stud. Class. (Turin) 25 (1977) 30-55.

Pozzi, Dora C., "Thucydides ii. 35-46: A Text of Power Ideology," CJ 78 (1983) 221-231.

Ridley, Ronald, "Exegesis and Audience in Thucydides," Hermes 109 (1981) 25-46.

Rokeah, D., "ta deonta peri ton aiei paronton: Speeches in Thucydides: Factual Reporting or Creative Writing?" Athenaeum 60 (1982) 386-401.

Schieber, A. S., "Thucydides and Pausanias," Athenaeum 58 (1980) 396-405.

264

Westlake, H. D., "Thucydides, Brasidas, and Clearides," <u>GRBS</u> 21 (1980) 332-39.

Wilson, John, "What Does Thucydides Claim for His Speeches?" <u>Phoenix</u> 36 (1982) 95-103.

III. The Athenian Empire/Athens and Her Allies

Bradeen, Donald W., "The Popularity of the Athenian Empire," <u>Historia</u> 6 (1960) 257-69.

Bruell, Christopher, "Thucydides' View of Athenian Imperialism," <u>American Political Science Review</u> 68 (1974) 11-17.

Campbell, William F., "Pericles and the Sophistication of Economics," <u>Hist. Pol. Econ.</u> 15 (1983) 122-135.

French, A., "Athenian Ambitions and the Delian Alliance," <u>Phoenix</u> 33 (1979) 134-141.

Galpin, Timothy J., "The Democratic Roots of Athenian Imperialism in the Fifth Century B.C.," <u>CJ</u> 79 (1983/84) 100-109.

Mattingly, Harold B., "The Tribute Districts of the Athenian Empire," <u>Historia</u> 33 (1984) 498-499.

Pecirka, Jan, "Athenian Imperialism and the Athenian Economy," <u>Eirene</u> 19 (1982) 117-125.

Robertson, Noel D., "The True Nature of The Delian League," <u>AJAH</u> 5 (1980) 64-96.

IV. Athenian Domestic Politics

Allison, June W., "Pericles' Policy and the Plague," <u>Historia</u> 32 (1983) 14-23.

Andrewes, A., "The Opposition to Pericles," <u>JHS</u> 98 (1978) 1-8.

Knight, D.W., "Thucydides and the War Strategy of Pericles," <u>Mnemosyne</u> 23 (1970) 150-161.

Merritt, B.M., & Wade-Gery, H.T., "Athenian Resources in 449 and 431 BC," <u>Hesperia</u> 26 (1957) 163-197.

V. Spartan Domestic Politics

Allison, June W., "Sthenelaidas' Speech: Thucydides 1.86," <u>Hermes</u> 112 (1984) 9-16.

Bloedow, Edmund F., "The Speeches of Archidamus and Sthenelaidas at Sparta," Historia 30 (1981) 129-143.

Bloedow, Edmund F., "Archidamus the 'Intelligent' Spartan," Klio 65 (1983) 27-49.

Brunt, P.A., "Spartan Policy and Strategy in the Archidamian War," Phoenix 19 (1965) 255-280.

Connor, W.R., "Pausanias 3.14.1 A Sidelight on Spartan History in 440 BC?" TAPA 109 (1979) 21-27.

Hamilton, Charles D., "The Early Career of Archidamus," Class. Views 1 (1982) 5-20.

Kelly, D. H., "Policy-Making in the Spartan Assembly," Antichthon 15 (1981) 47-61.

Rahe, Paul A., "The Selection of Ephors at Sparta," Historia 29 (1980) 385-401.

Rhodes, P.J., "The Selection of Ephors at Sparta," Historia 30 (1981) 498-502.

VI. Athens/The West/Corcyra-Epidamnus

Cogan, Marc, "Mytilene, Plataea, and Corcyra: Ideology and Policy in Thucydides Book Three," Phoenix 35 (1981) 1-21.

Madsen, David & McGregor, Malcolm F., "Thucydides and Egesta," Phoenix 33 (1979) 233-238.

Stadter, Philip A., "The Motives for Athens' Alliance with Corcyra (Thuc. 1.44)," GRBS 24 (1983) 131-136.

Raubitschek, Antony E., "Corinth and Athens Before the Peloponnesian War," in Greece and the Eastern Mediterranean in History and Prehistory, K. H. Kinzl, ed. (New York: de Gruyter, 1977) 266-269.

Wick, T.E., "Megara, Athens, and the West in the Archidamian War: A Study in Thucydides," Historia 28 (1979) 1-14.

Wick, T.E., "The Date of the Athenian Egestan Alliance," CP 76 (1981) 118-121.

VII. The Megarian Decree(s)

Brunt, P.A., "The Megarian Decree," AJPh 72 (1951) 269-282.

Connor, W.R., "Charinus' Megarian Decree Again," Rev. des Etud. Gr. 83 (1970) 305-308.

Fornara, Charles, "Plutarch and the Megarian Decree," YCS (1975) 213-228.

French, A., "The Megarian Decree," <u>Historia</u> 25 (1976) 245-248.

Legon, R.P., "The Megarian Decree and the Balance of Greek Naval Power," <u>CP</u> (1973).

MacDonald, Brian R., "The Megarian Decree," <u>Historia</u> 32 (1983) 385-410.

Losada, L.A., "Megara and Athens: Thucydides and the Motivation for Treason," <u>Class. et Med</u>. 30 (1969) 145-157.

Tuplin, C., "Thucydides 1.42.2 and the Megarian Decree," <u>CQ</u> 29 (1979) 301-307.

VIII. Miscellaneous

Fornara, Charles, "On the Chronology of the Samian War," <u>JHS</u> (1979) 7-19.

Kelly, Thomas, "Thucydides and the Spartan Strategy in the Archidamian War," <u>AHR</u> 87 (1982) 25-54.

MacDonald, Brian R., "The Importance of Attic Pottery to Corinth and the Question of Trade During the Peloponnesian War," <u>JHS</u> 102 (1982) 113-123.

SPECIAL PERIODICAL LITERATURE SUPPLEMENT

THE PUNIC WARS

Breckenridge, James D., "Hannibal as Alexander," <u>Anc. World</u> 7 (1983) 111-128.

Carney, T. F., "The Aims of Roman Military and Foreign Policy in the Last Quarter of the Third Century B.C.," <u>Proc. African Class. Assoc.</u> 1 (1958) 19-26.

Ekstein, A. M., "Perils of Poetry: The Roman 'Poetic Tradition' and the Outbreak of the First Punic War," <u>AJAH</u> 5 (1980) 174-192.

Ekstein, A. M., "Two Notes on the Chronology of the Outbreak of the Hannibalic War," <u>Rhein. Mus</u>. 126 (1983) 255-272.

Heichelheim, Fritz, "New Evidence on the Ebro River Treaty," <u>Historia</u> 3 (1954/5) 211-219.

Hoyos, B. D., "The Carthaginian and Roman Commanders in 264: Who Was Who," <u>Liverpool Class. Monthly</u> 8 (1983) 120-122.

Hoyos, B. D., "Hannibal: What Kind of Genius?" <u>G&R</u> 30 (1983) 171-180.

Hoyos, B. D., "The Romano-Punic Pact of 279 B.C.: Its Problems and its Purpose," <u>Historia</u> 33 (1984) 402-439.

Salmon, E. T., "The Strategy of the Second Punic War," <u>G&R</u> 7 (1960) 131-140.

Spann, Philip O., "Saguntum vs. Segontia," <u>Historia</u> 33 (1984) 116-119.

Walbank, F. W., "Polybius and the <u>Aitiai</u> of the Second Punic War," <u>Liverpool Class. Monthly</u> 8 (1983) 62-63.

SPECIAL PERIODICAL LITERATURE SUPPLEMENT

THE ROMAN CIVIL WAR

Balsdon, J. P. V. D., "Roman History, 65-50 B.C.: Five Problems," JRS (1962) 134-141. [Dispatch of Cn. Calpurnius Piso to Spain in 65; over-bidding of the publicani for the Asiatic tax contract in 61; Caesar's requests in 56 and Cicero's 'palinode'; consular provinces for the consuls of 55; and 'Absentia Ratio'--standing for election in absentia.]

Bauman, R. A., "Tribunician Sacrosanctity in 44, 36, and 35 B.C.," Rhein. Museum 124 (1981) 166-183.

Beare, Rhona, "The Imperial Oath under Julius Caesar," Latomus 38 (1979) 469-473.

Bernstein, A. H., "The Accidental Revolution," Historian 41 (1979) 513-520.

Boren, Henry C., "Cicero's Concordia in Historical Perspective," Laudatores Temporis Acta (1963) 51-62.

Boren, Henry C., "Rome: Republican Disintegration, Augustan Re-integration: Focus on the Army," Thought 55 (1980) 51-64.

Brunt, P. A., "The Army and the Land in the Roman Revolution," JRS 52 (1962).

Cuff, P. J., "The Terminal Date of Caesar's Gallic Command," Historia 7 (1958) 455-471.

Fantham, Elaine, "The Trials of Gabinius in 54 B.C.," Historia 24 (1975) 425-443.

Gardner, Jane F., "The 'Gallic Menace' in Caesar's Propaganda," Greece & Rome 30 (1983) 181-189.

Geiger, Joseph, "Contemporary Politics in Cicero's de Republica," CP 79 (1984) 38-43.

Green, Peter, "Caesar and Alexander: Aemulatio, Imitatio, Comparatio," AJAH 3 (1978) 1-26.

Gruen, Erich, "M. Licinius Crassus: A Review Article," AJAH 2 (1977) 117-128.

Hilliard, T. W., "P. Clodius Pulcher 62-58 B. C.: 'Pompei Adfinis et Sodalis'," PBSR 50 (1982) 34-44.

Keaveny, Arthur, "Young Pompey: 106-79 B.C.," Antiq. class. 51 (1982) 111-139.

Keaveney, Arthur, "The King and the Warlords: Romano-Parthian Relations Circa 64-53 B.C.," American Journal of Philology 103 (1982) 412-428.

Levick, Barbara, "Morals, Politics, and the Fall of the Roman Republic," G&R 29 (1982) 53-62.

Lintott, A. W., "Cicero and Milo," Journal of Roman Studies 64 (1974) 62-78.

Marshall, B. A., and G. R. Stanton, "The Coalition Between Pompeius and Crassus, 60-59," Historia 24 (1975).

Marshall, B. A., "Faustus Sulla and Political Labels in the 60's and 50's," Historia 33 (1984) 199-219.

Mc Dermott, W. C., "C. Asinius Pollio, Catullus, and C. Julius Caesar," Anc. World 2 (1979) 55-60.

Mitchell, Thomas, "The Inevitability of the Principate," Thought 55 (1980) 18-55.

Pelling, C. B. R., "Plutarch's Method of Work in the Roman Lives," JHS 99 (1979) 74-96.

Ridley, Ronald T., "The Economics of Civil War," Helikon 20-21 (1980/81) 27-41.

Ridley, Ronald T., "The Extraordinary Commands of the Late Republic," Historia 30 (1981) 280-297.

Ridley, Ronald T., "Pompey's Commands in the 50's: How Cumulative?" Rhein. Mus. 126 (1983) 136-148.

Rosivach, Vincent J., "Caelius' Adherence to the Caesarian Cause," CW 74 (1981) 201-212.

Ruebel, James, "The Trial of Milo in 52 B.C.: A Chronological Study," TAPA 109 (1979) 231-249.

Rundell, W. M. F., "Cicero and Clodius: The Question of Credibility," Historia 28 (1979) 301-328.

Sirianni, Frank A., "Caesar's Decision to Cross the Rubicon," Antiq. Class. 48 (1979) 636-638.

Sumner, G. V., "The Coitio of 54 B.C., or Waiting for Caesar," HSCP 86 (1982) 133-139.

Syme, Sir Ronald, "Caesar, the Senate and Italy," PBSR 14 (1938) 1-31.

Taylor, Lily Ross, "On the Chronology of Caesar's First Consulship," AJPh 72 (1951) 254-268.

Towend, G. B., "A Clue to Caesar's Unfulfilled Intentions," Latomus 42 (1983) 601-606.

Tyrrell, W. B., "Labienus' Departure from Caesar in January 49 B.C.," Historia 21 (1972) 424-440.

Ward, Allen M., "The Conference of Luca: Did It Happen?" <u>AJAH</u> 5 (1980) 48-63.

Weinrib, E. J., "The Prosecution of Magistrates-Designate," <u>Phoenix</u> 25 (1971).

CLS 350/550
GREEK AND ROMAN WARFARE   Janice Gabbert
Winter 1983   Wright State Universi

<u>COURSE OUTLINE</u>

This course is organized as a seminar, in which all students are expected
to participate. The first half of the course will consist primarily of
lectures by the instructor, although discussion from students is encouraged.
The major periods and events of Classical warfare will be covered, as
indicated below. The second half of the course will be discussion of
specific topics related to Classical warfare, directed by the instructor
with one or more individual students designated as primary discussants,
based on the topics of research they have chosen.

The only required textbook is:

Warry, John. <u>Warfare in the Classical World</u>
(New York: St. Martin's Press, 1980).

Students will be expected to be thoroughly familiar with the contents of
that book, and to do additional reading as appropriate from the attached
reading list.

Attendance and informed participation in class is extremely important,
and will account for about 40% of the final grade. Approximately 60%
of the final grade will be based on a research paper on an aspect of
Classical warfare chosen by the student in consultation with the instructor.
A separate page of instructions for preparation of the research paper is
attached. The length of the paper is not as important as the thoroughness
of research and the content; however as a general guideline, the paper will
be between fifteen (15) and forty (40) pages in length. The definition of
the topic, a preliminary outline and bibliography must be submitted not
later than Feb. 7th.

LECTURES

Lecture	Date	Topic
1	Jan. 3	Introduction; Overview of course; Warfare in the Archaic period.
2	Jan. 5	The Persian Wars.
3	Jan. 10	The Peloponnesian War; The fourth century.
4	Jan. 12	The campaigns of Philip II and Alexander the Great.
5	Jan. 17	The successors of Alexander.
6	Jan. 19	Rome; War in the Early Republic.
7	Jan. 24	The Punic and Macedonian Wars.

272

Lecture	Date	Topic
8	Jan. 26	Rome; War in the Late Republic.
9	Jan. 31	Julius Caesar.
10	Feb. 2	Civil War at Rome.
11	Feb. 7	The maintenance and defense of empire.

RESEARCH PAPER: BIBLIOGRAPHY AND OUTLINE DUE

The following topics of discussion are tentative and subject to revision based on the topics of research which have been chosen. Each student can expect to be designated as a primary discussant at least once, whenever the topic of discussion closely corresponds to the area of research chosen for the paper. That is, each student is expected to become somewhat of an expert in a particular event or area, and to share that expertise with the class.

12	Feb. 9	Infantry.
13	Feb. 14	Cavalry.
14	Feb. 16	Auxiliary troops; Guerilla war.
15	Feb. 21	Artillery.
16	Feb. 23	Naval warfare.
17	Feb. 28	Logistics.
18	Mar. 2	Intelligence.
19	Mar. 7	Strategy and grand strategy.
20	Mar. 9	Last day of class; Summary.

A due date for the submission of the research papers will be established for each student individually, and will be between Feb. 28th and March 9th. Each student is expected to meet the deadline, and failure to do so will be taken into consideration in the determination of the grade for the paper.

273

CLS 350/550
GREEK AND ROMAN WARFARE
Winter 1983

Schedule of Topical Discussions

All persons should be sufficiently familiar with the topic to be able to ask
intelligent questions, and to understand the presentations.

The individuals listed for each topic should informally summarize the results
of their research and state their conclusions. Note the time constraints. Be
prepared to cover the material in about twenty minutes.

Date	5:20 - 5:50	6:10 - 6:40	
Wed., Feb 9	Gabbert: Grand Strategy	Jim St. Peter Strategy: the Indirect Approach (esp. Diadochan and 2nd Punic War)	(F28)
Mon., Feb. 14	Roberta Semmett Intelligence and Covert Operations	Eric Sykes Hoplite Equip. & Tactics	(F28)
Wed., Feb. 16	Michael Hoffman The Classical Spartans	Steve Keller Alexander the Great	(F28)
Mon., Feb. 21	Eric Hutzel Cannae and Zama	Leif Kenney The Use of Elephants	(M2)
Wed., Feb. 23	Bob Jacobs Development & Use of Artillery	Joe Hjelm Defensive war: fortifications	(M2)
Mon., Feb. 28	Terry McClurg Warship Construction	John Breyer The Athenian Imperial Navy	(M4)
Wed., Mar 2	Dave Allbaugh The Roman Conquest of Britain	Steve Walters The Deployment of Roman Forces in Palestine (62 B.C.-135 A.D.)	(M7)
Mon., Mar. 7	Kristine King Battlefield Medicine	Jacqueline Ahburn Camp Followers	(M9)
Wed., Mar. 9	(last day of class) Retrospective: general discussion.		

Completed papers are due by the date
indicated in abbreviated form in the
right margin.

CLS 350
Greek and Roman Warfare

AGENDA FOR DISCUSSION
March 9, 1983

1. War has often brought out the best in men, and the worst. For example, there
    would be no _Iliad_ without war.[1]   Comment. Give examples.

2. The pursuit of peace requires an understanding of war. [1]   Comment.

3. What has a study of Greek and Roman Warfare taught us about Greeks and Romans?
    and What does that knowledge tell us about ourselves? [1]

4. "The...idea of victory..[is]...the one notion that gives defeat its meaning. If
    war can serve no worthwhile national purpose, ... it follows that victory can have
    no substantive content, and remains only as the empty goal of a compulsive
    machismo....if war [is] futile, victory [is not] a proper goal of statecraft...
    it follows inevitably that defeat too must lose its meaning, since the very act
    of waging war is in itself the only real defeat. ...War cannot after all serve
    any good purpose, since its cruelties will exceed any benefit that victory might
    secure. ... Either we rehabilitate the notion of victory, or else the United States
    will lose its capacity to use military power, thus consigning the future to those
    less inhibited." (2)   Comment.

5. "Great powers will abandon lesser allies when the cost of their protection exceeds
    their worth..." (2)   Examples?

6. "...the price of involvement [must be] clear..... so that [one] can weigh the
    probable costs of involvement against the dangers of noninvolvement. For there
    are worse things than war." (3)   Comment.

7. "War is death and destruction. The American way of war is particularly violent,
    deadly, and dreadful. We believe in using "things" - artillery, bombs, massive
    firepower - in order to conserve our soldiers' lives..." (3)
            Comment. Is this attitude totally foreign to anything we have
    learned about classical warfare?

8. The true aim of a military strategist "is not so much to seek battle as to seek
    a strategic situation so advantageous that if it does not of itself produce the
    decision, its continuation by a battle is sure to do so." (4)   Comment.

Course critique:

9. What have we _not_ covered in class?

10. Did you learn anything about the _methodology_ of research and investigation?

Other.

Notes
(1) JG. The thoughts are not original.
(2) Edward N. Luttwak, in the Dayton _Journal Herald_, 1/28/83.
(3) General Weyand, U.S.Army (last commander in Viet Nam), as quoted by Fox Butterfield
     in the New York Times Magazine, 2/13/83.
(4) B. H. Liddell Hart, _Strategy_ (N.Y., 1954), p. 339.

Politics and Culture in the Age of the Hannibalic War

First Session: The Origins of the Hannibalic War

Polybius, II, 1, 13, 36, XII, 6-15, 17, 20-35, 39-56, IV, 37
Livy, XXX, 1-21
Appian, Hann. 1-4, Iber. 4-13
Dio, XII.48, XIII (Zonares, VIII.21-22)
Diodorus, XXV, 1-16
Asconius, 3 (Clark)

Badian, Foreign Clientels, 47-54
Cassola, I gruppi politici, 233-240, 245-258, 285-284
De Sanctis, Storia dei Romani, III.1, 406-432; III.2, 1-15
Ebel, Transalpine Gaul, 16-25
Eucken, Probleme der Vorgeschichte des 2. punischen Krieges, 1-121
Errington, Dawn of Empire, 49-61
Frank, Roman Imperialism, 119-125
Harris, War and Imperialism, 200-205
Lazenby, Hannibal's War, 1-28
Proctor, Hannibals's March in History, 13-80
Rich, Declaring War in the Roman Republic, 28-44, 109-118
Schwarte, Der Ausbruch des zweiten punischen Krieges, 37-74
Scullard, Roman Politics, 39-42
Walbank, Commentary on Polybius (on relevant passages)

Reid, JRS (1913)
Otto, Historische Zeitschrift (1931-2)
Oertel, RhMus (1932)
Gelzer, Hermes (1933)
Kramer, AJP (1948)
Hoffman, RhMus (1951)
Scullard, RhMus (1952)
Dorey, Humanitas (1959-60)
Sumner, PACA (1966)
Astin, Latomus (1967)
Sumner, MSCP (1967)
Errington, Latomus (1970)
Liebmann-Frankfort, Latomus (1971)
Sumner, Latomus (1972)
Hampl, ANRW, I.1 (1972)
Cuff, RivStorAnt (1973)
Walbank, Studies for Salmon (1974)
Welwei, Talanta (1977)
Ruschenbusch, Historia (1978)
Walbank, LCM (1983)
Eckstein, RhMas (1983)

276

Second Session: Fabian Strategy and its Opponents (218-213)

Polybius, III.39-118, VII.9, VIII.3-7, 24-34 (esp. III.60-61,
69-75, 77-94, 101-118)
Livy, XXI.21-XXV.1 (esp. XXI.52-57, 63, XXI.1, #-14, 23-27, 30-31,
33-35, 38-45, 53-61, XXIII.14, 21-25, 30-32, 35-37, 41, 48-49,
XXIV.7-11, 18-19, 43-44, XXV.1)
Appian, Hann, 4-31, Iber, 13-15
Zenaras, VIII.23 - IX.4
Plutarch, Fabius, 2-19; 24; Marcellus, 9-18

Bleicken, Das Volkstribunat der klassischen Republik, 37-42
Cassola, I gruppi politici, 293-320, 336-346, 361-381
De Sanctis, Storia dei Romani, III.2, 15-64, 211-287
Errington, Dawn of Empire, 62-78, 80-83
Jahn, Interregnum und Wahldiktatur, 116-128
Lazenby, Hannibal's War, 29-105
Lippold, Consules, 147-174, 256-261, 337-349
Hunzer, Romische Adelsparteien, 72-76, 124-126
Scullard, Roman Politica, 39-61, 274-276
Walbank, Commentary on Polybius, (on relevant passages)

Reid, JES (1915)
Patterson, TAPA (1942)
Mueller-Seidel, RhMus (1953)
Staveley, Historia (1954)
Dorey, Orpheus, (1955)
Dorey, JRS (1955)
Carney, PACA (1958)
Dorey, RhMus (1959)
Brown, Historia (1959)
Crake, Phoenix (1963)
Pinsent, Phoenix (1964)
Ridley, Latomus (1975)
Sumner, Phoeniz (1975)
Gruen, CSCA (1978)
Rebuffat, REI (1982)
Twyman, CP (1984)

Third Session: Senatorial Politics in the War's Middle Years (212-206)

Polybius, VIII.37, IX.3-11a, X.1-20, 32-40, XI.1-3, 20-33
Livy, XXV.1 - XXVII.37 (esp. XXV.1-5, 22-31, 36, 40-41, XXVI.1-3,
12-22, 26-37, XXVII.3-12, 15-16, 20-22, 25, 33-35, 38, 40,
43-44, 48-51, XXVII.9-12)
Appian, Hann. 32-54; Iber. 16-37
Zonaras, IX.5-10
Plutarch, Fabius, 19-23; Marcellus, 19-30
Val. Max. 4.2.2

Cassola, Igrappi politici, 321-336, 408-410, 413, 421-423
De Sanctis, Storia dei Romani, II.2, 287-316, 336-347, 445-507
Errington, Dawn of Empire, 78-79, 83-95

277

Jahn, Interregnum und Wahldiktatur, 128-140

Lazenby, Hannibal's War, 105-151
Lippold, Consules, 174-198, 261-270
Munzer, Romische Adelsparteien, 126-129, 183-191
Rillinger, Der Einfluss des Wahlleiters, 186-200
Schur, Scipio Africanus, 9-43
Scullard, Roman Politics, 61-74
Scullard, Scipio Africanus, 35-107
Walbank, Commentary on Polybius (on relevant passages)

Reid, JRS (1915)
Patterson, TAPA (1942)
Salmon, Phoenix (1957)
Carney, PACA (1958)
Davis, Phoenix (1959)
Crake, Phoenix (1963)
Nicolet, Annales (1963)
Develin, Athenaeum (1977)

Fourth Session: Scipio Africanus and the Final Struggle (205-201)

Polybius, XI.33, XIV.1-10, XV.1-19
Livy, XXVII.38 - XXX.45 (esp. XXVIII.38, 40-46, XXIX.6-10, 13-22,
    37-38, XXX.1-2, 11-16, 19-27, 36-45)
Diodorus, XXVII.4-18
Appian, Hann. 55-61; Pun. 6-66; Iber. 38
Zonaras, IX.11-14
Plutarch, Fabius, 25-27

Cassola, I gruppi politici, 281-288, 393-396, 406-408, 410-420
De Sanctis, Storia dei Romani, II.2, 507-560
Errington, Dawn of Empire 96-101
Jahn, Interregnum und Wahldiktatur, 140-150
Waywood, Studies on Scipio Africanus, 45-58
Lazenby, Hannibal's War, 151-232
Lippold, Consules, 198-221, 276-280, 358-367
Munzer, Romische Adelsparteien, 135-146
Schur, Scipio Africanus, 44-68
Scullard, Roman Politics, 75-83, 277-280
Scullard, Scipio Africanus, 108-160, 166-173
Walbank, Commentary on Polybius (on relevant passages)

Patterson, TAPA (1942)
Dorey, Orpheus (1956)
Carney, PACA (1958)
Dorey, AJP (1959)
Gabba, Athenaeum (1975)

Fifth Session: The Coming of the Magna Mater

    Livy, X.47, XXII.9-10, 57, SSIII.11, 30-31, XXV.12, XXVIII.45,
        XXIX.10-12, 14
    Ovid, Fasti, IV.179-190, 207-214, 2470348; Met. XV.626-744
    Varro, LL, 6.15; Dion. Hal. II.19; Diodorus, XXXIV/XXXV.33.2-3
    Cicero, Pro Cael. 34; Har. Resp. 27-28; Strabo, XXII.5.3
    Catullus, 63.1-38; Propartius, IV.11.51-52; Silius Ittal. XVII.1-47
    Val. Max. 1.8.2, 7.5.2, 8.15.3; Suetonius, Claud. 25
    Plutarch, Fabius, 18; Marcellus, 8; Appian, Hann. 27, 56
    Justin, XXVIII.1-2; Herodian, I.11; Dio, fr. 57.61
    Vir.Ill. 22.1, 46.1; Julian, Or. 5.159-161; Amm. Marc. XXII.9.5
    Gage, Apollon romain, 270-279
    Graillot, Le Cult de Cybele, 25-69
    Holleaux, Rome, la Grece, et les Monarchies Hellenistiques, 5-22, 46-58
    Latte, Romische Religionsgeschichte, 223-227, 258-262
    Schmitt, Kultubertragungen, 1-30
    Vermaseren, Cybele und Attis, 24-32, 38-43
    Warde Fowler, Religious Experience of the Roman People, 223-247, 316-334

    Kuiper, Mnemosyne (1902)
    Vogt, Hermes (1933)
    Koves, Historis (1963)
    Bomer, RHI (1963)
    Weber, WS (1972)
    North, PBSR (1976)
    Develin, J.Rel.Hist. (1978)
    Gerard, REL (1980)
    Porte, Klio (1984)

Sixth Session: Poetry and Politics: The Beginnings of Latin Literature

    Cicero, Brutus, 60, 72-73, 75; De Sen. 20, 49-50; De Rep. 4.10.11-12;
        Tusc. Disp. 1.3, 4.3; De Orat. 2.2.49; Verr. 1.29
    Gellius, I.24.2-3, III.3.15, VII.8.5-6, XI.2.4, XVII.21.42-45
    Plautus, Miles, 209-212
    Varro, LL, VII.107, IX.78
    Livy, VII.2, XXVIII.9-10, XXIX.36-37, XXXI.12
    Horace, Epist.11.1.69-71, 161-163; Pliny, NH, XXXIV.19, XXXV.66
    Charisius, in Keil, GL, I, 208, 210, 216; Bassus, in Keil, GL, VI, 266
    Jerome, Chron. ad ann 201 BC, 187 BC; Cassiodorus, Chron. ad ann 239 BC
    Suetonius, De Gramm. 1; Plutarch, Cato, 25; Val. Max. 2.4.4, 3.7.11
    Festus, 32, 83, 446-448, Lindsay; Ps.Ascon. 215, Stangl; Pan. Lat. 9.7.3

    Dahlmann, Studien zu Varro, De Poetis, 65-100
    MacBain, Prodigy and Expiation, 65-71, 127-135
    Marmorale, Naevius Poeta, 9-141
    Palmer, Roman Religion and Roman Empire, 94-108
    Suerbaum, Untersuchungen zur Selbstdarstellung rom. Dichter, 27-42, 297-
                                                                        300

Sihler, AJP (1905)
Frank, AJP (1927)
Kroll, Hermes 1931)
Barwick, Philologus (1933)
Boyce, TAPA (1937)
Herrmann, Latomus (1937)
Beare, CQ (1940
Till, Neue Jahrbucher (1940)
Ferrero, Mondo Classico (1941)
Cousin, RHR (1942-3)
Rowell, MAAR (1949)
Smith, CQ (1951)
D'Anna, RendIstLomb (1954)
Mattingly, CQ (1957)
Mattingly, Historia (1960)
Waszink, Mnemosyne (1960)
Tamm, Opuscula (1961)
Richter, Gymnasium (1962)
Mette, Lustrum (1964)
Preux, Latomus (1966)
Marconi, MemAccadLinc (1966)
Jocylyn, Antichthon (1969)
Jory, Hermes (1970)
Wright, RhMus (1972)
Waszink, ANRW, I.2 (1972)
Crowther, Latomus (1973)
Killen, CP (1973)
More, Grazer Beitrage (1975)
Horsfall, BICS (1976)
Martina, Labeo (1980)
Martina, DialArch (1981)

Political and Social Upheaval
in the Age of the Gracchi, Marius, and Sulla

1st Session: Tiberius Gracchus: Reformer or Revolutionary?

Appian, BC, I.1-20
Plutarch, Ti. Gracchus
Greenidge and Clay, Sources for Roman History, 133-70 BC, 1-24

Astin, Scipio Aemilianus, 190-241, 345-346
Badian, Foreign Clientelae, 168-179
Bernstein, Ti. Sempronius Gracchus, 71-230
Earl, Ti. Gracchus, 7-40, 66-119
Gabba, Appian, BC, Lib. Prim., 3-66
Gruen, Roman Politics and the Criminal Courts, 45-78
Meier, Res Publica Amissa, 95-99, 128-131
Schneider, Wirtschaft und Politik, 270-293
Scullard, From the Gracchi to Nero, 1-33
Stockton, The Gracchi, 6-86, 206-216
Toynbee, Hannibal's Legacy, II, 155-210, 296-312

Brown, CJ (1947)
Tibiletti, Athenaeum (1948)
Tibiletti, Athenaeum (1949)
Drexler, Emerita (1951)
Boren, AHR (1958)
Boren, AJP (1958)
Boren, AJP (1961)
Badian, Historia (1962)
Taylor, Athenaeum (1963)
Nicolet, REA (1965)
Earl, Athenaeum (1965)
Taylor, Athenaeum (1966)
Cuff, Historia (1967)
Sterckz, RIDA (1969)
Schochat, Athenaeum (1970)
Hadot, REL (1970)
Nagle, Athenaeum (1970)
Nagle, Athenaeum (1971)
Frederiksen, Dialoghi (1971)
Badian, ANRW, I.1 (1972)
Molthagen, Historia (1973)
Flach, HZ (1973)
Gabba, Studies for Salmon (1974)
Briscoe, JRS (1974)
Morgan and Walsh, CP (1978)
Bauman, Historia (1980)

2nd Session: The Gracchan Reform Program and the Reaction

Appian, BC, I.18-26
Plutarch, C. Gracchus
ILLRP, #467-474
Greenidge and Clay, Sources, 13-49

Astin, Scipio Aemilianus, 227-241
Badian, Foreign Clientelae, 176-191, 299-301
Carcopino, Autour des Gracques, 129-209
Eder, Das Vorsullanische Repetundenverfahren, 120-152
Gabba, Appian, BC, Lib. Prim., 55-92
Galsterer, Herrschaft und Verwaltung, 171-184
Gruen, Roman Politics and the Criminal Courts, 60-98, 293-296
Hill, Roman Middle Class, 104-112
Jones, Criminal Courts of the Roman Republic and Empire, 45-52
Meier, Res Publica Amissa, 64-76, 131-134
Nicolet, L'Ordre equestre, 467-527
Schneider, Wirtschaft und Politik, 291-309
Scullard, From the Gracchi to Nero, 31-43
Stockton, The Gracchi, 87-205, 226-239
Venturini, Studi sul crimen repetundarum, 1-49

Fraccaro, Studi storici (1912)
Fraccaro, RendIstLomb (1919)
Fraccaro, Athenaeum (1925)
Balsdon, PBSR (1938)
Bernardi, NuovRivStor (1944-5)
Bruwaene, Phoibos (1950-1)
Tibiletti, Athenaeum (1953)
Badian, AJP (1954)
Boren, CJ (1956)
Miners, CQ (1958)
Ewins, JRS (1960)
Jones, PCPS (1960)
Badian, Historia (1962)
Rowland, TAPA (1965)
Hands, Latomus (1965)
Brunt, JRS (1965)
Rowland, Phoenix (1969)
Brunt, in Seager, Crisis of the Roman Republic (1969)
Mattingly, JRS (1969)
Mattingly, JRS (1970)
Badian, Dialoghi (1970)
Pico, RendIstLomb (1971)
Nicolet, ANRW, I.1 (1972)
Hall, Athenaeum (1972)
Sherwin-White, JRS (1972)
Griffin, CQ (1973)
Molthagen, Historia (1973)
Flach, ZSS (1973)
Mattingly, Latomus (1975)
Mattingly, CQ (1975)
Bianchini, RendIstLomb (1975)
Meister, Chiron (1976)
Hall, Athenaeum (1977)
Reiter, Athenaeum (1978)
Nicolet, Historia (1979)
Bauman, Historia (1980)   282

3rd Session: The Rise of Marius

Plutarch, Marius, 1-10
Sallust, BJ, 1-46, 63-65, 73, 82-86
FIRA, #8
Greenidge and Clay, Sources, 50-77

Badian, Foreign Clientelae, 192-198
Badian, Studies in Greek and Roman History, 235-242
Brunt, Italian Manpower, 391-415
Carcopino, Autour des Gracques, 244-303
Carney, A Biography of Marius
De Sanctis, Problemi di storia antica, 187-214
Gabba, Appian, BC, Lib. Prim., 93-96
Gabba, Republican Rome: Army and Allies, 1-19
Gruen, Roman Politics and the Criminal Courts, 98-156
Harmand, L'armeé et le soldat à Rome, 11-20
Hill, Roman Middle Class, 113-121
Johannsen, Die Lex Agraria des Jahres 111 v. Chr.
Koestermann, Sallustius BJ, passim
Ooteghem, Caius Marius, 56-93, 143-151
Saumagne, La Numidie et Rome, 121-261
Schur, Das Zeitalter des Marius und Sulla, 46-67
Scullard, From the Gracchi to Nero, 44-52
Syme, Sallust, 157-177

Bloch, Mel. d'Hist. Anc. (1909)
Hardy, JP (1910)
Passerini, Athenaeum (1934)
D'Arms, AJP (1935)
Allen, CP (1938)
von Fritz, TAPA (1943)
Sherwin-White, JRS (1956)
Badian, JRS (1956)
Douglas, AJP (1956)
Hands, JRS (1959)
La Penna, AnnPisa (1959)
Badian, Historia (1962)
Timpe, Hermes (1962)
Mattingly, Hommages Grenier (1962)
Suerbaum, Hermes (1964)
Ooteghem, LEC (1964)
Earl, Latomus (1965)
Hinrichs, ZSS (1966)
Douglas, AJP (1966)
Seager, CR (1967)
Bicknell, Latomus (1969)
Levick, CQ (1971)
Mattingly, Latomus (1971)
Sordi, Athenaeum (1972)
Deniaux, Philologus (1973)
Flach, HZ (1973)
Shatzman, AncSoc (1974)
Meister, Historia (1974)
Sumner, Phoenix (1976)
Rowland, Historia (1976)

4th Session: Marius and the Demagogues

Appian, BC, I.28-33
Plutarch, Marius, 11-30
FIRA, #6
JRS (1974), 195-220
Greenidge and Clay, Sources, 77-111

Badian, Foreign Clientelae, 198-210
Bauman, The Crimen Maiestatis, 38-58
Carney, A Biography of Marius, 29-44
Gabba, Appian, BC, Lib. Prim., 96-115
Gruen, Roman Politics and the Criminal Courts, 157-184
Hill, Roman Middle Class, 121-127
Jones, Criminal Courts, 52-55'
Nicolet, L'Ordre equestre, 529-549, 555-558
Ooteghem, Caius Marius, 232-253
Robinson, Marius, Saturninus und Glaucia, 23-131
Schneider, Wirtschaft und Politik, 309-318
Scullard, From the Gracchi to Nero, 52-62

Jones, JRS (1926)
Lengle, Hermes (1931)
Passerini, Athenaeum (1934)
Balsdon, PBSR (1938)
Schur, Klio (1938)
Tibiletti, Athenaeum (1953)
Badian, CR (1954)
Gabba, Athenaeum (1955)
Schönbauer, RIDA (1955)
Sherwin-White, JRS (1956)
Yarnold, AJP (1957)
Carney, WS (1960)
Carney, RhM (1962)
Badian, Historia (1962)
Gruen, TAPA (1964)
Gruen, Latomus (1965)
Seager, CR (1967)
Levick, CR (1967)
Gruen, CR (1969)
Mattingly, CR (1969)
Hinrichs, Hermes (1970)
Gabba, ANRW, I.1 (1972)
Hands, CR (1972)
Griffin, CQ (1973)
Bianchini, MemIstLomb (1975)
Lintott, ZPE (1976)
Smith, Athenaeum (1977)
Ferrary, MEFRA (1977)
Lintott, Hermes (1978)
Giovannini and Grzybek, MH (1978)
Sumner, GRBS (1978)
David, MEFRA (1979)

5th Session: Roman Politics and Eastern Policy in the 90s

Appian, <u>Mithr</u>. 10-11
Justin, XXXVII.4 - XXXVIII.3
Greenidge and Clay, <u>Sources</u>, 111-128

Badian, <u>Foreign Clientelae</u>, 210-215
Badian, <u>Studies in Greek and Roman History</u>, 34-70, 157-178
Carney, <u>A Biography of Marius</u>, 45-50
Gruen, <u>Roman Politics and the Criminal Courts</u>, 185-198, 201-206
Hill, <u>Roman Middle Class</u>, 127-132
Magie, <u>Roman Rule in Asia Minor</u>, 199-207
Ooteghem, <u>Caius Marius</u>, 254-267
Reinach, <u>Mithridate Eupator</u>, 81-106
Schur, <u>Das Zeitalter des Marius und Sulla</u>, 67-99
Scullard, <u>From the Gracchi to Nero</u>, 63-64

Passerini, <u>Athenaeum</u> (1934)
Balsdon, <u>CR</u> (1937)
Gabba, <u>Athenaeum</u> (1953)
Broughton, <u>Historia</u> (1953)
Frank, <u>CJ</u> (1953)
Badian, <u>Athenaeum</u> (1956)
Badian, <u>Historia</u> (1957)
Carney, <u>Athenaeum</u> (1958)
Badian, <u>Athenaeum</u> (1959)
Carney, <u>WS</u> (1960)
Carney, <u>RhM</u> (1962)
Gruen, <u>Historia</u> (1966)
Seager, <u>CR</u> (1967)
Luce, <u>Historia</u> (1970)
Gabba, <u>ANRW</u>, I.1 (1972)
Desideri, <u>Athenaeum</u> (1973)
Marshall, <u>Athenaeum</u> (1976)
Smith, <u>Athenaeum</u> (1977)
Sherwin-White, <u>JRS</u> (1977)
Glew, <u>Athenaeum</u> (1977)
Sherwin-White, <u>CQ</u> (1977)
Vardelli, <u>Aevum</u> (1978)
Sumner, <u>Athenaeum</u> (1978)
David, <u>MEFRA</u> (1979)

7th Session: The Impact of the Social War

Appian, <u>Mithr</u>. 11-22
Greenidge and Clay, <u>Sources</u>, 136-137, 141, 149-150, 159-162

Badian, <u>Foreign Clientelae</u>, 226-232
Bauman, <u>Crimen Maiestatis</u>, 59-68
Gruen, <u>Roman Politics and the Criminal Courts</u>, 215-226
Hill, <u>Roman Middle Class</u>, 136-141
Magie, <u>Roman Rule in Asia Minor</u>, 208-218
Meier, <u>Res Publica Amissa</u>, 215-216
Nicolet, <u>L'Ordre equestre</u>, 570-572
Reinach, <u>Mithridate Eupator</u>, 107-120
Schur, <u>Das Zeitalter des Marius und Sulla</u>, 114-130
Scullard, <u>From the Gracchi to Nero</u>, 68-71

Biedl, <u>WS</u> (1930)
Biedl, <u>WS</u> (1931)
Frank, <u>AJP</u> (1933)
Gelzer, <u>AbhBerlin</u> (1941)
Gruen, <u>JRS</u> (1965)
Seager, <u>Historia</u> (1967)
Wiseman, <u>CQ</u> (1967)
Hamilton, <u>CQ</u> (1968)
Badian, <u>Historia</u> (1969)
Yavetz, <u>Colloques Nat. du Centre Nat.</u> (1970)
Luce, <u>Historia</u> (1970)
Lintott, <u>CQ</u> (1971)
Gabba, <u>ANRW</u>, I.1 (1972)
Griffin, <u>CQ</u> (1973)
Mitchell, <u>CP</u> (1975)
Bianchini, <u>MemIstLomb</u> (1975)
Glew, <u>Athenaeum</u> (1977)
Sherwin-White, <u>JRS</u> (1977)
Katz, <u>RhM</u> (1977)
Keaveney, <u>CQ</u> (1978)
La Coscio, <u>Athenaeum</u> (1979)

6th Session: The Origins of the Social War and the Enfranchisement of Italy

    Appian, <u>BC</u>, I.34-53
    Greenidge and Clay, <u>Sources</u>, 128-136, 138-140, 142-149, 151-159

    Badian, <u>Foreign Clientelae</u>, 210-227
    Carney, <u>A Biography of Marius</u>, 51-53
    Gabba, <u>Appian, BC, Lib. Prim.</u>, 115-158
    Gabba, <u>Republican Rome: Army and Allies</u>, 70-96
    Galsterer, <u>Herrschaft und Verwaltung</u>, 184-204
    Gruen, <u>Roman Politics and the Criminal Courts</u>, 198-201, 206-214
    Harris, <u>Rome in Etruria and Umbria</u>, 212-231
    Hill, <u>Roman Middle Class</u>, 132-136
    Meier, <u>Res Publica Amissa</u>, 208-215
    Nicolet, <u>L'Ordre equestre</u>, 559-570
    Ooteghem, <u>Caius Marius</u>, 267-275
    Schur, <u>Das Zeitalter des Marius und Sulla</u>, 106-113
    Scullard, <u>From the Gracchi to Nero</u>, 64-67

    Hardy, <u>CR</u> (1912)
    Hardy, <u>CR</u> (1913)
    Seymour, <u>EHR</u> (1914)
    Carcopino, <u>BullAssocBudé</u> (1929)
    Thomsen, <u>ClMed</u> (1942)
    Bernardi, <u>NuovRivStor</u> (1944-5)
    Gabba, <u>Athenaeum</u> (1953)
    Gabba, <u>PP</u> (1956)
    Ewins, <u>JRS</u> (1960)
    Badian, <u>Historia</u> (1962)
    Salmon, <u>Phoenix</u> (1962)
    Brunt, <u>JRS</u> (1965)
    Gruen, <u>Historia</u> (1966)
    Lewis, <u>Athenaeum</u> (1968)
    Weinrib, <u>Historia</u> (1970)
    Luce, <u>Historia</u> (1970)
    Hands, <u>Phoenix</u> (1972)
    Gabba, <u>ANRW</u>, I.1 (1972)
    Fuks-Geiger, <u>Studi Volterra</u> (1972)
    Badian, <u>Dialoghi</u> (1972)
    Griffin, <u>CQ</u> (1973)
    Seleckij, <u>Klio</u> (1976)
    Marshall, <u>Historical Papers</u> (1976)

7th Session: The Impact of the Social War

Appian, Mithr. 11-22.
Greenidge and Clay, Sources, 136-137, 141, 149-150, 159-162

Badian, Foreign Clientelae, 226-232
Bauman, Crimen Maiestatis, 59-68
Gruen, Roman Politics and the Criminal Courts, 215-226
Hill, Roman Middle Class, 136-141
Magie, Roman Rule in Asia Minor, 208-218
Meier, Res Publica Amissa, 215-216
Nicolet, L'Ordre equestre, 570-572
Reinach, Mithridate Eupator, 107-120
Schur, Das Zeitalter des Marius und Sulla, 114-130
Scullard, From the Gracchi to Nero, 68-71

Biedl, WS (1930)
Biedl, WS (1931)
Frank, AJP (1933)
Gelzer, AbhBerlin (1941)
Gruen, JRS (1965)
Seager, Historia (1967)
Wiseman, CQ (1967)
Hamilton, CQ (1968)
Badian, Historia (1969)
Yavetz, Colloques Nat. du Centre Nat. (1970)
Luce, Historia (1970)
Lintott, CQ (1971)
Gabba, ANRW, I.1 (1972)
Griffin, CQ (1973)
Mitchell, CP (1975)
Bianchini, MemIstLomb (1975)
Glew, Athenaeum (1977)
Katz, RhM (1977)
Keaveney, CQ (1978)
La Coscio, Athenaeum (1979)

8th Session: The Age of Sulla

Appian, BC, I.55-84, 95-106
Appian, Mithr. 51-63
Plutarch, Sulla, 6-10, 20-28, 31-38
Cicero, Pro Roscio Amerino
Livy, Per. 77-90
Greenidge and Clay, Sources, 160-232

Badian, Foreign Clientelae, 226-251
Badian, Studies in Greek and Roman History, 206-234
Bennett, Cinna and his Times
Brunt, Italian Manpower, 294-312
Carcopino, Sylla, 37-245
Carney, A Biography of Marius, 54-70
Gabba, Appian, BC, Lib. Prim., 161-222, 253-292
Gabba, Republican Rome, Army and Allies, 131-150
Gruen, Roman Politics and the Criminal Courts, 221-278
Hill, Roman Middle Class, 141-150
Meier, Res Publica Amissa, 216-266
Nicolet, L'Ordre equestre, 573-591
Ooteghem, Caius Marius, 276-324
Schur, Das Zeitalter des Marius und Sulla, 130-223
Scullard, From the Gracchi to Nero, 71-87
Valgiglio, Silla e la crisi repubblicana, 53-233

Hill, CQ (1932)
Syme, PBSR (1938)
Afzelius, ClMed (1942)
Balsdon, JRS (1951)
Brunt, Latomus (1956)
Carney, Acta Classica (1961)
Badian, Historia (1962)
Badian, JRS (1962)
Bulst, Historia (1964)
Valgiglio, RivStudClass (1967)
Crawford, PCPS (1968)
Shatzman, Athenaeum (1968)
Badian, Historia (1969)
Badian, Todd Memorial Lecture (1970)
Ward, Phoenix (1970)
Luce, Historia (1970)
Frier, AJP (1971)
Lintott, CQ (1971)
Twyman, ANRW, I.1 (1972)
Gabba, ANRW, I.1 (1972)
Bauman, Athenaeum (1973)
Marino, AttiAccadPalermo (1974)
Hahn, ActaClassDebreciensis (1974-5)
Mitchell, CP (1975)
Buchhut, Historia (1975)
Ridley, WS (1975)
Twyman, Athenaeum (1975-76)
Katz, AC (1975)
Katz, AC (1976)
Katz, RhM (1977)
Glew, Athenaeum (1977)
Keaveney, CQ (1978)
Lo Coscio, Athenaeum (1979)
Katz, RhM (1979)

The Age of Cicero

The following books from which required readings are assigned should be purchased:

Caesar, <u>Conquest of Gaul</u> (Penguin paperback)
Catullus, <u>The Complete Poetry</u> (Ann Arbor paperback)
Cicero, <u>Letters to Atticus</u> (Penguin paperback)
Cicero, <u>Letters to his Friends</u>, vol. 2 (Penguin paperback)
Cicero, <u>Selected Political Speeches</u> (Penguin paperback) (this includes
   <u>On the Command of Cnaeus Pompeius</u>; <u>Against Catilina</u>, I-IV; <u>In
   Defense of M. Caelius Rufus</u>; <u>In Support of M. Claudius Marcellus</u>;
   <u>Philippic</u> I)
Cicero, <u>Selected Works</u> (Penguin paperback) (this includes <u>On Duties</u> III;
   <u>Against Verres</u> I; <u>Philippic</u> II)
Cicero, <u>On the Good Life</u> (Penguin paperback) (this includes <u>On the
   Orator</u> I; <u>On Duties</u> II; <u>The Dream of Scipio</u>)
Lucretius, <u>On the Nature of the Universe</u> (Penguin paperback)
Plutarch, <u>Fall of the Roman Republic</u> (Penguin paperback)
Sallust, <u>The Jugurthine War, The Conspiracy of Catiline</u> (Penguin paperback)
Scullard, H.H., <u>From the Gracchi to Nero</u>, 5th edition (Methuen paperback)

The following books are recommended reading and may be consulted in the library:

Duff, J.W., <u>Literary History of Rome, Golden Age</u>
Frank, T., <u>Economic Survey of Rome</u>, vol. I
Jolowicz, H.F., <u>Historical Introduction to Roman Law</u>
Laistner, M.L.W., <u>The Greater Roman Historians</u>
Taylor, <u>Party Politics in the Age of Caesar</u>

The Age of Cicero

Lecture Schedule

First Week (March 28-April 3)

March 28: Introduction

March 30: The Constitutional and Political Structure

Scullard, From the Gracchi to Nero, pp. 1-9
Jolowicz, Historical Introduction to Roman Law, pp. 16-55
(recommended)
Taylor, Party Politics in the Age of Caesar, III-IV (recommended)

April 1 : Roman Religion

Scullard, pp. 10-12

Second Week (April 4-10)

April 4 : The Economic Situation

Scullard, pp. 12-21

April 6 : Sulla

Plutarch, Life of Sulla
Scullard, pp. 61-84

April 8 : Cicero's Formative Years

Third Week (April 11-17)

April 11: The Aftermath of Sulla

Cicero, Against Verres I
Scullard, pp. 85-95

April 13: Army and Provincial Administration

April 15: Piracy and the Mithridatic Wars

Cicero, On the Command of Gnaeus Pompeius
Scullard, pp. 72-76, 95-104

Fourth Week (April 18-24)

April 18: Pompey, Caesar, and Cicero

Sallust, Conspiracy of Catiline, 1-22
Scullard, pp. 105-108

April 20: The Conspiracy of Catiline

        Cicero, Against L. Sergius Catilina, I-IV
        Sallust, Conspiracy of Catiline, 23-conclusion
        Scullard, pp. 108-110

April 22: The First Triumvirate

        Cicero, Letters to Atticus, #12-14, 16-19, 21, 23, 26, 27,
            29, 30, 36, 38-42, 52, 55, 60, 68
        Scullard, pp. 110-117

Fifth Week (April 25-May 1)

April 25: The Conference of Luca

        Cicero, Letters to Atticus, #69, 73-75, 80, 82-87
        Cicero, In Defense of M. Caelius Rufus
        Scullard, pp. 117-119

April 27: Military Conflict: Parthia and Gaul

        Caesar, Conquest of Gaul, I, VII
        Scullard, pp. 123-134

April 29: Midterm Examination

Sixth Week (May 2-8)

May 2 : Rhetoric and Political Theory

        Cicero, On the Orator I
        Cicero, The Dream of Scipio
        Scullard, pp. 200-204

May 4 : Lucretius and Ciceronian Philosophy

        Lucretius, On the Nature of the Universe, I-II
        Cicero, On Duties, II-III
        Scullard, pp. 204-207

May 6 : Catullus and the New Poetry

        Catullus, #2, 7, 8, 11, 29, 49, 53, 57, 58, 68, 76, 79, 83,
            85, 86, 93
        Scullard, pp. 192-196
        Duff, Literary History of Rome: Golden Age, pp. 202-254
          (recommended)

Seventh Week (May 9-15)

May 9 : Sallust and Historical Writing

        Sallust, Jugurthine War, 1-5, 37-42, 84-92, 102-113
        Scullard, pp. 196-200
        Laistner, The Greater Roman Historians, pp. 23-64 (recommended)

May 11 : Caesar as Historian and Propagandist

Caesar, Conquest of Gaul, I-IV

May 13 : Upper Class Society and Roman Women

Scullard, pp. 172-178
Frank, Economic Survey of Ancient Rome, I, pp. 347-402
(recommended)

Eighth Week (May 16-22)

May 16 : The Lower Classes and Urban Violence

Scullard, pp. 178-181

May 18 : Cicero's Private Life

Plutarch, Life of Cicero

May 20 : Prelude to Civil War

Cicero, Letters to Atticus, #88-95, 104, 122, 124, 126-132
Scullard, pp. 119-122

Ninth Week (May 23-29)

May 23 : Provincial Government: Cicero in Cilicia

Cicero, Letters to Atticus, #106-111, 113-121
Scullard, pp. 181-187

May 25 : Civil War and Dictatorship

Cicero, Letters to his Friends, II, #316
Cicero, Letters to Atticus, #134, 135, 139, 144-146, 151, 153,
158, 161, 163, 165A, 171, 174, 178A, 185, 187, 199,
199B, 217
Scullard, pp. 134-151

May 27 : Conspiracy and Aftermath

Cicero, Letters to his Friends, II, #248, 249, 255-258, 260,
325, 327, 329, 336, 345, 348, 349
Cicero, Letters to Atticus, #286, 293, 294, 298, 299, 343, 348,
353, 355, 364-366, 367A, 368, 387, 389, 415
Cicero, In Support of M. Claudius Marcellus
Scullard, pp. 151-153

Tenth Week (May 30-June 5)
May 30 : Holiday

June 1: Cicero and Antony

   Cicero, <u>Letters to his Friends</u>, II, #363-367, 380, 385, 388, 394,
        401, 408
   Cicero, <u>Letters to Atticus</u>, #418, 419
   Cicero, <u>Letters to Brutus</u>, #5, 9-11, 18, 21, 24-26
   Cicero, <u>Philippics</u>, I-II
   Scullard, pp. 154-160

June 3: Retrospect: Cicero and the Fall of the Republic

The First Imperial Dynasty of Rome

<u>1st Session</u>: The Augustan Constitution

Ancient Sources:
>   Augustus, <u>Res Gestae</u>
>   Dio Cassius, XLVI, 55; XLVIII, 54; XLIX, 15; L, 1-2, 4, 6-7; LI, 1, 19, 22;
>   LIII, 1-22, 28-33; LIV, 1-3, 6, 8, 10-17
>   Suetonius, <u>Aug.</u> 7, 17, 28, 35, 47, 52, 56, 66; <u>Tib.</u> 8
>   Tacitus, <u>Ann.</u> III, 56
>   Vell. Pat. II, 89, 91, 93, 126
>   Appian, <u>Ill.</u> 28; <u>BC</u>, IV, 7; V, 95, 132
>   Braund, #10, 13, 19, 71, 73, 544, 720

Books:
>   Earl, <u>Age of Augustus</u>, 55-71
>   Grant, <u>From Imperium to Auctoritas</u>, 408-453
>   Hammond, <u>The Augustan Principate</u>, 19-84
>   Pelham, <u>Essays</u>, 60-88
>   Scullard, <u>From Gracchi to Nero</u>, 208-219
>   Syme, <u>Roman Revolution</u>, 313-348, 509-524

Articles:
>   Chilver, <u>Historia</u> (1950)
>   Jones, <u>JRS</u> (1951)
>   Salmon, <u>Historia</u> (1956)
>   Atkinson, <u>Historia</u> (1960) --
>   Stockton, <u>Historia</u> (1965)
>   Swan, <u>HSCP</u> (1966)
>   Cuff, <u>RivFilol</u> (1973)
>   Benario, <u>Chiron</u> (1975)
>   Daly, <u>Historia</u> (1978)
>   Lacey, <u>JRS</u> (1979)

2nd Session: The Divinity of the Emperor

Ancient Sources:
Augustus, Res Gestae, 9-11
Vergil, Eclogues, I, 6-10, 40-45; IV, 15-16, 48-49; IX, 46-49;
    Georgics, I, 21-35, 497-504; IV, 559-562; Aeneid, I, 286-289;
    VI, 791-794; VIII, 678-681; IX, 640-642
Propertius, III.4, 1, 19-20; IV.1, 3, 46-47; IV.6, 23; IV.11, 58-60
Horace, Odes, I.2, 41-49; I.12, 46-50; III.3, 9-12; III.5, 1-4; IV.5, 29-40;
    Epistles, II.1, 15-17
Ovid, Ars Amatoria, I, 203-204; Fasti, I, 587-616; IV, 949-952; V, 143-146;
    Metamorphoses, XV, 858-860; Tristia, I.3, 38; I.5, 43-44; II, 53-54,
    169-175; III.1, 77-78; III.6, 22-23; IV.8, 52; V.2, 50; Ponto, I.2, 71-74,
    97-98; I.4, 43-44; I.6, 45-46; II.2, 50, 92; IV.9, 107-108
Nicolas of Damascus, FGH, 90, F125
Livy, Periochae, 139
Pliny, NH, II, 94
Vell. Pat. II, 124
Cicero, Ad Q. Fr. I.1, 26; Ad Att. V.21, 7; XII.18, 1; XII.19; XII.36, 1; XIV.11, 1
Dio Cassius, XLV, 1, 7; XLVII, 18; XLIX, 15; LI, 19-20; LIII, 16, 27; LIV, 10, 27, 32;
    LV, 6, 10, 10a; LVI, 42, 46
Plutarch, Flamininus, 16
Quintilian, Inst. Orat. VI.3, 77
Tacitus, Ann. I, 10, 39, 57, 78; IV, 37, 56
Appian, BC, II, 148; V, 132
Suetonius, Iul. 88; Aug. 7, 31, 52, 59, 94, 98, 100
Braund, #58, 66, 122, 125-127, 129-138, 148, 166, 170, 171, 368, 640a, 650

Books:
Earl, Age of Augustus, 166-176
Hopkins, Conquerors and Slaves, 197-242
Liebeschuetz, Continuity and Change in Roman Religion, 65-78
Price, Rituals and Power, 23-59, 207-248
Scullard, From Gracchi to Nero, 233-236
Taylor, Divinity of the Roman Emperor, 142-246

Articles:
Scott, TAPA (1930)
Charlesworth, HTR (1935)
Charlesworth, PBSR (1939)
Price, JRS (1980)
Price, JHS (1984)

<u>3rd Session:</u> War and Peace in the Augustan Age

    Ancient Sources:
        Augustus, <u>Res Gestae</u>
        Vergil, <u>Eclogues</u>, I, 64-66; <u>Georgics</u>, II, 169-174; III, 30-33; IV, 560-562;
            <u>Aeneid</u>, I, 257-296; VI, 791-807, 851-853; VII, 601-615; VIII, 704,
            714-728
        Horace, <u>Odes</u>, I.2, 21-26, 41-52; I.12, 49-57; I.21, 13-16; I.29, 1-5;
            I.35, 29-40; II.9, 19-24; II.13, 17-19; III.3, 43-64; III.4, 25-36;
            III.5, 2-12; III.6, 9-16; IV.5, 17-28; IV.14, 41-52; IV.15, 4-24;
            <u>Carmen Saeculare</u>, 33-34, 53-59; <u>Epistles</u>, I.12, 25-28; I.18, 56-57;
            II.1, 232-241, 250-259; <u>Epodes</u>, VII, 3-10; <u>Satires</u>, II.1, 10-15;
            II.5, 62-64
        Propertius, II.1, 25-36; II.10, 13-18; II.14, 23-24; II.15, 41-46; II.16, 41-42;
            III.1, 16; III.4, 1-9; IV.3, 7-11, 35-40, 63-69; IV.6, 79-84
        Ovid, <u>Ars Amatoria</u>, I, 177-228; <u>Remedia Amoris</u>, 155-158; <u>Fasti</u>, I, 277-278,
            697-704, 709-722; II, 683-684; III, 881; IV, 383, 407-408, 925-926;
            V, 550-596; VI, 92, 465-468; <u>Metamorphoses</u>, XV, 746-749, 820-834;
            <u>Tristia</u>, II, 169-172; II, 225-232; III.12, 45-48
        Livy, I, 19; IX, 17-19
        Vell. Pat. II, 91, 94, 100-102, 122
        Tacitus, <u>Ann</u>. I, 11; II, 1-4
        Pliny, <u>NH</u>, XXXIV, 48; XXXV, 93-94; XXXVII, 10
        Plutarch, <u>Alexander</u>, 2; <u>Antony</u>, 80
        Josephus, <u>Ant</u>. XV, 105; XVIII, 39-50
        Justin, XLII.5, 4-12
        Orosius, VI.21, 19-21, 29
        Appian, <u>BC</u>, V, 130
        Eutropius, VII, 9
        Strabo, III.2, 15; III, 156; XI.4, 6; XVI.1, 28; XVII.1, 54
        Dio Cassius, XLV, 1; XLVII, 41; LI, 1, 3, 6, 16, 18, 22; LIII, 10, 33; LIV, 7-9, 35;
            LV, 9-10a; LVI, 33
         Suetonius, <u>Aug</u>. 18, 21, 29, 31, 50, 56, 94; <u>Tib</u>. 9, 16
        Braund, #2-4, 6-8, 14, 20, 29-32, 38, 43-46, 60

    Books:
        Debevoise, <u>Political History of Parthia</u>, 135-153
        Earl, <u>Age of Augustus</u>, 134-165
        Levick, <u>Tiberius the Politician</u>, 24-26, 145-147
        Scullard, <u>From Gracchi to Nero</u>, 243-259
        Seager, <u>Tiberius</u>, 16-18, 96-103

    Articles:
        Benario, <u>TAPA</u> (1960)
        Weinstock, <u>JRS</u> (1960)

Toynbee, _JRS_ (1961)
Brunt, _JRS_ (1963)
Seager, _Athenaeum_ (1980)
Ober, _Historia_ (1982)

4th Session: Tiberius: The Making of an Emperor

Ancient Sources:

Tacitus, _Ann._ I, 1-15, 53; II, 39-40; III, 56; IV, 57
Vell. Pat. II, 94-126
Suetonius, _Aug._ 61-65, 100-101; _Tib._ 1-25
Ovid, _Ars Amatoria_, I, 194; _Metamorphoses_, XV, 836-837
Gellius, XV.7, 3
Dio Cassius, LIII, 26-28; LIV, 9-10, 18-19, 22, 25, 27-28, 31, 33-36; LV, 1-2,
        6, 8-13, 22, 28-34; LVI, 11-17, 23-26, 30-33, 43-47; LVII, 1-7
Braund, #28, 59, 63, 71

Books:

Levick, _Tiberius the Politician_, 19-81
Marsh, _Reign of Tiberius_, 30-58
Scullard, _From Gracchi to Nero_, 217-219, 268-270
Seager, _Tiberius_, 14-57
Syme, _Roman Revolution_, 387-405, 413-439
Syme, _Tacitus_, 364-374, 408-411

Articles:

Pappano, _CP_ (1941)
Allen, _TAPA_ (1947)
Weller, _Phoenix_ (1958)
Shotter, _CP_ (1967)   --
Wellesley, _JRS_ (1967)
Detweiler, _CJ_ (1970)
Levick, _Latomus_ (1972)
Jameson, _Historia_ (1975)
Birch, _CQ_ (1981)
Kehoe, _CJ_ (1985)

<u>5th Session</u>: Tiberius, Germanicus, and the Senatorial Opposition (14-21 AD)

Ancient Sources:
Tacitus, <u>Ann.</u> I, 31-55, 62, 69, 72-75, 79; II, 5, 26-43, 51, 53-61, 64,
68-84; III, 1-19, 22-24, 29, 49-51; IV, 17
Suetonius, <u>Tib.</u> 25-39, 49, 52
Dio Cassius, LVII, 4-20
Vell. Pat. II, 127-131

Books:
Levick, <u>Tiberius the Politician</u>, 82-115, 148-157
Marsh, <u>Reign of Tiberius</u>, 58-133
Rogers, <u>Criminal Trials and Legislation under Tiberius</u>, 12-64
Scullard, <u>From Gracchi to Nero</u>, 270-275
Seager, <u>Tiberius</u>, 58-122
Syme, <u>Tacitus</u>, 392-393, 399-401

Articles:
Marsh, <u>AHR</u> (1926)
Marsh, <u>CP</u> (1926)
Marsh, <u>CW</u> (1926)
Allen, <u>TAPA</u> (1941)
Leon, <u>CJ</u> (1957)
Shotter, <u>Historia</u> (1968)
Shotter, <u>Historia</u> (1972)
Shotter, <u>Historia</u> (1974)
Levick, <u>Greece and Rome</u> (1975)
Rapke, <u>Acta Classica</u> (1982)

<u>6th Session</u>: Tiberius and the Conspiracy of Sejanus

Ancient Sources:

Tacitus, <u>Ann.</u> I, 24; III, 29, 35, 56, 72; IV, 1-4, 7-12, 17-20, 26, 28-36,
38-41, 52-60, 67-71, 74; V, 1-11; VI, 3-5, 7-9, 14, 19-20, 23-27,
29-30, 45-51
Suetonius, <u>Tib.</u> 40-76; <u>Cal.</u> 7-13
Dio Cassius, LVII, 19 - LVIII, 23; LIX, 1; LXV, 14
Vell. Pat. II, 127
Josephus, <u>Ant.</u> XVIII, 179-182, 205-225
Philo, <u>Legatio ad Gaium</u>, 32-61
Braund, #98-104

Books:
>Levick, _Tiberius the Politician,_ 157-179, 201-219
>Marsh, _Reign of Tiberius,_ 160-229, 304-310
>Rogers, _Criminal Trials and Legislation under Tiberius,_ 64-166
>Scullard, _From Gracchi to Nero,_ 275-283
>Seager, _Tiberius,_ 178-223
>Syme, _Tacitus,_ 378-385, 401-406, 420-434, 752-754

Articles:
>Marsh, _AHR_ (1926)
>Rogers, _TAPA_ (1931)
>Allen, _TAPA_ (1941)
>Sealey, _Phoenix_ (1961)
>Boddington, _AJP_ (1963)
>Sumner, _Phoenix_ (1965)
>Bird, _Latomus_ (1967)
>Shotter, _CP_ (1974)
>Nicols, _Historia_ (1975)

7th Session: Caligula: Madman or Misunderstood?

Ancient Sources:
>Suetonius, _Caligula_
>Dio Cassius, LIX, 1-30
>Philo, _Legatio ad Gaium_; _In Flaccum_
>Josephus, _Ant._ XVIII, 257-309; XIX, 1-126, 201-211; _Jewish War,_ II, 181-203
>Braund, #175-176, 188-190

Books:
>Balsdon, _The Emperor Gaius,_ 24-219
>Box, _Philo, In Flaccum,_ xiii-lvi; 68-124 (_passim_)
>Griffin, _Seneca,_ 43-59
>Scullard, _From Gracchi to Nero,_ 283-287
>Smallwood, _Philo, Legatio ad Gaium,_ 3-36, 151-325 (_passim_)

Articles:
>Charlesworth, _CHJ_ (1933)
>Balsdon, _JRS_ (1934)
>Stewart, _AJP_ (1953)
>Davies, _Historia_ (1966)
>Bicknell, _Historia_ (1968)
>Phillips, _Historia_ (1970)
>Sherwin-White, _Latomus_ (1972)

Massaro and Montgomery, _Latomus_ (1978)
Massaro and Montgomery, _Latomus_ (1979)
Simpson, _Latomus_ (1981)

<u>8th Session</u>: Claudius: the Man and his Court

Ancient Sources:
Tacitus, _Ann._ VI, 46; XI, 1-7, 11-13, 23-38; XII, 1-9, 22-27, 41-42, 52-54,
58-59, 64-69; XIII, 1-4
Dio Cassius, LX, 1-8, 12-18, 27-35
Suetonius, _Claudius_, 1-13, 25-45
Seneca, _Apocolocyntosis_
Josephus, _Ant._ XIX, 127-200, 212-291
Braund, #568, 570, 571

Books:
Momigliano, _Claudius_, 1-38
Scramuzza, _Claudius_, 35-79, 89-98, 145-156
Scullard, _From Gracchi to Nero_, 288-304
Syme, _Tacitus_, 259-260

Articles:
Bagnani, _Phoenix_ (1946)
Leon, _TAPA_ (1948)
McAlindon, _AJP_ (1956)
McAlindon, _AJP_ (1957)
Carney, _Acta Classica_ (1960)
Yessey, _AJP_ (1971)
Levick, _AJP_ (1978)
Ehrhardt, _Antichthon_ (1978)

<u>9th Session</u>: Nero, his Mother, and his Advisers (54-62 AD)

Ancient Sources:
Tacitus, _Ann._ XII, 8; XIII, 1-6, 10-25, 42-47; XIV, 1-16, 22, 47-65
Dio Cassius, LXI, 1-20; LXII, 13-14
Suetonius, _Nero_, 6-10, 28, 33-35, 51-52
Seneca, _Apocolocyntosis_
Braund, #235-237, 240

Books:
- Bishop, <u>Nero, the Man, and the Legend</u>, 19-70
- Griffin, <u>Seneca</u>, 59-133
- Griffin, <u>Nero</u>, 37-99
- Henderson, <u>Life and Principate of the Emperor Nero</u>, 31-149
- Scullard, <u>From Gracchi to Nero</u>, 304-308
- Syme, <u>Tacitus</u>, 261-263, 549-553

Articles:
- Rogers, <u>TAPA</u> (1955)
- McAlindon, <u>AJP</u> (1956)
- Currie, <u>AC</u> (1962)
- Gillis, <u>PP</u> (1963)
- Baldwin, <u>Phoenix</u> (1964)
- Athanassakis, <u>TAPA</u> (1974)

<u>10th Session</u>: Nero: The Decline and Fall (62-68 AD)

Ancient Sources:
- Tacitus, <u>Ann.</u> XII, 44-51; XIII, 5-9, 34-41, 49; XIV, 12, 23-36; XV, 1-74; XVI, 6-35
- Dio Cassius, LXII, 15-29; LXIII, 1-29
- Suetonius, <u>Nero</u>, 11-16, 29-32, 35-50, 57
- Braund, #260-261

Books:
- Bishop, <u>Nero, the Man, and the Legend</u>, 71-166
- Charles-Picard, <u>Augustus and Nero</u>, 85-159
- Griffin, <u>Nero</u>, 100-118, 131-133, 164-182, 224-230
- Henderson, <u>Life & Principate of the Emperor Nero</u>, 153-195, 231-302, 379-423
- Scullard, <u>From Gracchi to Nero</u>, 308-321
- Syme, <u>Tacitus</u>, 263-265, 515-517, 554-562

Articles:
- Hammond, <u>HSCP</u> (1934)
- Clayton, <u>CQ</u> (1947)
- Charlesworth, <u>JRS</u> (1950)
- Rogers, <u>TAPA</u> (1952)
- Rogers, <u>TAPA</u> (1955)
- McAlindon, <u>AJP</u> (1956)
- Gilmartin, <u>Historia</u> (1973)
- Roper, <u>Historia</u> (1979)

University of California at Los Angeles

ROMAN LAW

History 118   Office Hours: T 11-12
Ronald Mellor   W 1-3
Spring 1981   Bunche Hall 5256 (x54157)
2:00 - 3:15 p.m.

April 7 - Introduction
April 9 - Historical Background

April 14 - The XII Tables
April 16 - Legal Procedure in Early Rome

April 21 - The Sources of Roman Law
April 23 - Roman Citizenship

April 28 - Law of Persons: Patria Potestas & the Family
April 30 - Law of Persons: Marriage

May 5   - Law of Persons: Slavery
May 7   - Law of Property: Possession

May 12   - MID-TERM EXAMINATION
May 14   - Law of Property: Succession I

May 19   - Law of Property: Succession II
May 21   - The Development of Legal Procedure

May 26   - Law of Obligations: Contracts
May 28   - Law of Obligations: Delicts

June 2   - Criminal Law
June 4   - Roman Statutes

June 9   - Roman Legal Science
June 11 - The Character of Roman Law

Each student will be assigned to a discussion section which will have three
meetings.

     Required Reading: B. NICHOLAS An Introduction to Roman Law (Oxford)
                        W. KUNKEL An Introduction to Roman Legal and
                                        Constitutional History (Oxford)
                        J. CROOK Law and Life at Rome (Cornell)
                        GAIUS Institutes (Handouts)

     Evaluation: There will be several quizzes on matters of definition
                  as well as a Mid-Term examination. But the principal
                  means of evaluation (66%) will be the "Projects". The
                  class will be divided into sections at which the
                  projects will be presented and scrutinized. Section
                  assignments will be arranged in the first week. There
                  will be no Final Examination.

ROMAN LAW

History 118
Ronald Mellor
Autumn 1981

BIBLIOGRAPHY

Required Reading:
B. NICHOLAS An Introduction to Roman Law
The best short introduction to private law, but weak on procedure.

*W. KUNKEL An Introduction to Roman Legal and Constitutional History
An excellent brief treatment with an invaluable annotated bibliography
on all aspects of Roman public and private law. Useful to us for
criminal and constitutional law.

*J. CROOK Law and Life at Rome

General:
*A. BERGER Encyclopedic Dictionary of Roman Law

Texts:
*GAIUS The Institutes (ed. by F. DE ZULUETA) 2 volumes
The best ancient textbook of Roman private law; sections will be
distributed. Vol. 1- text and translation; vol. 2- commentary.

*Corpus Juris Civilis - Justinianic Codification (Code; Institutes; Digest)
Multi Volume Translation by SCOTT on reserve.

History of Roman Law: (cf. KUNKEL above)
*H. JOLOWICZ Historical Introduction to the Study of Roman Law
The basic text in English on both the history of Roman law as well as a
treatment of Roman public law. In most cases, KUNKEL is enough.

Roman Private Law:
*W.W. BUCKLAND A Textbook of Roman Law
The most extensive discussion of Roman private law and procedure in
English. Your basic reference tool in preparing cases.

*F. SCHULZ Classical Roman Law
An excellent book, with different emphasis than Buckland.

*M. KASER Roman Private Law
A translation (for the South African law students) of Kaser's university
level textbook. Very useful; a much abridged version of KASER's German
reference books on Roman Private Law & Roman Procedure Das römische
Privatrecht (2 vol.) and Das römische Zivilprocessrecht.

Criminal Law:
  T. MOMMSEN Römisches Staatsrecht (3 vol.)

  J. STRACHAN-DAVIDSON Problems of Roman Criminal Law (2 vol.)

  A.H.M. JONES The Criminal Courts of the Republic and Principate

Public (or Constitutional) Law:
  T. MOMMSEN Römisches Staatsrecht (3 vol.) (1887-1888)
  This remains the basic text on the Roman constitution.

  F. DE MARTINO Storia della constituzione romana (5 vol.)
  A recent controversial (Marxist) treatment of the constitution.

  There is no extended English treatment of the Roman constitution.
  One must rely on Jolowicz and Kunkel.

Other Books of Interest:
  W. BUCKLAND & A. McNAIR Roman Law and Common Law

  W. BUCKLAND The Roman Law of Slavery

  D. DAUBE Forms of Roman Legislation

  F. SCHULZ Principles of Roman Law
  A more abstract analysis of general categories of Roman Law.

  F. SCHULZ History of Roman Legal Science
  A History of Roman Jurisprudence

  A. WATSON A series of monographs dealing with specific aspects of Roman
  law in the later Republic: marriage; obligations; succession.

Roman Law
Autumn 1981
Project I

Succession

Answer as many questions as possible using Nicolas, Buckland and (if necessary) the Digest and Institutes.

M. Fabius Rufus is an elderly widower with a great deal of wealth. He has three sons and three daughters:
1) T. Fabius Crassus is married with two sons and two daughters.
2) M. Fabius Longus, unmarried, has disappeared on military service.
3) P. Fabius Felix is married with three sons.
4) Fannia is married without manus into a good family and has two sons.
5) Fabia is married with manus and has two daughters.
6) Fabiola has become a Vestal Virgin.

*   *   *

Rufus has a Spanish mistress and two sons by her. He is not terribly fond of his old family since they had a fallen out during the Civil Wars of 69 AD. He would like to leave his money to Hispania and her sons. What is their status? Are there ways of changing their status? Can he have them legitimized? How?

How many of his descendents are still in his potestas? Who else is in his potestas? Would it be to their advantage or to Rufus' own for him to emancipate them?

Tiberius is worried about the financial future of his children in case he should die before his father. How can he prevent them remaining in their grandfather's potestas?

Publius has acquired an estate in Gaul during his quaestorship there. How can he keep it out of his father's hands?

Marcus appears with a foreign looking lady who, he says, is his wife. For the purposes of the eventual will of Rufus, how will Marcus prove he is legally married and that his ten year old son is legitimate?

If Rufus dies without making his will, who gets what? And what is the status of each of his children?

Roman Law
Autumn 1981
Project II

PROPERTY

Under the Roman Empire, Marcus brings his flocks each fall from their mountain summer pastures down to the lowlands. An earthquake panics the animals but Marcus manages to round up most of his beasts by abandoning a few stragglers and by burying his moneybag near an odd shaped tree hoping to retrieve it on his return six months hence.

Gaius finds a sheep, a goat and a horse wandering on his property after the earthquake. The earthquake has also uprooted a tree and when Gaius is chopping it up for firewood, he is delighted to discover a bag of gold.

As it happens, Marcus takes another route in the autumn and does not return to Gaius' land until the following spring -- about 53 weeks after the storm. When he finds the tree uprooted, he confronts Gaius and demands his money and asks about his animals. The goat has been sold to Sextus, and Gaius refuses to return the sheep or horse despite Marcus's clear brand on them. Only half the gold is left -- the other half has been sold to the jeweler Quintus which, however, was stolen by Spurius, a shady character. Quintus is about to bring an action against Spurius and refuses to reimburse Marcus.

Marcus decides to bring actions against Gaius, Sextus, Quintus and Spurius. No one denies the facts as given, save Spurius who claims he was given the bracelet for handyman work around the jewelry shop.

What actions are possible? Which will be successful? Under Roman law, who owns what? Who may keep what?

Roman Law
Autumn 1981
Project III

CONTRACT

Gaius and Marcus are brothers who have long farmed communally on their
adjoining farms. They used Gaius' horse, Equus, and Marcus' horse, Caballus,
as a team for plowing. But a disaster has struck and a great flood has washed
away the topsoil from most of their hillside farms. Publius, who has a nearby
farm and forest, is interested in the team for hauling timber down to the main
road. But he is uncertain how good these horses will be at that job. He
wishes to try them out and, if they work well, he will hire Gaius to work with
them. In return, he proposes to pay Marcus 40 bushels of wheat (which he has
on hand) and twenty large trees to be be delivered later to Marcus' new
homesite in the village (where he will live and sell wood carvings). This is
for Caballus. For Equus, Publius proposes to pay Gaius 60 bushels of wheat and
he will give Gaius an additional 20 bushels and 200 sesterces for 6 months work
with the team. Of course Publius is interested in both horses as part of the
package deal and is uninterested in either one singly.

Try to devise a contract (or contracts) or agreement (or agreements) that
will facilitate this exchange and protect all parties. Be particularly
concerned with protecting Publius against accidents (e.g. a horse becoming
lame). Make these contracts or agreements as brief as possible, but append
some explanations of what you are doing.

ROMAN LAW

History 118
Spring 1981
Ronald Mellor

BAR EXAM (Project #4)

We are now ready to see if you are ready to practice law in Rome. It is the simple everyday problems with which you will have to deal in your practice, so the following problems will enable you to apply your theory to a lawyer's ordinary business.

Your Client Marcus Cornelius Felix has been blessed with much wealth and many children. Here is his family:

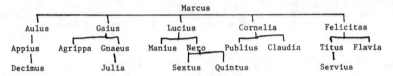

1. Marcus has an estate of 1,000,000 HS (sesterces). He feels that his children are reasonably well situated: Cornelia is married with manus while Felicitas is married without manus; Aulus married an heiress who was so besotted by his dark curls that she married him with manus; Lucius did extraordinarily well in the army and has a small fortune in his peculium castrense; and Gaius has been adopted into the family of Marcus' wealthy friend, Tullius (though his children remain in Marcus' potestas). Marcus feels he can pass over his children and wishes you to write a will giving them as little as possible and dividing the rest equally among his grandchildren. Write the will, making provision for the possibility that someone may predecease him.

* * *

2. You may be a careful lawyer, but you are a slow one. While you were writing the will, Lucius and Nero were killed when their chariot overturned and your client Marcus expired soon afterwards of a broken heart. As he died intestate, how will his 1,000,000 HS get divided up?

mellor1/sos2

History 1080cc:Religion and Society from Alexander to Julian
W 2-4 in Robinson 207
Fall term 1985   Harvard University

Mr. Georges
office: Robinson L-
tel. 5-3085
office hours: Monda
10:15-noon and Wed-
nesday after 4 pm;
also by appointment

Required texts: Iliad, tr. Lattimore or Fitzgerald
Herodotus, tr. Rawlinson for preference
Plato, Republic, tr. Cornford
The Essential Plotinus, ed. O'Brien
Augustine, Confessions, tr. Warner or Ryan
Aeneid, tr. Fitzgerald
Apuleius, Golden Ass, tr. Graves for preference

Recommended are: W. Burkert, Greek Religion
H. Liebeschuetz, Continuity and Change in Roman Religion
R. MacMullen, Roman Paganism

This course is an introduction to the religious sensibilities and social realities of
Greco-Roman civilization, intended for students who have some (but not necessarily much)
background in the ancient world, including graduate students interested in reading for an
ancient field or desiring some knowledge of the environment of the early Christians.
Depending on enrolment, each student will be asked to briefly present two or more topics for
discussion during the term, and to submit from among these two formal and substantial papers.

Meetings (second week onward)

i.   The inherited conglomerate: Homer, the high gods, and the religions of the warri
and the home. The nature of belief.

*Readings (R): Iliad, Herodotus, Aeschylus Oresteia

*Consult (C): Dodds, Greeks and the Irrational; Nilsson, Greek Folk/Popular
Religion; Burkert, Greek Religion; Geertz in Anthrop. Approaches
to...Religion

ii.   Social Control I: religion and the Greek state. Delphi.

R: Herodotus; Plato, Republic & Laws

C: Fontenrose, Delphic Oracle; Pritchett, Greek State at War iii: Religion;
Michell, Sparta

iii. Alexander the god.

R: Plutarch, Alex. & Demetrius; Arrian, Anabasis of A.; Curtius Rufus; Aristotle
Politics & Ethics; anon. Ithyphallic Hymn to Demetrius (ap. Athenaeus); inscriptions.

C: Tarn, A the Great; Badian "Deification of A" UCB/GThU Colloquium 1976;
id. "A & the Unity of Mankind" Historia 8.1958.425; Classen "Zeus Ammon"
Historia 9.1959.349

iv.   Social Control II: religion and the Roman state.

R: Livy, Dion. Hal.; Vergil Aeneid; Res gestae divi Augusti; Dio; Suetonius,
Gaius; Herodian; SHA

C: Liebeschuetz, Continuity & Change in Rom. Rel.; Mellor, Goddess Roma (in ANRW)
Fishwick "Augustus deus..." in Hommages À Vermaseren; Price "...Sacrifice",
JRS 70.1980.28

v.   The social realities.

   R: Lucretius, Seneca; Tacitus; Pliny, Letters; Juvenal; Artemidorus, Interpret-
      ation of Dreams; martyrologies in Eusebius etc.; Ausonius; Prudentius;
      Digest.

   C: Crook, Law & Life of Rome; MacMullen, Roman Social Relations; Garnsey, Social
      Status & Legal Privilege; Hopkins, Conquerors & Slaves, Death & Renewal;
      Finley, Ancient Slavery & Modern Ideology

vi. The supernatural landscape: magic, dreams, and the daimonic.

   R: Apuleius, Metamorphosis ("Golden Ass"); Artemidorus; Lucian; papyri

   C: MacMullen, Roman Paganism; id. "...Astrology" AncSoc 2.1975.105; Remus,
      "Magic or Miracle!" Second Century 2.1982.127; Brown, "Sorcery..." in Rel.
      & Society in the Age of St. Aug.; Collectanea pap. (F'schrift Youtie)

vii. Needs I: Exorcists, Miracle Workers, Holy Men.

   R: Plutarch, Pyrrhus; Suetonius, Vespasian; Philostratus, Life of Apollonius;
      Lucian; Gospel of Luke; Porphyry, Life of Plotinus.

   C: MacMullen, Roman Paganism; Thiessen, Sociology of Early Pal. Xity; Brown,
      "Holy Man" JRS 61.1971.80; Smith, "Divine Men ..." JournBibLit 90.1971.174;
      id., Jesus the Magician

viii. Needs II: Personal Saviors.

   R: Edelstein, Asclepius: Testimonies; Aristides, Sacred Tales (ed. Behr);
      Apuleius; Plutarch On Isis and Osiris

   C: Dunand, Culte d'Isis; Witt, Isis; Griffiths Apuleius; The Mysteries (Eranos
      Papers 2); Mithraic Studies, ed. Hinnells; Collectanea p. (F. Youtie)

ix. Needs III: Consolations of philosophy.

   R: M. Aurelius, To Himself ("Meditations"); Plato, Phaedrus; Plotinus.

   C: Cambridge History of Later Greek & Early Medieval Philosophy; Armstrong,
      Introd. to Loeb Plotinus; Brunt, "M.Aurelius & the Xians" in Studies in
      Lat. Lit. & Rom. Hist., ed. Deroux

x.   Jews, "Godfearers," Christians.

   R: Tacitus, Histories; Josephus, Jewish War; Pliny, Letters (Book x); Acts of
      the Apostles; I Thessalonians, I & II Corinthians; Nag Hammadi Library;
      Apocrypha; Didache

   C : Thiessen, Sociology of E. Pal. Xity; Meeks, First Urban Xians; Brown, Mak'
      of Late Antiquity; Scroggs, NT Sociology F'bericht in NTS 26.1980.164;
      Ste. Croix, "Why Xians Persecuted" Past & Present 26.1963.6; Smith "Pauli
      Worship as Seen by Pagans" HTR 73.1980.241; Sherwin-White "Persecutions" JT
                                                           n.s. 3.1952.199

xi. Church and Empire

   R: Eusebius, Hist. Eccl. & Vita Const.

   C: Dodds, Pagan & Xian in an Age of Anxiety; Jones, Later Roman Empire;

L'Orange, <u>Art Forms & Civic Life in the Later Roman Empire</u>;
Momigliano, ed.; <u>Conflict of Paganism & Christianity in the
4th Century</u>; Baynes, <u>Constantine ... ;& the Christian Church</u>

xii.   The Age of Julian & Augustine.

        R: Ammianus Marcellinus; Julian; Augustine, <u>Confessions</u> etc.

        C: Jones, <u>LRE</u>; Bowersock, <u>Julian</u>; Kantorowicz, "Gods in
           Uniform" <u>PAPhS</u> 105. 1961.368; Chadwick et al. "Bishops
           in Ancient Society" UCB/GThU Colloquium 1980; Brown, <u>Aug.
           of Hippo</u> & <u>Religion and Society in the Age of St. Aug.</u>;
           Momigliano, ed. <u>Conflict</u>

                        * * * * * * * * *

*Excerptions are <u>not</u> indicated throughout

The Dialogue of Paganism and Judaism in the Greek and Roman World

Prof. Louis H. Feldman, Yeshiva University

I. Required text:
    Victor Tcherikover, Hellenistic Civilization and the Jews (Atheneum, paper).

II. Examinations: A mid-term and a final examination covering Tcherikover and the lectures: 10 of 16 objective questions to be answered in two or three sentences; one of two essay questions. Each part of the examination counts 50%.

III. Term paper:
    A term paper will be due two weeks before the last lecture. There are no limits as to length, although approximately 3000 words are recommended. All papers must be typewritten, double-spaced. The topic must be selected within one month of the start of the semester and must be approved by the instructor. The paper must be a critical paper using primary and secondary sources, which are to be cited on the spot for every major point made. It must be in good English and must be proofread; if it is not it will be returned unread. Any topic within the scope of the course may be selected. The following are among those suggested:
    1. An analysis of the Greek and Jewish elements in Ezekiel the dramatist's tragedy Exodus, and a comparison of it with Euripides.
    2. An analysis of the Greek and Jewish elements in Philo the Elder's epic poem On Jerusalem and Theodotus' On Shechem, and a comparison with Homer.
    3. A comparison of the Greek and Jewish elements in the political theory of Philo.
    4. An analysis and comparison of the Greek and Jewish elements in Philo's views of education.
    5. A comparison of Philo and Gnosticism.
    6. A comparison of two views of Platonism (the subject being limited to a single aspect) in the Hellenistic-Roman Age: Philo vs. Plutarch.
    7. Wolfson vs. Goodenough: a comparison and critique of their analyses of a given aspect of Philo.
    8. A critique of the theory that the Septuagint is a Sadducean document.
    9. A critique of Azariah dei Rossi's comments and theories concerning the Septuagint.
    10. A comparison of the treatments of a given Biblical episode (e.g., the binding of Isaac, the story of Joseph and Potiphar's wife, the early life of Moses, the story of Samson, the life of Saul, etc.) in the Hebrew Bible, the Septuagint, Philo, Pseudo-Philo's Biblical Antiquities, Apocrypha and Pseudepigrapha, Rabbinic Midrashim, etc.
    11. Josephus as apologist for Judaism as compared with the Talmud with respect to some aspect of Judaism.
    12. Hellenistic philosophies of history: a comparison of Josephus with a pagan historian (e.g., Polybius, Dionysius of Halicarnassus, etc.) of the Hellenistic period, as seen in treatments of similar episodes.
    13. A comparison of Josephus with Tacitus, Suetonius, or Dio Cassius where they deal with the same episode (e.g., Parthian affairs, the assassination of Caligula, the great war against the Romans).

14. A critique of Pines' explanation of the variations in the Arabic version of Agapius of the Testimonium Flavianum of Josephus.

15. A critical analysis of E. R. Goodenough's thesis in his **Jewish Symbols in the Greco-Roman Period** that Rabbinic teachings had little influence on the practices of the Hellenistic Jewish community and/or the Palestinian Jewish community with respect to the laws pertaining to art and art objects.

16. A critique of H. M. Kallen's The Book of Job as a Greek Tragedy.

17. A critique of Rozelaar's attempt (in Eshkolot, 1954, pp. 33-48) to view the Song of Songs as a Hellenistic work.

18. A critique of a section of Schürer's History of the Jewish People.

19. A critique of Henry A. Fischel's Rabbinic Literature and Greco-Roman Philosophy.

20. A critique of Yitzchak Baer's Yisrael Ba-amim.

21. A critique of a chapter in Saul Lieberman's Greek in Jewish Palestine, or in his Hellenism in Jewish Palestine.

22. A comparison of the legal documents (e.g. loans, divorce) found in Egyptian Jewish papyri with the format of such documents as discussed in Talmudic literature, and conclusions as to the relevance of such evidence in evaluating the degree to which Alexandrian Jewry was "Orthodox."

23. A critique of the evidence as to whether the Jews were citizens of Alexandria.

24. An analysis of a particular aspect of Judaism (e.g., the Sabbath, festivals, dietary laws, circumcision) or of Jewish history or of the description of the land of Israel as seen in Greek and Latin writers.

25. A critique of the views of Bickermann, Tcherikover, and Hengel with regard to the role of Antiochus Epiphanes in the Maccabean revolt.

26. An analysis of the Greek ideas in Eleazar ben Jair's speeches at Masada.

IV. Lecture Topics:
No attempt will be made to cover all aspects of the subject. Instead, a selected number of topics will be considered which seem to be of particular interest and importance:

1. Cultural contacts in Palestine before the Maccabees

   Recommended primary readings: Homer, Iliad, Books 1, 9, and 24 (Achilles as a Greek hero)
   Bible: Genesis, chaps. 12-50 (Abraham, Isaac, Jacob, and Joseph as Hebrew heroes)

   Recommended secondary readings: Cyrus H. Gordon, Before the Bible: The Common Background of Greek and Hebrew Civilizations (New York: Harper, 1962; rpt., Arno, 1973).
   Martin Hengel, Judaism and Hellenism: Studies in Their Encounter in Palestine during the Early Hellenistic Period, vol. 1 (Philadelphia: Fortress, 1974).
   Louis H. Feldman, "Hengel's Judaism and Hellenism in Retrospect," Journal of Biblical Literature 96 (1977) 371-382.
   S. K. Eddy, The King Is Dead: Studies in Near Eastern Resistance to Hellenism 334-31 B.C. (Lincoln, Nebr., 1961).

Additional (supplementary) secondary readings:
(*=works of particular interest)
Michael C. Astour, Hellenosemitica: An Ethnic and Cultural Study
    in West Semitic Impact on Mycenaean Greece (Leiden, 1965).
*Cyrus H. Gordon, "Homer and Bible: The Origin and Character of
    East Mediterranean Literature, Hebrew Union College Annual
    26 (1955) 43-108.
H. Gressmann, "Foreign Influences in Hebrew Prophecy," Journal of
    Theological Studies 27 (1926) 241-254.
*Fergus Millar, "The Background to the Maccabean Revolution: Reflections
    on Martin Hengel's 'Judaism and Hellenism,'" Journal of Jewish
    Studies 29 (1978) 1-21.

Questions: 1) How can we arrive at definitions of Hellenism and of
                Hebraism?
            2) How can Homer's depiction of Achilles and the Bible's
                portrait of the forefathers help us toward this end?
            3) Why were there so few contacts between Greeks and
                Jews before the time of Alexander?
            4) How valid is Cyrus Gordon's thesis that there were
                meaningful contacts before Alexander?
            5) How valid is Hengel's theory that Palestine was deeply
                Hellenized before the Maccabees?

2. The Rabbis' attitude toward the Greek language, literature,
    and philosophy

        Recommended primary readings: Talmud, Baba Kamma 82b-83a and
            Menahoth 99b (Is the study of Greek culture permitted?
            What is meant by Greek wisdom in this passage?).
        Talmud, Hagigah 14b-15b (Elisha ben Abuyah, the rabbi who was
            led astray by Greek "melodies").

        Recommended secondary readings: Saul Lieberman, Greek in
            Jewish Palestine (New York: Jewish Theological
            Seminary, 1942; rpt. Feldheim, 1965).
        Saul Lieberman, Hellenism in Jewish Palestine (New York:
            Jewish Theological Seminary, 1950; rpt. Ktav, 1962).
        Saul Lieberman, "How Much Greek in Jewish Palestine?" in
            Philip W. Lown Institute of Advanced Judaic Studies,
            Brandeis Univ.: Studies and Texts, vol. 1: Biblical
            and Other Studies, ed. Alexander Altmann (Cambridge,
            Mass.: Harvard, 1963) 123-141.
        Henry Fischel, Rabbinic Literature and Greco-Roman
            Philosophy (Leiden: Brill, 1973).

        Additional (supplementary) secondary readings:
        *Yitzhak Baer, Yisrael Ba-amim (in Hebrew=Israel among the
            Nations)(Jerusalem, 1955).
        Judah Bergmann, "Die Stoische Philosophie und die jüdische
            Frömmigkeit," in Judaica: Festschrift Hermann Cohen
            (Berlin, 1913) 143-166.

David Daube, "Rabbinic Methods of Interpretation and Hellenistic Rhetoric," Hebrew Union College Annual 22 (1949) 239-264.

*Henry A. Fischel, "Story and History: Observations on Greco-Roman Rhetoric and Pharisaism," American Oriental Society, Middle West Branch, Semi-Centennial Vol., Asian Studies Research Institute, Oriental Series #3 (Denis Sinor, ed.) 59-88.

*Henry A. Fischel, Essays in Greco-Roman and Related Talmudic Literature (New York: Ktav, 1977).

T. F. Glasson, Greek Influence in Jewish Eschatology, with Special Reference to the Apocalypses and Pseudepigraphs (London, 1961).

E. E. Hallewy, "The Writers of the Agada and the Greek Grammarians" (in Hebrew), Tarbiz 29 (1959-60) 47-55.

E. E. Hallewy, "Biblical Midrash and Homeric Exegesis" (in Hebrew), Tarbiz 31 (1961-62) 157-169, 264-280.

Armand Kaminka, "Les rapports entre le rabbinisme et la philosophie stoïcienne," Revue des Études juives 82 (1926) 232-252.

R. Meyer, Hellenistisches in der rabbinischen Anthropologie (Beiträge zur Wissenschaft vom Alten (und Neuen) Testament IV, 22) (1937).

Siegfried Stein, "The Influence of Symposia Literature and the Literary Form of the Pesach Haggadah," Journal of Jewish Studies 8 (1957) 13-44.

Geza Vermes, Scripture and Tradition in Judaism: Haggadic Studies (Leiden: Brill, 1961).

Questions: 1) If the rabbis were so opposed to Greek, how can we explain the presence of so many Greek words in the Talmudic corpus, as well as the similarity between rabbinic and Greek methods of exegesis?

2) Was the Hellerization of the rabbis different in degree and kind from that of the other Jews in Palestine and in the Diaspora?

3) Is the Talmudic method of dialectic due to Greek influence?

4) How does the Talmudic method differ from the Socratic method?

5) Why does the Talmud not even mention Socrates, Plato, and Aristotle?

3. Josephus as an interpreter of Judaism to the Greeks

Recommended primary readings: Josephus, Antiquities, Book 1, sections 1-256 (Josephus' paraphrase of Genesis through the death of Abraham).

Recommended secondary readings: Harold W. Attridge, The Interpretation of Biblical History in the Antiquitates Judaicae of Flavius Josephus (Missoula, Montana: Scholars Press, 1976).

Louis H. Feldman, "Hellenizations in Josephus' Account of Man's Decline," in Studies in the History of Religions, 14 (E. R. Goodenough Memorial Vol., ed. Jacob Neusner; Leiden, Brill, 1968) 336-353.

Louis H. Feldman, "Abraham the Greek Philosopher in Josephus," Transactions of the American Philological Association 99 (1968) 143-156.

Louis H. Feldman, "Flavius Josephus Revisited: the Man, His Writings, and His Significance," Aufstieg und Niedergang der römischen Welt 2. 21 (Berlin: de Gruyter, 1983).

Thomas W. Franxman, Genesis and the 'Jewish Antiquities' of Flavius Josephus (Rome: Biblical Institute Press, 1979).

Henry St. John Thackeray, Josephus the Man and the Historian (New York: Jewish Institute of Religion, 1929; rpt., Ktav, 1967).

Additional (supplementary) secondary readings:

Martin Braun, History and Romance in Graeco-Oriental Literature (Oxford, 1938).

*Shaye J. D. Cohen, Josephus in Galilee and Rome: His Vita and Development as a Historian (Leiden: Brill, 1979).

*Louis H. Feldman, "Hellenizations in Josephus' Version of Esther," Transactions of the American Philological Association 101 (1970) 143-170.

*Louis H. Feldman, "Josephus as an Apologist to the Greco-Roman World: His Portrait of Solomon," in Elisabeth S. Fiorenza, Aspects of Religious Propaganda in Judaism and Early Christianity (Notre Dame: Notre Dame Univ., 1976) 69-98.

*Louis H. Feldman, "Josephus' Commentary on Genesis," Jewish Quarterly Review 72 (1981-82) 121-131.

*Louis H. Feldman, "Josephus' Version of the Binding of Isaac," Society of Biblical Literature: 1982 Seminar Papers 21 (1982) 113-128.

*Louis H. Feldman, "Josephus' Portrait of Saul," Hebrew Union College Annual 53 (1982) 45-99.

David J. Ladouceur, Studies in the Language and Historiography of Flavius Josephus (diss., Brown Univ., 1976).

*Tessa Rajak, Josephus (Berkeley, Calif.: Univ.of California, 1983).

Salomo Rappaport, Agada und Exegese bei Flavius Josephus (Wien, 1930).

Willem C. van Unnik, "Josephus' Account of the Story of Israel's Sin with Alien Women in the Country of Midian (Num. 25. 1 ff.)," in Travels in the World of the Old Testament: Studies Presented to Professor M. A. Beek (Assen, 1974) 241-261.

Questions: 1) How could Josephus say that he has neither added to nor subtracted from the Bible when he has so manifestly done so?

2) Are there consistent principles underlying Josephus' version of the Biblical stories?

3) To what extent can we identify the sources which Josephus used in his "Hellenization" of the Biblical narrative?

4) To what extent was Josephus influenced by the attempt to answer the criticism of the Bible "critics" of his day?

5) To what degree was Josephus influenced by the popular Hellenistic philosophical schools of his day?

4. Greek Influence in Hellenistic Jewish Art

Recommended primary readings: none

Recommended secondary readings: Erwin R. Goodenough, Jewish Symbols
   in the Greco-Roman Period, vol. 4: The Problem of Method (New
   York: Pantheon, 1954); vol. 12: Summary and Conclusions (New
   York: Pantheon, 1965).
Jacob Neusner, Early Rabbinic Judaism (Leiden: Brill, 1975) 139-215.
Morton Smith, "Goodenough's Jewish Symbols in Retrospect," Journal
   of Biblical Literature 86 (1967) 53-68.
Morton Smith, "The Image of G-d: Notes on the Hellenization of
   Judaism with Especial Reference to Goodenough's Work on Jewish
   Symbols," Bulletin of the John Rylands Library 40 (1957-58) 473-512.

Additional (supplementary) secondary readings:
Joseph Gutmann, The Dura-Europos Synagogue: a Re-evaluation (Scholars
   Press, 1973)

Joseph Gutmann, The Synagogue: Studies in Origins, Archaeology
   and Architecture (New York: Ktav, 1975).
Mordecai Margaliot, Sepher ha-Razim: A Newly Discovered Book of
   Magic from the Talmudic Period (in Hebrew)(1966).
Jacob Neusner, "Notes on Goodenough's Jewish Symbols," Conservative
   Judaism 17 (1963) 77 ff.
Jacob Neusner, Judaism in the American Humanities (Scholars Press,
   1981) 91-106.
Jacob Neusner, Take Judaism for Example (Chicago: Univ. of Chicago.
   Press, 1982) 1-28, 215-226.
Michael Avi-Yonah, Oriental Art in Roman Palestine (Studi Semitici,
   vol. 5: Istituto di Studi del Vicino Oriente, Università di
   Roma, Centro di Studi Semitici)(Rome, 1961).
Joseph Gutmann, "The 'Second Commandment' and the Image in Judaism,"
   Hebrew Union College Annual 32 (1961) 161-174.
Rudolf Meyer, "Die Figurendarstellung in der Kunst des späthellenistischen
   Judentums," Judaica 5 (1949) 1-40.

Questions: 1) Is it true that the Jews, as compared to the Greeks,
             have an innately defective sense of color, as some
             have charged?
          2) How can one determine what is a Jewish and what is a
             Greek symbol?
          3) To what degree does Jewish art have symbolic value and
             show Greek influence and to what degree is it merely
             decorative?
          4) Is there any significance in the increase of decoration
             after the destruction of the Temple in the year 70?
          5) To what degree does the evidence of art indicate a
             "popular" Judaism independent of rabbinic influence?

5. Diaspora Contacts: The Septuagint

Recommended primary readings: Septuagint, Genesis, chapters 1 through 50.

Recommended secondary readings: Charles H. Dodd, The Bible and the
   Greeks, 2nd ed. (London, 1954).
Gillis Gerleman, "The Septuagint Proverbs as a Hellenistic Document,"
   Oudtestamentische Studien 8 (1950) 15-27.
Sidney Jellicoe, The Septuagint and Modern Study (Oxford, 1968;
   rpt., Eisenbrauns, 1978).
Ralph Marcus, "Jewish and Greek Elements in the Septuagint," in
   Louis Ginzberg Jubilee Vol. (New York, 1965) 227-245.
Harry M. Orlinsky, "The Septuagint as Holy Writ and the Philosophy
   of the Translators," Hebrew Union College Annual 46 (1975) 89-114.

Additional (supplementary) secondary readings:
*Elias Bickermann, "The Septuagint as a Translation," Proceedings of
   the American Academy for Jewish Research 28 (1959) 1-39.
Sheldon H. Blank, "The Septuagint Renderings of Old Testament Terms
   for Law," Hebrew Union College Annual 7 (1930) 259-283.
*Jacob Freudenthal, "Are There Traces of Greek Philosophy in the
   Septuagint?", Jewish Quarterly Review, old series, 2 (1889-90)
   205-222.
Leo Prijs, Jüdische Tradition in der Septuaginta (Leiden, 1948).
W. Schwarz, Principles and Problems of Biblical Translation
   (Cambridge, 1955).

Questions: 1) What significance can we attach to such external
              phenomena as Greek metrical forms in the Septuagint?
           2) To what extent is there Platonism in the Septuagint's
              account of creation?
           3) To what extent is the account of the banquet for the
              translators in the Letter of Aristeas a symposium in
              the tradition of Plato, Plutarch, Athenaeus, and others?
           4) To what extent does the Septuagint's theology (as
              compared with that of the Hebrew text) reveal Greek
              influence or an attempt to answer such ideas?
           5) To what degree can we discern apologetic motifs in the
              Septuagint that are intended to reply to anti-Semitic
              charges?

6. Philo as Greek and as Jew

Recommended primary readings: Philo, On Abraham (Loeb Library trans.
   of Philo, vol. 6, pp. 5-135).

Recommended secondary readings: Erwin R. Goodenough, An Introduction
   to Philo Judaeus, 2nd ed. (Oxford: Blackwell, 1962; rpt.
   Allenson, 1962).
Samuel Sandmel, Philo's Place in Judaism: A Study of Conceptions of
   Abraham in Jewish Literature (Cincinnati: Hebrew Union Coll., 1956).
Samuel Sandmel, Philo of Alexandria: An Introduction (Oxford: Univ.
   Press, 1979).

Harry A. Wolfson, Philo: Foundations of Religious Philosophy in
Judaism, Christianity and Islam, 2 vols. (Cambridge, Mass.:
Harvard Univ., 1947; 2nd ed., 1962).

Additional (supplementary) secondary readings:
Samuel Belkin, "The Philonic Exposition of the Torah in the Light of
the Ancient Rabbinic Midrashim" (in Hebrew), Sura 4 (1960) 1-68.
Samuel Belkin, Philo and the Oral Law: The Philonic Interpretation of
Biblical Law in Relation to the Palestinian Halakah (Cambridge,
Mass.: Harvard, 1940).
K. Bormann, Die Ideen- und Logoslehre Philons von Alexandrien: eine
Auseinandersetzung mit H. A. Wolfson (Diss., Köln, 1955).
*Erwin R. Goodenough, By Light, Light! The Mystic Gospel of Hellenistic
Judaism (New Haven: Yale, 1935).
Erwin R. Goodenough, The Politics of Philo Judaeus: Practice and
Theory (New Haven: Yale, 1938).
*Erwin R. Goodenough, rev. of Wolfson's Philo, in Journal of Biblical
Literature 67 (1948) 87-109.
*Isaak Heinemann, Philons griechische und jüdische Bildung: Kultur-
vergleichende Untersuchungen zu Philons Darstellung der jüdischen
Gesetze (Breslau, 1932).
H. Neumark, Die Verwendung griechischer und jüdischer Motive in den
Gedanken Philons über die Stellung Gottes zu seinen Freunden
(Würzburg, 1937).
Valentin Nikiprowetzky, Le Commentaire de l'Écriture chez Philon
d'Alexandrie: Son Caractère et sa Portée (Leiden: Brill, 1977).
S. G. Sowers, The Hermeneutics of Philo and Hebrews: Comparison of
the Interpretation of the Old Testament in Philo Judaeus and the
Epistle to the Hebrews (Richmond, 1965).

Questions: 1) To what degree is there a correlation between Philo's
deviation from rabbinic norms and the deviations found
in Jewish art?
2) To what degree is there a correlation between Philo's
Hellenism and that of Josephus?
3) To what degree is Philo's account of Abraham dependent
upon the Hebrew Biblical text, and to what degree is it
dependent upon the Septuagint?
4) To what degree does Philo's Platonism show parallels
with rabbinic literature?
5) Has time been kinder to Goodenough's or to Wolfson's
characterization of Philo?

7. Implications: The Jews and Their Neighbors: Philo-Semitism, Anti-Semitism,
Jews as Missionaries

Recommended primary readings: Josephus, Against Apion, Book 1 (Loeb
Library trans. of Josephus, vol. 1, pp. 163-291).

Recommended secondary readings: Louis H. Feldman, "Philo-Semitism
among Ancient Intellectuals," Tradition 1 (1958) 27-39.

Louis H. Feldman, "The Jews in Greek and Latin Literature," in
   Menahem Stern, ed., The Jewish Diaspora in the Second Temple
   Period (World History of the Jewish People, vol. 4, Second
   Temple series)(New Brunswick: Rutgers, 1983).
Louis H. Feldman, "Proselytism and Syncretism," in Menahem Stern,
   ed., The Jewish Diaspora in the Second Temple Period (World
   History of the Jewish People, vol. 4, Second Temple series)
   (New Brunswick: Rutgers, 1983).
Bernard J. Bamberger, Proselytism in the Talmudic Period (Cincinnati:
   Hebrew Union Coll., 1939; rpt., New York: Ktav, 1968).
John G. Gager, Moses in Greco-Roman Paganism (Nashville: Abington, 1972).
Jan N. Sevenster, The Roots of Pagan Anti-Semitism in the Ancient
   World (Leiden: Brill, 1975).

Additional (supplementary) secondary readings:
William C. Braude, Jewish Proselyting in the First Five Centuries of
   the Common Era (Providence: Brown Univ., 1940).
P. Dalbert, Die Theologie der hellenistisch-jüdischen Missionsliteratur
   unter Ausschluss von Philo und Josephus (Theologische Forschung,
   4)(Hamburg, 1954).
John G. Gager, Moses in Greco-Roman Paganism (Nashville: Abingdon, 1972).
Jerry L. Daniel, "Anti-Semitism in the Hellenistic-Roman Period,"
   Journal of Biblical Literature 98 (1979) 45-65.
Isaak Heinemann, "Antisemitismus," in August Pauly and Georg Wissowa,
   edd., Realencyclopädie der klassischen Altertumswissenschaft,
   Suppl. 5 (1931) 3-43.
*Ralph Marcus, "Anti-Semitism in the Hellenistic-Roman World," in
   Koppel S. Pinson, ed., Essays on Antisemitism (2nd ed., New
   York, 1946) 61-78.
*P. Krüger, Philo und Josephus als Apologeten des Judentums(Leipzig, 1906).
Max Radin, The Jews among the Greeks and Romans (Philadelphia:
   Jewish Publication Society, 1915), esp. 163-327.
J. S. Raisin, Gentile Reactions to Jewish Ideals with Special Reference
   to Proselytes (1953), esp. 154-172.
Menahem Stern, Greek and Latin Authors on Jews and Judaism, 2 vols.
   (Jerusalem: Israel Academy of Sciences and Humanities, 1974-80).

Questions: 1) How can we explain that the earliest references to Jews
               by Greeks are so favorable, whereas the later ones are
               usually virulently anti-Semitic?
            2) Did the increasing Hellenization of the Jews contribute
               to greater or lesser anti-Semitism?
            3) How can we explain the fact that there was so much more
               anti-Semitism in certain regions of the ancient world
               than in others?
            4) Why did the Jews so suddenly become an active missionary
               religion?
            5) How can we explain the extraordinary success of the Jews
               in proselyting during the Hellenistic period?

8. Implications: Hellenistic Judaism and the Rise of Christianity

   Recommended primary readings: New Testament--Book of Acts

   Recommended secondary readings: Erwin R. Goodenough and At.T. Kraabel, "Paul and the Hellenization of Christianity," in Jacob Neusner, ed., Religions in Antiquity: Essays in Memory of Erwin Ramsdell Goodenough (Studies in the History of Religions, 14; Leiden: Brill, 1968) 23-68.
   Frederick C. Grant, Roman Hellenism and the New Testament (Edinburgh, 1962).
   Samuel Sandmel, The First Christian Century: Certainties and Uncertainties (New York, 1969).
   Samuel Sandmel, Judaism and Christian Beginnings (Oxford: University Press, 1978).

   Additional (supplementary) secondary readings:
   David Daube, The New Testament and Rabbinic Judaism (London, 1956).
   *William D. Davies, Paul and Rabbinic Judaism (London, 1948).
   Donald A. Hagner, "The Vision of G-d in Philo and John: A Comparative Study," Journal of the Evangelical Theological Society 14 (1971) 81-93.
   Joseph Klausner, From Jesus to Paul (London, 1944; rpt., New York: Menorah, 1979).
   Claude G. Montefiore, Judaism and St. Paul (London, 1914).
   *Samuel Sandmel, The Genius of Paul: A Study in History (New York, 1958).
   *Jan N. Sevenster, Do You Know Greek? (Leiden, 1968).
   Ronald Williamson, Philo and the Epistle to the Hebrews (Arbeiten zur Literatur und Geschichte des hellenistischen Judentums, vol. 4) (Leiden, 1970).

   Questions: 1) To what degree is Paul a synthesis of Hellenistic mystery cults and Hellenistic Judaism?
   2) To what degree is there a correlation between Paul and the motifs of Hellenistic Jewish art?
   3) To what degree is there a correlation between Paul and Philo, and to what degree is Paul more "rabbinic" than Philo?
   4) Is there a correlation between the degree of Hellenization of Jews and the degree to which Christianity was successful in converting them?
   5) Why did Christianity, in the process of Hellenization, not disintegrate into a thousand sects (as it was later to do); or is it perhaps true that this Hellenization was a solid front against more acute Hellenization?

V. Background Bibliographies

   1. Introductory Books on Jewish History
      Max I. Dimont, Jews, G-d, and History (New York: Simon and Schuster, 1962).
      Abba Eban, My People: The Story of the Jews (New York, 1968).
      Isidore Epstein, Judaism: A Historical Perspective (Baltimore: Penguin, 1959).
      Solomon Grayzel, A History of the Jews (rev. ed., New York: Mentor, 1968).

Max Margolis and Alexander Marx, A History of the Jewish People
(Philadelphia: Jewish Publication Society, 1960).
Chaim Potok, Wanderings: A History of the Jews (New York: Knopf, 1978).
Abram Sachar, History of the Jews (New York: Knopf, 3rd ed., 1948).
Leo W. Schwarz, Great Ages and Ideas of the Jewish People (New York:
Random, 1956).

2. More Extensive Works on Jewish History
Salo W. Baron, A Social and Religous History of the Jews, 17 vols.
to date (New York and Philadelphia: Jewish Publication Society,
1952-present).
Haim H. Ben-Sasson, ed., A History of the Jewish People (Cambridge,
Mass., Harvard University, 1976).
Louis Finkelstein, ed., The Jews, Their History, Culture, and
Religion, 3 vols. (4th ed., New York: Harper, 1970).
Benzion Netanyahu, ed., The World History of the Jewish People, 12
vols. to date (New Brunswick: Rutgers University, 1964-present).

3. Books on Ancient Jewish History
Michael Avi-Yonah, The Holy Land from the Persian to the Arab Conquests
(536 B.C. to A.D. 640): A Historical Geography (Grand Rapids, 1966).
Laurence H. Browne, From Babylon to Bethlehem: The Story of the Jews
for the Last Five Centuries before Christ (Cambridge, 1951).
Henry L. Ellison, From Babylon to Bethlehem: the Jewish People from
the Exile to the Messiah (Exeter, 1976).
Donald E. Gowan, Bridge between the Testaments: A Reappraisal of
Judaism from the Exile to the Birth of Christianity (Pittsburgh, 1976).
W. Stewart McCullough, The History and Literature of the Palestinian
Jews from Cyrus to Herod: 550 B.C. to 4 B.C. (Toronto, 1975).
Charles F. Pfeiffer, Between the Testaments (Grand Rapids, 1959).
Bo Reicke, The New Testament Era: The World of the Bible from 500
B.C. to A. D. 100 (Philadelphia, 1968).
Norman H. Snaith, The Jews from Cyrus to Herod (London, 1949).
Henry Voogd, Seedtime and Harvest: A Popular History of the Period
between the Testaments (Washington, 1977).

4. Books on the Hellenistic Period Generally
J. B. Bury et al., The Cambridge Ancient History, vol. 6: Macedon
401-301 B.C. (1927); and vol. 7: The Hellenistic Monarchies.
John Ferguson, The Heritage of Hellenism: The Greek World from 323
to 31 B.C. (New York: Harcourt, Brace, 1973).
Michael Grant, From Alexander to Cleopatra: The Hellenistic World
(New York: Scribner's, 1982).
Moses Hadas, Hellenistic Culture: Fusion and Diffusion (Norton, 1959).
Francis E. Peters, The Harvest of Hellenism: A History of the Near
East from Alexander the Great to the Triumph of Christianity (New York,
1970).
Michael Rostovtzeff, The Social and Economic History of the Hellenistic
World, 3 vols. (1941).
W. W. Tarn and G. T. Griffith, Hellenistic Civilisation (3rd ed.,
London: Arnold, 1952).
C. Bradford Welles, Alexander and the Hellenistic World (Toronto,
1970).

5. Works on Hellenistic Judaism Generally
Salo W. Baron, A Social and Religious History of the Jews, vols.
1 and 2 (2nd ed., Philadelphia, 1952).
Salo W. Baron and Joseph L. Blau, edd., Judaism: Postbiblical and
Talmudic Period (New York, 1954).
G. H. Box, Judaism in the Greek Period from the Rise of Alexander
the Great to the Intervention of Rome (Oxford, 1932).
Louis H. Feldman, "Hellenism and the Jews," Encyclopaedia Judaica
8 (1971) 295-301.
Louis H. Feldman, "Judaism, History of: Hellenistic Judaism (4th
Century BCE-2nd Century CE)," Encyclopaedia Britannica (Macropaedia)
10 (1974) 310-316.
Martin Hengel, Judaism and Hellenism, 2 vols. (Philadelphia: Fortress,
1974).
Ralph Marcus, "The Hellenistic Age," in Leo W. Schwarz, ed., Great
Ages and Ideas of the Jewish People (New York: Random House, 1956) 95-139.
Robert H. Pfeiffer, History of New Testament Times with an Introduction
to the Apocrypha (New York: Harper, 1949).
Emil Schürer, History of the Jewish People in the Age of Jesus Christ
(175 B.C.-A.D. 135), revised by Geza Vermes and Fergus Millar
(Edinburgh, 1973 and 1979), vols. 1 and 2.
Victor A. Tcherikover et al., Corpus Papyrorum Judaicarum, 3 vols.
(Cambridge, Mass.: Harvard, 1957-64), esp. Prolegomena by Tcherikover,
vol. 1, pp. 1-111.
Solomon Zeitlin, The Rise and Fall of the Judaean State: A Political,
Social and Religious History of the Second Commonwealth, 3 vols.
(Philadelphia: Jewish Publication Society, 1962-78).

6. Bibliography on Hebraism and Hellenism Generally
G. F. Abbott, "Hebraism and Hellenism," in his Israel in Europe
(London, 1907).
Matthew Arnold, "Hebraism and Hellenism" (many editions); see A. Dwight
Culler, Poetry and Criticism of Matthew Arnold (Houghton Mifflin).
James Barr, "Athens or Jerusalem? The Question of Distinctiveness,"
in his Old and New in Interpretation (New York, 1966) 34-64.
Th. Boman, Hebrew Thought Compared with Greek (London, 1960).
W. L. Courtney, "Jewish Philosophy and the Hellenic Spirit,"
Fortnightly Review 82 (1907) 806-813.
David J. DeLaura, Hebrew and Hellene in Victorian England: Newman,
Arnold, and Pater (Austin, Texas: University of Texas, 1969).
John Ferguson, Moral Values in the Ancient World (London, 1958).
Isaac Herzog, several essays in his collected works, edited by
Jacob Herzog.
David Hill, Greek Words and Hebrew Meanings: Studies in the Semantics
of Soteriological Terms (Cambridge: University Press, 1967).
Milton Himmelfarb, "Hebraism and Hellenism Reconsidered," in his
Essays in Modernity.
Maurice Hutton, The Greek Point of View (London, no date).
John Kelman, "Hebraism and Hellenism," Prophets of Yesterday and Their
Message for Today (Cambridge, 1924) 3-37.
Ben Kimpel, Philosophies of Life of the Ancient Greeks and Israelites
(An Analysis of Their Parallels) (New York: Philosophical Library, 1981).

Hans Kohn, "Israel and Hellas," in his The Idea of Nationalism (New York: Macmillan, 1967) 27-60.
Richard W. Livingstone, "Christianity and Hellenism," in his Greek Ideals and Modern Life (Cambridge, Mass.: Harvard, 1935).
Grace H. Macurdy, The Quality of Mercy; the Gentler Virtues in Greek Literature (New Haven: Yale, 1940).
Bernard Martin, Great Twentieth Century Jewish Philosophers (New York; 1969) (on Lev Shestov).
Helen North, Sophrosyne: Self-Knowledge and Self-Restraint in Greek Literature (Ithaca: Cornell, 1966).
Lev Shestov, Athens and Jerusalem (trans. by Bernard Martin)(Athens, Ohio: Ohio University, 1966).
Joseph B. Soloveitchik, "Confrontation," Tradition 6 (1964) 5-29; rpt. in Leon D. Stitskin, Studies in Judaism in Honor of Dr. Samuel Belkin (New York, 1974) 45-68.
Joseph B. Soloveitchik, "Catharsis," Tradition 17 (1978) 38-54.
V. S. Zukovsky, A History of Russian Philosophy (New York: Columbia University, 1953), pp. 780-791 (on Lev Shestov).
E. R. Dodds, The Greeks and the Irrational (Berkeley, Calif: Univ. of California, 1951; rpt., Boston: Beacon, 1957).
Erich Auerbach, "The Scar of Odysseus," in his Mimesis: The Representation of Reality in Western Literature (tr. by W. R. Trask) (Princeton, 1953).
William Barrett, Irrational Man: A Study in Existential Philosophy (Garden City, 1958).
Martin Buber, Israel and the World (New York, 1958).
Charles H. Dodd, The Bible and the Greeks (London, 1954).
Horace M. Kallen, Art and Freedom (New York, 1942).
Kalman J. Kaplan and Moriah Markus-Kaplan, "Covenant versus Contract as Two Modes of Relationship Orientation: On Reconciling Possibility and Necessity," Journal of Psychology and Judaism 4 (1979) 100-116.
Ludwig Lewisohn, Midchannel: An American Chronicle (New York, 1929).
Moriah Markus-Kaplan and Kalman J. Kaplan, "The Typology, Diagnosis, Pathologies and Treatment-Intervention of Hellenic versus Hebraic Personality Styles: A Proposal on the Psychology of Interpersonal Distancing," Journal of Psychology and Judaism 3 (1979) 153-167.
Reinhold Niebuhr, Faith and History (New York, 1949).
Reinhold Niebuhr, "The Two Sources of Western Culture, in E. Fuller, ed., The Christian Idea of Education (New Haven, 1957).
Robert H. Pfeiffer, "Hebrew and Greek Verse of Tragedy," The Joshua Bloch Memorial Volume (New York, 1960) 54-64.
Max Pohlenz, "Stoa und Semitismus," Neue Jahrbücher für Wissenschaft und Jugendbildung 2 (1926) 257-269.
H. Ranston, Ecclesiastes and Early Greek Wisdom Literature (London, 1925).
Maurice Samuel, The Gentleman and the Jew (New York, 1950).

7. Bibliographical Works for Hellenistic Judaism
   S. F. Brock et al., A Classified Bibliography of the Septuagint (Leiden, 1973).
   *Gerhard Delling, Bibliographie zur Jüdisch-Hellenistischen und Intertestamentarischen Literatur 1900-1970 (2nd ed., Berlin 1975).
   *Louis H. Feldman, Scholarship on Philo and Josephus (1937-62) (New York, 1963).
   *Louis H. Feldman, Josephus and Modern Scholarship (Berlin, de.Gruyter, 1983).

George S. Glanzman and Joseph A. Fitzmyer, An Introductory
Bibliography for the Study of Scripture (rev. ed., Rome, 1981).
Erwin R. Goodenough, The Politics of Philo Judaeus, Practice
and Theory, with a General Bibliography of Philo by Howard L.
Goodhart and Erwin R. Goodenough (New Haven: Yale, 1938).
Earle Hilgert, "A Bibliography of Philo Studies, 1963-1970,"
Studia Philonica 1 (1972) 57-71; 2 (1973) 51-54; 3 (1974-75)
117-125; 4(1976-77) 79-85; 5 (1978) 113-120; 6 (1979-80) 197-200.
John C. Hurd, Jr., A Bibliography of New Testament Bibliographies
(New York, 1966).
*Ralph Marcus, "Selected Bibliography (1920-1945) of the Jews in
the Hellenistic-Roman Period," Proceedings of the American Academy
for Jewish Research 16 (1946-47) 97-181.
*Uriel Rappaport, "Bibliography of Works on Jewish History in the
Hellenistic and Roman Period, 1946-1970," in B. Oded et al., edé.,
Studies in the History of the Jewish People and the Land of Israel
(=Mehkarim, in Hebrew) 2 (Haifa, 1970) 247-321.
*Uriel Rappaport, Bibliography of Works on Jewish History in the
Hellenistic and Roman Periods, 1971-1975 (in Hebrew) (Jerusalem:
Institute for Advanced Studies, The Hebrew University, 1976).
*Menahem Mor and Uriel Rappaport, Bibliography of Works on Jewish
History in the Hellenistic and Roman Periods, 1976-1980 (in Hebrew
and English) (Jerusalem: The Zalman Shazar Center, The Historical
Society of Israel, 1982).
Andrew J. Mattill and Mary B. Mattill, A Classified Bibliography
of Literature on the Acts of the Apostles (Leiden, 1966).
Bruce M. Metzger, Index to Periodical Literature on Christ and the
Gospels (Leiden, 1966).
*Heinz Schreckenberg, Bibliographie zu Flavius Josephus (Leiden:
Brill, 1968).
*Heinz Schreckenberg, Bibliographie zu Flavius Josephus: Supplementband
(Leiden: Brill, 1979).

8. Regularly Appearing Current Annotated Bibliographies of
Hellenistic Judaism

Internationale Zeitschriftenschau Bibelwissenschaft und Grenzgebiete
(1951 ff.).
*New Testament Abstracts (1956 ff.).
Journal for the Study of Judaism in the Persian, Hellenistic and
Roman Period (1970 ff.).
Zeitschrift für die alttestamentliche Wissenschaft (1881 ff.).
Zeitschrift für die neutestamentliche Wissenschaft (1900 ff.).

CLASSICAL AND CHRISTIAN WORLDS
Carole Straw
Mount Holyoke College

This course will examine the continuities and contrasts in classical and Christian traditions. We will pursue what Clifford Geertz has called a "thick description" of culture, noting how ideas, social patterns, political institutions, and economic conditions interlock to form a distinct society. We will focus on three major problems: 1.) What does it mean to be human? Can we detect an increasing recognition of the complexity of man's and woman's personality and psychology in the sources? Is there what one historian has termed "a development of conscience"? 2.) What is mankind's relationship to the gods (or God)? How does the definition of a god reflect human characteristics and human needs? What does this relationship between mankind and god tell us about mankind's control of the environment? 3.) How are the political, social and economic patterns of a culture somehow an expression of a complete thought world, rather than simply the product of sheer necessity? In other words, to what extent is history determined by external events, or created by personalities and ideas interacting with an environment?

This course will emphasize teaching the student how to interpret primary sources and how to write an analytical essay. We shall discuss guidelines for writing a paper in history at a later date.

Books to be purchased:

Aeschylus, The Oresteian Trilogy (Penguin)
Augustine, The City of God (Image)
Augustine, The Confessions (Image)
Barrow, R.W., The Romans (Penguin)
Chadwick, Henry, The Early Church (Penguin)
Finley, M.I., ed., The Portable Greek Historians (Penguin)
Grant, M. ed., Cicero: Selected Works (Penguin)
Hadas, M. ed., The Stoic Philosophy of Seneca (Norton)
Jowett, B. tr., The Works of Plato (Modern Library)
Kitto, H.D.F., The Greeks (Penguin)
Plutarch, The Fall of the Roman Republic (Penguin)
Paolucci, H., The Political Writings of St. Augustine (Gateway)

Rieu, ed., <u>Homer: The Odyssey</u> (Bantom)
St. Pachomius, <u>Rule</u> (Eastern Orthodox Press)
Staniforth, ed., <u>Early Christian Writings</u> (Penguin)
Tacitus, <u>The Annals</u> (Penguin)
Waddell, Helen, <u>The Desert Fathers</u> (Ann Arbor)
Ward, B., <u>The Wisdom of the Deserrt Fathers</u> (Fairacres)

Requirements:

1. Preparation for and participation in class discussion.
2. Completion of short quizzes in class.
3. Midterm of five to seven pages due March 20. Late papers are
   penalized 1/2 grade per day. The midterm may be rewritten within
   one week of its return to the student.
4. A final paper will be due May 11. Late papers are penalized
   1/2 grade per day.

Class Meetings:

1.   Introduction

2.   Kitto, pp. 7-64.

3.   Homer, <u>The Odyssey</u>, bks. 1-5.
      Kitto, pp. 169-205

4.   Homer, <u>The Odyssey</u>, bks. 6-11.

5.   Herodotus, in <u>The Portable Greek Historians</u>, pp. 81-157.
      Kitto, pp. 64-109.

6.   Herodotus, pp. 157-215.
      SHORT QUIZ

7.   Plutarch, <u>Solon</u>
      Selections of Solon's poems
      (begin next assignment of Kitto)

8.   Kitto, pp. 109-69.
      Aeschylus, <u>The Agamemnon</u>, in <u>The Oresteia Trilogy</u>, pp. 41-100.

9.   Aeschylus, <u>The Choephori</u> and <u>The Eumenidies</u>, in <u>The Oresteia</u>
      Trilogy, pp. 103-182.

10.   Sophocles, <u>Oedipus the King</u> and <u>Antigone</u>, in <u>The Complete</u>
      <u>Plays of Sophocles</u>, 77-114, and 117-147.

11.   Euripides, <u>Electra</u>
      SHORT QUIZ

328

12. Plato, Phaedo, in The Works of Plato, pp. 109-189.

13. Plato, Selections from the Republic, in The Works of Plato
    pp. 397-478.

14. Midterm paper due.
    Thucydides, Pericles' "Funeral Oration" in The Portable Greek
    Historians, pp. 265-274.
    Plutarch, Pericles, in The Rise and Fall of Athens pp. 165-206.

15. HOLIDAYS (begin Barrows)

16. Plutarch, Cicero, in The Fall of the Roman Republic, pp. 311-361.

17. Cicero, On Old Age, in Selected Works, pp. 213-46.
    Barrow, The Romans, pp. 9-78.

18. Tacitus, The Annals, pp. 29-40; 88-101; 126-52.
    Barrows, pp. 79-111.

19. Seneca, On Providence and On Tranquility, in The Stoic
    Philosophy of Seneca, pp. 27-45, 75-106.

20. St. Paul, I Corinthians

21. Chadwick, The Early Christian Church, pp. 23-32, 54-73.
    Clement of Rome, Epistle, in Early Christian Writing,
    pp. 42-54.
    Ignatius of Antioch, pp. 119-130, in ECW
    SHORT QUIZ

22. Waddell, The Desert Fathers, pp. 60-126.

23. Waddell, The Desert Fathers pp. 126-201.

24. Augustine, The Confessions, bk. 1-5.

25. Augustine, The Confessions, bks. 6-10.

26. Augustine, The City of God, pp. 39-118.

27. Augustine, Political Writings, pp. 153-83, 211-219.

28. Final paper due.

329

The Editors

Sarah B. Pomeroy received her Ph.D. from Columbia University. She is professor of Classics at Hunter College and the Graduate School, C.U.N.Y., and in 1984-85 was the Blegen Visiting Distinguished Research Professor at Vassar College. She is the author of <u>Goddesses, Whores, Wives, and Slaves: Women in Classical Antiquity</u> (1984), and of <u>Women in Hellenistic Egypt from Alexander to Cleopatra</u> (1984), and has written articles and review essays on papyrology, social history, numismatics, Roman law, and Greek literature. She is currently editing a Teubner text and writing a social and economic commentary on Xenophon, <u>Oeconomicus</u>.

Stanley M. Burstein graduated from the University of California, Los Angeles where he received his B.A., M.A. and Ph.D. degrees in history. He is professor of Ancient History at California State University, Los Angeles. He is the author of <u>Outpost of Hellenism: The Emergence of Heraclea on the Black Sea</u> (1976), <u>The Babyloniaca of Berossus</u> (1978) and <u>The Hellenistic Age from Battle of Ipsos to the Death of Kleopatra VII</u> (1985) and co-editor of <u>Panhellenica: Essays in Ancient History and Historiography in Honor of Truesdell S. Brown</u> (1980). He has published numerous articles on various aspects of the history of Greece and the Near East in the Hellenistic Period and is currently preparing a translation and commentary on the <u>Concerning the Erythraean Sea</u> of Agatharchides of Cnidus.

330